Lexical Studies in the Bible and Ancient Near Eastern Inscriptions

Lexical Studies in the Bible and Ancient Near Eastern Inscriptions

The Collected Essays of Hayim Tawil

Edited by
Abraham Jacob Berkovitz,
Stuart W. Halpern, and Alec Goldstein

THE MICHAEL SCHARF PUBLICATION TRUST
OF THE YESHIVA UNIVERSITY PRESS
NEW YORK

ISBN 978-1-60280-212-4

Layout: Marzel A.S — Jerusalem

Distributed by
KTAV Publishing House, Inc.
888 Newark Avenue, Suite 119
Jersey City, NJ 07306
orders@ktav.com • www.ktav.com
(201) 963-9524 • Fax (201) 963-0102

To my students everywhere
and especially to my students
at Yeshiva University

בְּטַח אֶל יְקֹוָק בְּכָל לִבֶּךָ וְאֶל בִּינָתְךָ אַל תִּשָּׁעֵן
(משלי ג : ה)

Hayim Tawil

Contents

Editors' Preface 9
Publication Acknowledgements 11
Common Abbreviations 13

Lexicographical Notes

Hebrew צלח/הצלח, Akkadian ešēru/šušuru:
A Lexicographical Note 19

Hebrew סלף, Mishnaic Hebrew צלף, Akkadian ṣalāpu/ṣullupu:
A Lexicographical Note II 33

Hebrew שׂכל-סכל, Akkadian Saklu:
A Lexicographical Note III 53

Late Hebrew-Aramaic ספר, Neo-Babylonian Sirpu/Sirapu:
A Lexicographical Note IV 69

Late Hebrew-Aramaic לעס, Akkadian Na'āsu:
A Lexicographical Note V 75

Was Chiropractic Known In Biblical Times? Hebrew חלץ:
A Lexicographical Note VI 79

Hebrew נַפֵּץ יָד = Akkadian qāta napāṣu: A Term of
Non-Allegiance: A Lexicographical Note VII 91

Two Biblical and Akkadian Comparative Lexical Notes:
A Lexicographical Note VIII 99

Hebrew יסר, Akkadian Esēru: A Term of Forced Labor:
A Lexicographical Note IX 107

The Semantic Range of the Biblical Hebrew חלל:
A Lexicographical Note X 117

Two Biblical Architectural Images in Light of Cuneiform
Sources: A Lexicographical Note XI 123

Biblical Essays

ʿAzazel The Prince of the Steppe: A Comparative Study 151

The Historicity of 2 Kings 19:24 (= Isaiah 37:25): The Problem of Yeʾōrê Māṣôr 175

Amos' Oracles against the Nations: A New Interpretation . . . 195

Bathing in Milk (Songs 5:12): A New Look 209

Tāphat the Daughter of Solomon 215

Paved with Love (Song of Songs 3:10d): A New Interpretation. 229

"If the Sun Has Risen Upon Him" (Exodus 22:2): Legal Terminology in Light of Akkadian Texts from Ugarit . . 237

The Lion and the Birds: Isaiah 31:4–5 in the light of Neo-Assyrian Royal Inscriptions 249

Northwest Semitic Inscriptions

A Note on the Aḥiram Inscription 263

The End of the Hadad Inscription in the Light of Akkadian. . . 267

Some Literary Elements in the Opening Sections of the Hadad, Zākir, and the Nērab II Inscriptions in the Light of East and West Semitic Royal Inscriptions 277

A Curse Concerning Crop-Consuming Insects in the Sefîre Treaty and in Akkadian: A New Interpretation 311

Two Notes on the Treaty Terminologyof the Sefîre Interpretations 321

Hebrew Section

"אִם זָרְחָה הַשֶּׁמֶשׁ עָלָיו" (שמות כב, ב) מונח משפטי לאור הטקסטים האכדיים מאוגרית 333

הערה לכתובת אחירם 341

Indices

Sources Indices 345

Editors' Preface

The articles contained in this volume represent only a minor fraction of the contributions of Prof. Hayim Tawil. His erudite studies on the Bible and Northwest Semitics complement and parallel his great impact on the Jewish community. Over the course of his illustrious career, Prof. Tawil has made tremendous efforts in assisting the Jews of Yemen, has plumbed the depths of Semitic philology, and has mastered a diverse array of texts and methodologies. More importantly, his scholarly contributions go hand in hand with his steadfast dedication to his students. As a denizen of the fifth floor of the Yeshiva University library, he engaged in his own studies while taking a deep interest in the work of others. His encouragement and advice brought to fruition a diverse collection of scholarship. We, as his students, therefore, are proud to present his collected essays in this volume.

This book consists of four general sections. The first contains, for the first time, a complete collection of Prof. Tawil's lexicographical notes. These notes represent groundbreaking word studies in which he uncovered linguistic nuances by employing an inductive comparative Semitic methodology. The second section contains studies on the Hebrew Bible. In these articles, Prof. Tawil presents his unique and creative perspective on the study of the Hebrew Bible. These essays attest to his broad interest and mastery, ranging from studies devoted to a specific word to examinations of large methodological questions. The third section contains his work on Northwest Semitic inscriptions. These studies best demonstrate Prof. Tawil's unique contribution to the study of Aramaic idioms. The final section contains the Hebrew versions of two articles appearing in this volume.

As these articles, with the exception of one, first appeared in various publications, we imposed their topical reordering as described above. Additionally, we have tried to strike a balance between consistency of style throughout the book while largely maintaining the original form of the essays as they first appeared. As that entails much subjectivity and compromise, we hope the readers will indulge the results of that effort.

This book represents the reciprocal dedication of students to teachers. While it is impossible to fully repay one's teachers, many of Prof. Tawil's students expressed their gratitude to him by adding their efforts to this project. As such, we wish to thank Michael Siev for his hours of work on the Akkadian content of this book, and David Lasher for his efforts in laying the book's groundwork. We also wish to offer our appreciation to the following individuals for their various efforts on behalf of the project: Tali Adler, Tuvia Brander, Jina Davidovich, Jack Djmal, Ahuva Gandara, Leah Greenstein, Tamar Warburg Gross, Yigal Gross, Dovid Halpern, David Marks, Joseph Offenbacher, Shmuel Rosenblatt, Michael Rubin, Shaul Seidler-Feller, Daniel Sherman, Chaim Siev, Yehuda Sommer, Sarah Stern-Strobel, Yaakov Taubes, Gabi Weinberg, and Shlomo Zuckier.

In addition, we would like to thank Yeshiva University's own Dr. Richard White and Zvi Erenyi for their assistance and guidance, as well as the highly professional and supportive staff of KTAV, whose publishing of this book as well as Prof. Tawil's Akkadian Lexicon demonstrates their commitment to making Dr. Tawil's works accessible to a large audience.

This publication is made possible by the support of the Michael Scharf Publication Trust of Yeshiva University Press, which for many decades has plaid a vital role in the publication of scholarship under the auspices of Yeshiva University.

Abraham Jacob Berkovitz
Stuart W. Halpern
Alec Goldstein

Publication Acknowledgements

The following are the original publication details for those chapters that were previously published. Permission to republish them herein is gratefully acknowledged.

"Hebrew הצלחה/צלח, Akkadian *ešēru/šūšuru*: A Lexicographical Note," *Journal of Biblical Literature* 95 (1976), 405–13.

"Hebrew סלף, Mishnaic Hebrew צלף, Akkadian *ṣalāpu/ṣullupu*: A Lexicographical Note II," *Beit Mikra* 146 (1996), 276–92.

"Hebrew סכל–שׂכל, Akkadian *saklu*: A Lexicographical Note III," *Beit Mikra* 153 (1998), 203–16.

"Late Hebrew-Aramaic ספר, Neo-Babylonian *sirpu/sirapu*: A Lexicographical Note IV" *Beit Mikra* 154–5 (1998), 339–44.

"Late Hebrew-Aramaic לעס, Akkadian *na'āsu*: A Lexicographical Note V," *Beit Mikra* 156 (1998), 94–6.

"Was Chiropractic Known in Biblical Times? Hebrew חלץ: A Lexicographical Note VI," *Nahala* 2 (2000), 1–13.

"Hebrew יד נפץ, Akkadian *qāta napāṣu*. A Term of Non-Allegiance: A Lexicographical Note VII," *Journal of American Oriental Society* 122 (2002), 79–82.

"Two Biblical and Akkadian Comparative Lexical Notes: A Lexicographical Note VIII," *Journal of Semitic Studies* 47 (2002), 209–14.

"Hebrew יסר, Akkadian *esēru*: A Term of Forced Labor: A Lexicographical Note IX" in *Teshûrôt LaAvishur* (eds. M. Heltzer and M. Malul; Tel Aviv-Jaffa: Archaeological Center Publications, 2004), 185–90.

"The Semantic Range of the Biblical Hebrew חלל: A Lexicographical Note X," *Zeitschrift Für Die Alttestamentliche Wissenschaft* 117 (2005), 91–4.

"Two Biblical Architectural Images in Light of Cuneiform Sources: A Lexicographical Note XI," *Bulletin of the American School of Oriental Research* 341 (2006) 37–52.

"ʿAzazel the Prince of the Steppe: A Comparative Study," *Zeitschrift Für Die Alttestamentliche Wissenschaft* 92 (1980), 43–59.

"The Historicity of 2 Kings 19:24 (= Isaiah 37:25): The Problem of *Yeʾōrê Māṣôr*," *Journal of Near Eastern Stuides* 41 (1982), 195–206.

"Amos' Oracles Against the Nations: A New Interpretation," *Beit Mikra* 146 (1996), 376–88.

"Bathing in Milk (Song of Songs 5:12): A New Look," *Beit Mikra* 151 (1997), 388–92.

"Tāpat the Daughter of Solomon," *Beit Mikra* 159 (1999), 372–384.

"Paved with Love (Song of Songs 3:10d): A New Interpretation," *Zeitschrift Für Die Alttestamentliche Wissenschaft* 115 (2003), 266–71.

"'If the Sun Has Risen Upon Him' (Exodus 22:2): Legal Terminology in Light of Akkadian Texts from Ugarit," *Lešonēnu* 69 (2008), 30–8.

"A Note on the Aḥiram Inscription," *The Journal of the Ancient Near Eastern Society of Colombia University* 3 (1971), 32–6.

"The End of the Hadad Inscription in the Light of Akkadian," *Journal of Near Eastern Studies* 32 (1973), 477–82.

"Some Literary Elements in the Opening Sections of the Hadad, Zākir, and Nērab II Inscriptions in the Light of East and West Semitic Royal Inscriptions," *Orientalia* 43 (1974), 40–65.

"A Curse Concerning Crop-Consuming Insects in the Sefîre Treaty and in Akkadian: A New Interpretation," *Bulletin of the American School of Oriental Research* 225 (1977), 59–62.

"Two Notes on the Treaty Terminology of the Sefîre Inscriptions," *The Catholic Biblical Quarterly* 42 (1980) 30–7.

Common Abbreviations

AASOR	*The Annual of the American Schools of Oriental Research*
AB	Anchor Bible
ABL	R.F. Harper, *Assyrian and Babylonian Letters*
AfO	*Archiv für Orientforschung*
AHw	W. von Soden, *Akkadishes Handworterbuch*
AJSL	*American Journal of Semitic Languages and Literatures*
AKA	E.A.W. Budge and L.W. King, *The Annals of the Kings of Assyria*
AMT	R.C. Thompson, *Assyrian Medical Texts*
ANEP	J.P. Pritchard (ed.), *The Ancient Near East in Pictures Relating to the Old Testament*
ANES	*Ancient Near Eastern Studies*
ANET	J.P. Pritchard (ed.), *Ancient Near Eastern Texts Relating to the Old Testament*
AnSt	*Anatolian Studies*
AOAT	*Alter Orient und Altes Testament*
AOB	*Altorientalische Bibliothek*
ARM	*Archives royales de Mari*
AS	*Assyriological Studies*
ASOR	American Schools of Oriental Research
BAR	*Biblical Archeology Review*
BASOR	*Bulletin of the American Schools of Oriental Research*
BBR	H. Zimmern, *Beiträge zur Kenntnis der babylonischen Religion*
BBSt	L.W. King, *Babylonian Boundary Stones*
BDB	F. Brown, S.R. Driver, and C.A. Briggs, *A Hebrew and English Lexicon of the Old Testament*
BKAT	*Biblischer Kommentar Altes Testament*
BRM	*Babylonian Records in the Library of J. Pierpont Morgan*
BWL	W.G. Lambert, *Babylonian Wisdom Literature*
BZAW	*Beihefte zur Zeitschrift für die alttestamentliche Wissenschaft*

CAD	*The Assyrian Dictionary of the Oriental Institute of the University of Chicago*
CBQ	*Catholic Biblical Quarterly*
CH	R.F. Harper, *The Code of Hammurabi*
CIS	*Corpus Inscriptionum Semiticarum*
CT	*Cuneiform Texts from Babylonian Tablets*
CTA	A. Herdner, *Corpus des tablettes en cunéiformes alphabétiques découvertes à Ras Shamra-Ugarit de 1929 à 1939*
DISO	C.F. Jean and J. Hoftijzer, *Dictionnaire des inscriptions sémitiques de l'ouest*
EA	J.A. Knudtzon, *Die El-Amarna-Tafeln*
FRLANT	*Forschungen zur Religion und Literatur des Alten und Neuen Testaments*
HAT	Handbuch zum Alten Testament
HUCA	*Hebrew Union College Annual*
IAB	*Alian Baal (Part 1)*
IB	tablets in the Pontificio Istituto Biblico, Rome
ICC	International Critical Commentary
IEJ	*Israel Exploration Journal*
JANES	*Journal of the Ancient Near Eastern Society*
JANESCU	*Journal of the Ancient Near Eastern Society of Columbia University*
JBL	*Journal of Biblical Literature*
JCL	*Journal of Cuneiform Literature*
JCS	*Journal of Cuneiform Studies*
JJS	*Journal of Jewish Studies*
JNES	*Journal of Near Eastern Studies*
JPOS	*Journal of the Palestine Oriental Society*
JQR	*Jewish Quarterly Review*
JSOT	*Journal for the Study of the Old Testament*
KAH	*Keilschrifttexte aus Assur historischen Inhalts*
KAI	H. Donner and W. Röllig, *Kanaanäische und aramäische Inschriften* I–III
KAR	*Keilschrifttexte aus Assur religiösen Inhalts*
KAT	*Kommentar zum Alten Testament*
KB	L. Koehler and W. Baumgartner, *Lexicon in Veteris Testamenti libros*
KJ	*King James*
LAPO	*Littératures ancienne du Proche-Orient*
LBAT	*Late Babylonian Astronomical and Related Texts*

LKA	E. Ebeling, *Literarische Keilschrifttexte aus Assur*
MDP	*Mémoires de la Délégation en Perse*
MSL	*Materialien zum sumerischen Lexikon*
NAB	*New American Bible*
Nbn	J.N. Strassmaier, *Inschriften von Nabonidus*
NEB	*New English Bible*
NJPS	*The New JPS Translation on according to the Traditional Hebrew Text*
NSI	*North Semitic Inscriptions*
OECT	*Oxford Editions Cuneiform Texts*
OIP	Oriental Institute Publications
OLZ	*Orientalistische Literaturzeitung*
OTL	Old Testament Library
OTS	*Oudtestamentische Studiën*
PBS	*Publications of the Babylonian Section,* University Museum, University of Pennsylvania
PEQ	*Palestine Exploration Quarterly*
PRU	Ch. Virolleaud, *Le Palais royal d'Ugarit*
RA	*Revue d'assyriologie et d'archéologie*
RAr	*Revue archéologique*
RevQ	*Revue de Qumran*
RHR	*Revue d l'histoire des religions*
RS	Field numbers of tablets excavated at Ras Shamra
RSV	*Revised Standard Version*
STC	L. King, *The Seven Tablets of Creation*
SVT	*Supplements to Vetus Testamentum*
TDP	R. Labat, *Traité akkadien de diagnostics et prognostics médicaux*
TMB	F. Thureau-Dangin, *Textes mathématiques babyloniens*
TuL	E. Ebeling, Tod und Leben nach den Vorstellungen der Babylonier
VAB	*Vorderasiatische Bibliothek*
VAS	*Vorderasiatische Schriftdenmäler*
VT	*Vetus Testamentum*
VTE	*Vassal Treaties of Esarhaddon*
YOS	*Yale Oriental Series,* Babylonian Texts
ZA	*Zeitschrift für Assyriologie*
ZAW	*Zeitschrift für die alttestamentliche Wissenschaft*
ZDMG	*Zeitschrift der Deutschen Morgenländischen Gesellschaft*
ZDPV	*Zeitschrift des Deutschen Palästina-Vereins*

Lexicographical Notes

Hebrew צלח/הצלח, Akkadian *ešēru/šušuru*: A Lexicographical Note

Hebrew צלח is etymologically equated by most Hebrew[1] and Aramaic lexica with the Aramaic[2] verb צלח, "to split." This equation is based mainly on the biblical verse וצלחו הירדן (2 Sam. 19:18)[3] and the expression צלח על/אל רוח (Judg. 14:6, 19; 15:14; 1 Sam. 10:6; 16:13; 18:10). BDB, on the other hand, divides the Hebrew into צלח I (= Aramaic/Syriac צלח, "to split/cleave") "to rush," and צלח II (= Aramaic צלח, "to prosper") "to advance/prosper."

The distinction between the two verbs as well as the etymologies proposed above are open to question. (a) While צלח, "to split," is attested only in Aramaic[4] and Syriac,[5] there is no clear indication that in Biblical Hebrew צלח originally denoted "to split." (b) One would have expected Targum Jonathan to render the biblical expression וצלחו הירדן by either צלח "to split," or the common Aramaic verb בזע.[6] Interestingly enough, Targum Jonathan reads here וגזו ירדנא, "they passed the Jordan (with speed)."[7] (c) Based on the above Aramaic equation, some biblical expressions employing the verb צלח cannot sufficiently be explained. (d) It is difficult to accept the alleged semantic development of צלח, "to split/cleave" > צלח, "to succeed/prosper."

To understand fully the various meanings of צלח, an inductive method disclosing the semantic origin of the verb and its lexical relation to other Semitic languages is required. This replaces the use of etymology alone.

S. Lieberman has indicated that the LXX renders the expression ותצלח עליו רוח ה' by the Greek ἅλλομαι. "It is obvious," he says, "that the LXX understood the verb צלח, as an equivalent to קפץ, 'to jump, leap.'" He points out further that צלח, meaning קפץ, is well attested in rabbinic literature.[8] Thus, it would seem that Lieberman's observation (צלח = קפץ/ז) makes it improbable to equate semantically Hebrew צלח (in וצלחו הירדן and ותצלח עליו רוח

(ה') with the Aramaic verb צל, "to split." Similarly, in the *Piyyûṭîm,* where, as pointed out by H. Yalon,[9] the verb צלח (= קפץ = מהר = בא) denotes "to pass/proceed (with speed)." The semantic development of Hebrew צלח is, then, as follows: "to proceed/pass/to go (with speed) > to advance > progress > prosper > succeed"; it should in all probability be kept apart from its Aramaic homonym, צלח, "to split." This calls to mind the semantic development of the Akkadian verb *ešēru/šūšuru* "to proceed/march on/to, go straight towards," which then becomes "to advance/prosper > thrive/succeed."

It is the purpose of this paper to study some other usages of Hebrew הצלח/צלח in the light of Akkadian *ešēru/šūšuru.*

At the outset, it should be stressed that the exact semantic and etymological equivalent[10] of Akkadian *ḫarrāna ešēru/šūšuru*[11] is Hebrew ישר/הושר דרך.[12] No different in function and meaning is the Hebrew expression, הצלח דרך, "to cause one's way to succeed, prosper."[13] That is, Akkadian *urḫa/ḫarrāna/padāna ešēru/šūšuru (šutēšuru)* is to be equated not only with Hebrew ישר הושר דרך/ארח/מעגל, but also with הצלח דרך. Similarly, Akkadian *kibsu išaru*[14]*/ḫarrāna išartu*[15] corresponds to Hebrew דרך/ארח ישר/מישור, "successful path"[16] as well as to Late Hebrew דרך צלחה.

Another correspondence between Akkadian *ešēru* and Hebrew צלח may be seen in the expression *ina šipir/lipit qāti/idi ešēru/šūšuru*[17] = Hebrew הצלח במעשה/ביד "to be/cause to be successful in one's undertaking."[18]

Alongside the above usage, Akkadian *ešēru* is specifically employed in reference to the thriving of crops[19]; *ešēru* in this particular sense immediately calls to mind the attestation of Biblical Hebrew צלח (Ezek. 17:9, 10) in this very meaning. Such is also the case in post-biblical literature[20]; particularly relevant here is the Aramaic expression אצלח זרעא אפלא/(חרפא),[21] which semantically is the exact correspondent of Akkadian *še'u uppulu/(ḫarpu) šūšuru* "to cause late (early) barley to thrive."[22] Furthermore, the Akkadian idiom *ešēru eli*,[23] "to proceed to/straight towards/against": *ša utukku lemnu elīšu īšeru,* "towards whom the evil demon proceeded"[24]; and *kakkum mertappidum elīšu līšer,* "may the pursuing weapon go straight toward him,"[25] is semantically equivalent to Hebrew צלח על, as well as to the Late Hebrew idiom קפץ על, "to rush upon."[26]

In the light of the above Akkadian-Hebrew semantic correspondences, the clause (גבר) לא יצלח, employed in Jer. 22:30, may be better explained. Following the LXX, P. Volz[27] omits the clause, גבר לא יצלח בימיו. In this he is followed by J. Bright, who doubts "that these words are original."[28] Such an emendation, however, is not without difficulties. The resulting verse is unbalanced, leaving the term ערירי without any parallel.[29] Rather, the clause גבר לא יצלח, taken with what precedes, serves as a parallel interpretation of the term ערירי,[30] while צלח in the following clause (i.e., מזרעו לא יצלח) serves as a play on words. Such an understanding is strengthened when one notes that the phrase לא יצלח, in the sense of "unenergetic/unproductive" (parallel to ערירי, "a non-prosperous person"), may be viewed alongside the Akkadian phrase *lā išaru* employed in the following *ŠU.ILA* passage: *ašar tappallasī iballuṭ mītu itebbi marṣu iššer lā išaru,* "wherever you (Ishtar) look, the dead comes to life, the sick gets well (lit., rises), the unproductive man becomes prosperous."[31]

Yet another instance of הצלח in the Book of Jeremiah may be better understood in view of a different usage of Akkadian *ešēru/šūšuru*. The somewhat puzzling text of Jer. 5:28 reads as follows:

שמנו עשתו גם עברו דברי רע
דין לא דנו דין יתום ויצליחו
ומשפט אביונים לא שפטו

Following the interpretation of Qimḥi, modern biblical scholarship renders ויצליחו as "that they shall prosper/succeed,"[32] with the wicked as the subject of יצליחו. Such is also the rendering of G. R. Driver who argued that "clearly the text is distorted and the residual דין יתום, ומשפט אביונים לא שפטו, being unrhythmical, is a gloss on דין לא דנו explaining what kind of a דין they neglected."[33] T. Gaster equates יצליחו with Theiopic *ṣalḥawa,* "deceive, defraud," rendering v. 28b as follows: "In the case of the fatherless they cheat, and mete no justice to the poor."[34] On the other hand, J. Bright,[35] following D. Winton Thomas[36] and K. Rudolph,[37] claims that the subject of יצליחו is יתום (lit., "that they the orphans may have success."). A. Ehrlich[38] transfers ויצליחו to the end of v. 27, reading על כן גדלו ויעשירו ויצליחו, while P. Volz,[39] followed by N. H. Tur-Sinai,[40] argues that the verb belongs to the end of the first clause of v. 28, following דברי רע.

One would, however, expect an interpretation of v. 28b, דין יתום, ויצליחו that is less dependent upon a rearrangement of the verse. One of the attested meanings of Akkadian *ešēru*/*šūšuru* (*šutēšuru*) is "to provide/render justice — to see that justice is done."[41] The cognate usage of Akkadian *ešēru* is employed in Isa. 1:17, where אשר seems to be the exact etymological as well as semantic equivalent of the Akkadian term. As noted already by Ibn-Ezra and Qimḥi, the verb אשרו (רבו//שפטו//), used of a socially deprived individual, e.g., חמוץ (אלמנה//יתום//) "oppressed[42] (// orphan//widow)" is to be understood as ישרו,[43] "provide justice."[44] Similarly, in the sense of providing justice, הצלח is the semantic equivalent of Akkadian *šūšuru* and is used of deprived individuals, i.e., אביונים, יתום. Thus, the prophet condemns evildoers for the justice withheld from the orphan. In parallelism[45] with לא דנו and לא שפטו, we propose to render MT ויצליחו as ו(לא) יצליחו, in which the negative participle is understood from the preceding clause. Such an ellipsis, or double duty of one negative participle in subsequent clauses, is attested in both Ugaritic[46] and Hebrew poetry.[47] In Jer. 5:28, we encounter the triple duty of the negative participle, i.e., the negative is expressed in clauses a and c, but is understood in clause b. Such an omission of the negative in one of three clauses is found with nouns in 2 Sam. 1:21; there the negative participle is omitted in clause c: אל טל ואל מטר עליכם ושדי תרומות, "(Hills of Gilboa), let not dew not rain (fall) on you, nor upswelling of the deeps."[48] With verbs, on the other hand, this phenomenon is clearly attested in Isa. 38:18, where the negative is omitted in clause b but retained in clauses a and c: כי לא שאול תודך מות יהללך לא ישברו יורדי בור אל אמתך, "For it is not Sheol that praises you, not the Netherworld that extols you; nor do they who descend into the pit hope for your grace."[49] Furthermore, while in some cases the negative particle involving two clauses is totally omitted,[50] in other numerous instances a *waw* precedes the vocable in place of the negative; this happens with nouns[51] and verbs.[52] It seems, then, somewhat safe to assume that *waw* is used as a poetic device, and is functionally employed to serve as an indicator for the negative particle. Though it involves three clauses, such seems to be the case in Jer. 5:28, where the *waw* of ויצליחו stands for ולא יצליחו.

In light of these observations, the structure of Jer 5:28 b–c is best viewed as comprising three distinct cola:

(a) דין לא דנו
(b) דין יתום ויצליחו
(c) ומשפט אביונים לא שפטו

These are to be rendered:

(a) They (the wicked) judge not the cause
(b) the cause of the orphan they do not justly render
(c) nor do they provide justice to the cause of the poor.[53]

Finally, a word should be said about the difficult usage of צלח in Amos 5:6:

פן יצלח כאש בית יוסף ואכלה ואין מכבה לבית אל.

The problem centers on the employment of צלח with אש and the subject of the verse. Medieval commentators (Ibn-Janāḥ, Ibn-Ezra, Qimḥi) equated צלח with בקע, "to split"; they considered God's wrath (i.e., חמתו) as the hidden subject of the verse, rendering the clause, "lest (God's wrath) shall split the house of Joseph like fire." But as pointed out above,[54] there seems to be no clear indication that Hebrew צלח is semantically related to בקע; and צלח with a person as object (i.e., בית יוסף) is always followed by the preposition על or אל. Further, if one grants that the hidden subject is God's wrath, one would expect the feminine form of the word (תצלח) to be employed. A number of modern biblical scholars, considering the subject to be God, propose the following emendations: W. R. Harper,[55] ישלח אש, "cast fire";

Koehler-Baumgartner,[56] following K. Budde,[57] ישלח אש ב. On the other hand, those who argue that the subject is either אש or בית יוסף offer numerous emendations: J. Rieder, ילחך אש "(lest) the fire lick…";[58] Tur-Sinai, following Rieder, reads ילחך אש (Niphʿal), "will be licked by fire";[59] Grätz, followed by Ehrlich,[60] emends to ישלח באש (Niphʿal), while W. Rudolph[61] reads יצלח באש, equating it with the Akkadian *ṣelû.* Rudolph's emendation, however, is farfetched. Akkadian *ṣelû* is never used of people being burnt, but rather of *qutrinnu,* "incense," or other fumigants.[62] Hebrew צלח refers only to the roasting of meat.[63] Two other interesting interpretations are noteworthy: that of F. Perles, who equates צלח with Akkadian *ṣiriḫtu*, "in Brand setzen,"[64] as well as that of J. Blau,[65] who argues that Biblical Hebrew has two homonyms: צלח I, "to split > succeed,"[66] related to Aramaic צלח; and צלח II, "to burn," attested only in Amos 5:6, to be equated with Syriac *ṣrḥ.*

The LXX, Tg. Jonathan, Peshiṭta, and the Vulgate all translate צלח as "to burn/kindle." This also the opinion of M. Margolis,[67] who advocates no emendation. While not elaborating on either the etymological origin of צלח, "to burn," or on the semantic development of צלח, "to succeed" > צלח, "to burn," he does refer to the problematic usage of צלח in Sir. 8:10.

Most of the emendations discussed above suggest for Amos 5:6 the meaning of "to burn." Such a meaning is obviously required in this verse. Thus, an interpretation without involving an emendation would be to take צלח in the sense of "to burn." It should be recalled that Hebrew הצלח/צלח, the proposed semantic equivalent of Akkadian *ešēru*/*šūšuru*, is a *verbum movendi*, referring to an action of speech and rush. The verb דלק, attested nine times in the Hebrew Bible, is also employed as a *verbum movendi*, meaning "to pursue/rush after,"[68] as well as "to burn."[69] This also seems to be true of Hebrew בער, which commonly means "to burn," but also has the meaning (in the Piʿel) "to sweep away."[70] In Ugaritic, *bʿr* is also employed as a *verbum movendi*, twice meaning "to lead": *ybʿr lṯn aṯṯh lm nkr mdth*, "he (the newly wed) leads his wife to another, his beloved to a stranger"[71]; *qdš yuḫdm šbʿr amrr kkbkm lpnm*, "Qadesh proceeds to lead,

Amrur like a star in front."[72] It is also used to mean "to burn/kindle."[73] In Akkadian, an identical pattern prevails, exactly as in Northwest Semitic: verbs which express speed and rush may have two interrelated aspects, "to rush/proceed/advance (with speed)," or "to burn." Thus, while Akkadian *ešēru/šūšuru*, the proposed semantic equivalent of Hebrew צלח/הצלח, does not take on the related meaning of "to burn," one may refer, with different thematic vowels, to the relation between Akkadian *ḫamāṭu,* "to hurry/hasten"[74] and *ḫamāṭu*, "to burn."[75] With the same thematic vowels, this is also the relation of Akkadian *ṣarāḫu*, "to send quickly/to hurry,"[76] to *ṣarāḫu*, "to heat/scorch"[77] (= Aramaic/Syriac *ṣrḥ*).[78] In short, in Amos 5:6 צלח (without any emendation) is similar to the use of Hebrew דלק, "to rush" and דלק, "to burn"; to Hebrew/Ugaritic בער, "to sweep away"/"to lead" and בער, "to burn"; to Akkadian *ḫamāṭu/ṣarāḫu*, "to hurry"/"send quickly" and *ḫamāṭu/ṣarāḫu*, "to burn/scorch." Thus, Hebrew צלח shares this much related aspect: צלח, "to proceed/advance (with speed)" and צלח, "to burn" (employed in Amos 5:6).

NOTES

1. Ibn Janāḥ, *Sepher Haschoraschim* (ed. W. Bacher; Berlin: H, Itzowski, 1896), 430; D. Qimḥi, *Hebraeum bibliorum lexicon* (eds. H. R. Biesenthal and F. Lebrecht; Berlin: G. Bethge, 1847), 313a; W Gesenius and H. Buhl, *Hebräsches und aramäsches Handwörterbuch über das Alte Testament* (17th ed.; Berlin: Springer, 1949), 683; F. Brown, S. R. Driver, and C. A. Briggs, *Hebrew and English Lexicon of the Old Testament* (Oxford: Clarendon, 1906), 852.
2. *Aruch Completum* (ed. A. Kohut; Vienna: Beth Raphael, 1878–85), 7, 18–19; J. Levy, *Chaldäisches Wörterbuch über die Targumim* (Leipzig: J. Meltzer, 1881), 190–1; G. H. Dalman, *Atramäisch-neuhebräisches Handwörterbuch zu Targum, Talmud und Midrasch* (Göttingen: E. Pfeiffer, 1938), 363; M. Jastrow, *A Dictionary of the Targumim, the Talmud Babli and Yerushalmi, and the Midrashic Literature* (2 vols.; New York: Choreb, 1926), 1283b.
3. Note that the equation is based on Tg. Onqelos (וצלח אעי לעלתא), rendering the Hebrew ויבקע עצי עולה (Gen. 22:3). While Rashi renders וצלחו הירדן as בקעוהו בתריסהון, "they split it by their shields," Qimḥi provides

two possible interpretations: (a) כמו עברו, basing it on Targum Jonathan וגזו ירדנא; (b) ובקעו, as the rendering of Tg. Onqelos of Gen. 22:3. Further, note that S. D. Luzzatto (*Erläuterungen über einen Theil der Propheten und Hagiographen* [ed. M. Lamberg; reprinted, Jerusalem: Maqor, 1969], 22) equates Hebrew צלח (in 2 Sam. 19:18) with עבר, "to pass."

4. It seems that the first attestation of Aramaic צלח, "to split," is employed in *Aḥiqar* 125 (A. E. Cowley, *Aramaic Papyri of the Fifth Century B.C.* [Oxford: Clarendon, 1923], 216): איש מצלח עקז בחשוכא ולא חזה כאיש... גנב זי שתר בי, "a man may chop wood in the dark without seeing, like a thief who demolishes a house and...." This verb is attested also in the targumim rendering the Hebrew בקע עץ (cf. Tg. Onq., Gen. 22:3; Tg. Neb., 1 Sam. 6:14); בקע במחנה (Tg. 1 Chr. 11:18); גזר ים (Tg. Ket., Ps. 136:13). Elsewhere, in the Babylonian Talmud the verb צלח, "to split," is attested at least six times in reference to תכתקא, "stool" (b. *Šabb.* 129a); פתורא, "table" (ibid.); שרשיפא, "chair" (ibid.); ציבא, "wood chips" (b. *Šabb.* 119a; b. *B. Meṣ.* 79a); דיקלא, "twigs/reeds" (b. *B. Qam.* 113b), as well as the noun צלחתא, "splitting-headache"' (b. *Šabb.* 90a; b. *Git.* 68b).

5. Note that C. Brockelmann (*Lexicon Syriacum* [2d ed.; Halle: Niemeyer, 1928], 629) clearly distinguishes between the Aramaic/Syriac צלח, "to split," and Hebrew צלח, "to succeed/prosper."

6. Cf. Tg. Ps.-J., Exod. 14:16; Tg. Isa. 63:12; Tg. Ps. 74:15; 78:13; Job 28:10, and others.

7. Observe that targumic usage of (ירדנא) וגזו rendering the Hebrew (הירדן) וצלחו is, indeed, not incidental. Aramaic גוז, the sematic equivalent of Hebrew עבר/צלח, is clearly employed in cases referring to "passing sea/river." See Tg. Neb., Isa. 10:29: זגו עברו ירדנא = עברו מעברה, "they passed the Jordan (with speed)"; Tg. Isa. 51:10 שוית עומקי ימא אורח למיגז משיזביא = השמה מעמקי ים דרך, לעבר גאולים, "who made the ocean's depths a path for the ransomed to pass"; Tg. Nah. 1:12: ויגוזון ית = נגוזו ועבר דגלת ויעברון ית פרת, "they passed the Tigris with speed, they passed the Euphrates." Such is also the case in the b. *Yoma* 72b: לא תיזיל בספינת ציידין ובורני רבתא לא תנוזינה (Tg. Isa. 33:21), "(where) no ship can sail and no mighty vessel can pass." So too, in the Midrashim we encounter the following usages: *Gen. Rab.* 10:7: מגיזה יתה נהרא, "(a frog bearing a scorpion) causing it to pass the river"; *Lev. Rab.* 22:4: אגיזתא נהרא, "she (the frog) causing him (the scorpion) to pass the river"; ibid., 37:2: גוזין בחד נהרא (rd. מן דגיזין), "as they were passing the river." In Hebrew, the verb גוז (Num. 11:31, ויגז שלוים; Nah. 1:12, נגוזו ועבר; Ps. 90:10, כי גז חיש ונעופה) denotes an action of speed and rushing. Although *Aruch Completum* (2. 259–60); J. Levy (*Chaläisches Wörterbuch,* 129); M.

Jastrow (*Dictionary,* 220) semantically relate Aramaic גוז, "to pass with speed," to Aramaic גזז, "to cut," it is best, however, to keep the two verbs apart. Note that Hebrew גזז, exactly as its Akkadian semantic equivalent *gazāzu,* means only "to shear (sheep and goats)." While in Aramaic גזז by a later extension comes to connote "to cut" and grammatically is interchangeable with the "hollow" root גוז (cf. Hebrew סבב-סוב; קמם-קום; ערר-עור; רמם-רום, etc.), one fails to see any semantic relation between Aramaic גוז-גזז, "to shear, cut." and גוז "to pass with speed."

8. "Two Lexicographical Notes," *JBL* 65 (1946), 67–69; see further יונית ויונות בארץ ישראל (Jerusalem: Bialik Institute, 1963), 127–28: (a) the phrase ותצלח עליו רוח ה׳, translated by the Palestinian Talmud as שקפצה עליו רוח הקדש, "that the holy spirit leapt upon him"; (b) according to Pseudo-Rashi on *Gen. Rab* 86, Tg. Neb., 2 Sam. 19:18 rendered וצלחו by קפצו; (c) we read in *Gen. Rab.* 86, ויהי איש מצליח ר׳ ברכיה אמר גבר קפוז היך דאת אמרת וצלחו הירדן, "and he was a successful man" (Gen. 29:2). R. Berekhia said איש מצליח means here a jumping (i.e., energetic) man, as it says, וצלחו, "they jumped over the Jordan"; (d) Hebrew צלח ורכב (Ps. 45:5) and *ʾAggadat Šîr Haššîrîm* 2:14:ועלח פרעה על הסוס והקב"ה צלח כנגדו שנאמר צלח רכב, "and Pharaoh leaped (rushed) on the horse and the Holy One, blessed be He, leaped (rushed) to meet him, as it says, 'And do thou, Thy majesty, leap (or, and) ride.'"

9. "שווה שמשמעותו תנועה מהירה, טרופה," *Lešonénu* 27–28 (1963–64), 82.

10. Akkadian *haṭṭu išartu (OIP,* 2. 117:5)/*ḫaṭṭi mīšarim* (*RA* 39 [1940–44] 10:113–14), "just sceptre/sceptre of justice" = Hebrew שבט מישור (Ps. 45:7); Akkadian *awāt mīšarim* (*CH,* 25:64–67), "words of justice" = Hebrew אמרי ישר (Job 6:25); Akkadian *mīšara dabābu* (*CT* 46:44 II 12), "to speak righteousness" = Hebrew נגד מישרים/דבר (Isa. 33:15; 45:19; Prov. 23:16); Akkadian *mīšaru(m) dânu* (*BBSt,* 31:6), "to render justice" = Hebrew דון/שפט מישר/מישרים (Ps. 9:9; 58:2; 67:5; 75:3; 96:10; 98:9); Akkadian *mīšara šakānu* (*YOS* 9, 62, 11; *V A B* IV, 216:1–2), "to make an equitable arrangement/to establish justice" = Hebrew עשה/כנן מישרים (Ps. 99:4; Dan. 11:6); Akkadian *rāim mēšari* (*OIP* 2/4, 1:15), "lover of justice" = late Hebrew אוהב את המישרים (m. *ʿAbot* 6:6) — abbreviations of Akkadian sources are those employed in *CAD,* 1/1 (1964) xxiv–xxxiv.

11. E.g., Ebeling, *Handerhebung,* 52C:17 (*muštēšer urḫī)*; ibid., 8:24 (*urḫī lidmiq//padānī līšer).*

12. Ps. 5:9; Prov. 3:6; 11:15.

13. Gen. 24:21, 40, 42, 56; Deut. 28:29; Jos. 1:18; Judg. 18:5; Isa. 48:15; Jer. 12:1. For the semantic relation between Biblical Hebrew צלחה הדרך

and late Hebrew קפצה הדרך, see N. M. Bronznick, "למקורו ולהוראתו של המונח קפיצת הדרך" *Lešonénu* 37 (1973), 15–20.

14. E.g., *kibsa išara ina šēpēya šuk[un]* "(Marduk) led me (lit., set my feet) in a successful course" (Ebeling, *Handerhebung,* 108:16). Note that the latter phrase drawn from a *ŠU-ILA* prayer to Marduk corresponds to the following Biblical passages employed in the Psalms: תנחני בארץ מישור, "lead me into successful land" (Ps. 143:10); ונחני בארץ מישור, "lead me on a successful path" (Ps. 27:11).
15. E.g., *ša elīka ṭâbu ḫarrāna išarta tapaqqissu,* "you (Marduk) set the one who pleases you on a successful road" (*VAB,* IV, 122:58–60).
16. Jer. 31:9; Ps. 27:11; Prov. 2:13; cf. also Prov. 4:11.
17. E.g., *CT,* 39, 4:39: *lipit qātišu iššer,* "his endeavor will prosper"; *OIP* II, 81:29–30: *ana ilāni rabûti utninma suppêya išmûma lipit qātēya,* "I prayed to the great gods, so they heard my prayers and caused my undertaking to succeed..."; *YOS* 10 54 r. 25: *ina šipir [id] īšu iššer,* "he will be successful in his undertaking; cf. M. Held, "A Faithful Lover in an Old Babylonian Dialogue," *JCS* 15 (1961), 25a.
18. Gen. 39:3, Isa. 53:10; 2 Chr. 32:30; Ezra 5:8 (Aramaic).
19. Cf. *CAD,* E 354a.
20. *Gen. Rab.* 13:2.
21. b. *Roš Haš.* 16a.
22. E.g., B. Langdon, "Babylonian Proverbs," *AJSL* 28 (1911–12), 228–56 (cf. B. Landsberger, "Jahreszeiten im Sumerisch-Akkadischen," *JNES* 8[1949], 284 n. 118): *še'i ḫarpu iššer minâmmi nīdi še'u uppulu iššer minâmmi nīdi*, "how can we know whether the early barley will thrive (or) the late-barley will thrive"; *LKA* 142:30: *še'i ḫarpu uppula tušeššir še'u uppula tušeššir ḫarpa* "you can make late barley thrive on the (field suitable for) early barley; you can make early barley thrive on the (field suitable for) late (barley)."
23. Cf. also Akkadian *ešēru ana panī* (*YOS* 10 20 r. 26; *CT* 16 44: 110–11), lit., "to proceed straight towards/against," and Akkadian *ešēru ana* (*CT* 16 2:63f) = Hebrew צלח אל (1 Sam. 16:13; 18:10).
24. 5 *R* 50i, 41–42.
25. *Babylonica* 12, pl. 13, 15:3 (*Etana-susa* version); ibid., 14:5.
26. Note the following usages: b. *Ta'an.* 52, זקנה קופצת עליו, "old age rushes towards him"; y. *Giṭ. 6,* קפץ עליו החלי, "the disease attacked him"; y. *Ketub.* 10 קפצה עליהן ירואת תורה, "the legal succession according according to the legal law proceeded towards them"; *Gen. Rab.* 40:2, קפץ עליו רעבון, "hunger attacked him"; *Num. Rab.* 10, יצר הרע קופץ עליו, "an evil impulse attacks him"; *Sifra* 44:4, קפצה פורענות על נדב, "punishment came upon Nadab..."; קפץ הדבר על, "the word (of God) leaped upon

X," (see S. Lieberman, *Greek in Jewish Palestine* [New York: Jewish Theological Seminary, 1942], 165–66; *JBL* 65 [1946], 68).

27. *Studien zum Text des Jeremia* (Leipzig: Hinrichs, 1920), 188–90.
28. J. Bright, *Jeremiah* (AB 21; Garden City: Doubleday, 1965), 143.
29. Contrast Bright (ibid.), who argues that the words "one who'll have no success in his life time" interrupt the close connection between "childless" and the remainder of the verses which explains it.
30. Observe that the term ערירי(ם) (Gen. 15:2; Lev. 20:20, 21), which traditionally has been rendered "childless," can hardly fit the context in this verse, since Jehoiakim had children (for a discussion, see J. Bright, *Jeremiah,* 143). Sensing the contextual difficulty, *The New English Bible* (Oxford: Clarendon, 1970), 942, loosely translates the term as "stripped of all honour." In the light of the parallel clause, גבר לא יצלח, Luzzatto's interpretation is to be preferred (*Erläuterungen über einem Theil der Propheten und Hagiographen,* 76): וכאן ענינו דרך כלל נעדר מכל טוב וכמו שפירש גבר לא יצלח בימיו.
31. King, *STC,* 2. pl. 78:40–41.
32. See S. R. Driver, *The Book of the Prophet Jeremiah* (London: Hodder and Stoughton, 1906), 32; J. P. Hyatt, "Jeremiah," *The Interpreter's Bible* (New York: Abingdon, 1956), 853.
33. "Textual Problems: Jeremiah," *JQR* 28 (1937), 102.
34. "Jeremiah 5.28," *ExpTim* 56 (1944–45), 54b.
35. *Jeremiah,* 40.
36. "Jeremiah 5.28," *ExpTim* 57 (1946–47), 54–55.
37. *Jeremiah* (HAT 12; Tübingen: Mohr Siebeck, 1968), 40.
38. *Mikra Ki-Pheschuto* (reprinted, New York: Ktav, 1969), 3. 186.
39. *Studien zum Text,* 43–44; his reading of v. 28a is:שמנו ועבו גמ עשו דברי רע ויצליחו.
40. פשטו של מקרא (Jerusalem: Kiryath Sepher, 1967), 3/1. 171; his reading of v. 28a is: שמנו עשתו גם עבו דִּבְרֵי ויצליחו.
41. Cf. *CAD* E 361–63.
42. i.e., חמוץ, "oppressed" (following the rendering of the LXX, Tg. Neb., Pešiṭta, Sacadia, Radaq, and Luzzatto) = Akkadian *ḫamāṣu,* "to rob" (*AHw*, 315b); cf, also Hebrew חמוץ, "oppressor" (Ps. 71:4), and Tag. Neb. חמץ (מעיקא) for חמץ (רמס//שודד//) in Isa. 16:4.
43. For the interchange between roots *primae* aleph and *primae* yodh in Ugaritic, cf. *yḥd*, "solitary man" (1K: 96) and *aḥd* (ibid., line 184); Ugaritic *aḥdy*, "I alone" (IIA B 7:49) and Amarna yaḫudunni, "I myself" (RA 19[1922], 97–98: 24–25, Canaanite for anāku). For the interchange in Biblical Hebrew, cf. יש, "there is" and יש (2 Sam. 14:19; Mic. 6:10); in Old Aramaic, יש (KAI 216:16); Biblical Aramaic, איתי;

Ugaritic, *iṯ*. Cf. Also Hebrew ארשת, "request" (Ps. 21:3) and ירשת (Ps. 61:6); Akkadian *erištu*; Ugaritic *ʾrš*.1

44. Note that the *Tg. Neb.* Renders the MT אשרו חמוץ as זכו דאנים.
45. Note that the Akkadian also employs the verb *šutēšuru* (= Hebrew הצלח), "to provide justice," in parallelism with *dânu* (= Hebrew שפט// דון); cf. Ebeling, *Handerhebung*, 130:25–26: *dīn baʾūlāti ina kiti u mīšari tadinnī attī tuppallasī ḫabla u šagša tuštešerī uddakam*, "you (Ištar) in truth and justice judge the case of mankind, daily, you look favorably upon and see the case of the homeless girl"; Eberling, *Handerhebung*, 125:20: *tadân dīn tēnišēti tuštešura ikâ ekūtim*, "you (Šamaš) judge the case of mankind, render justice to the unjustly treated, the weak, the homeless girl."
46. *VAB* IV: 49–50; *IV A B* II:4–5.
47. See P. Joüon, *Grammaire de l'hébreu biblique* (Rome: Biblical Institute, 1947), X 160g.
48. For this rendering, see H. L. Ginsberg, "The Ugaritic Texts and Textual Criticism," *JBL* 62 (1943), 111–12.
49. For this translation, see H. L. Ginsberg, *The Book of Isaiah* (Philadelphia: Jewish Publication Society, 1973), 77.
50. Cf. 1 Sam. 2:3; Isa. 23:4; 38:18; Ps. 9:19; 75:6; Job 3:11; 30:25.
51. Gen. 49:10; Num. 23:19; Ps. 38:2 (= Ps. 6:2); 50:8; Prov. 31:4; Job 32:9.
52. Ex. 28:43 (= Lev. 22:9); Lev. 22:15–16; Ezek. 13:5; Amos 8:8; Ps. 44:19; 59:16.
53. Note that this rendering is also advocated by *NEB*, 916.
54. Cf. pp. 403–6 above.
55. *Amos and Hosea* (ICC; Edinburgh: Clark, 1905), 112–13.
56. *Lexicon in veteris Testamenti libros* (Leiden: Brill, 1958), 804a.
57. "Zu Text und Auslegung des Buches Amos," *JBL* 43 (1924), 107.
58. "Contributions to the Scriptural Text," *HUCA* 24 (1952–53), 95.
59. פשוטו של מקרא, 3/2. 463.
60. *Mikra Ki-Pheschuto* 3, 409.
61. *Joel-Amos-Abadja-Jona* (KAT 13/2; Gutersloh: Mohn, 1971), 189.
62. Cf. *CAD* Ṣ 124b.
63. 1 Sam. 2:15; Isa. 44:16, 19.
64. *Analekten zur Textkritik des Alten Testaments* (Leipzig: T. Achermann, 1922), 94.
65. "Über Homonyme und angeblich Homonyme Wurzeln II," *VT* 7 (1957), 100–101.
66. Contrast Blau; see above.
67. "Notes on Some Passages in Amos," *AJSL* 17 (1900–1), 171.
68. Cf. Gen. 31:36; 1 Sam. 17:53; Lam. 4:19. Note also the observation of

Ibn Janāḥ (*Sepher-Haschoraschim*, 110) that in parallelism to ירדפו, ידליקם (= ידלקו) in Isa 5:11 should be rendered as "they pursue."

69. Cf. Ezek. 24:10; Obad. 18; Prov. 26:23.
70. Cf. 1 Kings 14:10; 16:3; 21:21.
71. IK: 101–2; 190–191; cf. H. L. Ginsberg, "The Legend of King Keret: A Canaanite Epic of the Bronze Age," *BASOR* Supplementary Studies 2–3 (New Haven: ASOR, 1946), 16.
72. *II A B*, IV: 16–17; cf. *ANET*[3], 133a.
73. *VAB* IV: 69–70.
74. Cf. *CAD* Ḫ 62–64.
75. Cf. *CAD* Ḫ 64–66.
76. Cf. *CAD* Ṣ 100b–101a.
77. Cf. *CAD* S, 98b–99b.
78. Cf. Akkadian *ṣiriḫti libbi* (e.g., Streck, *Ašb* 46 V. 37)/*ṣiriḫti ša libbi* (e.g., *AMT* 39, I I 40), "inflammation of the heart" = Aramaic צירחא דליבא (Tg. Ps.-J., Deut. 28:22; b. *Giṭ*. 69b).

Hebrew סלף, Mishnaic Hebrew צלף, Akkadian *ṣalāpu/ṣullupu*: A Lexicographical Note II[1]

לטָפַּת, אריה ונעמי

"בכל דרכיך דעהו
והוא יישר ארחתיך"
(משלי ג:ו)

I

The suggested origin and etymology of the biblical סלף is open to serious questions on both etymological and semantic grounds. While modern biblical lexica offered unsound etymological derivations of the root, the various recent translations vary as to the precise rendering of the verb within its proper semantic context. At the end of the last century, S. R. Driver confessed that "the precise meaning" of the verb סלף "is uncertain; prob. to twist, pervert, fig. to subvert, ruin."[2] Uncertain as to the primary meaning of סלף more than a quarter century later, E. Dhorme[3] maintained that "the exact connotation" of the verb "is suggested by the context: sometimes 'falsify' the word (Exod. 23:8, Deut. 16:19; Prov. 22:12), sometimes 'make treacherous a path' (Prov. 19:3), finally, 'to plunge into misfortune' (Prov. 21:12) or 'overthrow' (Prov. 13:6)." Indeed, a doubt as to the precise etymological origin and the semantic connotation of the root is reflected in some of the recent English translations of the Hebrew Bible. The NJPS and NEB, for example, differ as to the proper rendering of the verb. While the NJPS rendering of סלף throughout the Hebrew Bible is consistent, the NEB's translation varies as to the proper connotation of the verb. Modern biblical lexica suggest one main possible etymological derivation for the root סלף. Although they basically maintain two meanings: 1. "to twist, pervert" 2. "subvert, turn upside down, ruin," etymologically they equate סלף with the Arabic verb *sálafa*, which means "to pass, pass away, come to naught." While in KB[4] it is asserted that the Heb. סלף is related to the Arabic *sálafa* "plough up," KB[1] equates the verb סלף with the Akk. noun *ṣullupu*, rendered by them as "dates turned about (for drying)." KB[1]'s etymological equation is somewhat puzzling, for it is difficult to follow the semantic relationship between the Heb. verb סלף and the Akk. noun *sullupu* (Sum. *ZÛ-LUM.MA*). Akk. *sullupu*, which is a borrowed noun from Sumerian, means "dates."[5] The vocable is attested only as a noun without any verbal form, allegedly meaning "to turn about," as maintained in KB[1]. Likewise, on semantic grounds, it is difficult to accept the etymological equation of Heb. סלף with Arabic *sálafa* as suggested by various lexica.[6] Arabic *sálafa* is not utilized at all in the same context as the Heb. סלף. This fact is clearly recognized when one notes that as understood by Sa'adya, the Arabic semantic equivalent of the Heb. סלף is *zāfa* (= Aram. זיף) "to counterfeit, to declare something to be false." Thus, Sa'adya consistently renders all the attestations of biblical סלף by the Arabic *zāfa*[7] and never by *sálafa*.

Likewise, following Sa'adya's rendering, Solomon ben Abraham Parchon, the medieval Jewish (12th cent.) lexicographer,[8] equates the Heb. סלף with the Aramaic זיף. Further, in the medieval Jewish literature, the verb סלף is often employed in synonymous parallelism[9] with זיף. On the other hand, Ibn-Ezra and Qimḥi equate סלף with the verb עות, which like סלף, is predominantly employed in the biblical wisdom literature in the sense of "to pervert (justice)/to falsify."[10]

The root סלף is employed nine times in BH. While the verbal form is attested (in the Pi'el) seven times,[11] the segolate nominal form סֶלֶף is employed only twice.[12] Contextually, the vocable is exclusively utilized (seven times) in the wisdom literature. The remaining two cases are found in the poetic parallel verses in Exod. 23:8 and in Deut. 16:19, which similarly have strong affinity with the wisdom literature.[13] Contextually, the root סלף is employed in parallelism with עור "to make blind"[14] and שלל.[15] סלף is also attested twice as the antonym of נצר "to guard, protect."[16] Additionally, the segolate noun סֶלֶף is employed as the antonym of תמה "completeness, integrity"[17] and of מרפא "healing."[18] This verb is likewise employed twice in the post-biblical wisdom books of Ben-Sira. There, סלף is utilized in parallelism with the verb הפך "to overturn."[19]

It is likewise noteworthy to idiomatically compare the usage of סלף in light of its biblical counterpart עקש. The root עקש is attested twenty times in BH. It is rendered fifteen times by the Targumim by the Aramaic עקם "to curve, twist"[20] (i.e., not straight) and once by קלקל.[21] Similar to סלף, the vocable עקש is predominantly employed twelve times in the wisdom literature, in the sense of "to pervert justice"; utilized six times as the antonym of תמם "to be complete, perfect, wholesome;"[22] and it is employed eight times in the idiom עקש דרך/נתיבה/ארח "to make a way[23]/path[24]/road[25] crooked/twisted" (i.e., "to prevent justice") = BH[26]/Ben-Sira[27] סלף דרך. However, unlike סלף the verb/noun עקש/מעקש/עקשות clearly functions as a concrete and physical vocable. It is employed figuratively in the idioms עקש פה/שפתיים/לב "to twist the mouth[28]/lips[29]/heart[30]," idioms that may have originally served as medical terms, to connote physical impediment of the body. עקש/מעקש is also utilized as the synonym of פתל "to twist"[31] and as the antonym of ישר/מישור "straight, leveled country."[32] Accordingly, although the root סלף at first glance seems to serve in BH as an abstract verb/noun, nevertheless from its usage as an antonym of נצר/מרפא/תמה "to guard/healing/completeness," and its employment with שֶׁבֶר "break"[33] שדד "to ruin,"[34] הפך "to overturn,"[35] סלף may have originally functioned in BH as a physical concrete vocable as well.

II

The purpose of the present paper is thus twofold; first we will re-investigate the etymological origin of the biblical root צלף and thereby to fully establish its primary meaning. This will be accomplished by stressing inductively the lexical and the semantic relation with its Akk. counterpart *ṣalāpu*. Second, we will establish the etymological and the semantic inner-relation between the biblical סלף, the difficult Mishnaic Heb. צלף and the Aram. צלב. It is indeed noteworthy that the proposed etymological-semantic equation of Akk. *ṣalāpu*, BH סלף, Mishnaic Heb. צלף, and Aramaic צלב[36] was hardly noticed by either East or by North West Semitic lexicographers.[37] However, to my knowledge, the only scholar who openly equates the biblical סלף with the Mishnaic צלף, seeing a dissimilation between *ṣade* and *samekh*,[38] and understanding the Mishnaic verb to mean "to turn aside" (i.e. נטה), is the Yemenite Yiḥya Saliḫ (= Mahariṣ, 1715–1805 CE).[39]

Unlike Heb. צלף, the Akk. root *ṣalāpu* is clearly employed to express both something physical/concrete, as well as a developed abstract notion. It should be observed that in the lexical lists Sum. *BAR*, *BAR NUN*, is the equivalent of Akk. *ṣalāpu* in all its attested grammatical forms.[40] Akk. *ṣalāpu* is likewise equated with Sum. *KU*.[41] Accordingly, to express the verb's concrete and physical notion, Sum. *ku$_5$-ku$_5$-ru* is equated in the lexical lists with Akk. *nakāsu* "to cut off," *pussusu* "to erase," *nukkusu* "to cut to pieces,"[42] *qalāpu* "to peel off,"[43] as well as with Akk. *ṣalāpu* "to cross out." The physical act of crossing out/canceling a clay or a wooden tablet is expressed by the Akk. *ṣullupu* (D stem) "to cross out/to cancel": a) [*gab-ri*] *Bābili ša kīma ṣirpi DIR šaṭāri ṣullupu* "copy of a (tablet/from) Babylon, according to a... baked clay tablet a canceled document."[44] b) *kî pī li'um ša ana pī šaṭātri ṣullupu* "according to the wording of a wooden tablet, which (lit., *ṣullupu* was in its writing) corresponds to a cancelled document."[45]

Accordingly, the act of cancellation is expressed by drawing a straight line by the parties involved. This line ran diagonally across the tablet, from the left upper angle to the lower right angle. Indeed, from OB onwards, Sum. *BAR.NUN* is equated in the lexical texts with the Akk. substantive *ṣiliptu*, and comes to connote "diagonal or hypotenuse."[46] Thus, in Akk. mathematical texts *ṣiliptu* is utilized as: a) "hypotenuse" (of a right-angled triangle), e.g., *šiddu pūtu u ṣiliptu 40 u 2 eqlu 15 šiddu [8 pūtu 17 ṣiliptu*]... "the short side, the long side, and the hypotenuse are 40, and the area is two. The short side is 15, the long side is [8, the hypotenuse is 17]."[47] b) diagonal of a square, e.g., *ṣilipti tamḫarti* 10 *ammātu* "ten cubits in the diagonal of a square"[48]; *bābum mušlu* 2 *ammātu mēlûm* 2 *ammātu rupšum ṣiliptašu minûm* "a door, one half minda two cubits height, two cubits what is its diagonal"[49]? c) diagonal of a trapezoid, e.g., *1.20 ṣilipti ša apsammikki* "1.20 is the diagonal of the trapezoid."[50] Furthermore, in medical contexts, the Akk. root *ṣlp* is likewise utilized as a concrete vocable to describe a physical malfunction of the human body.[51] The term *ṣalpu,* which is somewhat synonymous with Akk. *egru* (= LH. חגר),[52] means "slanted, twisted, perverse," in both physical as well as the abstract sense.[53] Thus, while the physical sense of the Heb. סלף is not apparent, nevertheless, from the usage of its Akk. counterpart *ṣalāpu*, it seems safe to assume that Heb. סלף, likewise has this very extended semantic development, from the physical to the abstract sense. Similar to the usage of סלף, Akk. *ṣalāpu* is mainly attested in the Babylonian wisdom literature connoting "to distort, pervert (justice)." Accordingly, in the Babylonian wisdom literature, and especially in the perceptive hymns to the god of justice Šamaš, Akk. *ṣalpu* "crooked/dishonest (i.e., not straight)," is employed in negative parallelism with *lā muštēšeru* "not to keep (things) straight, i.e., not to give correct judgment": *dayāna ṣalpa mēsira tukallam māḫir ṭaʾti lā muštēšeru tušazbal arna* "you (Shamash) show the prison to the crooked judge, (the judge) who accepts bribe yet does not give correct judgment you make him bear his punishment."[54] It is also interesting to note that in this passage, the Akk. sequential order *ṣalāpu — ṭaʾta maḫāru* is semantically comparable (in reverse order) to the biblical סלף — לקח שחד "to accept a bribe — to distort."[55] Furthermore, in both Babylonian wisdom literature and in neo-Assyrian annals, Akk. employs the idioms *ṣalipta dabābu/awû* "to speak/utter treacherous/distorted words": a) *ṣaklāti ša lišāna dābibu ṣa[lpāti] ša kima erpēti lā iša pāna u [bāba]* "those with a foolish tongue, who speak treacherous words, (words) which like clouds have neither head nor tail."[56] b) *Ḫattî dābibū ṣalipti bēlūssu izêrūma PN urabbû elišun* "The Hittites, who (always) speak treachery hated his rule and made PN… their overlord."[57] Here the Akk. expression *ṣalipta dabābu* "to speak distorted (i.e., not straight) words," may be associated with the Heb. idiom סלף דברי (צדיקים) "to distort the words of (the just men)."[58] This idiomatic expression is attested once more in Prov. 22:12: עֵינֵי ה' נָצְרוּ דָעַת וַיְסַלֵּף דִּבְרֵי בֹגֵד "The eyes of the Lord watch the wise man, he distorts the word of the treacherous." Contextually similar to this proverbial verse, Shamash the god of the sun and the lord of justice is likewise portrayed as one who watches the evildoers: *Šamaš dayān šamê u erṣiti ḫāʾit ṣalpat ayābi mušerû ṣēni* "the judge (ruler) of heaven and underworld, who watches over the treachery of the enemy, who inspect the wicked."[59] Akk. *ṣalpat ayābi* "the treachery of the enemy," may be the semantic equivalent of the Heb. idiom סֶלֶף בֹּגְדִים "the treachery of the treacherous," e.g., תֻּמַּת יְשָׁרִים תַּנְחֵם וְסֶלֶף בֹּגְדִים יְשָׁדֵּם "The integrity of the upright guides them, the treachery of the treacherous will destroy them."[60] It is noteworthy that in Prov. 11:3 תֻּמָּה "integrity" (lit., "completeness/fullness"), is employed as the antonym of the segolate noun סֶלֶף "crookedness" (lit., fracture, i.e., "not straight/complete/wholesome"). Likewise, is the case in Akk., where *kittu* "truth" is attested as the antonym of *ṣaliptu* "crookedness/treachery": *anāka Aššuraḫeinddina šar mat Aššur šar kibrat erbetti ša kittu irammuma ṣaliptu ikkibšu* "I Esarḫaddon the king of Assyria, the king of the four quarters of the world, who loves truth and abhors treachery."[61] Finally, one may similarly compare the Heb. verbal idiom סלף (דברי) הצדק "to distort (words of) justice"[62] with its nominal Akk. expression *ṣilip dīni* "distorted justice."[63]

III

While the Heb. root סלף is employed three times in post-biblical Heb., twice in the wisdom books of Ben-Sira,[64] and once in the

Temple Scroll,[65] our proposed Akk. equivalent *ṣalapu*, may similarly be found as צלף in Mishnaic Hebrew. The Mishanic *hapax* verb צלף is attested in m. *Yoma* 5:2–3.[66] This chapter relates that on the Day of Atonement, after making his second confession, the High Priest slaughtered his bullock and received its blood in a bowl, he then gave it to a priest who stirred it, lest it congeal, until he returned to sprinkle it, after offering the incense:

> נטל את הדם ממי שהיה ממרס בו נכנס למקום שנכנס, ועמד במקום שעמד, והזה ממנו אחת למעלה ושבע למטה ולא היה מתכון להזות לע למעלה ולא למטה אלא כמצליף. וכך היה מונה: אחת, אחת ואחת, אחת ושתים, אחת ושלש, אחת וארבע, אחת וחמש, אחת ושש, אחת ושבע, יצא והניחו על כן של זהב שבהיכל
>
> He took the blood from the one who was stirring it, he entered the place where he entered, and he stood in the place he stood, and he sprinkled from it one upwards and seven downwards, and he would not intend to sprinkle upwards or downwards, rather as *maṣlip*. And thus he would count: "One, one and one, one and two, one and three, one and four, one and five, one and six, one and seven." He came out and placed it on the golden stand in the Sanctuary.

The verb כמצליף (Hiph'il), employed in the phrase ולא היה מתכון להזות לא למעלה ולא למטה אלא כמצליף, "And he (the High Priest) did not aim (intend) to sprinkle either above, or below, rather like one who is *maṣlip*," created a philological as well as contextual problem, noted already by the Amoraim, the sages of the Talmud, namely: a) The accurate connotation of the *hapax* verb צלף. b) The manner of which the blood was sprinkled on the curtain, facing the Ark. The Babylonian Talmud[67] asks מאי כמצליף "What does *kemaṣlip* mean?" Consequently the Babylonian Talmud provides the scholarly opinion of Rav Judah מחוי רב יהודה כְּמַנגְּדָנָא "Rav Judah showed it to mean 'as one swinging a whip.'"[68]

The employment of the Aram. verb חוא/חוי "to show/demonstrate," is indeed revealing. Rav Judah explained the problematic

מצליף by physically demonstrating (i.e., מחוי) the action, hence imitating the movement of the lasher. Accordingly, the Aram. *nomen agentes* מנגדנא "lasher/whipper," derived from the root נגד "to lash/whip,"[69] was understood by Rav Judah as the correspondence of the Mishnaic מצליף "lasher/whipper." Although from Rav Judah's statement it is not clear at all as to the actual movement of the lasher and therefore the manner of sprinkler's gesture, Rashi,[70] who is followed by Bertinoro,[71] elaborates: כמכה ברצועה שמתחיל מן הכתפיים ומכה והלוך למטה "As one who lashes with a strap he starts from the shoulders and he continually whips downward." While Rashi acknowledges that ולשון מצליף לא נודע לי "The meaning of the (word) *maṣlip* is unknown to me,"[72] he asserts that the lasher did not whip in one place: כשליח בית דין המכה ברצועה זו למטה מזו שאינו מכה מבקום אחד "Like the court messenger who whips with a strap one (lash) below the other (lash), he does not whip in one place."[73] On the other hand, Rabad,[74] who follows Rabbenu Ḥananel,[75] maintains that the "lasher" (i.e., the sprinkler) whips (i.e., sprinkles) in one place: כמלקה הזה שפעמים שמגביה את ידו, ופעמים שמורידה, וכולן במקום אחד, כך היה מזה למעלה ולמטה בהגבהת יד ובהורדתה "Like this lasher that sometimes raises his hand and sometimes lowers it, but all (lashes) in one place. Thus, he was sprinkling upwards and downwards by raising and lowering his hand."

Hameiri disagrees with Rabad that the High Priest sprinkles in one place, and maintains that the lasher (i.e., the sprinkler) whips whatever he desires:

> ויש לפרש כמצליף כמגדנא כלומר שאינו מכוין להכות במוקם ידוע אלא באי זה מקום שיזדמן לו... אלא כמלקה זה שמגביה היד ומכה ואינו מכוין באי זה מקום אלא כמו שיארע לו...
>
> And one should interpret *kemaṣlip* as 'a lasher,' that is to say that he (the lasher) does not aim to whip in a specific (lit., known) place, rather in any spot that occurs to him... but like a whipper who raises a hand and lashes and he does not aim in a specific spot rather as it happens to him.[76]

Furthermore, alongside כמנגדנא "like a lasher," the Babylonian Talmud offers another explanation as to the question מאי כמצליף "what does *kemaṣlip* mean":

> תנה: כשהוא מזה – אינו מזה על הכפורת אלא כנגד עוביה של כפורת. כשהוא מזה למעלה – מצדד ידו למטה וכשהוא מזה למטה ידו למעלה
>
> A Tanna taught: as he sprinkled he did so not upon the ark-cover, but against its thickness and when he is to sprinkle upwards he first *meṣadded* his hand down, and when he is to sprinkle downwards he first *meṣadded* his hand up.[77]

Accordingly, the Tanna equates the Mishnaic vocable כמצליף with the word מצדד (Pi'el participle) from צדד, a denominative from the noun צד "side,"[78] rendered in our case by the majority of the medieval scholars as "to turn" (the hand).[79]

The explanation is provided by the Jerusalem Talmud. As to the question מהוא כמצליף "what does *kemaṣlip* mean?" they answer: ר' שמואל בר חנניה בשם ר' לעזר כמטוורד "Rabbi Shmuel bar Hananiah[80] in the name Rabbi Le'ezer like *metavred*."[81] It should be observed that the Jerusalem Talmud's כמטוורד, which seems to be the equivalent of the Mishnaic כמצליף, is rendered by the majority of scholars as כמטברר.[82] This vocable was analyzed as: a) denominative of the Aram. טְבּוֹר (Heb. טַבּוֹר) "navel." Thus, Rabbenu Ḥananel explains that the hand movement of the lasher/sprinkler as follows: פי' יש מי שאמרים שמטה ידו עד טבורו "Its explanation, there are some who say that he (the lasher/sprinkler) extends his hand till his navel."[83] b) H. Yalon[84] analyzes the Aram. טורד i.e., טברר as טבריז derived from the Syriac (by way of Persian) טברזא. He thus states: פי' קרדום, ומכאן מכת קרדום "its explanation: 'hatchet' and therefore the strike of a hatchet." c) The Yemenite Midrash *Hammidraš Haggadol* equates the Babylonian Talmud כמנגדנא "like a lasher" with the Jerusalem Talmud כמטוורד, i.e., כמטבריר, stating that כולהון לשון הכאה "all means striking."[85]

Accordingly, while the etymology of the Jerusalem Talmud's verbal *hapax* מטוורד (i.e., מטבריר) is indeed problematic, nevertheless the equation of the Mishnaic מצליף, Babylonian Talmud מנגדנא, Jerusalem Talmud מטוורד (i.e., מטבריר) understood by *Hammidraš Haggadol* as כולהו לשון הכאה "all means striking,"[86] is revealing. Further, although both medieval, as well as modern Talmudic scholars are in agreement that the Mishnaic מצליף comes to connote "lasher/whipper," thus considering the hand-gesture of the sprinkler to be the same as the hand-movement of the lasher, nevertheless, they are indecisive as to the actual hand-movement, whether lashing or sprinkling. From our Mishnaic passage, one action is evidently clear, namely, that the High Priest on the Day of Atonement did not sprinkle the blood, "either above or below." So, the question remains as to how he sprinkled? The verb צלף, in the sense of "to strike/whip/lash," is employed neither in Biblical Hebrew nor in Late Hebrew. It seems that its first occurrences are to be found twice in Aramaic: a) Tg. Pseudo- Jonathan renders the Heb. ארבעים יכנו לא יוסיף "He shall flog him forty (lashes) but no more" (Deut. 25:3) as ארבעין יצליף וחסיר חד "He shall flog (him) forty (lashes) less one." It is interesting to note that while in Tg. Pseudo- Jonathan צלף, is parallel to the more common Aram. verb לקה "to beat," in Tg. Onqelos, however, Aram. לקה is parallel to מחא "to strike." b) Tg. Ketuvim renders the Heb. יודע כמביא למעלה "as though bringing upward," Ps. 74:5 = Tg. Ket. יצלף בקורנסא "he shall strike with a mallet." Although, contextually it seems somewhat certain that the Mishnaic/Aram. verb צלף means "to flog/whip/lash," the etymology and the origin of the vocable is unclear.

As noted above in the Babylonian Talmud, the Tanna equates מצליף with מצדד, while R. Judah associates it with מנגדנא. Both Rabbis employed different Aramaic verbs to explain the actual way which the High Priest sprinkled the blood. Accordingly, in order to understand the precise hand-movement of the sprinkler it is worthwhile to contextually study the Late Hebrew/Aramaic denominative מצדד — the other term equated by the Tanna with *maṣlip* — as employed in post-biblical times. Let us bring forward the following four cases:

a) *Genesis Rabbah* 8:11 relates that a man glance diagonally (i.e., מצדד) at 45 degrees, without turning his face sideways, and an animal cannot.
b) In the Babylonian Talmud, in b. *Menaḥot* 98b, we learn that from both sides the six candlesticks were diagonally facing the middle one, e.g., מלמד שהיו מצדדין פניהם כלפי הנר האמצעי "That teaches us, that they (the candlesticks) were diagonally facing the middle light."

The Aramaic idiom צדד פנים "to slightly turn the face sideway," i.e., "to diagonally direct one's face," is similarly employed in c) b. *Yoma* 53a. There, we are told that the Priests, Levites, and the Israelites, in order not to turn their back to the Holy Ark — out of respect — they would leave their respected posts walking diagonally backwards, e.g., וכן תלמיד הנפטר מרבו לא יחזיר פניו וילך אלא מצדד פניו והולך "Thus also a disciple taking leave of his master, must not turn his face back to go away, but must turn his face diagonally and depart." The denominative צדד is unmistakably attested to convey the idea of positioning oneself diagonally behind his Rabbi out of respect. Also, in the Babylonian Talmud in d) b. *Yoma* 37a, we read: והתניא המהלך כנגד רבו הרי זה בּוּר אחורי רבו הרי זה מגסי הרוח דמצדד אצדודי "But has it not been taught, one who walks in front of his teacher is a 'boor,' one who walks behind him is arrogant? [it is assumed here] that he [the student walked] diagonally behind him." From the above Talmudic passage, it is rather obvious that both the left and right side of the master are reserved for the master's deputy and the head of the family, and forbidden to a regular student. It is likewise clear that a regular student is being advised not to walk either in the front or in the back of his master. Consequently the only choice left for the student is to position himself diagonally at 45 degrees behind his master on his either sides i.e., דמצדד אצדודי.

Our assumption that the verb צדד (employed in the above four cases) comes to express the notion of positioning oneself or an object diagonally may gain further ground by us noting that in the Babylonian Talmud *B. Bat.* 99a, some of the Talmudic sages argue that the placement of the Cherubs on the Ark, is identical to the body movement of a student when he takes leave of his master. Consequently, among the various opinions expressed, three are relevant to our study:

a) R. Aha bar Jacob (3rd–4th generation Amora) maintains that the Cherubs were positioned diagonally, e.g., ודלמא באלכסונא הוו קיימי "They might have been standing diagonally."
b) the Amora asserts: דמצדדי אצדודי "They were slightly turned sideways (i.e., they were positioned diagonally)."
c) Onqelos the proselyte (2nd century CE, Tanna) states that כרובים מעשה צעצועים הם ומצודדים פניהם כתלמיד הנפטר מרבו "The Cherubs are of sculptured work and their face and their face turned slightly sideways (i.e., diagonally) as a student who takes leave of his master."

It seems thus somewhat clear, that the employment of the noun אלכסונא "diagonal"[87] (= λοεον[88]) by the early Amora R. Aha bar Jacob (325 CE), is semantically parallel to the usage of the LH/Aram. verb צדד as attributed to Onqelos and the Amora. That is to say that both the noun אלכסונא, and the verb מצדד, come to express the notion of positioning and object/oneself diagonally.

IV

In light of the above usage of the LH/Aram. verb צדד, we would like to propose a more definite explanation as to why the Tanna depicted the verb מצדד, to interpret the Mishnaic כמצליף. At the outset it should be observed that unlike the Tanna, in order to explain the Mishnaic כמצליף, R. Judah found it necessary to demonstrate (i.e., חוי) the gesture of the lasher/whipper (i.e., כמנגדנא), as related to the movement of the sprinkler. Whereas R. Judah was obviously familiar with the hand movement of the lasher at the time of the whipping, we are left in the dark as to this actual gesture. However, from the usage of מצדד, as it was advanced by the Tanna to explain the word מצליף, we may finally better understand the actual movement of the "lasher." That is to say, if our conclusion that in the above cited examples, צדד comes to connote not only "to turn aside" but also "to position oneself/an object diagonally" at 45 degrees is correct, than the lasher's hand movement may be explained as follows: the lasher holding the whip in his hand, whipping the accused diagonally across his back from the left to the right side alternatively. Consequently, R. Judah's interpretation of the Mishnaic כמצליף as כמנדנא "like a lasher," and his demonstration (i.e., חוי) of the gesture, is to be understood as follows: on the Day of Atonement, the High Priest did not aim to sprinkle (the blood) either above or below, i.e., vertically, (i.e., לא למעלה ולא למטה) rather diagonally "like a lasher" (i.e., אלא כמצליף). Thus, the Tanna and R. Judah using different terminologies agree that the Mishnaic *hapax* צלף express the notion of a hand movement that is positioned diagonally.

More specifically, our internal philological analysis of the above Talmudic passages attempted to show that the Mishnaic צלף comes to express a gesture executed diagonally. The present thesis may be strengthened noting that the Mishnaic צלף, is likewise the etymological and the semantic equivalent of the Akk. verb *ṣalāpu/ṣullupu* "to cross out"[89] as well as the substantive/adjective *ṣalpu/ṣiliptu*, which comes to connote the mathematical concept of a diagonal (line).

NOTES

1. See H. Tawil, Hebrew הצלח/צלח, Akkadian *ešēru/šūšuru*. A Lexicographical Note, *JBL* 95 (1976), 405–13. I would like to thank Hakham Isaac S. D. Sassoon for his comments. I am also grateful to the staff of Yeshiva University for their kind assistance.
2. S. R. Driver, *A Critical and Exegetical Commentary on Deuteronomy* (International Critical Commentary; Edinburgh: T &T Clark, 1902), 200–201.
3. E. Dhorme, *A Commentary on the Book of Job* (trans. Harold Knight; London: Nelson, 1967), 177.
4. *KB*[1] (1958), 660. Note that in *KB*[3] (1983), 716 the Akk. etymology is abandoned.
5. See *AHw*, 1057; *CAD*, S, 373–377.

6. *BDB*, 701; *KB 3* (1983), 716.
7. See J. Dernbourg, *Ouevres Completes de R. Saadia ben Iosef Al-Fayyoume* (Paris, 1893), Vol. I, 114 (Exod. 23:8 = ויזיף), 278 (Deut. 16:19 = ותזיף); ibid., Vol. II, 70 (Prov. 13:16 = יזיפאן), 100 (Prov. 19:3 = יזיף), 117 (Prov. 21:12 = זיף), 125 (Prov. 22:12 = ויזיף). Likewise, the noun סלף is rendered by Sa'adya as זיף, cf. ibid., 62 (Prov. 11:3), 78 (Prov. 15:4 = ואלזיף), 41 (Job 12:19 = יזיפהם).
8. *Lexicon Hebraicum* (מחברת הערוך) reprint (Jerusalem 1970), 45b (Heb.)
9. E. g., כי אימת הזיפים//ופחד המסלפים נפלה עליו "because the fright of the dishonest (lit., the counterfeiters) and the fear of the crooked fell upon him." Eliezer ben Yehuda, *A Complete Dictionary of Ancient and Modern Hebrew* (Vol. 5; New York, London: T Yoselof, 1959), 5:4801b (hereafter, Ben-Yehuda dictionary) (Heb.)
10. Am. 8:5; Ps. 146:9; Job 8:3 = Job 34:12; Lam. 3:36, 59; Eccl. 1:15; 7:13.
11. Exod. 23:8; Deut. 16:19; Prov. 13:6; 19:3; 21:12; 22:12 (all employed in the earliest collection of Prov. 10–29); Job 12:19.
12. Prov. 11:3; 15:4.
13. See U. Cassuto, *A Commentary on the Book of Exodus* (trans. Israel Abrahams; Jerusalem: Magnes, 1967), 299; M. Weinfeld, *Deuteronomy and the Deuteronomic School* (Oxford: Clarendon Press, 1972), 245, 273, 362.
14. Exod. 23:8.
15. Job 12:19 (= 12:17).
16. Prov. 13:6.
17. Prov. 11:3.
18. Prov. 15:4.
19. Sir. 11:33.
20. Deut. 32:5; Isa. 59:8; Mic. 3:9; Ps. 101:4; Prov. 2:15; 4:24; 6:12; 8:8; 10:9; 11:20; 17:20; 19:1; 22:5; 28:6, 18.
21. Job 9:20.
22. Prov. 10:9; 11:20; 19:1; 28:6, 18; Job. 9:20.
23. Mic. 3:9; Prov. 10:9; 22:5; 28:6, 18.
24. Isa. 59:8.
25. Prov. 2:15.
26. Prov. 19:13.
27. Sir. 11:33.
28. Prov. 4:24; 6:12.
29. Prov. 19:1.
30. Ps. 101:4.
31. Deut. 32:5; Prov. 8:8.
32. Mic. 3:9; Prov. 8:8.
33. Prov. 15:4.

34. Prov. 11:3.
35. Sir. 11:33: סלף דרך//הפך ברית "to make the way crooked//to overturn a treaty."
36. Note that the Mishnaic/Aramaic/Mandaic noun/verb צלב/צליבה "crucify/to impale" seems to be a loanword from the Neo-Assyrian *ṣilbu* "crosswise arrangement (of bandages or woods)," equated by the *CAD* (Ṣ 187) with *ṣalāpu*. Cf. also M. Dietrich "Zum Mandaischen Wortschatz," *Biliotheca Orientalis* 24 (1967), 302; N. Waldman, "Akkadian Loanwords and Parallels in Mishnaic Hebrew" (Ph.D. diss. University of Pennsylvania, 1973), 133–34, esp. see n. 33. Note also that the extended meaning of צלף in Modern Hebrew comes to connote "to snipe/sniper/marksman" — namely, an expert who aims his arrows/bullets directly at the center point (of his target) where the two diagonal lines crisscross each other. See A. Even-Shoshan, *The New Dictionary* (vol. V; Jerusalem: Kiryat Sepher, 1968), 5:234 (Heb).
37. Note that while W. von Soden (*AHw*, 1076b) equates Akk. *ṣalāpu* only with the Syr. *slp*, Nahum Waldman depicts the relationship without fully elaborating as to the precise connotation of the Mishnaic Hapax צלף. Likewise, M. Moreshet does not shed any new light on the Mishnaic verb צלף. See M. Moreshet, *A Lexicon of the New Verbs in Tannaitic Hebrew* (Ramat-Gan: Bar Ilan University Press, 1980), 307 (Heb.).
38. For the dissimilation of *ś*>*s*>*ṣ* cf. e.g., Akk. *sullû/(ṣullû)* = Aram. צלא = Ugr. *ṣly*; Akk. *ṣâḫu* = Heb. צחק/שחק = Late Hebrew סחק = Ugr. *ṣḥq* "to laugh"; Akkadian *ṣaḫātu* = Heb. שחט = Late Heb. סחט "to press grapes and other fruits." See. E. Y. Kutscher *Words and their History*, (Jerusalem: Kiryat Sepher, 1965), 1-4-105 (Heb.); M. Moreshet -צחק שחק/יצחק-ישחק, *Beit Mikra* 35/4 (1968), 127–130; H. R. (Chaim) Cohen, *Biblical Hapax Legomena in the Light of Akkadian and Ugaritic* (Missoula, Montana: Scholars Press, 1978), 56. nn. 29–31; R. C. Steiner *Affricated Sade in the Semitic Languages* (New York: American Academy for Jewish Research, 1982).
39. See Yaḥya Saliḫ's commentary *'Eṣ Ḥayyim* on the Tiklal (Yemeni prayer book), Vol. III, 96–97 (ed. Y. Hasid, Jerusalem 1961 [Heb.]): לשון מצליף ענין הטיה כמו ויסלף דברי צדיקים בחלוף צדי בסמך כלומר שיהיה מטה לכאן ולכאן "And the meaning of *maṣlip* is a matter of turning aside, like: 'He will destroy the words of the righteous.' There is (here) a substitute of *ṣade* with *samekh*. Namely, that he (the High Priest) turns (his hand) aside in both directions."
40. *CAD* Ṣ 71, 86, 188 (Lexical Section) cf. also *AHw*, 1076, 1100.
41. B. Landsberger, *Materialien zum Sumerischen Lexicon,* (Roma:

Pontificium Institutum Biblicum; Chicago, Ill.: Distributed by Argonaut Inc. 2, 1960), 4:150 (hereafter *MSL*).

42. *MSL* 13, 17 (= *Izi* DII:24–27).
43. *MSL* 14, 229 (= *ana ittišu* 16:167–169).
44. W. G. Lambert, *Babylonian Wisdom Literature* (Oxford: Clarendon Press, 1960), 66, n. 1 (hereafter, *BWL*); *CAD* Ṣ 240.
45. *BWL* 66 n. 1; *CAD* Ṣ 240.
46. E.g. *MSL* 1, 54:43–36 (*ana ittišu*): Sum. *a.šà šu.ri.àm* = Akk. *eqel mišlāni* (line 43). Sum. *a.ša sùr.ra* = Akk. *eqel ḫirri* (line 44). Sum *sùr. še sag.e.dè* = Akk. *ana ḫarāri* (line 45). Sum. *BAR.NUN BAR NUN še. ib.ta.e* = Akk. *ṣilipta ana ṣilipte ušēsi* (line 46). Translation: Line 43 "field of the half (half lease)." Line 44 "field for digging." Line 45 "to dig up (with the hoe)." Line 46 "diagonal upon diagonal he leased."
47. F. Thureau-Dangin, *Text Mathèmatiques Babylonies* (Leiden, 1938), 77 No. 156 (Hereafter *TMB*).
48. *TMB* 78 No. 158.
49. *TMB* 130 No. 232:1, ibid., No. 233:1.
50. See A. Draffkorn Kilmer, "Two Lists of Key Numbers," *Orientalia* 29 (1960), 285 D, 2.
51. E.g. *šumma ina šumēl marti ina šepīma ana panīšu ana arkišu turrat* "If at the left of the gall bladder in the… there is a foot and it is slanted towards its front, turned towards its back" *CAD* S 86.
52. See "*Ḥgr* I and *Ḥgr* II," *JANES*, 3 (1971), 126, n. 39.
53. Note the sequence *ṣalpu egru lā šēmû* "crooked, dishonest, disobedient" in a broken text in *AfO* 19 (1959), 65:53. Cf. also *BWL*, 128:61: *tutarra ṣalpu ša lamu* "you (*Šamaš*) dismiss (lit., return back) the crooked who is surrounded." Note also that the verbal adj. *ṣalpu* "crooked," is equated in the synonym list with *ṣēnu* "wicked" (*AHw*, 1097a) = *ṣalpat* (*ayābi*)//*ṣēni* (cf. *op. cit.* n. 58). The Akk. expression *ša libbašu ṣalpu* (= Sum. *lú.ša.bar.ra*) "whose heart is crooked," employed in the lexical list (*CAD* S, 86a) is to be compared to the idiom *libba egēru* (cf. ibid., n. 51) e.g., *itgur libbašunuma*//*malû tuššāti* "their hearts are crooked//they are full of malice" (*CAD* E, 42a). Both the *libba ṣalpu*/*egēru* are likewise the semantic equivalent of Heb. עשק לב "crooked heart" employed in Prov. 11:20 עשק לב//תמימי דרך "crooked heart//righteous"; Prov. 17:20 עשק לב//נהפך בלשונו "crooked heart//one who speaks duplicity."
54. *BWL* 132:97–98.
55. Exod. 23:8, Deut. 16:19, See also 1 Sam. 8:3: לקח שחד//הטה משפט "to accept a bribe//to subvert justice."
56. *BWL* 136:167–168 (Šamaš Hymn).
57. A.G. Lie *The Inscription of Sargon II, King of Assyria* (Paris: Librarie

orientaliste P. Geuthner, 1929), lines 253–254 (hereafter Lie, Sar.). Note also the pair *kāpid (u) limnēti//dābib ṣalipti* "who plots evil//who speaks treachery." H. Winckler, *Die Keilscrifttexte Sargons* (Leipzig: J. C. Hinrichs, 1889), 45F 19. Note also the sequence *egru//lemutta qabû// [l]ā bānita qabû//ṣalipta šudbubu* "crooked//to speak evil//to speak [u]nseemly things//to cause treachery to be spoken," E. Reiner, *Šurpu* (= *AfO Beiheft* 11 [1958] II:10–15. For *ṣalipta tamû* in an omen text, see *AfO* 11 (1936–1937), 223:22–23: *[šum]ma in dabābišu qaqqara inaṭal ṣilipta itamû* "if when he talks he looks down (lit. at the ground) he will speak treachery."

58. Exod. 23:8; Deut. 16:19.
59. E.A. Wallis Budge and L.W. King, *Annals of the Kings of Assyria: The cuneiform texts with translations, transliterations, etc., from the original documents in the British Museum* (London: The Museum, 1902), 29 i7:8 (hereafter *AKA*).
60. Prov. 11:3.
61. R. Borger, *Die Inschriften Asarhaddon Konigs von Assyrien* (= *AFO beihef* 9, Graz 1956), 54 IV:25–26.
62. Yigael Yadin (ed.) *The Temple Scroll,* (Jerusalem: Society for the Study of Israel and its Antiquity, 1983), Vol. 2, 228, 51:13. As noted by Yadin, "the change in the scroll is surely a reflection of the importance of the term צדק in the sectarian usage, and especially of the title מורה צדק."
63. *BWL* 207:6–7: *[...] ēpiš enīti bābil pāni [...] ṣilip dīni* "Doer of iniquity, the one who shows favor [...] who administrates crooks justice." Note that the biblical sequence הכר פנים – סלף דברים "to show favor — to distort words" in Deut. 16:19 corresponds to Akk. order *bābil pāni — ṣilip dīni*. Further, the biblical idiom הכר פנים lit. "to recognize a face," seems to be the semantic equivalent of נשא פנים "to lift up a face." Both expressions connote "to show favor." While נשא פנים is employed in its general sense ten times (Gen. 19:21; 32:21; Num. 6:26; Deut. 28:50; Mal. 1:8,9; Job. 22:26; 32:21; 42:8; Lam. 4:16), הכר פנים is attested only once (Prov. 28:21). Both expressions הכר/נשא פנים are the semantic correspondence of the Akk. idiom *pāna wabālu* "to favor, to show preference." Both the Heb. and Akk. idioms are likewise employed in the legal sense. While הכר פנים (במשפט) is attested three times (Deut. 1:17; 16:9; Prov. 24:23), נשא פנים is utilized only once (Deut. 10:17). For Akk. *pāna wabālu,* which is commonly attested in the legal sense, see the following three examples: a) *awīlum pāni awīlim in bāb Ištar lā ūbal* "one must show any preference at the Ištar Gate (i.e., in a law court)," *Vorderasiatiche Schriftdenkmaler* 16 (1917), 88:14–15. b) *ina ubbubika pānišuna lā tubbal* "you must not show any favoritism when you clear (them) of obligations," *Archives Royal de Mari* (Paris, 1950),

Vol. I, No. 82:16–17 (hereafter *ARM*). c) *uluma awāt ekallim uluma awāt* "should the place, or should Kibridagan have a law case against you I shall not show you favor," *ARM* II, No. 94:16–19.

64. Sir. 11:7, 31.
65. Cf. n. 61.
66. See also t. *Kipp*. 3:20 (Zuckermandel 186); *Sefra Ahare Mot*, chap. 3.
67. b. *Yoma* 15a; 54b; b. *Zeb*. 38a.
68. Ibid.
69. For the Aramaic verb/noun נגד/מנגדנא "to lash/lasher (at court)," see M. Jastrow, *Dictionary* (vol. 2; New York: Pardes Publishing House, 1950), 796, 872; Nathan ben Jechielis, *Aruch Completum* (vol. 5; New York: Pardes Publishing House, 1955), 172, 305 (hereafter *Aruch)*. Note further that in Maindaic *ṣilpa* means "whip/blow/stroke." See E.S. Drower and R. Macuch, *A Mandaic Dictionary* (Oxford: Clarendon Press, 1963), 393.
70. See Rashi's commentary on b. *Yoma* 54b.
71. See Obadiah ben Abraham Bertinoro's (1415–1500) commentary on m. *Yoma* 5:2–3.
72. See Rashi's commentary on b. *Yoma* 15a.
73. Ibid.
74. See Abraham Ben David's (= Rabad) commentary on *Sifra*, Aḥare Mot, chap. 3 = *Sifra Debey Rav. Torat Kohanim* (Jerusalem 1969), 79. (Heb.).
75. See Ḥananel ben Hushiel's (died 1055) *Commentary on the Talmud* (Jerusalem 1973), 75 on b. *Yoma* 55a (Heb.).
76. See Menachem ben Shalom Meiri's (1249–1316) *Commentary on m. Yoma* 5:2 (ed. Menahem Meshi Zahav; vol. 2; Jerusalem: Itri Press, 1971), 371–372 (Heb.).
77. b. *Yoma* 15a.
78. For the Aramaic denominative צדד, see Jastrow, *Dictionary,* Vol. 2, 1261; *Aruch,* Vol. 7, 7; Ben Yehuda, *Dictionary,* Vol. 6, 5380–5381; cf. also Moreshet, *Lexicon,* 302 (cf. Ibid., n. 36).
79. See Rashi's commentary on b. *Yoma* 55b.
80. Rabbi Shmuel bar Hananiah is a 3rd generation Palestinian Amora (290–320 CE).
81. y. *Yoma* 5:4.
82. See Jastrow, *Dictionary*, Vol. 2, 519; *Aruch,* Vol. 2, p. 13; Moshe Kosovsky, *Concordance to the Talmud Yerushalmi* (vol. 4; Jerusalem: Magnes Press, 1990), 4:39; *Otzar Hageonim* (ed. B.M. Levin, vol. 6; Jerusalem, 1934), 6:56; *Sefer Ahavat Zion and Jerusalem on b. Yoma* (ed. Baer Ratner, Vilna 1909), 63. For a full discussion of כמצליף =

כמטברר cf. S. Liberman, *Tosefta ki-Feshutah* (vol. 4; New York: Mechon Meir Lev Press, 1962), 4:774.

83. Cf. ibid., n. 74.
84. H. Yalon, *Pirqe Lashon* (Jerusalem: Mosad Biyalik, 1971), 397–8 (Heb.).
85. *Hammidrash Haggadol on Leviticus* (Ed. N. Rabinowitz, New York, 1930), 423.
86. Ibid.
87. See Jastrow *Dictionary* I, 70.
88. See S. Krauss, *Griechische und lateinische lehnwörter in Talmud, Midrasch und Targum,* (Berlin: S. Calvary, 1988), 54.
89. Note that this idea of two diagonal lines crisscrossing one another is expressed in post-biblical Heb. by the Greek letter *chi* = *x* = Heb. כי. The Greek letter *X* = *chi* = כי is employed twice in the Mishnah as follows: a) m. *Kelim* 20:7 מחצלת שעשה לה קנים לארכה טהורה וחכמים אומרים עד שיעשה כמין כי "A piece of matting whereon reeds are laid lengthwise is not susceptible to uncleanness; but the sages say: only if they are laid crosswise (i.e. in the form of [the Greek letter] *chi*)." b) m. *Men.* 6:3 החולת טעונות בלילה והרקיקים משוחים כיצד מושחין? כמין כי "The cakes required to be mingled (with oil) and the wafers to be anointed. How did they anoint them? In the form of (a cross like the Greek letter) *chi"* (cf. also t. *Men.* 8:9; t. *Ter.* 4:9). In the Babylonian Talmud they elaborate מאי כמין כי אמר רב כהנא כמין כי יוני "What is the meaning of 'in the form of *chi'*? Said R. Kahana, in the form of the Greek letter *chi"* (b. *Men.* 75a; 106a). As to the question in what manner kings and priests are anointed the Babylonian Talmud states: תנו רבנן כיצד מושחים את המלכים כמין נזר ואת הכוהנים כמין כי מאי כי אמר רב מנשיא בר גדא כמין כי יוני "Our Rabbis taught: How were the kings anointed? In the shape of a wreath. And the priests in the shape of a *chi.* R. Menasha b. Gadda replied: in the shape of a Greek *X.*" b. *Hor.* 12a; b. *Ker.* 5b; cf. also y. *Ter.* 42b; y. *'Erub.* 18:3. For a discussion of the Greek letter *chi* in post biblical Heb. see E. Fink "Schriftgeschichtliche Beobachtungen an den beiden griechischen Buchstaben T und X, dren sich der Talmud zur Bezeichnung von Gestalten bedient," *HUCA*, 10 (1935), 169–183. Cf. also S. Krauss, *Griechische und lateinische lehnwörter*, 284; S. Lieberman, *Tosefta Ki-Feshutah, Order Zeraim* pt. I (Jerusalem, 1992), 523.

Hebrew שׂכל-סכל, Akkadian *Saklu*: A Lexicographical Note III

The BH roots שׂכל and סכל are considered by various modern lexicons and commentators to be three distinct lexemes. The BDB[1] and KB,[2] for example, list them in three different entries: a) 1 שׂכל. "to be prudent" 2. "to have an insight" 3. "to succeed, prosper." b) שׂכל "to lay crosswise" (*hapax legomenon*). c) סכל "to be foolish, to act foolishly."[3]

The etymological origins and semantic relationship between these words have not been sufficiently clarified. The purpose of the present paper is twofold. First, we will reinvestigate the etymological and the semantic relationship between alleged *hapax* שׂכל II "to lay crosswise" and סכל. The word סכל is unsatisfactorily rendered as "to be foolish, to act foolishly."[4] We will attempt to establish its primary connotation by stressing inductively its lexical and semantic relationship with its Akkadian (adjective/ substantive) counterpart *saklu.* Second, we will identify two additional attestation of שׂכל II in BH, and further clarify the relationship between שׂכל I and שׂכל II.

I. שׂכל II "to lay crosswise, to crisscross"

The alleged *hapax* שׂכל II is employed in Gen. 48:14 in context of Jacob's blessing:

> וישלח ישׂראל את־ימינו וישׁת על־ראשׁ אפרים והוּא הצעיר
> ואת־שׂמאלו על־ראשׁ מנשׁה שִׂכֵּל את־ידיו כי מנשׁה הבכור

NJPS renders:

> But Israel stretched out his right hand and laid it on Ephraim's head, though he was younger, and his left hand on Manasseh's head — thus crossing his hands-although Manasseh was the firstborn.

Both lexicons, the BDB and KB3, equate שׂכל II with the Arabic *šakala*, which primarily connotes "to bind the legs of a beast, plait locks of hair."[5] This etymological equation was rejected by numerous scholars as a "secondary and so remote analogy,"[6] and "unacceptable."[7] Indeed, one should expect Sa'adya's translation to reflect the Arabic *šakala*. However, following Tg. Onq., he renders the idiom שִׂכֵּל את־ידיו as אחכם ידיה "he (Jacob) gave his hand good sense."[8] It should be further observed that Rabbi Nehemiah, a second generation tannaitic scholar, likewise follows Tg. Onq. and comments: ר' נחמיה אמר: ניתחכמו ידיו של אבינו יעקב ליתן בכורה לאפרים "Rabbi Nehemiah said: 'the hands of our father Jacob were wise to bestow the birthright on Ephraim.'"[9] Consequently, the majority of medieval Jewish commentators, such as Rashi, Ibn-Ezra, and Qimḥi followed Tg. Onq., rendering the idiom as אחכימנון לידוהי "he (Jacob) smartly (directed) his hands." This equates שׂכל in Gen. 48:14 with שׂכל I "to be prudent, wise, to have insight."[10]

On the other hand, contrary to the opinion advocated by Rabbi Nehemiah (i.e. שׂכל = חכם), Rabbi Judah states: רבי יהודה אמר: נִישְׂתכלו ידיו של אבינו יעקב מליתן בכורא למנשה "Rabbi Judah said: 'Jacob's hands canceled themselves from bestowing the birthright on Manasseh.'"[11] It should be noted that Albeck, without elaboration, interprets נִישְׂתכלו ידיו as נשמטו ידיו "his (Jacob's) hands dropped."[12] We, however, maintain that in this specific context נִישְׂתכלו has the following semantic range: (his hands) were *crossed* > *entangled* > *cancelled themselves* (from bestowing the birthright to Manasseh). This can be strengthened by noting Rabbi Judah's comment in *Pesiqta Rabbati*: אמר רבי יהודה שִׂכֵּל ידיו של יעקב בבכרתו של מנשה "Rabbi Judah said: 'Jacob cancelled (i.e., nullified) his hands from the birthright of Manasseh.'"[13]

Furthermore, Tgs. Pseudo-Jonathan and Yershalmi render: פרג ידוהי "he Jacob reversed/changed his hands." Tg. Neofiti translates שלחף ית ידוהי "he (Jacob) reversed his hands." Rabbenu Ḥananel explains שִׂכֵּל ידיו as הרכיב ידיו זו על גב זו "he mounted his hands one upon the other."[14] Baḥya elaborates: וכונתו לאמר כי לא

החליף את הנערים ולא שנה את מקומם אבל החליף את ידיו והרכיבם זו על גבי זו, ושׂם את ימינו על ראש הצעיר ושׂמאלו על ראש מנשה שהיה הבכור "And he (Ḥananel) meant to say that he (Jacob) did not change the boys' (place), but he reversed his hands and mounted one upon the other. He placed his right hand on the head of the younger (boy) and his left on the head of Manasseh, which was the firstborn."[15]

Rashbam seems to be the first exegete to stick to the simple meaning of the text. He compares the verb שִׂכֵּל with the noun שָׂכָל, and further equates it with the Heb. פתל and the Aram. עקם "to twist, to be crooked:"

> שִׂכֵּל אֶת־יָדָיו, כמו שָׂכָל שהוא לשון אדם מעוקם ונפתל. כִּי מְנַשֶּׁה הַבְּכוֹר, ויודע היה יעקב שיוסף בנו הביאם שיהא מנשה לימינו של יעקב ואפרים לשׂמאלו והוא רצה לתת ימינו על ראש הצעיר ושׂמאלו על ראש הבכור.
>
> *śikkel et yādāw,* similar to (like) *śākāl*, which means a twisted and crooked man. 'Because Manasseh is the firstborn,' and Jacob knew that Jospeh brought them, so that Manasseh will be at the right side of Jacob, and Ephraim to his left. But he (Jacob) wanted to place his right (hand) on the head of the young and left (hand) on the head of the firstborn.

Rashbam's philological insight equating the alleged verbal *hapax* שִׂכֵּל "to lay crosswise," with the noun שָׂכָל (spelled in BH with *samekh* i.e., סכל) and rendered by him as "crooked, twisted man" is indeed revealing. Rashbam considered the verbal form שִׂכֵּל in Gen. 48:14 as a dissimilation[16] of the late form of סכל. One sees such dissimilation of שִׂכְלוּת in Ecc. 1:17, and סִכְלוּת in Ecc. 2:3, 12, 13; 7:25, 10:1, 13.

II. Heb. סכל = Akk. *Saklu*

The root סכל is attested to twenty-one times in BH: eight times as a verb,[17] seven times as a masc. noun (i.e., סָכָל),[18] six times as an abstract fem. noun (i.e., סִכְלוּת),[19] and once as a segolate masc. noun (i.e. סֶכֶל).[20] This lexeme is universally rendered by various lexicons, commentators, and Bible translations as "to be foolish, to behave foolishly" (verb) and "foolish, fool, foolishness" (noun). This describes the mental faculties of a person who is empty-headed and lacking good sense of judgment. It should be observed, however, that although the above rendering may contextually apply in BH to some cases, it is lacking and explains neither the etymological origin of the root סכל, nor the full range of its semantic development.

Six employments of the noun סָכָל appear relatively late. It is twice attested to in the Book of Jeremiah in negative parallelism, i.e., סכל//אין לב "foolish//devoid of intelligence" (Jer. 5:21), and סכלים//לא נבונים "foolish//not intelligent" (Jer. 4:22). The remaining four cases occur late in the book of Ecclesiastes: as the antonym of חכם "wise" (Ecc. 2:19), in sequence with לב חסר "wanting mind" (Ecc. 10:3), modifying "wickedness" (Ecc. 7:17), and describing "much talking" (Ecc 10:14). Similarly, the abstract noun שִׂכְלוּת/סִכְלוּת "folly," is employed only in Ecclesiastes: twice as the antonym of חכמה "wisdom" and once in parallelism with חֹשֶׁךְ "darkness" (Ecc. 2:3, 13; 10:1). סכלות I is thrice attested to in hendiadys and parallelism with הוללות "madness" (Ecc. 2:12; 7:25; 10:13). Accordingly, Rashbam's equation of שִׂכֵּל "to lay across, to crisscross, i.e., entangle" with שָׂכָל (BH סָכָל), defined by him as a twisted and crooked man, may apply only to one range of the meaning of the root of סכל. Namely, the nouns סָכָל/סֶכֶל/סִכְלוּת, seem to refer to a person who is awkward, crooked, entangled, and twisted; more specifically, a person who is foolish, devoid of intelligence, and lacking a straight mind.

The verb סכל, furthermore, appears in Middle Heb. It is attested six times: twice in the Piʿel (2 Sam. 15:31; Isa. 44:25), twice in Hiphʿil (Gen.31:28 1 Sam. 26.21), and four times in the Niphʿal (2 Sam. 24:10, 1 Chr. 21:18; 1 Sam. 13:13; 2 Chr. 16:9). The verb is employed five times in context involving political conflict between a) Samuel and Saul (1 Sam. 13:13); b) Samuel and David (1 Sam. 26:21); c) David and Absalom (2 Sam. 15:32); d) Hanani the Seer and Asa concerning the treaty with Aram (2 Chr. 16:9); e) Jacob and Laban (Gen. 31:28). The verb is likewise employed in the context of David's transgression against God concerning the census (2 Sam. 24:10 = 2 Chr. 21:8) and God's manifested strength against pagan diviners (Isa. 44:25). Lexicographically, the verb appears in negative parallelism, i.e., נסכלת-לא שמרת "you have acted crookedly (i.e., not straight) — you did not observe (i.e., you were unwholesome)."[21] סכל is also employed in sequence with חטא and שגה, i.e., a) חטאתי-נסכלתי "I have transgressed — I have acted crookedly"[22] (i.e. treacherously). b) חטאתי-הסכלתי-אשגה "I have transgressed — I have acted crookedly — I went astray."[23] סכל is likewise employed in some sort of idiomatic antonym with לב שלום. Namely, Hanani the Seer rebukes king Asa as follows: "the Lord gives support to those who are לבבם שלם אליו 'wholeheartedly with Him.' But you (Asa) נסכלת על זאת 'have acted treacherously' (i.e., unwholesomely) in this matter, and henceforth you will be beset by wars."[24] Similarly, Laban blames Jacob with various deceptions: "you stole my mind" (i.e., kept me in the dark); "you flee in secrecy"; "you misled me and did not tell me"; "הסכלת עשׂו" "you have acted deceitfully"[25] (i.e., not straight). Finally, the twice-attested Pi'el of the verb סכל clearly expresses the idea of crisscrossing — thus having the extended meaning of "to cancel, nullify." Accordingly, in 2 Sam. 16:31 סכל נא את עצת אחיתפל "crisscross (i.e., cancel) Ahitophel's counsel," is substituted two verses later (2 Sam. 16:34) by והפרת לי את עצת אחיתפל "nullify Ahitophel's council for me." Likewise, the verb סִכֵּל is employed in Isa. 44:25 in parallelism with פרר lit., "to break (i.e., blot)"; מפר אותות בדים... ודעתם יסכל "he (God) nullifies the omens of the diviners... and cancels the council (of the wise)." Indeed, the idiom of סכל עצה/דעת is semantically equivalent to the expression פרר עצה (= Akk. *tēma parāru)* "to break (i.e., cancel) advice."[26] This expression is also employed in 2 Sam. 17:14, Isa. 8:10, Ezek. 4:5, Ps. 33:10, and Neh. 4:9.

In light of the above contextual and lexicographical aspects, the root סכל comes to connote in general — as Rashbam defined it — a crooked, twisted man. Accordingly, while the nouns סִכְלוּת/סֶכֶל/סָכָל express the abstract idea of foolishness and stupidity, the Hiph'il and Niph'al verbal conjugations of סכל has yet another semantic range of meaning: a person whose mind is devious and morally oblique. On the other hand, the employment of סִכֵּל (in the Piʿel) seems to historically reflect the more concrete and physical notion of the verb, i.e., to crisscross, cross-over, to cancel, nullify. These two semantic connotations of Heb. סָכָל, expressing both mental foolishness and moral crookedness, likewise characterizes the Akkadian adjective/substantive *saklu.*[27]

Akk. *saklu*, which is attested in both lexical and literary texts, refers basically to a socially simple person, a person of a lower class. In a Neo-Assyrian letter we read: *ina bīt ili ātamaršunu gabbu saklūte šunu memēni issu libbi qinnāti ša Ninua Labīrūti laššu* "I looked then over in a temple — they are all simple men, none belonging to the old families of Nineveh."[28] Another meaning, however, exists. Mentally, *saklu* refers to a person who is devoid of intelligence: a fool. Thus, in the lexical lists *saklu* is equated and employed in sequence with the following mentally deprived people: 1*) i-dím BAD = saklu, sakku, sukkuku* "fool, obtuse, half-witted";[29] 2) *[LÚ] umuš (TÚG) nu.tu[ku] = dunnamû = saklu* "stupid = fool;"[30] 3) *hašiku = sukkuku, hašiku* "not intelligent = obtuse, not intelligent fool";[31] 4) *saklu* "fool" is employed in sequence with *nûʾu* "stupid" and *guzallu* "rascal;"[32] 5) in the commentary of the Babylonian Theodicy *saklu* "fool" explains *isḫappu* "rogue;"[33] 6) similarly, in cuneiform literary texts, especially in the middle and Neo-Babylonian *kudurrus* ("boundary stones"), *saklu* "fool" appears in sequence with the mentally impaired *samû* "inept," *lā mudû* "ignorant," and *lā nāṭilu* "imbecile" (i.e., a person who can't see).[34] Accordingly, the standard warning-curse not to instigate the destruction of a boundary stone reads: *matima... sakla sakka nuʾâ isḫappa lā nāṭila umaʾaruma narâ anna ušaššûmma* "whenever (an official) gives an order to remove this stele to an obtuse, fool, stupid, rogue, imbecile,"[35] or *ša... skla sakka samû u lā mudâ umaʾaru* "He who sends a fool, half-wit, or an inept person (to remove his stele)."[36] Furthermore, not unlike the Heb. root סכל, Akk. *saklu* has yet another semantic connotation. Contextually, the adjective/substantive appears in military context. In Old Babylonian lexical lists, *saklu* is preceded by *raggu* "wicked" and *ayābu* "enemy."[37] It is equated with *edku* "fierce."[38] The lexeme comes likewise to express the idea of treacherous acts (> acts which are not straight). It is employed in parallelism with *arnu* "wrong-doing"[39] and *lemnētu* "evil deeds."[40] Similarly, the Gutain king Agum-Kakrime designated himself as *šar Gutî nišî saklāti* "the king of the Gutians, intricate (devious) people."[41] The Akk. compound *nîši saklāti* is semantically equivalent to the Heb. idiom עם סכל (Jer. 5:21). Furthermore, to express the notion of "treacherous, devious, tongue, language" (i.e., forked tongue), Akk. utilizes the express *lišānu sakiltu*. More specifically, the abstract notion of a crooked (i.e., not a straight) tongue is conveyed in Akk. by the nominal phrase *saklati ša lišāna* "to speak treacherous words:" *saklāti ša lišāna dābibu ṣal[ipti] ša kîma erpēti lā íšâ pāna u [baba]* "Those with crooked tongue, who speak treacherous words, (words) which like clouds have neither head nor tail."[42]

In our study, "Hebrew סלף, Mishnaic Hebrew צלף, Akkadian *ṣalāpu/ṣullupu*,"[43] we attempted to demonstrate that the Heb. סלף has the same semantic development as Akk. verb *ṣalāpu* — from the concrete to the abstract. Namely, "to crisscross, crossover > to cancel > to distort," i.e., not to keep things straight. Accordingly, in the light of the employment of *ṣaliptu* in parallelism with *sakiltu* in the above Akk. source, we maintain that Heb. שׂכל/סכל and Akk. *saklu* went through an identical semantic development, i.e., "to crisscross > to cancel> to obliterate." It is especially significant that biblical wisdom literature uses the pair שׂכל//סכל in Prov. 21:12. This is similar to the employment of Akk. *sakiltu*// *ṣaliptu* in parallelism in the above Babylonian wisdom literary text.

III. a) Proverbs 21:12

Prov. 21:12 reads:

מַשְׂכִּיל צַדִּיק לְבֵית רָשָׁע
מְסַלֵּף רְשָׁעִים לָרָע

NJPS renders:

> The Righteous One observes the house of the wicked man. He subverts wicked men to their ruin.

This verse contains two problems: 1) who is the subject of the verse? Does the lexeme צַדִּיק refer to God? Does it depict "a righteous man"? 2) What is the precise meaning of the verb מַשְׂכִּיל (Hif'il participle)? In the light of the above philological and syntactical questions, the rendering of the first clause of Prov. 21:1 is considered as: "Uncertain;"[44] "details are obscure and it is difficult to elucidate;"[45] "the problem as it lies before us is far more intelligible."[46] Accordingly, Rashi, who is followed by numerous modern scholars and translators, maintains that "the righteous one" refers to God — צדיקו של עולם הוא הקב"ה "the Righteous One of the world is the Holy One Blessed be He." As previously noted, apart from Job 34:17, צדיק can hardly refer to God. Additionally, one should expect the noun to be spelled with the definite article, i.e., הַצַּדִּיק "the Righteous One." On the other hand, Joseph, Moses, and David Qimḥi, followed by the modern commentators and translators, understand the subject of the verse as pertaining simply to "a righteous man."[47] Secondly, as to the meaning of the verb מַשְׂכִּיל, the majority of medieval and modern students derive it from שׂכל I "to be prudent, to have an insight, to observe." Accordingly, the following main translations were adduced for verse 12a: "The righteous *considers* the house of the wicked man;"[48] "a just man *reads the thoughts* of the wicked man;"[49] "The righteous one *has control* over the wicked man's household;"[50] "the Just God makes the wicked man's home *childless*;"[51] "The righteous one *observes* the house of the wicked."[52] Indeed, the Tg. on Proverbs renders verse 12a as מסתכל צדיקא בביתיה דרשיעא "The righteous man observes the house of the wicked." Contextually, David Qimḥi elaborates הצדיק הוא מתבונן על בית הרשע שבנאו מגזלה ועשק "The righteous man observes the house of the wicked who built it by means of theft and oppression." So too, Rabbi Levi ben Gershom (Ralbag) derives the verb מַשְׂכִּיל from the root שׂכל I, rendered by him as "prosper:" הצדיק המצליח לבית הרשע וזה יהיה כשיעמוד בביתו כי אז יברך ביתו בגלל הצדיק "The righteous man causes the house of the evildoer's to prosper. And it will happen when (the righteous) will stand in his (the evildoer's) house. Only then the Lord will bless his (the evildoer's) house on the account of the righteous man." On the other hand, it is interesting to observe that while Rashi derives מַשְׂכִּיל from שׂכל I, rendering the verb as נותן לב "sets (his) mind," he further completes the idea of verse 12a by inserting the verb להכרית "to destroy:" צדיקו של עולם הוא הקב"ה נותן לב להכרית בית רשע כגון זכר עמלק "The Righteous One of the world, who is God, sets his mind *to destroy* the house of the wicked, (e.g., the remembrance of Amalek)."

Although the verb מַשְׂכִּיל in Prov. 21:12a is universally equated with שׂכל I, we prefer to equate it with שׂכל II (Gen. 48:14) "to crisscross, cross out > obliterate, destroy." Our assumption may be strengthened by noting that Hebrew employs מַשְׂכִּיל in parallelism with מְסַלֵּף in a similar fashion to the usage of the Akk. pair *sakiltu//ṣaliptu*. Accordingly, in the light of the above discussion, our rendering of Prov. 21:12a will read:

The righteous one crisscrosses (i.e., destroys) the house of the wicked man. He (the righteous one) crosses out (i.e., obliterates) the evildoers to (their) ruin.

Consequently, the structural link between vv. 11 and 12 is chiastic. Both contain the verb שׂכל in its two opposite meanings:[53]

a)	v. 11	בְּהַשְׂכִּיל	בַּעֲנָשׁ
	v. 12	מְסַלֵּף	מַשְׂכִּיל
b)	v. 11	חָכָם	לֵץ
	v. 12	רָשָׁע	צַדִּיק

Furthermore, another case where the root שׂכל II occurs may be found in Amos 5:13[54]

Amos 5:13 reads:

לָכֵן הַמַּשְׂכִּיל בָּעֵת הַהִוא יִדֹּם
כִּי עֵת רָעָה הִיא

NJPS renders:

> Assuredly, in such a time the prudent man keeps silent,
> for it is an evil time.

Shalom Paul summarizes the vexing problems encountered by the students of Amos as follows:

> Verse 13 is generally interpreted as either late wisdom or apocalyptic gloss or is assumed to be misplaced in its present position…a further vexing problem is the meaning of מַשְׂכִּיל. If the מַשְׂכִּיל refers, as some think, to Amos, why would he, of all people, be silent? It refers to this 'prudent one' in general, for what reason need he keep silent: to protect his own skin? Or is it merely the cautionary wisdom of not questioning God's actions? Does מַשְׂכִּיל refer to the prudent one at all?[55]

While Paul does not offer any alternative solution, Shemaryahu Talmon and Esti Eshel[56] adopt Sillini's[57] well-known suggestion to relate our lexeme with the word that appears as a superscription to several psalms. Accordingly, they render מַשְׂכִּיל in Amos 5:13 as "the joyful song (will be silent)."

In the light of such divergent exegesis, yet another suggestion might be offered for consideration. Namely, to equate מַשְׂכִּיל in Amos 5:13 with שׂכל II = סכל = Akk. *saklu,* which as noted above comes also to connote a person who is morally crooked. If our assumption that מַשְׂכִּיל is employed by Amos to refer to the crooked and the devious is correct, then verse 13 is not a gloss or misplaced. Rather, verses 12–13 comprise one unified literary unit: verse 13 is the result and punishment of the corruption described in verse 12. The prophet decries those whose "crimes are many" (רַבִּים פִּשְׁעֵיכֶם); whose "sins are countless" (עֲצֻמִים חַטֹּאתֵיכֶם); who are "the enemies of the righteous" (צֹרְרֵי צַדִּיק); who are the "takers of bribes" (לֹקְחֵי כֹפֶר); who "subvert in court the cause of the needy" (אֶבְיוֹנִים בַּשַּׁעַר הִטּוּ). These crooked and treacherous people will be punished. Consequently, as always, Amos introduces the actual punishment, in our case a total annihilation (i.e., יָדֹם),[58] with the particle לכן,[59] "therefore." Our rendering of verse 12 reads:

> Therefore the crooked men will be incapacitated (lit. silenced, destroyed) for it is a time of calamity.

IV

The philological relationship between Heb. roots סכל//שׂכל II and שׂכל I falls into the category of *Addād*: "a word that has two contrary meanings," words that, according to the definition of Arab philologists, have two meanings opposite each other.[60] Henceforth, the verb סכל//שׂכל II comes to originally express the idea of a deed, action, or state of being or a person, which is not straight. Namely, the root has the following semantic development progressing from the concrete to the abstract: a) to lay across, crisscross > to cancel, nullify > to act crookedly, deviously (for verbs). b) A person whose mind is not straight > a fool, stupid, mentally or crooked, treacherous, devious, morally (for nouns). שׂכל I has mutually opposed meanings. Although unapparent, it seems that שׂכל I comes to express the notion of a straight (free of curves) action or a person > a successful, prosperous deed or person. This basic meaning of שׂכל I seems to be reflected at least in seventeen cases[61] where the idea of a person whose actions are straight and upright — absent of crooked and twisted deeds — is a successful and prosperous man.

Accordingly, the verb is employed three times in Proverbs as an antonym of בוש, i.e., עבד/בן משׂכיל — בן מֵבִישׁ "a successful slave/son- an incompetent son."[62] It is once utilized in a negative parallelism, i.e., לא השׂכילו//בשו "they shall be incompetent//they shall not be successful."[63] The verb refers to אשה מַשְׂכָּלֶת "successful, prosperous woman;"[64] גבור מַשְׂכִּיל (read: מַשְׂכִּיל) "a successful hero."[65] In this sense, הִשְׂכִּיל/מַשְׂכִּיל/שָׂכָל is likewise employed in reference to David, Solomon, Hezekiah, servant of God, people of Israel, and Joshua.[66] More specifically, in Josh. 1:8 the verb השׂכל is employed in parallelism with הצלח. As previously noted, the idiom הצלח דרך is not different in function and meaning from its equivalent הושׁר דרך, lit., "to cause one's way to be straight," i.e., to succeed, prosper."[67] So too, the thrice-employed expression השׂכל דרך has this very basic meaning, "to cause one's way to be straight," i.e., "to succeed, prosper." This can clearly be affirmed from Prov. 21:17: אדם תועה מדרך השׂכל בקהל רפאים ינוח "A man who strays from the straight/right path will rest in the company of ghosts." Here דֶּרֶךְ הַשְׂכֵּל is the exact semantic equivalent of דרך/ארח יָשָׁר/מישור "a straight > successful path, way."[68]

NOTES

1. F. Brown, S.R. Driver, C.A. Briggs, *Hebrew and English Lexicon of the Old Testament* (Peabody, MA: Hendrickson Publishers, 1997), 698, 968.
2. Ludwig Koehler and Walter Baumgartner, *The Hebrew and Aramaic Lexicon of the Old Testament (*Leiden, New York: E. J. Brill, 1994–2000), 754–5; 1328–30 (English translation and editing under the supervision of M.E.J. Richardson).
3. Cf. *op. cit*., 4–8.
4. See for example the translations of *NEB* and *NJPS*.
5. Cf. Brown, Driver, Briggs, *Hebrew and English Lexicon*, 698, 968; Koehler and Baumgartner, *The Hebrew and Aramaic Lexicon*, 754–5; 1328–30.
6. C.H. Toy, *A Critical and Exegetical Commentary on the Book of Proverbs* (The International Critical Commentary, Edinburgh: T & T Clark, 1959), 402. (Hereafter, ICC).
7. Eliezer ben Yehudah, *A Complete Dictionary of Ancient and Modern Hebrew* (Vol. 8; New York, London: T Yoselof), 8:7567, n. 2.
8. See, J, Dernbourg, *Ouvres Completes de R. Saadia Ben Iosef Al-Fayyoume,* (Paris 1983) 1: 76.
9. H. Albeck, *Bereshit Rabba* (vol. 3; Jerusalem: Shalem, 1996), 3:1244.
10. Cf. n. 5 above.
11. Cf. ibid., n. 9.
12. Ibid.
13. M. Friedman, *Midrash Pesiqta Rabbati* (Wien, 1880), 3:4.
14. *Torat Ḥayyim: Five Books of the Law* (Ed. M.L. Katzenelenbogen; Jerusalem: Mosad Ha-Rav Kook, 1987).
15. Ibid.
16. For the merger of שׂ (ś*)* and *(s)*, see especially E.Y. Kutscher,

"Contemporary studies in North-Western Semitic," *JSS* 10 (1965), 39–41. *Idem. History of the Hebrew Language* (ed. Raphael Kutscher; Jerusalem: Magnes Press; Leiden: Brill, 1982), 14.

17. Gen. 31:28, 1 Sam. 13:12, 26:21, 2 Sam. 15:31, 24:10, 1 Chr. 21:8, 2 Chr. 15:9.
18. Jer. 4:22, 5:21, Ecc. 2:19, 7:17, 10:3 (twice); 10:14.
19. Ecc. 2:3, 12, 12, 7:25, 10:1, 13.
20. Ecc. 10:6.
21. 1 Sam. 13:13.
22. 2 Sam. 24:10.
23. 1 Sam. 26:21.
24. 2 Chr. 16:9.
25. Gen. 31:28. It is interesting to note that Don Isaac Abarbanel, in his commentary on Gen. 48:14, equates שׂכל II with the verb הסכל/סַכֵּל: ופירושו שִׂכֵּל כמו סכל נא את עצת אחיתופל, ועתה הסכלת עשׂה כי הסמ"ך והשׂי"ן מתחלפים "And the meaning of שִׂכֵּל is similar to 'crisscross Ahitophel's advice,' and now you have acted deceitfully because the *samekh* and *śin* interchange.
26. *AHw*. 830a. 4.
27. *CAD* 80; *AHw*. 1012. Note that M. Held, "Studies in Comparative Lexicography" in *B. Landsberger Fesrschrift* (Chicago: Chicago University Press, 1965), 406 suggests to equate Akkadian *saklu* with Hebrew כסל "stupidity."
28. *ABL* 437 n.15.
29. *CAD* S 80 (lexical section).
30. Ibid.
31. Ibid.
32. Ibid.
33. *BWL* 83.222.
34. *CAD* S 80b a): 78a.
35. *BBSt*. No. 7 II:9.
36. *RA* 66 (1972), 166:34. For a full discussion of this standard warning-curse cf. H. Tawil, "The end of the Hadad Inscription in the Light of Akkadian," *JNES* 32 (1973), 477–82.
37. *CAD* S 80b (lexical section).
38. Ibid.
39. *CAD* S 80a c).
40. Ibid.
41. *5R* 33:39.
42. *BWL* 136:167 (hymn to Šamaš).
43. H. Tawil, "Hebrew סלף, Mishnaic Hebrew צלף, Akkadian *ṣalāpu*/

ṣullupu," *Beit Mikra* 146 (1996), 276–96. See pages 23–42 in this volume.

44. *ICC*, Prov. 904.
45. W. McKane, *Proverbs: a New Approach* (Philadelphia: Westminster Press, 1970), 561.
46. Cf. Keil and F. Delitzche, *Commentary on the Old Testament* (Peabody, Mass: Hendrickson 1989), Vol. 6, 73.
47. Frank Talmage, *The Commentaries on Proverbs of the Kimhi Family* (Jerusalem: Magnes, 1990), 107, 265, 427.
48. *ICC*, 402; *IB*, Prov. 904.
49. R.B.Y. Scott, *Proverbs, Ecclesiastes* (Anchor Bible; New York: Doubleday, 1965), 124.
50. McKane, *Proverbs*, 243.
51. *NEB* 908 (read מַשְׂכִּיל).
52. *NJPS* 1319.
53. Cf. *op. cit.* n. 60.
54. For a full discussion and bibliography of this verse, see S. M. Paul, *Amos: A Commentary on the Book of Amos* (Minneapolis: Fortress Press, 1991), 175. Cf. Also M. Weiss, *The Book of Amos* (Jerusalem: Magnes, 1992), Vol. I, 150; Vol. II 263.
55. Paul, *Amos*. For a review of שׂכל I, see Hans Kosmala, "Maskil," *JNESCU* 5 (1973), 235–241. Note also the remarks of Francis I. Andersen and David Noel Freedman that הַמַּשְׂכִּל ידם connotes "the wise man remains silent." See F. Anderson and D. Freedman, *Amos: Translation and Commentary* (Anchor Bible; New York: Doubleday, 1989), 503–504.
56. S. Talmon and E. Eshel "ידם והמשׂכיל בעת ההיא," *Shnaton: an annual for Biblical and Ancient Near Eastern Studies* (1986–87), 115–22 (Heb.).
57. E. Sellin, "Zwölfprophetenbuch", *KAT* (Leipzig, 1929) vol. XII/I, 239–40.
58. While Paul proposes to equate Heb. דמם II in Am. 5:13 with the Akk. *damāmu* and Ugr. *Dmm* "to mutter, moan, groan, sigh," the majority of commentators equate our verb with Heb. דמם I "to be silent." It seems that KB³, 226 errs in listing דמם III "to be devastated, perish" in a separate entry. דמם I "to be silent," comes likewise to connote "to be destroyed, perish" (cf. *BDB* in such cases as Jer. 25:37: וְנָדַמּוּ נאות השלום "and the peaceful meadows shall be silenced, i.e., wiped out;" Jer. 51:6 נסו מתוך בבל ומלטו איש נפשו אל תִּדַּמּוּ בעונה "flee from the midst of Babylon and save your lives, each of you! Do not be silenced, i.e., perish for your iniquity;" Jer. 8:14 האספו ונבוא אל ערי המבצר וְנִדְּמָה שם כי... ה' אלקינו הֲדִמָּנוּ "Let us father into the fortified cities and be silenced. i.e., destroyed us...." More specifically, note that in Jer. 49:26 = 50:30

נפל//דמם "to fall//to perish" are parallel: וכל אנשי המלחמה יִדַּמּוּ ביום ההוא... לכן יפלו בחוריה ברחבתיה//"assuredly, her young men shall fall in her squares will be destroyed that day..." Finally, not unlike Am. 5:13, יִדֹּם־כי עת רעה היא "will be destroyed-for it is a time of calamity," Jer. 51:6 likewise utilized a identical juxtaposition, i.e., (אל) — עת נקמה היא תִּדַּמּוּ "(do not) perish — for it is a time of vengeance."

59. For the particle לכן in the oracles of Amos introducing the actual punishment, cf. W. Rudolf, *Joel-Amos-Obadiah-Jonah* (KAT 23/2; Gütersloh: Gerd Mohn, 1971), 185.
60. For a full discussion of *Addād* in Semitic languages, cf. Nöldrkr, *Newe Beiträge zür Semitischen Sprachwissemschaft* (Strassburg, 1919), 72–89; Robert Gordis, "Some Effects of primitive Thought on Languages," *AJSL* 55 (1938), 270–8.
61. Deut. 29:8; Josh. 1:7,8; 1 Sam. 18:5,14,15,30; 1 Kings 2:3; 2 Kings, 18:7; Isa. 52:13; Ps. 101:2; Prov. 10:5, 14:35; 17:2, 8, 19:14, 21:16.
62. Prov. 17:2.
63. Jer. 20:11.
64. Prov. 19:14.
65. Job 50:19 See ibid., n.61.
66. Ps. 5:9; Prov. 3:6, 11:15.
67. Cf. H. Tawil, *JBL* (1976), 405–13.
68. Jer. 31:9; Ps. 27:11; Prov. 2:13; 4:11. It should be noted that the modern Heb. Word for frustration is תִּסְכּוּל. The word was first introduced by the Academy of Hebrew Language in its twenty-eighth meeting in March 1959. However, תסכול "frustration" was finally accepted by the Academy only twenty years later in its one hundred-fortieth meeting in April 1979. I am indebted to Ms. Malkah Zemeli from the Academy for this information.

Late Hebrew-Aramaic ספר, Neo-Babylonian *Sirpu/Sirapu*: A Lexicographical Note IV

לצבי ארני

איש רעים להתרעע
(משלי י"ח:כד)

The Late Heb-Aram. root ספר "to cut the hair, to shear" is not employed in BH. Jastrow[1] confused the lexeme with its homonym ספר "to count, to converse," thus listing both vocables under one entry. While it is generally accepted that these two words are to be listed separately, nevertheless, no cognate was found earlier than Tannaitic Heb. (i.e., 0–300 CE). The purpose of the present note is to chronologically fix the earliest possible attestation of ספר "to cut the hair, to shear" and thereby establish the etymologic and semantic origin of the root.

At the outset, it should be observed that Nahum Waldman[2] attempted to etymologically equate the LH-Aram. ספר with the Akk. *ṣepēru* "to stand, to dress (hair), to trim, decorate (with stone)." Waldman's etymological equation was rejected by Moreshet[3] as extremely vague and contextually dependent upon obscure interpretations. Indeed, as admitted by Waldman,[4] Akk. *ṣepēru* "does not mean 'to cut' exclusively." The verb is used in Akk. in connection with stranding, dressing hair, stranding linen, and trimming an object with precious stones. Akk. *ṣepēru* does not imply "to cut the hair, to shear."[5] Accordingly, von Soden[6] does not offer any Northwest Semitic equivalents.

The verb ספר "to cut the hair; to shear," the nouns מִסְפֶּרֶת/מַסְפֶּרֶת/מִסְפּוֹרֶת/תִּסְפּוֹרֶת/מִסְפָּרַיִם "scissors, (gardener's) shears, shearing knife, chipping tool, hair-cut,"[7] and the *nomen agentis* סַפָּר "hair cutter" (i.e., "a barber") first appear in LH.[8]

The semantic equivalent to the LH-Aram. root ספר is the

BH גלח "to shave the head, hair, beard." The verb is attested twenty-three times. However, in the Pentateuch, גלח is employed thirteen times. Although, it is exclusively rendered in Tg. Neof. by the Aram. ספר, Tg. Onq. renders the vocable twelve times by the Heb. גלח[9] and only once by ספר.[10] Tg. J., on the other hand, translates the verb four times by the Heb. גלח[11] and nine times by the Aram. ספר.[12] It should be likewise observed that the BH noun תער "razor," is employed six times. While Heb. תער is rendered by both Tg. Onq. and Tg. Neof. as מַסְפַּר (Num. 6:5; 8:7). Tg. J. translates the noun as גְּלָב. The root גלב is a *hapax* in BH, employed only in Ezek. 5:1 in the idiom תער הַגַּלָּבִים "barber's razor," and rendered by Tg. J. as מספר גלביא = Akk *paṭri gallābi.*[13] The Heb. *hapax* גַּלָּב is clearly loanword from Akk. *gallābu* "barber" (employed from Old Akk. onward).[14] Aramaic (Phoenician, Punic, Nabatean)[15] גלב may likewise be regarded as an Akk. loanword and not a cognate. The reason is that Aram. commonly employs the root ספר "to cut the hair, to shear," and rarely גלב.[16] It should be further noted that in both East and Northwest Semitic the verb "to cut hair, shear" is not employed in the Qal.

The etymological and the semantic equivalent of the LH-Aram. ספר may be found in the Neo-Babylonian metathesized substantive *sirpu/sirapu* "shears, scissors,"[17] not included as a cognate in von Soden's dictionary.[18] The Neo-Babylonian *sirpu/sirapu* is employed mainly in the inscriptions of Nabu-nāid (555–539 BCE) and Cambyses II (530–522 BCE). *sirpu/sirapu* is employed beside *ḫaṣṣinnu* "an axe," and *nalpattu*[19] "(a barber's) handle." It is modified by *parzillu* "iron:" *sirpu parzilli kî niššaʾ umma niksu nikkisima ultu bīt kīli nuṣʾi* "we brought iron shears saying: 'Let us make a breach and get out of prison.'"[20] Although *sirpu/sirapu* is not employed in Neo-Babylonian cuneiform texts in contexts involving cutting/shaving the hair of a human, it is utilized in the context involving shearing: 40 *sirpi parzilli ana gizzi* "forty shears for the shearing"[21]; *ana epeš sirapi parzilli ša gizzi* "for making shears of iron for shearing."[22] It should be observed that while in Neo-Babylonian *sirpu/sirapu* is utilized solely for shearing, in LH and Aram., however, ספר is employed for cutting/shearing the hair of humans, goats, cutting the foliage-cover for the booth, and cutting vegetables: מספרת שנחלקה לשנים ר' יהודה מטמא, מפני שהוא בתחילה חותך בה את הסכך ועכשיו הוא חותך בה את הסכך וחכמים מטהרים "Shears divided into two R. Judah declares unclean, because in the first place one cuts the branches with it and now one cuts the branches with it"[23]; אין מספרין את הירק במספרת אבל מספרין את הקונדס ואת העכביות "we may not trim the vegetable with a shear, but we may cut the Kundas and the Ackabious"[24]; שמשא מספר עזייא דששי "the servant shears Sheshai's goats."[25]

In summation, it seems that the ספר "to cut the hair, to shear" is an original Aramaic lexeme that was preferred by the Aramaic speaking Neo-Babylonian scribes over the then less frequently used Akk. word *gullubu*. This Aramaic loanword seems to enter Neo-Babylonian cuneiform inscriptions in metathesized form. It later re-appeared in Late Heb.-Aramaic in its original form ספר.

There are various occurrences of either cognates or loanwords (LW) that are passed from one language to the other in metathesized form. Cases include: Akk. *dišpu* — Heb. דבש "honey"; Akk. *būṣu*[26] — Heb. צבוע[27] "hyena"; Akk. *simmiltu*[28] — Heb. סלם[29] "ladder, stairway"; Akk. *eqlu*[30] — Aram. חלק — Heb. חלק (א) "field"; Heb. נמלה — Akk. *lamattu*[31] "ant"; Akk. *rapādu*[32] — Heb. רדף "to pursue"; Akk. *karābu*[33] — Heb. ברך "to pay homage, bless"; LH-Aram. קדרה[34] — Akk. *diqaru*[35] "cooking/drinking vessel."

Further, the phenomenon of metathesis[36] commonly occurs when the liquid ר is involved. It happens in BH when the liquid ר is metathesized between the first and second radicals, e.g., הערל–הרעל (Hab. 2:6); צרח–רצח (Ezek. 21:27). The liquid ר is metathesized (at least once) between the first and third radicals, e.g., גער–רגע (Isa. 51:15; Jer. 31:34). Likewise, between the first and third radicals, e.g., LH טרש–רטש,[37] Aram. (מ)זרח(יא)–(מ)רזח(יא);[38] נגרא–רגלא.[39]

Furthermore, the liquid ר is metathesized (first with second radical) between the cognate languages as follows, e.g., Heb. רמח — Ugr. *mrḥ*[40] "spear, lance"; Heb. רחל — Akk. *laḫru*[41] — "ewe, lamb"; Aram. רגובל(א)[42] — Akk. *purkullu*[43] "stone, seal cutter."

More specifically, the liquid ר is most commonly metathesized between the second and third radicals in such cases as שניר–שריון (Deut. 3:9); פצר-פרץ (1 Sam. 28:23; 2 Sam. 13:25, 27; 2 Kings 5:23); חגר-חרג (2 Sam. 22:27 = Ps. 18:46); דבר-ברד (Ps. 78:48); (מ)בחר(יו)-(מ)ברחו (Ezek. 17:21); גזר–גרז (Ps. 31:23 = Lam. 3:54); אדר-ארד(י) (Gen. 46:21; Num. 26:40 = 1 Chr. 8:3); בחר(ומי)-ברח(מי) (2 Sam. 23:31 = 1 Chr. 11:33); תפראת (IQIsa[a]) — תפארת (Isa. 13:19); Aram. פטרוי–טַרְפוי (b. *Giṭ*. 1:5). The metathesis between the second and the third radicals of the liquid ר occurs also between the following cognate language, e.g., Aram. תרע — Heb. שער "gate;" Heb. שֵׁרות[44] — Akk. *semeru*[45] "bracelets" (LW); LH כרם[46] — Akk. *kamāru*[47] "to pile" (LW); Akk. *arad-ekalli* — LH אדריכל "a builder" (LW).

Accordingly, the Neo-Babylonian *sirpu/sirapu* is an additional example for a metathesis between the second and the third radical of the liquid ר in loanwords.

NOTES

1. M. Jastrow, *A Dictionary of Targumim, the Talmud Babli and Yerushalmi, and the Midrashic Literature* (2 vols.; New York: Peabody, 1950), 2:1017.
2. N. M. Waldman, "Akkadian Loanwords and Parallels in Mishnaic Hebrew," (Ph.D. Dissertation; Philadelphia, 1973), 221–3.
3. M. Moreshet, *A Lexicon of the Hebrew Verbs in Tannaitic Hebrew* (Ramat-Gan: Bar Ilan University Press, 1980), 252–4 n. 27 (Heb.).
4. Ibid., 222.
5. *CAD* S 132–3.
6. *AHw* 1082a.
7. Cf. e.g., m. *Kelim* 13:1; 15:8; t. *Kelim*; b. *Mes*. 3:2, 3; t. *Beṣ*. 3:19; t. *Mak.* 4:5; *Sifré* Aḥaré 86:1. See also b. *Šabb*. 9:2, 48:2. 58:2; b. *Mak.* 21:1; b. *Sanh*. 96:1. For a full discussion on shears, scissors, and clipping tools during the Talmudic period, see Daniel Sperber, *Material Culture in Eretz-Israel during the Talmudic Period* (Jerusalem: Yad Ben Tzvi Press, 1993), 91–96 (Heb.).
8. Cf. e.g., m. *Šeb.* 8:5; *Šabb*. 1:2; *Qidd*. 4:14; t. *Pesaḥ*. 3:18; *Yad*. 1:11; *Mek*. Nez. 1.
9. Cf. Tg. Onq. on Lev. 14:8, 9; 13:33; 21:5; Num. 6:9. 18. 19; Deut. 21:12.

10. Cf. Tg. Onq. on Gen. 41:14.
11. Cf. Tg. Onq. on Num. 6:9 (twice), 19; Jer 41:5.
12. Cf. Tg. Ps. J. Onq. on Gen. 4:14, Lev. 13:33 (twice), 14:8, 9 (twice); 21:5; Deut. 21:12.
13. *CAD* N 120b (lexical section).
14. *CAD* N 14b. Cf. also, Harold Cohen, *Biblical Hapax Legomena in the light of Akkadian and Ugaritic* (Ann Arbor: Scholars Press, 1978), 134.
15. Cf. J. Hoftijzer and K. Jongeling, *Dictionary of the North-West Semitic Inscriptions* (Leiden: Brill, 1995), 1:222.
16. Stephen A. Kaufman, *The Akkadian Influence on Aramaic (AS 19)* (Chicago: University of Chicago Press, 1974), 51.
17. *CAD* S 316a.
18. *AHw* 1037b.
19. *CAD* S 316a.
20. *YOS* 7 97:16.
21. *CT* 55 252:1, 6.
22. *Nbn* 867:2.
23. t. *Yoma* 3:19, b. *Beṣ*. 34 a.
24. m. *Kelim* 3:3.
25. MMDam Gen. 41:9. Cf. also Michael Sokoloff, *A Dictionary of Jewish Palestinian Aramaic of the Byzantine Period* (Ramat Gan: Bar Ilan University Press, 1990), 387.
26. *CAD* B 349a; *AHw*, 143a.
27. Jer. 12:19.
28. *CAD* S 273a; *AHw* 1045.
29. Gen. 28:12. For a full discussion cf. H. Cohen, *Hapax*, ibid., 34.
30. *CAD* E 249b; *AHw* 231b.
31. *CAD* L 67; *AHw* 533a. Note that Akk. *lamattu* which is employed once in the synonym list (*Malku* v:61 = *MSL* 8/2, 75, 61) with the standard Akk. word *kulbābu* "ant" (*CAD* K 501b), is a loanword from North West Semitic.
32. *AHw* 954a.
33. *CAD* K 192a; *AHw* 445b.
34. m. *Ḥul*. 8:3
35. *CAD* D 157b; *AHw* 172b. For a full discussion cf. N. Waldman, ibid.
36. For the question of metathesis, see the following major studies: Ibn Janāḥ, *Sefer Hariqma*, ed. Michael Wilensky, (Jerusalem, 1964), 352f.; N.H. Tur-Sinai, *The Language and the Book* (Jerusalem, 1954) vol. II, 106–149.
37. See M. Moeshet, *Lexicon*, 345.
38. m. *Ber*. 3:1.
39. b. *B. Qam*. 9:57; b. *B. Bat*. 9:88.

40. Cf. e.g., *IAB* I:23; *IIK I-II*:47, 51.
41. *CAD* L 42f; *AHw* 528b.
42. Tg. J. on 1 Kings 5:32.
43. *AHw* 834a.
44. Isa. 3:19.
45. *CAD* S, 219a; *AHw* 1036b.
46. E.g., m. *Kelim* 23:4. For a full discussion, cf. N. Walderman, "Akkadian loanwords," 173f.
47. *CAD* K 112b; *AHw* 430b.

Late Hebrew-Aramaic לעס, Akkadian *Naʾāsu*: A Lexicographical Note V

It is of interest to note that the vocable that comes to express the idea "to chew" is absent from the lexicon of Biblical Hebrew. The lexeme makes its first appearance in Tannaitic Hebrew (i.e., 0–300 CE) as לעס "to chew."[1] In the Mishnah and Tosefta, the verb is employed four times and the substantive לְעִיסָה, "chewing"[2] twice.

1. לא ילעס אדם חיטין מכתו בפסח מפני שהן מחמיצות

   "One may not chew wheat and place it on his wound on Passover, because it ferments."[3]

2. עושין כל צרכי מילה בשבת מוהלין ופורעין... אם לא שחק מערב שבת לועס בשיניו ונותן

   "One may do all the needs of circumcision on Shabbat; one may circumcise and tear... if he did not grind (it) before Shabbat, he may chew (it) with his teeth and apply."[4]

3. אין לועסין מוסתכי (מסטיכי) בשבת

   "One may not chew gum-matich on Shabbat."[5]

4. כשהשמש עומד ללעוס קופץ את פיו ולועס

   "When the attendant is ready to chew he must close his mouth and chew (the meat of the paschal lamb)."[6]

The first attestation of the Aramaic verb for "chew" is in the Babylonian Talmud, where it appears seven times: four times as לעס and three times as אלס — a metathesized form with the עֽ<אֽ interchange.[7] For example, אמר מר טחול יפה לשינים וקשה לבני מעיים מאי תקנתיה נלעסיה ונשדייה "The master said: spleen (meat) is beneficial for the teeth and harmful for the intestines. What is remedy? He should chew it and spit it out;"[8] and ההוא תורא לאלס ידיה דינוקא "An ox once chewed the hand of a child...."[9] Likewise, לעס is employed once in the Jerusalem Talmud.[10] It also appears once in the late Targum to Qoh. 12:3, which renders the phrase וּבָטְלוּ הַטֹּחֲנוֹת כִּי מִעֵטוּ "And the maids that grind (i.e., the teeth), grown few, are idle" as ויתבטלון כַּכֵּי פומך עד דלא יכלין לְמִלְעַס מיכלא "the teeth of your mouth will become useless such that they are unable to chew food."[11]

It is noteworthy that both Northwest and East Semitic lexicographers fail to depict the earliest etymological and semantic equivalent of LH-Aramaic verb לעס. Nahum Waldman does not provide any etymological parallels for לעס in his thesis "Akkadian Loanwords and Parallels in Mishnaic Hebrew."[12] Stephen Kaufman's study *The Akkadian Influence on Aramaic*[13] likewise does not identify any cognate for the Aramaic occurrence of the verb. Menahem Moreshet,[14] however, cities some parallels with Syriac. He also notes a late Arabic borrowing from Aramaic. However, there was no cognate found earlier than LH.

The earliest attestation of the verb לעס "to chew," however, is employed in "standard Babylonian," the literary Neo-Babylonian of the Neo-Assyrian period (934–610 BCE). The Akkadian verb appears as *na'āsu* in the lexical list (Proto-Ea),[15] but is equated with the Sumerian *ga-az GAZ* and it is syllabized as *na-Ḫa-su-um*. Akkadian *na'āsu* "to chew" seems to be used exclusively in ritual texts that list a combination of ritual actions and prayers designated for performance and recitation by the suppliant or the professional liturgist, the *mašmāšu*, acting for the supplicant. Accordingly, in the *Namburbû* ("undoing of such and such evil") ritual for dispelling of evil, we read: *ina ūmišu mašmāšu urqi kirî kalīšuni uṭaḫḫâšsu āšipu ina 'isma* "At the proper time the exorcist serves all the garden plants to him. The exorcist chews the plants for him."[16] Moreover, Akkadian verb *na'āsu* "to chew" is employed in parallelism with the commonly used Akkadian verb *lêmu* "to soften the food in the mouth"[17] in the following ritualistic text: *bārû... erēna ina pīšu ina'is (una'as) u Nisaba ina pīšu ilêm* "The diviner chews cedar in his mouth and softens grains in his mouth."[18]

In short, on the basis of למנ"ר interchange, the Akkadian verb *na'āsu* and the LH-Aram. לעס "to chew" are etymologically and semantically related.

NOTES

1. See Menahem Mosreshet, "A Lexicon of the Verbs in Tannaitic Hebrew," *Ramat-Gan* (1980): 202 n. 4 (Heb.).
2. m. *Nid.* 8:9, 9:7.
3. m. *Pesaḥ.* 2:7.
4. m. *Šabb.* 19:2.
5. t. *Šabb.* 12:8.
6. t. *Pesaḥ.* 6:11.
7. Cf. J.N. Epstein, *A Grammar of Babylonian Aramaic,* (Jerusalem: Magnes, 1960) (Heb.).
8. b. *Ber.* 44:2.
9. b. *B. Qam.* 84:1.
10. y. *Ter.* 45:2.
11. Alexander Sperber, *The Bible in Aramaic: Based on Manuscripts and Old Books* (vol. IV; Leiden: Brill, 1968), 3:167 (Heb.).
12. Nahum Waldman, "Akkadian Loanwords and Parallels in Mishnaic Hebrew" (Ph.D. diss. University of Pennsylvania, 1973).
13. Stephen Kaufman, *The Akkadian Influence on Aramaic* (Assyriological Studies, no. 19; Chicago: University of Chicago Press, 1974).
14. Ibid.
15. *MSL* 2, 140:10; *CAD* N/I 8 a; *AHw* 694a.
16. R. Caplice, "*Namburi* Texts in the British Museum II", *Orientalia* 36 (1967), 34:13–14.
17. *CAD* I. 127a. 2; *AHw* 543b.
18. *BBR* no. 74–78:16–17.

Was Chiropractic Known In Biblical Times? Hebrew חלץ: A Lexicographical Note VI

with Aryē J. Tawil

To Drs. Daniel Fenster
and Robert J. De Bonis

I.

The Biblical Hebrew verb חלץ appears forty-four times in the Bible: fourteen times in the Torah, nine times in the Nevi'im, and twenty-one times in the Ketuvim. The verb is attested to twenty-two times in the Qal (four in the Qal active[1] and eighteen in the Qal passive participle,[2] i.e., חלוץ). It occurs seven times in the Niph'al,[3] fourteen times in the Pi'el,[4] and once in the Hiph'il.[5]

It should be observed that while lexicons such as BDB,[6] Ben-Yehuda,[7] Even-Shoshan,[8] and DCH[9] account for two homonyms of the word חלץ, 1. "to draw off or out, withdraw," and 2. "equip for war" (primary idea of strength, vigor), KB³ maintains one entry of חלץ with two connotations: 1. "to draw off (a shoe)" and 2. "ready for fighting."[10] KB³ further equates Heb. חלץ with the Akkadian verb *ḫalāṣu*, rendered as "to squeeze out, to clean by combing."

However, KB³'s assertions are unwarranted on both semantic and etymological grounds. A) Semantic — It fails to show the semantic development of חלץ "to draw off, withdraw" > "ready for fighting." B) Etymological — While Akkadian *ḫalāṣu* and Heb. חלץ are related etymologically, they are semantically distinct. Akk. *ḫalāṣu*, which is employed in sequence with *ṣaḫāṭu*[11] (= Heb. שחט)[12] "to press" (grapes and other fruits), also means "to press." It seems better to equate Akk. *ḫalāṣu* with Heb. לחץ, "to press, oppress," invoking a metathesis which commonly occurs between those two languages.[13]

While KB[3] fails to convey the semantic development of חלץ "to pull off" > חלוץ "ready for fighting," Ibn Janāḥ, along with various other medieval commentators, advocates two possibilities. His first suggestion concerning the development of the primary meaning חלץ "to pull off" (i.e., שלף) > חלוץ goes as follows: וקרוב מן הענין הראשון 'ועבר לכם כל חלוץ' כל הפושטים בגדיהם לצאת למלחמה (Num. 32:21), "and very close to the first meaning (i.e., to pull off) is 'and all *ḥālūṣ* shall pass (the Jordan) before you,' which means those who take off their clothes to go to war."[14] Ibn Janāḥ's second possible interpretation is not concerned with the semantic development of the verb, and explains חלוץ as follows: וכבר פרשו במלות האל האזירה והחגירה למלחמה...ושני פרושים יכונו, "and it (i.e., חלוץ) was already explained in these words: the girding and belting (oneself) for war... and both interpretations are possible."[15]

Although Ibn Janāḥ presents his two explanations as mutually exclusive, Kutscher,[16] commenting on the vocable בחלץ employed in the Genesis Apocryphon,[17] attempts to reconcile Ibn Janāḥ's two definitions of חלוץ as follows:

> בחלץ cf. Syriac 'חליצותא' 'fortitudo.' That the Biblical root חלץ is sometimes close to this meaning is indicated by the fact that Targum Onqelous translates the root חלץ with זרז (e.g., Deut 3:18).... If this be true, we would have in all these instances a survival of the root חלץ 'strengthen' which probably is an offshoot of the root חלץ 'strip' etc. as a development from the word חלוץ 'equipped for war' (= stripped for fighting).

However, Kutscher's proposed semantic development of חלץ is not universally accepted. He confesses that "admittedly, the Midrash Wayyiqra Rabba 34, which deals with the different meanings of this root, does not explain it in this way." More significantly, Kutscher's theory is tenuous on semantic grounds, something we will have occasion to examine shortly.

II

The purpose of the present paper is to inductively study the verb חלץ in biblical and post-biblical Heb. and attempt to show that Heb. חלץ consists of one single root that has three distinct semantic denotations, one of which expresses the notion of chiropractic.

At the outset, it should be observed that the primary meaning of the verb חלץ is indeed physical and concrete. Thus, a) three times in the Qal it refers to חלץ נעל, "to pull off a sandal,"[18] rendered by Tg. Onq. שרה סינא, "to untie the sandal"; Tg. Neof. and Tg. J. שלף סנדלה, "to pull off the sandal" b) It is employed twice in the Piʿel in the idiom חלץ אבנים, "to pull out stones,"[19] rendered by Tg. Onq. שלף אבניא; Tg. Neof./Tg. J. שמט אבניה, "to detach stones" c) It is employed once in the Qal in the idiomatic *hapax* חלץ שד, "to pull off (i.e., expose) the breast,"[20] rendered by Tg. Ket. as טלען תד, "to take off the breast."

So, too, the verb חלץ "to pull off" is employed in post-biblical Hebrew in a concrete and physical sense in the following idioms: חלץ תפילין "to pull off phylacteries";[21] חלץ גידין ועצמות, "to pull off tendons and bones;"[22] חלץ בשר (מן העצם), "to pull off meat (from the bones)";[23] חלץ גלעין, "to pull off pit";[24] חלץ כתף (מן חלוק), "to expose the shoulder (from the garment)."[25]

The secondary connotation of חלץ is employed exclusively in wisdom literature: twelve times in the Piʿel and four times in the Niphʿal. Here, the verb חילץ/נחלץ expresses the notion of "to pull off" > "to save, rescue." Tg. Ket. renders the verb once by דחק "to push away," eight times by the verb פצה "rescue," and seven times by the verb שזיב "to save."

Indeed, this very specific connotation of the verb is attested to in both Punic and Old Aramaic inscriptions. In Old Aramaic, the verb is employed in the Paʿel as *ḥṣl*, a metathesis for חלץ "to save, rescue" (lit., "to pull off"). Thus, in the Zakur inscription we read: [ואנה א][ק]ם עמך ואנה אחצלך מן כל [מלכיא אל זי] מחצו עליך מצר, "and [I (Baal-Shamayn) shall stand] with you, (i.e., help you [Zakur]), and I shall deliver you from all [these kings who] have imposed a siege upon you."[26] Likewise, in Imperial Aramaic, the Adon papyrus from Saqqara (482 BCE), we read: למשלח חיל לחצלתי אל ישבקנ[י] "to send an army to deliver me (Adon), let him (the Pharaoh) not abandon me."[27] In Punic, however, we find the verb employed in the Qal passive participle in the sense of "to rescue, save" e.g., לעשתרת לפגמלין ידע מלך בן פדי חלץ אש חלץ פגמלין, "to Astarte, to Pygmalion, Yadaʿmilk son of Paday the saved one (i.e., *ḥālūṣ*) whom Pygmalion saved."[28]

The third connotation that the verb חלץ exhibits is attested solely in the passive, in both the Qal passive participle as well as in the Niphʿal. Besides appearing four times in the Niphʿal, where חלץ carries the connotation of "to pull off > to save" (from danger, calamity, evildoers, etc.),[29] the verb is likewise attested to three times in the Niphʿal in a military context: a) החלצו מאתכם אנשים לצבא (Num. 31:3); b) ואנחנו נחלץ חשים לפני ה' (Num. 32:17); c) אם תחלצו לפני ה' למלחמה (Num. 32:20). Following the rendering of LXX and the Peshiṭta, "to arm oneself," Tg. Onq./Tg. J. זרז, and Tg. Neof. זין, medieval and modern biblical scholarship understood the verb to mean "to equip, to arm, to take up arms."

However, this explanation is not without its problems. Specifically, the accepted translation of the Qal passive participle חלוץ as "equipped for war," or "ready for fighting," results in the unsatisfactory explanation of the semantic development from the primary meaning "to pull off, draw off" > "to equip, ready for war." Sensing the difficulties, Milgrom states that the NJPS rendering "Let [men] be picked out... although conjectural, is preferable."[30] Thus, NJPS consistently understood חלוץ to mean "picked for," "shock-fighter, troops," "vanguard."

The best solution to the present confusion is to take the Nifhʿal החלצו (Num. 31:3)/נחלץ (Num 32:17)/תחלצו (Num 32:20), as well as the Qal passive part. חלוץ, as a direct semantic offshoot of the primary meaning "to pull off, draw off, detach." According to this reconstruction, חלוץ would express the notion of a person or a group of persons who is (are) "pulled off, drawn off, detached," from the "main body of the people, army," i.e., "vanguard," as opposed to the מאסף "rearguard" (Josh. 6:9). Accordingly, the expression חלוצי/חלוץ צבא is in a sense similar to the idiom /יוצא יוצאי צבא "one who goes out to the army."[31]

The above interpretation of the military term חלץ is indeed strengthened by the Talmudic understanding of שלף=חלץ "to draw off, pull off," involving both non-military and military contexts:

> אמר ליה רב כהנא לשמואל ממאי דהאי וחלצה נעלו מעל רגלו מישלוף הוא דכתיב וחלצו את האבנים אשר בהם הנגע ואימא זרוזי הוא דכתיב החלצו מאתכם אנשים לצבא התם נמי שלופי מביתא לקרבא.

> Rabbi Kahana said to Shemuel: whence is it derived *'wêḥālêṣā* his shoe from his foot' signifies 'pulling off?' Because it is written, 'They shall take out the stones in which the plague is.' But I might suggest that the meaning is that of *zerūzē*, for it is written: *'hēḥālṣū* from among you men for the army'! [No,] there too [the meaning is] those who are *pulled off* from the house to war.[32]

III

The verb חלץ is likewise employed once in the Hiph'il in the idiomatic *hapax* החלץ עצמות in Isa. 58:11:

1. ונחך ה' תמיד
2. והשביע בצחצחות נפשך
3. ועצמתיך יחליץ
4. והיית כגן רוה וכמוצא מים
5. אשר לא יכזבו מימיו

1. The Lord will guide you continually
2. He will satisfy yourself in dry places
3. He will *yaḥaliṣ* your bones
4. so that You will be like a watered garden and like a source of water
5. whose waters never fail.

The verse raises both lexicographical and contextual problems, confronted by medieval and modern scholars alike: a) what is the precise connotation of the *hapax* expression ועצמתיך יחליץ? b) What is the contextual relationship between clauses *1–2/4–5* and *3*? Namely, what does the idiom ועצמתיך יחליץ have to do with the notion of quenching one's thirst in dry places and being like a well-watered garden and a spring whose waters fail not? In order to answer the above questions, one has to fully understand the denotation of the *hapax* expression ועצמתיך יחליץ.

Ancient translations, medieval commentators, and modern biblical scholars[33] dispute the exact meaning of this idiom. LXX and the Peshiṭta render it as "strengthen"; Tg. J. freely translates it as וגופך יחי, "He shall invigorate (lit., make live) your body." Medieval exegetes as well as modern biblical scholars have suggested two primary interpretations: 1. Strengthen — Saʿadya renders קוה אלעטאם "strengthen the bones";[34] Rashi reads יזין, "to make strong"; Isaiah of Trani offers לשון חזוק, "a meaning of strength"; Eliezer of Beaugency comments יזרז אבריך, "He shall strengthen your limbs." 2. The second explanation is semantically non-committed, that is, it translates the expression on contextual grounds. Accordingly, Ibn Janāḥ renders ירוה וירטיב, לפי הענין, "He will moisten, he will make wet, according to the context."[35] Such is also the interpretation of Qimḥi, who renders יחליץ as ידשן, "to make fat."

Ibn Ezra rejects both explanations and states:

> יש אומרים כמו 'ידשן,' בלי חבר. ואחרים אמרו 'יחזק' כמו חלוצי צבא (במ' לא, ה). ויש אומרים ש'יחליץ' – כמו 'יחלץ' (איוב לו, טו), כאשר מצאנו 'ישליח' (שמ' ח, יז) – 'ישלח' (תה' עח, מה); 'ישמיח' (תה' פט, מג) – 'ישמח' (איכה ב, יז). וזהו הנכון, כי הנה הוא 'שומר כל עצמותיו' (תה' לד, כא), והנה יחלצם משבר.
>
> Some will declare it to be a hapax legomenon, and explain it as 'He will make fat'; others render it 'He will strengthen,' comparing it with חלוצי 'armed' (Num. 31:5); still others think that *yaḥalīs* and *yeḥaleṣ* 'he delivers' (Job 36:15) are the same in meaning; as in the case with *yašliaḥ* (Exod. 8:17), and *yešallaḥ* 'he sends' (Ps. 78:45), with *yasmīaḥ* (Ps. 89:43) and *yesammaḥ* 'he causes to

> be glad' (Lam. 2:17). This latter explanation is right; cf. 'He keeps all his bones, [not one of them is broken]' (Ps. 34:21) — he is protecting them from breaking.

ועצמתיך יחליץ means, therefore, "He delivers his bones from the danger of being broken." Although some modern scholars unnecessarily resort to emending the verb יחליץ, rendering the idiom "(will make your bones) young and fresh again,"[36] the majority follow the medieval interpretation "to strengthen (the bones)."

Prior to discussing the idiomatic *hapax* ועצמתיך יחליץ, which may indeed constitute the first reference to the practice of chiropractic in biblical times, we should examine some of the post-biblical texts related to this matter. It is interesting to note that in the liturgy, in the prayer of קדוש החדש, "the sanctification of the New Moon" (i.e., the new month) on the Sabbath preceding the new month, the petition for חיים של חלוץ עצמות, "life of *ḥillūṣ* of the bones" is included. This appeal is based upon the prayer of Rav (3rd century CE) that appears in Babylonian Talmud *Berakhot* 16b:

> רב בתר צלותיה אמר הכי: יהי רצון מלפניך ה' א-לקינו שתתן לנו חיים ארוכים, חיים של שלום, חיים של טובה, חיים של ברכה, חיים של פרנסה, חיים של חלוץ עצמות.
>
> Rav, after his prayer (i.e., his שמונה עשרה prayer) would say: 'May it be your will, O Lord our God, that You give us a long life, a life of peace, a life of goodness, a life of blessing, a life of sustenance, a life of *ḥillūṣ* of the bones.'

Practically all understood the nominal idiomatic *hapax* חלוץ עצמות as lit., "strengthening of the bones" (i.e., "life of physical health").

In truth, the petition utilizing the verb החלץ is employed prior to Rav, in Mishnah *'Erub*. 3:9. There, R. Dosa b. Harkinas (first-second century CE) says:

> העובר לפני התיבה ביום טוב של ראש השנה אומר: החליצנו ה׳ אלקינו את יום ראש החדש הזה אם היום אם למחר.
>
> The person who passes before the Ark on the holiday of Rosh Hashanah says, "*haḥălīṣēnū*, O Lord our God on this day of Rosh Ḥodesh (i.e., the first of the new month), if today, if tomorrow."

Here again, the verb החליצנו is commonly rendered as "strengthen us."

One final post-biblical text in which the verb החליצנו appears is the Midrash *Leviticus Rabbah* 34:15, which alludes to the prayer that was later incorporated into the grace after meals on the Sabbath:[37]

> רצה והחליצנו ה׳ א־לקינו במצותיך ובמצות יום השביעי השבת הגדול והקדוש הזה, כי יום זה גדול וקדוש הוא לפניך, לשבת בו ולנוח בו באהבה כמצות רצונך.
>
> Let it be according to Your wishes *wêhaḥălīṣēnū* through Your commandments and through the commandment of the seventh day, this great and sanctified Sabbath. This day is indeed great and sanctified for You to abstain from work and to rest on it with loyalty according to Your will.

Here too, the majority of prayer books translate the verb והחליצנו as "strengthen us."

As noted above, there is no semantic justification for such a rendering. On the contrary, we have shown above that the verb חלץ has almost the opposite meaning, namely, the verb developed from its primary-concrete meaning "to pull off" > "to be detached (from the main body of people)" > "to rescue." To our mind, such is also the case concerning the idiomatic *hapax* ועצמתיך יחליץ in Isa. 58:11. The prophet Isaiah intentionally employs the concrete verb חלץ in the Hiph'il to express the idea of God separating, detaching, and pulling off one's bones from each other, a sign of relaxation and physical health. Indeed, the contextual relationship of clause "3" to clause "2" on the one hand, and clauses "4/5" on the other, demands an understanding of clause "3" which implies physical health. The clause, which according to our suggestion describes a chiropractic-like procedure, is taken as conducive to good health.

We know from elsewhere in the Bible that the bones are regarded as the seat of health and vigor; their weakened condition parallels the general state of deterioration in old age. Accordingly, note the following idioms: דבקה עצמי לבשרי, "my bones are charred from dryness" (Job 30:33; cf. also Ps. 102:4); בלו עצמי, "my bones are wasted away" (Ps. 32:3); עצמי עששו, "my bones are wasted away" (Ps. 31:11); צפד עורם על עצמם יבש היה כעץ, "their skin has shriveled on their bones it has become dry as a wood" (Lam. 4:8). The converse, of course, is that their sturdiness earlier in life is representative of the robust state of the rest of the body; see שמועה טובה תדשן עצם, "good news puts fat on the bones" (Prov. 15:30); ועצמותיכם כדשא תפרחנה, "your bones shall flourish like a tender grass" (Isa. 66:14); ומח עצמותיו ישקה, "his bone marrow is watered (i.e., juicy)" (Job 21:24).

It was out of recognition for the healthy, relaxed state conveyed by the idiom "החלץ עצמות" that R. Eleazar characterized it as the best of blessings:[38] הא דכתיב ועצמתיך יחליץ, ואמר רבי אלעזר, זו מעולה שבברכות, "[what explanation is there, however, for] the Scriptural text 'and he shall loosen up your bones,' of which Rabbi Eleazar said that this was the best of blessings...?" This very state of relaxation, rest, and repose expressed by separation and loosening up of one's bones is the reason for the inclusion of the petition in the liturgy of Rosh Hashanah (i.e., החליצנו...את יום ראש החדש הזה); in the prayer of Rav and in קידוש החדש (i.e., חיים של חלוץ עצמות); and in grace after meals on the Sabbath, where רצה והחליצנו, "let it be according to Your wishes and loosen us" (i.e., our bones) is followed and juxtaposed with ולנוח בו, "and to rest on it."[39]

Our understanding of the semantic range of חלץ, and more specifically the juxtaposition of החלץ עצמות with נוח "to rest," is clearly advocated in *Leviticus Rabbah* 34:15:

'ונחך ה' תמיד והשביע בצחצחות נפשך ועצמתיך יחליץ' – א"ר טביומי, אם עשית כן, הרי את כבוראך, כאותו שכתוב 'דודי צח ואדום' (שה"ש ה, י). 'ועצמתיך יחליץ,' ישמוט, יזיין, ויניח. ישמוט, כד"א 'וחלצה נעלו מעל רגלו' (דב' כה, ט); יזיין כד"א 'חלוצים תעברו לפני אחיכם בני ישראל' (שם, ג, יח); ישזיב, 'חלצני ה' מאדם רע' (תה קמ, ב); ויניח. מכאן קבעו חכמים לומר רצה והחליצנו בשבת. 'והיית כגן רוה וכמוצא מים אשר לא יכזבו מימיו' (יש' נח, יא), זה עדן.

"And the Lord will guide thee continually, and satisfy thy soul in *ṣaḥṣaḥot* and make loose thy bones." R. Tabyumi explained: If you have done this you will be like your Creator, of whom it is written, "My beloved is white (*ṣaḥ*) and ruddy" (Song 5:10). "And make strong (*yaḥaliṣ*) thy bones." '*Yaḥaliṣ*' means "He will loose," "He will arm," "He will deliver," and "He will give rest." "He will loose" is a meaning proved by the text, "and she pulled off his shoe from his foot" (Deut. 25:9). "He shall arm" is a meaning proved by the text "Ye shall pass over armed" (Deut. 3:18). "He shall deliver" is a meaning proved by the text, "Deliver me O Lord, from the evil man" (Ps. 140:2). "He shall give rest." It is for this reason that the Sages have ordained that one should say, "Be pleased and give us rest on the Sabbath." "And thou shalt be like a watered garden that is, literally, a garden. And like a spring of water, whose waters fail not" — this alludes to Eden.

IV

Our analysis of the verses in Isaiah implies that the prophet, in antiquity, anticipated what later became known as chiropractic. Separating the bones creates optimal space between them to promote proper fluid retention and nerve flow. If the space between the vertebrae is reduced, the fluid that lies between the bones and insures the health of the joint is impaired and the nerves that run between the bones are pinched. Of course, proper nerve flow is crucial for the body to function properly. If a nerve is damaged or constricted, the information that it carries is interrupted. Thus, without proper separation of the bone, mobility, nerve communication, and above all else optimal health are put at risk. Isaiah, prophesying some 2700 years ago, seems to have acknowledged the beneficial effects of this treatment.

NOTES

1. Deut. 25:9; Isa. 20:2; Hos. 5:6; Lam. 4:3.
2. Num. 31:5; 32:21, 27, 29, 30, 32; Deut. 3:18; 25:10; Josh. 4:13; 6:7, 9, 13; Isa. 15:4; 1 Chr. 12:23, 24; 2 Chr. 17:18; 20:21; 28:14.
3. Num. 31:3; 32:17, 20; Ps. 60:7; 108:7; Prov. 11:8, 9.
4. Lev. 14:40, 43; 2 Sam. 22:20 (= Ps. 18:20); Ps. 6:5; 7:5; 34:8; 50:15; 81:8; 91:15; 116:8; 119:153; 140:2; Job 36:15.
5. Isa. 58:11.
6. *BDB*, 322–3.
7. Eliezer Ben-Yehuda, *A Complete Dictionary of Ancient and Modern Hebrew* (New York: Thomas Yoseloff, 1959), 2:1564 (Heb.).
8. Abraham Even-Shoshan, *The New Dictionary* (Jerusalem: Kiryat Sefer, 1966), 2:779 (Heb.).
9. David J.A. Clines (ed.), *The Dictionary of Classical Hebrew* (Sheffield: Sheffield Academic Press, 1996), 4:239–240.
10. KB^3, 1:321–2.
11. *CAD Ḫ* 40a; *AHw* 1074a.
12. Gen 40:11; See Harold R. (Chaim) Cohen, *Biblical Hapax Legomena in the Light of Akkadian and Ugaritic* (Missoula: Scholars Press, 1978), 35.
13. H. Tawil, "Lexicographical Note IV," 340–1.
14. Jonah Ibn Janaḥ, *Sepher Haschorashim* (ed.Wilhelm Bacher; Berlin, 1896), 156–7 (Heb.).
15. Ibid.
16. E.Y. Kutscher, "The Language of the Genesis Apocryphon: A Preliminary Study," *Scripta Hierosolymitana* 4 (1965), 29.
17. J.A. Fitzmayer, *The Genesis Apocryphon of Qumran Cave I* (Rome: Biblical Institute Press, 1971), 52 2:8.
18. Deut. 25:9, 10; Isa. 20:2.
19. Lev. 14:40, 43.
20. Lam. 4:3.

21. C.J. Kasowski, *Thesaurus Talmudis* (Jerusalem: Ronald, 1965), 14:481 ff. (Heb.).
22. Ibid., 482.
23. Moshe Kosovsky, *Concordance to the Talmud Yerushalmi* (Jerusalem: Keter, 1984), 3:650 (Heb.).
24. Ibid.
25. Ibid.
26. John C.L. Gibson, *Textbook of Syrian Semitic Inscriptions* (Oxford: Clarendon Press, 1975), 8 A:12–15.
27. Ibid., 113 N-21:17.
28. Ibid., 3:69:1–6. cf. also J. Hoftijzer and K. Kongeling, *Dictionary of the North West Semitic Inscriptions* (Leiden: Brill, 1995), 1:378.
29. Ps. 60:7; 108:7; Prov. 11:8, 9.
30. J. Milgrom, *The JPS Torah Commentary: Numbers* (Philadelphia: The Jewish Publication Society of America, 1990), 255–256, n. 3.
31. Cf., e.g., Num. 1:3, 45; 26:2; 1 Chr. 12:9 and passim.
32. b. *Yeb.* 102b.
33. See, for example, E.J. Kissane, *The Book of Isaiah* (Dublin: Browne and Nolan, 1943), 23; John D. Watts, *Isaiah 34–66* (*WBC*; Waco: Word Books, 1987), 270–71; John L. McKenzie, *Second Isaiah* (AB; Garden City: Doubleday, 1964), 164.
34. See J. Dernbourg, *Oueovres Completes de R. Saadia ben Iosef Al-Fayyome* (Paris, 1893).
35. Ibid., n. 14.
36. See, for example, Claus Westermann, *Isaiah 40–66* (Philadelphia: Westminster Press, 1969), 352.
37. See the standard prayer books.
38. b. *Yeb.* 102b.
39. This idea is expressed even more clearly in the Yemenite and Sephardic books, where רצה והחליצנו במצותיך is followed by ובמצות יום המנוח השביעי הזה, "and through the commandment of the day of *rest*, this seventh day." See Yaḥya Saliḥ, *Tiklal* 1:169 (Hebrew) (ed. Y. Hasid; Jerusalem, 1961). Note that the Yemenite and the Sephardic prayer books seem to have a better version of the line that follows, i.e., נשבת בו ונגוח בו, "so *we* shall stop working on it, and *we* shall rest in it."

Hebrew נַפֵּץ יַד = Akkadian *qāta napāṣu*: A Term of Non-Allegiance: A Lexicographical Note VII

To: Harry Epstine

וקנה לך חבר (m. *Avot* 1:6)

The last chapter in Daniel, chapter twelve, has traditionally been divided into two basic units:[1] (a) an eschatological prophecy foreseeing the final victory of God's chosen ones — the ultimate victory of the righteous — introduced by the standard formula בָּעֵת הַהִיא "at that time" (Dan. 12:1–4),[2] and (b) an epilogue (vv. 5–13) involving two major subunits: 1. a celestial colloquy about the end in the form of a vision of two angels — one of whom states the duration of the troubles just foretold (vv. 5–7), and 2. an inquiry as to the conclusion of the age; the answer given is that the "final phase" (עֵת קֵץ) will be a time of purification, with personal bliss assured in the resurrection (vv. 8–13).

Our present concern is with the subunit of Dan. 12:5–7 in general, and with the *hapax* idiomatic expression (וּכְכַלּוֹת) נַפֵּץ יַד (עַם קֹדֶשׁ) in particular. Dan. 12:5–7 reads as follows:

5. וראיתי אני דניאל והנה שנים אחרים עמדים אחד הנה לשפת היאר ואחו הנה לשפת היאר
6. ויאמר לאיש לבוש הבדים אשר למעלה מימי היאר עד מתי קץ הפלאות
7. ואשמע את האיש לבוש הבדים אשר ממעל למימי היאר וירם ימינו ושמאלו אל השמים וישבע בחי העולם כי למועד מועדים וחצי וּכְכַלּוֹת נַפֵּץ יַד עַם קֹדֶשׁ תכלינה כל אלה

5. Then I, Daniel, looked and saw two others standing, one on one bank of the river, the other on the other bank of the river. 6. One said to the man clothed in linen who was above the waters of the river, "How long until the

> end of these awful things?" 7. Then I heard the man dressed in linen, who was above the water of the river, sear by the Ever-Living One as he lifted his right hand and his left had to heaven "for a time, times and a half a time and at the rumination of *nappēṣ yad* of the holy people all these things will come to an end."

The clause וככלות נַפֵּץ יַד עם קדש has been variously rendered: "and when an end is made to breaking in pieces the power of the Holy People" (ICC); "and when the breaking of the power of the holy people comes to an end" (NJPS, RSV); "and when the power of the holy people is no longer being shattered" (RV).

The idiomatic *hapax* נַפֵּץ יַד has elicited much comment from modern biblical scholars: "the final sentence is difficult"[3]; "it's entirely vague"[4]; "the conclusion of the verse is a puzzle"[5]; "the Heb. is unusual"[6]; "the last clause of 12:7 is obscure in the MT"[7]; "the MT is not impossible, but it is not clear to what point it would refer."[8] Accordingly, various emendations have been suggested. Charles emends the verb נַפֵּץ to נֹתֵץ "one who pulls down (a structure)," considering the MT "to be a corruption."[9] Ginsberg rejects this emendation as "too un-idiomatic in the context to be worth considerable alteration of the graphic picture which it involves."[10] The NEB revocalizes the verb to נְפֹץ, deriving the word from נפץ II "to disperse, scatter," hence translating the clause: "when the power of the holy people ceases to be dispersed." The most celebrated transposition of word and revocalization is that of Bevan, who transposes the word יַד and — revocalizing נַפֵּץ to נֹפֵץ — renders the clause as וּכִכְלוֹת יַד נֹפֵץ "when the power of the shatterer (of the holy people) should come to an end,"[11] referring to Antiochus IV. This widely accepted emendation was rejected by Ginsberg on both grammatical and historical grounds. Grammatically, Ginsberg maintains that the participle נֹפֵץ "would be a unique occurrence of the *qal* of this verb." Historically, he further argues, "Antiochus IV, however, did not subjugate the Jews, who had been subject to his two predecessors before him.... In any case, the military and political aspects of Antiochus IV's relations with the Jews were completely overshadowed by the religious."[12] Ginsberg, while rejecting the emendations of both Bevan and Charles, tentatively accepts "the changes of the word order."[13] However, he suggests the Heb. *nappēṣ* is here a mistranslation of the original Aramaic, which had *mps* (*mappes* = *mhappes*), "desecrator." Ginsberg likewise maintains "that the consonants of the latter can also be read *mippas*: which is the *qal* infinitive, or verbal noun of the same root and means 'dividing, taking apart.'" Accordingly, he reads the clause as וּכְכַלּוֹת יַד נַפֵּץ עַם קֹדֶשׁ, translating it as "and when the strength of the breading up of the holy people shall fail."[14]

An alternative solution to the above renderings, emendations, and transposition may be found in cuneiform inscriptions that are contextually similar to our case at hand. At the outset, however, it should be noted that Heb. נפץ "to shatter" is not only the etymological and semantic equivalent of the Akk. verb *napāṣu* "to smash, crush, tear down," but also comes to mean "to kick, strike, dash down."[15] This can be seen from the following Heb./Akk. idiomatic equivalents: Heb. (said of humans) נַפֵּץ גוים "to smash nations"[16] = Akk. *napḫar nišī amēlī nuppuṣu* "to crush all people"[17]; נַפֵּץ איש ואשה־זקן ונער־בחור בתולה "to crush man and woman — old and young — youth and maiden"[18] = Akk. *eṭlūti šuggušu ušaggaš ardāti ḫubbulu uḫabbal ṣiḫru nuppuṣu unappaṣ* "she (the *Lamaštu*-demon) indeed murders men, ruins women, smites the young"[19]; Heb. נַפֵּץ עוֹלָלִים "to crush descendants (lit., children)"[20]= Akk. (*adi ūm ṣâti*) *lippuṣū zerasu* "may they (forever) crush the offspring"[21]; Heb. (said of important people) נַפֵּץ פַּחוֹת וּסְגָנִים "to crush governors and prefects"[22] = Akk. (said of heroes, warriors) *qarrādī nuppuṣu* "to shatter warriors," e.g., *qarrādīšu ina pān abbulīšu kīma alsī unappiṣ* "I (Sargon II) crushed his warriors in front of the city gate like lambs"[23]; Heb. (to crush, mash an object) נָפוּץ/נַפֵּץ כדים/כלי יוצר/נבלים/אבני גיר/עצב "to crush, smash pitchers/potters ware/jars/blocks of chalk/clay"[24] = Akk. *kupra/dalta/sikkūra/bīta nuppuṣu* "to crush, smash bitumen/a door/a bolt/a house."[25]

More specifically, the idiomatic *hapax* נַפֵּץ יַד, which has created numerous difficulties for students of Daniel, can be completely clarified in the light of the rather common Akk. idiomatic gesture *qātam napāṣum*.[26] However, prior to our discussion of these Hebrew and Akkadian expressions, let us consider a now well-known symbolic gesture that is the reverse of this one: "seizing a hem of the cloak," a specific gesture that is relevant for our study. The idiomatic gesture "to grasp the hem (of a garment)"[27] has been identified in Akk. *sissikta ṣabātu* "to grasp the hem"[28]; *qannam ṣabātu* "to grasp the hem"[29]; *qaran ṣubāti ṣabātu* "to grasp the hem of a garment"[30] = Old Aramaic[31] אחז בכנף = Heb. החזיק בכנף[32] = Ugar. *ʾḫd bsin*.[33] It is derived from a gesture in which a suppliant beseeches or indicates his submission to his superior by grasping the latter's hem. More specifically, it is "not merely a submission, but an act of declaring an allegiance,"[34] a symbolic gesture of covenantal loyalty.

The Akk. idiomatic expression *qāta napāṣu*, on the other hand, has the opposite connotation; it denotes "to refuse, reject, push back," lit., "to thrust away the hand." It is derived from a gesture of refusing to hold a hand in an expression of unity allegiance. Pushing back, thrusting away a hand, is a symbolic gesture that expresses a rejection of a treaty allegiance. Akk. *qātam napāṣum* is employed primarily in Old Babylonian and Mari texts:

> *Awīl Ḫaššum awīl Uršum u awīl Karkemiš itti Sumu-epuḫ ina pānīya qātam inappaṣū*
>
> The ruler of Ḫaššum, the ruler of Uršum, and the ruler of Carchemiš before my arrival will refuse to make alliance (lit., thrust away a hand) with Sumu-epuḫ.[35]
>
> *4 ālāni ḫarbātim bēli uwašśeramma ina 4 ālāni ina Araitim qātī ippuṣū u muškēnam apālam ul eleʾī*
>
> For worthless cities my lord had released to me and my authority was withdrawn from four cities in Araitim. I cannot then give satisfaction to the *muškēnum* (Benjaminite citizen).[36]

Apart from reference to humans, this idiomatic gesture likewise pertains to a country or tribes that violate a treaty:

> *Mātum ša qāti bēlīša ippu[ṣu ana bēli]ša iturram*
>
> A land which has refused to obey (lit., pushed back the hand of) its overlord will return [to] its [overlord].[37]

As noted above, the gesture of "seizing the hem of a garment" symbolizing loyalty has its opposite expression by gesture of "pushing back the hand." These two gestures are attested together in the Mari letters:

> *Ana qabê mātīya qaran ṣubat bēlīya aṣbat bēlī qātī lā inappaṣ*
>
> At the request of my land, I seized the hem of my lord's garment. My lord must not reject me (lit., "push back my hand").[38]

In light of the above Akkadian examples, it seems rather clear that emendations, revocalizations, and transposition of the last clause of Dan. 12:7 are indeed unwarranted.[39] The idiomatic gesture נַפֵּץ יַד in Daniel seems to conform to traditional Mesopotamian covenantal technical terminology *qāta napāṣu*. In the eschatological vision of Zechariah, the prophet foresees a time when many nations and people will acknowledge the universal supremacy and authority of the God of Israel, expressed by the covenantal gesture of seizing the hem of a garment:

> בימים ההמה אשר יחזיקו עשרה אנשים מכל לשנות הגוים והחזיקו בכנף איש יהודי לאמר נלכה עמכם כי שמענו אלהים עמכם
>
> In those days, ten men from nations of every tongue will take hold — they will take hold of every Jew by the corner of his cloak and say "let us go with you, for we have heard that God is with you" (Zech. 8:23).

In Daniel's apocalyptic eschatology, however, the promise of redemption is executed by the traditional gesture of the angel's uplifting his hands in an oath-like gesture to the Ever Living-One: (i.e., וירם ימינו ושמאלו אל משמים וישבע בחי העולם). Not unlike in Zechariah, the stipulation of the oaths is likewise drawn from the legal-conventional physical gesture, namely, God's termination of the rejection of the holy people. When the appointed time arrives, God will renew his covenant with Israel, and all the "awful things" (הנפלאות) will come to an end. Accordingly, the last clause of Dan. 12:7 כי למועד מועדים וחצי וככלות נפץ יד עם קדש תכלינה כל אלא may be rendered anew:

> For a time, times, and a half a time, and at the time of the termination of thrusting the hand (i.e., of the covenantal rejection) of the holy people all these things will come to an end.

NOTES

1. J. J. Collins, *Daniel* (Minneapolis: Fortress Press, 1993), 371.
2. Cf. for examples, Collins, *Daniel*, 390a.
3. James A. Montgomery, *A Critical and Exegetical Commentary on the Book of Daniel* (Edinburgh: T & T Clark, 1927), 475. Montgomery further comments "It is best to remain by the text of M, which is intentionally obscure diction."
4. R. H. Charles, *A Critical and Exegetical Commentary on the Book of Daniel* (Oxford: Clarendon Press, 1929), 334.
5. *The Interpreter's Bible*, vol. VI (New York: Abingdon Press, 1956), 6:545.
6. John E. Goldingay, *Daniel* (Dallas: Word Books, 1989), 281.
7. Louis F. Hartman and Alexander A. Di Lella, *The Book of Daniel* (New York: Doubleday, 1978), 312.
8. Collins, *Daniel*, 399b.
9. Charles, *loc. cit.*
10. H. Louis Ginsberg, *Studies in Daniel* (New York,; JTS 1948), 83.
11. A. A. Bevan, *A Short Commentary on Daniel* (Cambridge: Cambridge Press, 1892), 206; K. Marti, *Das Buch Daniel* (Tubingen, 1901), 91; BDB 658b; *KB* II (1995), 711a.
12. Ginsberg, *Studies*, 83.
13. Ibid., 83.
14. Ibid., 84.

15. *CAD* N/I 285a; *AHw* 735b.
16. Jer. 51:20.
17. *CAD* N/1 285b, lex. section.
18. Jer. 51:20.
19. *CAD* N/I 287b.
20. Ps. 137:9.
21. *CAD* N/1 286b.
22. Jer. 20:23.
23. *CAD* N/1 287b.
24. Judg. 7:19; Ps. 2:9; Jer. 48:12; Isa. 27:9; Jer. 22:28.
25. *CAD* N/1, 286b.
26. *CAD* N/1, 286a.
27. Ronald A. Brauner, "'To Grasp the Hem' and 1 Samuel 15:27," *JANES* 6 (1974), 35–38; K. Lawson Younger, Jr., "Panammuwa and Bar-Rakib: Two Structural Analyses," *JANES* 18 (1986), 98 n. 31; Shalom M. Paul, "Gleanings from the Biblical and Talmudic Lexica in Light of Akkadian," in *Minḥah le-Nahum* (eds. Marc Brettler and Michael Fishbane; Sheffield: JOST Press, 1993), 244–48.
28. E.g., [*asḫur*]*ki aše'ki sissiktaki aṣbat kīma sissikti ilīya u ištarrīya*" [I turned] to you and sought you. I seized your hem (= importuned you) as if it were the hem of my god and goddess" (*CAD* S 324b and *passim*).
29. E.g., *qurbī ana* RN *ṣābit qanniki* "(Ištar), pronounce your blessings over RN, who grasps your hem" (*CAD* Q 83b and *passim*).
30. E.g *ištu ūmim ša qaran ṣubātīya iṣbatu matima ina mātīšu kaspam... mimma ul alqut* "Ever since he grasped the hem of my garment (i.e., gave me his allegiance), I have never exacted silver… from his country" (*CAD* Q 84b and *passim*).
31. E.g., פי אחז בכנף מראה מלך אשור ר[ב] "He (Panammuwa II) grasped the hem of his lord (Tiglath-Pileser III), the great king of Assyria" (*KAI* I 215:11, Bar-Rakib).
32. E.g., ויסב שמואל ללכת ויחזק כבנף מעילו ויקרע "Samuel turned to depart, but he (Saul) took hold of the hem of his cloak and it tore" (1 Sam. 15:27).
33. E.g., *tiḫd m[t] bsin lpš tšṣqnh bqṣ all* "She (Anat) seizes Mot by the hem of (his) garment, she presses him by the edge of (his) robe" (*CTA* 6, ii 9–11). This sole example from Ugarit was first pointed out by R. A. Brauner, "Aramaic and Comparative Semitic" *Gratz Annual of Jewish Studies* 6 (1977), 25- 27. For some reason this essay is not acknowledged by E. L. Greenstein, "To Grasp the Hem in Ugaritic Literature," *VT* 32 (1982), 217–18.
34. Paul, "Gleanings," 248.
35. *ARM* I 24 r. 14–15 (*CAD* N/1, 286a) = *LAPO* 16: 330 (pp. 512f.).
36. *ARM* II 55 r. 26–29 (*CAD*, N/1, loc. cit.) = *LAPO* 16: 705 (pp. 453ff.).

The idiom here is used with reference not so much to political allegiance as to administrative authority.

37. *YOS* 10 39:12 (*CAD* N/1, *loc. cit.*).
38. *ARM* VI 26 r. 9–10 (CAD N/1, loc. cit.) = *LAPO* 16: 359 (pp. 585ff.).
39. Note that Magen Broshi and Esther Eshel in "The Greek King is Antiochus IV (4 Q Historical Text = 4 Q 248)," *JJS* 48 (1997), 124, have proposed that this Qumran text was the source of Daniel. Accordingly, Broshi and Eshel read lines 9 and 10 as [*u-kehalot*] *nappēṣ yad ʿam ha*[*qodesh*]: "[and] when the shattering of the power of the holy people [is complete]." This would correspond to Dan. 12:7. However, as noted by J. J. Collins, *Encyclopedia of the Dead Sea Scrolls* (eds. Lawrence Schiffman and J. C. VanderKam; New York: Oxford Press, 2000), 178, "the actual reading of the key phrase is very doubtful. The *nun* of *nappēṣ* has to be reconstructed and other scholars read *b(bet)* instead of *p(pe)*." The article of Broshi and Eshel was called to my attention by my colleague Samuel Klein.

Two Biblical and Akkadian Comparative Lexical Notes: A Lexicographical Note VIII

I. Hebrew רִטֵּשׁ = Akkadian *šarāṭu/šurruṭu*

Biblical lexica differ as to the etymology of the BH verb רטשׁ. KB equates the lexeme with Heb. נטשׁ stating that it means "1. to smite, smash, dash to pieces; 2. to spread out > forsake, abandon." The first meaning is related to Arab. *laṭasa*, the second to נטשׁ, assuming a phonetic shift *nṭ* and *lṭ* > *rṭ*.[1] BDB equates the verb with the Targumic Aramaic רְטַשׁ, "to cast away, to reject," noting that it is possibly akin to לטשׁ, "hammer, sharpen."[2] Both KB's[3] and BDB's etymological equations and seem difficult to accept on semantic grounds. Namely, the alleged development of the verb: "to smite, smash > to spread out, forsake, abandon." Rather, it seems more appropriate to consider Targumic Aramaic רְטַשׁ as a למנ"ר interchange with the Heb. נטשׁ "to forsake," and semantically to keep BH רִטֵּשׁ "to tear apart" as a separate lexeme. This seems evident since Tg. J. renders Heb. רַטֵּשׁ/רְטַשׁ once as טרף "tear apart," once as בזע "split open," once as קטל "split open,"[4] and once as רְטַשׁ "to kill."[5] Never with Aram. רְטַשׁ.

The BH verb רטשׁ is employed six times, always in a context of warfare. It once describes the war between Aram and Israel,[6] and five times appears in Assyrian warfare tactics.[7] The verb is employed twice in the Piʿel in the idioms עלליהם תְּרַטֵּשׁ//והרתיהם תבקע "you shall tear apart their little ones//you shall rip open their pregnant women,"[8] and קשתות נערים תְּרַטַּשְׁנָה//ופרי בטן לא ירחמו "their bows shall dash the young//they shall show no pity to infants."[9] In the same context, the verb is likewise employed four times in the Puʿal: עלליהם יְרֻטְּשׁוּ//ונשיהם תשגלנה, "their babes shall be dashed to pieces//their wives shall be raped";[10] עלליהם יְרֻטָּשׁוּ//והריותיו יבקעו "their infants shall be dashed//their pregnant women ripped open";[11] אם על בנים רֻטָּשָׁה "mother together with (her) children is dashed";[12] עלליה יְרֻטָּשׁוּ בראש כל חוצות "her infants were dashed at every main street."[13] Heb.רִטֵּשׁ/רֻטַּשׁ employed in the above verses describing the brutal manner of the Assyrian war games, finds its parallel in the Akk. verb *šurruṭu* and Akk. *šarāṭu/ šurruṭu*. These words, in our mind, are a metathesized form of Heb. רטש, which is commonly employed since Old Babylonian to mean "to tear, to tear into strips, to shred specifically garments"[14] e.g., *naḫlapta/kitâ/ṣubāṭa/lubša šarāṭu/šurruṭu* "to tear/tear into strips cloaks/linen garments/clothing."[15]

More specifically, in the Middle Assyrian "heroic poem" celebrating the victories of the Assyrian king Tiglath Pileser I (1114–1076 BCE), the Akk. verb *šurruṭu* (D stem) = Heb. רַטֵּשׁ (Piʿel) is employed in once describing the king's brutal and murderous acts upon pregnant women:

> *ḫarrān šelalti ūmi irtedi [ ] adu la šamaš napāḫu ipirušunu anqullu ušerriṭi libbi arâti unappil lakûti ša dannūtišunu unakkis kišādāti*
>
> He (Tiglath Pileser I) pushes ahead a distance of three days even before the sun rose, the earth was aglow (?). He rips open the wombs of pregnant women, he blinds the infants, he cuts the throats of the strong ones.[16]

The employment of the Akk. verb *šurruṭu*, which is attested only once in the above Assyrian idiom *libbi arâti šurruṭu* "to tear apart the wombs of pregnant women," finds its semantic equivalent with the Heb. verb בִּקֵּעַ "to split open," similarly used in the twice attested idiom בַּקֵּעַ הָרוֹת "to split open the (wombs of) pregnant women." However, contrary to von Soden's etymological equation of Heb. שָׂרַט "to scratch, incise" with Akk *šarāṭu* "to tear, to tear into strips, dash"[17] — also followed by KB[18] — we propose etymologically and semantically to equate Heb. רִטֵּשׁ (metathesis) used in the idiom רַטֵּשׁ עללים/נערים/אם "to tear apart infants/ young/mothers"[19] with the Akk. verb *šurruṭu*, employed once in the expression *libbi arâti šurruṭu* "to split open the wombs of pregnant women."

II. Hebrew קָטֹן = Akkadian *qatnu/qutnu*

The etymological and the semantic equivalent of the BH צָעִיר is the Akk. lexeme *ṣiḫru* "young, small, child."[20] This can be seen, for example, from the following Heb.-Akk. idiomatic equivalents: Heb: רַב־צָעִיר "older-younger"[21] (sequential *hapax*) = Akk: *ṣiḫru-rabû* "young-old";[22] Heb. צָעִיר־יָשִׁישׁ "young-old"[23] = Akk. *šību-ṣiḫru* "old-young."[24] However, the semantic equivalent of Akk. *ṣiḫru* "young" is the Heb. adj. קָטֹן/קָטָן "young, small."[25] This can be seen, for example, from the idiomatic equivalent of Akk. *ṣiḫru-rabû* =Heb. קָטֹן־גָּדוֹל "young/small-old/big."[26] The Heb. verb קָטֹן "to be small" and the adj. קָטֹן/קָטָן "small/young" are the etymological equivalent of the Akk. verb *qatānu* and the adj. *qatnu*. Unlike the Heb. lexemes, these Akkadian words connote mainly "to become thin, narrow"[27] and "thin, fine, narrow" (adj.).[28] It should be observed, however, that Heb. קֹטֶן (i.e. קֹטֶן/קָטֹן*) seems to finds its semantic equivalent with Akk. *qatnu/ qutnu,* in the sense "thin, fine" in two cases.

The first case is to be found in 1 Kings 12:10, where the *hapax* substantive קֹטֶן* is employed as the antonym of the verb עָבָה "to be thick." That is to say, קָטָנִּי may be rendered as "my thinnest part (of the body)," probably "my small finger," as understood both by medieval and modern scholars alike. Similarly, Akk. employs the verb *qatānu* "to be thin" as the opposite of *kabāru* "to be thick,"[29] and the substantive *qutnu* "thin part" (referring also to thin parts of the body) as the opposite of *kabru* "thick."[30] 1 Kings 12:10a קָטָנִּי עָבָה מִמָּתְנֵי אָבִי may be rendered as "my thinnest part (of the body) is thicker than my father's loins."

The second case where Heb. קָטֹן seems to be the etymological and the semantic equivalent of Akk. *qatnu/qutnu* in the sense of "thin, fine" is in 1 Sam. 2:19 ומעיל קָטֹן תעשה לו אמו והעלתה לו מימים ימימה בעלותה את אישה לזבח את זבח הימים. This verse is traditionally rendered as: "and his (Samuel's) mother used to make him a *little*[31] robe and brought it to him every year when she went up wither her husband to sacrifice the yearly sacrifice." Among the medieval commentators, Qimḥi seems to be the only one who attempts to explain contextually the problematic usage of מעיל קטן in this verse. Qimḥi comments: עשתה לו מעיל ולא היתה מניחתו אצלו כדי שלא יעטה אותו בימות החול אלא ממועד למועד לכבוד היום והוא היה נער ולא נשמר מלעטתו לפיכך היתה מעלה אותו לו במועד ומחזירה אותו עד מועד אחר "she used to make him a robe but she did not leave it with him so that he should not wear it out during the week days, rather from one holiday to the other in honor of the day. Since he was a youth and was not careful from wearing it, therefore, she used to bring up to him on holiday and bring it back until the next holiday."[32] Ehrlich maintains that Qimḥi's interpretation is unsatisfactory. He states that "Radaq (Qimḥi) erred saying that the text refers to one coat that his mother brought him, and brought it back every year, but this is not correct... Radaq also erred since the coat was called little... as it is maintained that the text does not refer only to a coat that was made when Samuel was a young boy. And Qimḥi's explanation cannot be right since (it says) that Samuel continuously grew in height, and so the coat would have been too short for him and would not have fitted him after two or three years."[33] Accordingly, Erlich advances the following interpretation:

> and truly מעיל קטן means מעיל של קטן "a coat of small (unimportant person)" or מעיל כמעיל אשר ילבשו הקטנים, "or a coat like the coat that small (important people) wear." Because the coat served them as garments of honor, and most simple people did not wear it during their lifetime, and none of them wore it until his wedding, but the important people used to wear a coat even before that, as it is written "thus the virgin daughters of the kings used to wear coats" (2 Sam. 13:18), except that the coat of the little one or the youth was not made like the coat of the big one or the married person.[34]

The ICC, sensing no textual problem, comments:

> No English word corresponds to the Hebrew. The garment was worn over the tunic. There seems no reason

> to find fault with the statement on the ground that as the boy grew it would no longer be a *little* robe. The narrator has the earlier years especially in mind."[35]

An alternative solution may be found in the specific usage of the Akk. verb *qatānu* and the adj./sub. *qatnu/qutnu*, which etymologically and semantically may be the equivalent of קָטֹן as employed in 1 Sam. 2:19. The Akk. adj. *qatnu*, as well as the substantive *qutnu*, generally means "thin, fine" and "thin part of an object,"[36] respectively. However, both *qatnu* and *qutnu* are more specifically employed to describe the "fine" quality of textiles and fabrics.[37] Akk. *qatnu* depicts the fine quality of *naḫlaptu/ṣubātu/lubuštu* "textile/garments/wardrobe." *Qatnu* is likewise used in sequence with the adjectives *raqqatu/damiqtu/nasiqtu* "thin textile/fine quality/choice fabric." A few examples will suffice:

a) *1 naḫlaptu raqqatam damiqtam qatanam šāmanimma*

"buy for me a thin textile, textile of good quality with fine weave"[38]

b) *šūnātim 1 mana ulama 2 mana qatanātim damqātim šūbilma*

"send me one or two minas of *šūnu* textiles, fine and good quality ones"[39]

It is interesting to note that the substantive *qatnu*, which is equated in the lexical synonym list with *ṣubat rabû* "garment of a noble" and *ṣubat qalpu* "threadbare garment,"[40] denotes "a garment of good quality worn thin." Likewise, the more commonly employed (in OAkk., OB, SB) substantive *qutnu* expresses the idea of "a thin fabric of a good quality," e.g., *qutni ana lubušti awīlim lišēpiš*, "let him procure thin (fabrics) for the wardrobe of the boss."[41]

In short, it seems best to equate the *hapax* Heb. expression מְעִיל קָטֹן with the Akk. compound *naḫlaptu/ṣubatu qatnu*, "a thin textile garment of good quality."

NOTES

1. L. Koehler and W. Baumagartner, *The Hebrew and the Aramaic Lexicon of the Old Testament* (Leiden-New York: Koln 1996), 1223a.
2. Francis Brown, S.R. Driver, Charles A. Briggs, *Hebrew and English Lexicon of the Old Testament* (Oxford 1907), 936a.
3. Cf. Tg. J. on 2 Kings 8:12; Isa. 13:15–16; Hos. 14:1; Nah. 3:10.
4. Cf. Tg. J. on Isa. 13:18.
5. Cf. Tg J. on Hos. 10:14.
6. 2 Kings 8:12.
7. Isa. 13:16, 18; Hos. 10;14 14;1 Nah. 3:10.
8. 2 Kings 8:12.
9. Isa. 13:18.
10. Isa. 13:16.
11. Hos. 14:1.
12. Hos. 10:14.
13. Nah. 3:10.
14. *CAD* Š/2 59a-b; *AHw* 1186a.
15. *CAD* Š/2 59a 1. a; 2.; *AHw* 186a.
16. E. Zbeling "Literarische Keilschrifttexte aus Uruk" 62 r. 1–4; *CAD* Š 2 59b 2. For a detailed discussion for this brutal Assyrian practice cf. M. Cogan '"Ripping open Pregnant Women in light of an Assyrian Analogue," *JAOS* 10 (1983), 755–7.
17. *AHw* 1186a.
18. *KB*^{3} 1355b.
19. 2 Kings 8:12; Isa. 13:16; Hos. 14:1; Nah. 3:10; Isa 13:18; Hos. 10:14.
20. *CAD* Ṣ 179b.
21. Gen. 35:23.
22. E.g. *qinnī ṣiḫir rabi amur aššumišunu rēmanni naḫraka likšundanni* "have regard for my (whole) family young and old, be kind to me for their sake, may (some token of) your help reach me" (*CAD* Ṣ 184a, OB letter); *šumma attūnu tunkkaršūni issu libli aḫḫēšu ṣiḫrū rabū ina kumušu ina kussî Aššur tušešabāni* (you swear) "that you will not be hostile to him nor will you seat one of his brothers, older or younger on the throne of Assyria instead of him"; D.J. Wiseman "The Vassal-Treaties of Esarhaddon" *Iraq* (1958), 33; 56–7.
23. Job 32:6.
24. E.g. *amat šarri ana Rašaga šībūti u ṣaḫrūti* "message of the King to Rasaeans (both) old and young" (*CAD* Ṣ 184b 2').
25. Cf. the *hapax* pair קטן//צעיר e.g., הקטן יהיה לאלף//והצעיר לגוי עצום, "the smallest shall be a clan//and the young, a mighty nation" (Isa. 60:22).
26. Cf. e.g., 1 Sam. 30:19; 2 Kings 25:26; Jer. 8:10, etc.

27. *CAD* Q 163b.
28. *CAD* Q 173b.
29. *CAD* Q 163b 1. Note also that the verb *qatānu* to become thin is employed to describe parts of the body and likewise the finger, e.g., *šumma [rēšub]ānim iqtimma ana imitti ubānim iknuš* "if the top of the finger is thin and bends down to the right of the finger" (*CAD* ibid.).
30. *CAD* Q 332b 2.
31. Cf. for example NJPS and various other translations.
32. A. Ehrlich, *Mikra Ki-Pheschuto,* (Berlin 1900), 2:104–5 (Heb.).
33. Ibid.
34. Ibid.
35. H. Smith, *The International Critical Commentary on the Books of Samuel* (ICC; Edinburg-New York: T & T Clark, 1899), 19.
36. *CAD* Q 173b; 322b.
37. *CAD* Q 174a b; 322b 1.
38. *CAD* Q 174b.
39. Ibid.
40. *CAD* Q175b.
41. *CAD* Q 322b 1.

Hebrew יסר, Akkadian *Esēru*: A Term of Forced Labor: A Lexicographical Note IX

ליצחק

אַשְׁרֵי אָדָם מָצָא חָכְמָה
(משלי ג:יג)

I

The verbal root יסר occurs forty-two times in BH. It is employed twice in Qal (Ps. 94: 10; Prov. 9: 2), six times in Niphʿal,[1] and the rest in Piʿel. יסר is attested eight times in the Torah,[2] sixteen times in the Prophets (twice in former and fourteen times in Later Prophets),[3] and eighteen times in the Writings (mostly in the Wisdom Literature).[4] In the Torah, יסר is rendered by Targum Onqelos four times as אלף "to teach, instruct,"[5] three times as רדה "to discipline" (Lev. 26: 18, 23, 28), and once by לקה "to flog" (Deut. 22: 18). Targum Jonathan translates the verb in the Torah once by אלף (Deut. 4: 36), twice by ספר "to train" (Deut. 8: 5 [2x]), once by בסן "to rebuke" (Deut. 21: 18), once by לקה "to strike" (Deut. 28: 18), and three times by רדה (Lev. 26: 18, 23, 28). Targum Neofiti, on the other hand, is the most consistent. He renders the verb in the Torah always by רדה "to discipline." In the Prophets and the Writings, out of thirty four cases, the Targum renders the verb יסר once by דוי "to hurt" (Ps. 16: 7), once by חיב "to obligate" (Ps. 94: 10), four times by כסן "to rebuke, chastise" (Ps. 118: 18 [2x]; Job 4: 3), once by the term מרדותא "chastisement" (Ps. 2: 10), nine times by the idiom איתא יסורין "to bring sufferings,"[6] twice by אלף "to teach, instruct" (Isa. 8:11; 28:26), and in the majority of cases, fourteen times the Targum translates יסר by the verb רדה.

Moreover, the verb is attested in parallelism: twice as יָסֵר//חַזֵּק "to instruct//to strengthen" (Hos. 7:15; Job 4:3), once as הַשְׂכֵּל// הִוָּסֵר "to be mindful//to be instructed" (Ps. 2:10), once as יַסֵּר//לַמֵּד "to instruct//to teach" (Ps. 94:12), once by יַסֵּר//הוֹרָה "to instruct// to teach" (Isa. 28:26), and in the majority of cases, five times, as יַסֵּר//הוֹכֵחַ "to chastise//to rebuke."[7]

In the general semantic field of learning and instructing, the verb יסר specifically relates not to formal education, but to the instilling of values and norms of conduct by verbal means or even by physical chastisement. The subject of the verb can be either divine or human, in ordinary life or in life before God. As to the divine subject, the verb occurs twenty seven times concerning God's discipline: chastisement or punishment of "men,"[8] "nations" (Ps. 94:10), "rulers of the earth" (Ps. 2:10), and in the majority of cases of "Israel."[9] On the other hand, when יסר is employed with a human subject, it pertains twice to the fruitlessness of instructing a לֵץ "scorner" (Prov. 9:7), and an עֶבֶד "slave, servant" (Prov. 29:19). In the educational field, it pertains once to public instruction (Job 4:3), and five times with regard to parents disciplining/instructing their sons.[10]

At first glance, it seems that the biblical texts do not reveal the substratum-original connotation of the verb יסר. Accordingly, biblical lexica, translations, and interpretations consistently render the verb "to instruct, teach, rebuke, discipline," depicting only the verb's abstract and more general sense. The purpose of the present paper, however, is to attempt to narrow down as much as possible the original-basic meaning that the verb exhibits. Doing this, we will be able to follow its semantic development. To this end, יָסַר/יִסֵּר will be analyzed in light of its Akkadian etymological and semantic equivalent, the verb *esēru/ussuru.*

II

Among the forty two attestations of our verb, two cases are indeed conspicuous. They may reveal its substratum sense. These are Deut. 22:18–19 and 1 Kings 12:11, 14 (= 2 Chr. 10:11, 14). The latter reads:

וְעַתָּה אָבִי הֶעְמִיס עֲלֵיכֶם עֹל כָּבֵד וַאֲנִי אוֹסִיף עַל־עֻלְּכֶם
אָבִי יִסַּר אֶתְכֶם בַּשּׁוֹטִים וַאֲנִי אֲיַסֵּר אֶתְכֶם בָּעַקְרַבִּים

> And now my father imposed a heavy yoke on you but I shall add to your yoke; My father *yissar* you with whips and I will *[a]yassēr* you with 'scorpions.'

The use of יִסֵּר, employed here in the *hapax* idioms יִסֵּר בשוטים/ עקרבים, is considered difficult.[11] Nevertheless, it is universally rendered as "to chastise." However, in order to better conceive the precise meaning of the verb in 1 Kgs. 12:11, 14, one should study these idioms within the specific context of the narrative of Rehaboam's rejection at the assembly at Shechem (12:1–19). The circumstances that brought about the split of the Israelite Kingdom following the death of Solomon are the subject of 1 Kings 12:1–19. Whereas Judean authorities no doubt gave immediate recognition to Rehaboam as the legitimate heir to the throne following Solomon's death, the allegiance of the northern Israelite tribes was not to be taken for granted. The cause of the breach was the refusal of Rehaboam to accede to the demands of the northern tribes for the alleviation of the heavy burden of taxes and corvée imposed by his father Solomon. The negotiated settlement between the king and his northern subjects as depicted in 1 Kings. 12:1–19 is indeed heavy with technical terms and idiomatic expressions. They find their parallel equivalents in the royal cuneiform documents concerning the relationships between the Mesopotamian kings and their subjects.

At the outset, it should be noted that Malamat, in his article "Kingship and Council in Israel and Sumer: A Parallel,"[12] has detected a unique parallel between the Sumerian epic "Gilgamesh and Agga" and our biblical account, both in matters of content as well as in matters of terminology. The epic deals with the power struggle between Gilgamesh, the King of Uruk, and Agga, the ruler of Kish, for political hegemony in Sumer. The envoys of

Agga present Gilgamesh with an ultimatum to submit to Agga. Gilgamesh does not decide on his own, but turns instead to the two assemblies of Uruk — the council of the "elders" of the city = Sumerian *abba uru*, and the council of "men" = Sumerian *guruš*. This, according to Malamat, parallels the institution of "the elders" = Hebrew זְקֵנִים and the council of "young men" = Hebrew יְלָדִים, respectively, in the Rehaboam narrative.

In seeking advice from both councils, Weinfeld has further shown that the dialogue between Rehoboam, the two advisory bodies, and the representative of the northern tribes is heavy with technical-legal terminology drawn from the treaty-corvée lexicon of the ancient Near East.[13] Indeed, Held[14] was the first to call our attention to an important terminology involving "forced labor, corvée work" at the time of King Solomon. Accordingly, dealing with Solomon's appointment of Jeroboam as the overseer of the corvée workers in 1 Kings 11:28, the noun סֵבֶל is rendered by Held as lit., "basket," i.e., "forced labor, corvée work," and equated by him with the Mari and Amarna nouns *sablum*[15] (= Hebrew סֵבֶל) and *massu*[16] (= Hebrew מַס). Moreover, Held maintains that the idiomatic expression הַנֹּשְׂאִים בַּסֶּבֶל in Neh. 4:11 is not to be rendered as "they that bore burdens," "burden bearers," but rather "basket carriers." This very technical נֹשֵׂא סֵבֶל term is "hidden," according to Held, in 1 Kings 5: 29. According to him, the MT נֹשֵׂא סַבָּל should be rendered as נֹשֵׂא סֵבֶל//(בָּהָר חֹצֵב) "corvée workers" (lit. "basket carriers"//"mountain hewers"). Hebrew נֹשֵׂא סֵבֶל "is fully corroborated... by such well known Akkadian idioms as *nāš tupšikk/zābil tupšikki;*[17] *nāš kudurri/zābil kudurri*[18] 'corvée workers,' literally 'basket carriers.'" However, Weinfeld was the first to point out systematically the parallels between the biblical text of 1 Kings 12: 1–19 and the Akkadian royal-treaty inscriptions:

a) Those who serve (lit., stand before) the King:
Hebrew עמד לפני/את פני "to stand before" (1 Kings 12:6, 8) = Akkadian *uzzuzu ina pān* "to stand before" (i.e., "to serve").[19]

b) A treaty term of consent:
Hebrew ענה "to consent" (lit., "to answer") (1 Kings 12:7) = Akkadian *apālu* "to answer favorably" (i.e., "to consent").[20]

c) A term concerning a decision making by way of negotiation:
Hebrew דַּבֵּר דָּבָר "to negotiate" (lit., "to speak a word") (1 Kings 12: 7) = Akkadian *amātam dabābu* lit. "to speak a word" (i.e., "to negotiate").[21]

d) A treaty term concerning friendly relations:
Hebrew דברים טובים "friendly relations" (lit., "good things") (1 Kings 12: 7) = Akkadian *awātim damqātim* "good things, words" (i.e., "friendly relations").[22]

e) A terms concerning forced labor:
Hebrew עבודה קשה "harsh labor" (1 Kings 12: 4) = Akkadian *dullu dannu* "hard labor" (Weinfeld, *op. cit.,* p. 6: 20).

III

The last parallel between 1 Kings 12 and the Akkadian royal-treaty inscriptions is found in the Hebrew idioms עֹל כָּבֵד "heavy yoke" to be equated with the Akkadian expression *nīru kabtu* "heavy yoke,"[23] as well as הֶעְמִיס עֹל "to impose a yoke,"[24] to be likewise equated with Akkadian *nīra emēdu* "to impose a yoke." Both of these two Hebrew-Akkadian technical parallel terms are, interestingly enough, employed in the same verse with what seems yet another labor term יִסֵּר (בשוטים/בעקרבים) (1 Kings 12: 11). To our mind, the substratum origin of the verb יסר can be clarified in light of the Akkadian verb *esēru/ussuru*, which is employed from Old Assyrian and Old Babylonian on. It seems to connote "to press for payment due, to collect tribute, to put a pressure upon a person."[25] In the synonym lists, Akkadian *esēru* is equated with *sanāqu*, which is the common verb for "to press."[26] Akkadian *esēru/ussuru* is employed in the sense of "press for payment due, to collect" said of an individual as well as of a group of people. (1) Said of a person: see, e.g., *ilkum īsrannima naparkâm ul elî* "feudal duties pressed me hard, I could not get away";[27] *šumma awīlum kaspam itti tamkārim ilqīma tamkāršu īsiršuma mimma ša nadānim lā ibaššīšum* "if a man has borrowed money from a merchant and this merchant presses him for payment but he (the debtor) has nothing to give."[28] (2) Said of a group of people: see, e.g., *kaspu ša ultu* MN *ina qātē awīlī Nippurî ša ina qātē šakin māti ēsiru nadnu* "silver which they have collected from MN on, from the inhabitants of Nippur that under the governor, has been delivered"[29]; *napḫar 124 gammalē peṣûti [ut]tesiru* "a total of 124 white camels have been collected as tribute."[30]

Accordingly, although the traditional rendering of 1 Kings 12:11, 14 (בשוטים/בעקרבים) יסר "to chastise (with whips/scorpions)," is somewhat vague and imprecise, in light of the Akkadian usage of *esēru/ussuru*, and in light of the accumulative royal-treaty terms involving forced labor and tax collecting, we suggest to see in 1 Kings 12:11, 14 the substratum origin of the verb יִסֵּר. The verse may, therefore, be rendered anew as follows: "my father pressed you for taxes due by means of whips and I will put a pressure upon you by means of scourges."

Moreover, unlike Akkadian *esēru/ussuru,* Hebrew יִסֵּר seems to be employed once more in Deut. 22:18 in the sense of to put a pressure on an individual by means of lashing, on an individual in order to collect fines due. Indeed the verb יִסֵּר employed in Deut. 22:18–9: וְלָקְחוּ זִקְנֵי הָעִיר־הַהִוא אֶת־הָאִישׁ וְיִסְּרוּ אֹתוֹ וְעָנְשׁוּ אֹתוֹ מֵאָה כֶסֶף. NJPS renders the verses as follows: "the elders of that town shall then take the man and flog him and they shall fine him a hundred [shekels of] silver...." The verb יִסֵּר is rendered by both Targum Onqelos and Targum Jonathan by the verb לקה "to flog." Such was also the understanding of Josephus, who maintained that the husband received the legal forty stripes save one (cf. Deut. 25: 3). Following the *halakhic* explanation, the majority of the medieval Jewish commentators likewise interpret the verb יִסֵּר in Deut. 22:18 as "to flog." Unlike Hebrew יִסֵּר, the Akkadian verb *esēru/ussuru* seems not to have the connotation of "to press/to put a pressure for payment *by means of lashing.*"

The notion of putting pressure by means of a whip using the verb יִסֵּר seems to be restricted only to Hebrew. This also is seen from the *hapax* nominal expression שֵׁבֶט מוּסָר, "a rod of pressure," i.e., "discipline," e.g., אִוֶּלֶת קְשׁוּרָה בְלֶב־נָעַר שֵׁבֶט מוּסָר יַרְחִיקֶנָּה מִמֶּנּוּ "if folly settles in the heart of a lad, a rod of discipline will remove it" (Prov. 22:15). Indeed, שֵׁבֶט = מוּסָר "discipline" (lit., "pressure") = "rod," are twice equated, e.g., אַל־תִּמְנַע מִנַּעַר מוּסָר כִּי־תַכֶּנּוּ בַשֵּׁבֶט לֹא יָמוּת "do not withhold discipline from a child if you bit him with a rod he will not die" (Prov. 23:13) = חוֹשֵׂךְ שִׁבְטוֹ שׂוֹנֵא בְנוֹ וְאֹהֲבוֹ שִׁחֲרוֹ מוּסָר "he who spares the rod hates his son, but he who loves him put a pressure (i.e., disciplines him) on him early" (Prov. 13:24); and cf. also כַּאֲשֶׁר יְיַסֵּר אִישׁ אֶת־בְּנוֹ "as a man pressures (i.e., disciplines) his son" (Deut. 8:5).

In summation, like Akkadian *esēru/ussuru* "to press for payment due, to collect tribute, to put a pressure upon a person," the Hebrew verb יִסֵּר in 1 Kings. 12:11, 14; Deut. 22:18, and the noun מוּסָר in Prov. 13:24; 22:15; 23:13, have the basic meanings of "to pressure for taxes, fines due" and "pressure" by means of using a "whip, rod," respectively. The semantic development of Heb. יִסֵּר will then be "to pressure a person (by means of whip, rod) > to chastise > to discipline > to instruct."

NOTES

1. Lev. 26:23; Jer. 6:8; 31:18; Ezek. 23:48; Ps. 2:10; Prov. 29:19.
2. Lev. 26:18, 23, 28; Deut. 4:36; 8:5 (2x); 21:18; 22:18.
3. 1 Kgs. 12:11, 14; Isa. 8:11; 28:26; Jer. 2:19; 6:8; 10:24; 30:11; 31:18 (2x); 46:28; Ezek. 23:48; Hos. 7:12, 15; 10:10.
4. Ps. 2:10; 6:12; 16:17; 38:2; 39:12; 94:10; 118:8 (2x); Prov. 9:7; 19:18; 29:17, 19; 31:1; 2 Chr. 10:11, 14.
5. Deut. 4:36; 8:5 (2x); 21:18.
6. Jer. 2:19; 10:4; 30:11; 31:18 (2x); 46:28; Hos. 7:12, 15; 10:10.
7. Jer. 2:19; Ps. 6:2; 38:2; 94:12; Prov. 9:7.
8. Deut. 22:18; Jer. 10:24; 31:18; Ps. 6:2; 38:2; 39:12; 94:2; 118:18.
9. Lev. 26:18, 23, 28; Jer. 2:19; 6:8; 30:11; 46:28.
10. Deut. 2:18; 8:5; Prov. 19:18; 29:11; 31:1.
11. See, for example, W. A. van Gemeren (ed.), *Dictionary of Old*

Testament Theology and Exegesis (Grand Rapids, Mich.: Zondervan Pub. House, 1997), 2:480: 2a.

12. A. Malamat, "Kingship and Council in Israel and Sumer: A Parallel," *JNES* 22 (1963), 247–53.
13. M. Weinfeld, "The Advice of the Elders to Rehoboam (1 Kgs. 12: 7)," *Lešonenu* 36 (1971), 3–13 (Heb.). For the English version of Weinfeld's article see *Maarav* 3/1 (1982), 27–53. See also E. Lipiriski, "Le recit de 1 Rois XII 1–19 a la lumiere de usage de d'Hebreu et de nouveaux texts de Man," *VT* 24 (1974), 430–37.
14. M. Held "The Root *zbl/sbl* in Akkadian, Ugaritic and Biblical Hebrew," *JAOS* 88 (1968), 93b-96.
15. E.g., *aššu sablim ša ḫalṣiya TUR u SAL.TUR ana dannatim kamāsim bēlī išpuram* "Concerning the corvée workers from my district my lord ordered me to assemble male and female minors into the fortress," *ARM* 3, 38: 5–7; *CAD* D 89b.
16. E.g., *anumma anākuma errrēšu (*gloss:*aḫrišu) ina šunama u anākuma ubbalu LÚ.MEŠ (awīlūti) massa MEŠ* "now I alone am plowing in the town of Sunama and I am alone bringing the corvée workers," *RA* 19 (1922), 97–8: 10–14 (a letter from Megiddo).
17. E.g., *zābil tupašikki elīšun ukīn* "I imposed forced labor upon them" (*AKA* 273 I:67).
18. E.g., *zābil kudurri elīšun aškun* "I imposed forced labor upon them" (*AKA* 277 I: 67).
19. E.g., *ina maḫriya ina kīnāti izzizzuma* "who has served me (lit., stood before me) loyally" (*CAD* K 384b 2').
20. E.g., *ina kīnāte tarṣāti lā tātanappalšūni* "if you (the vassals) answer him (Assurbanipal) in truth and faithfulness; if you will not speak to him with your truthful heart" (*VTE* lines 97–99); cf. also ibid., line 236.
21. E.g., *ištu awātum ša idbubu ibbalakkitu* "if he will break off the word that he spoke" *(AASOR* 16 [1936], 55: 54).
22. E.g., *awātim damqātim birītiya u birītišu nīš ilim u riksātim dannātim nišakkan* "friendly relations (lit., good things) an oath and a loyal treaty we shall set between me and him" *(RA* 36 [1939], 51:10, Mari); cf. also the Amarna idiomatic expression *tabuta dababu itti* "to establish friendly relations" (*EA* 8: 8–9). See Moran *CBQ* 22 (1963), 173–6.
23. E.g., *nīr bēlūtiya kabta elišu ana ṣāt ūmē ukīn* "I (Tiglat-Pileser I) imposed on him heavy yoke of my rule forever" (*CAD* N/2, 263a 2')
24. E.g., *kabtu nīr bēlūtiya ēmissunūti* "I (Esarhaddon) imposed the heavy yoke of my rule on them" (*CAD* ibid.).

25. *CAD* E 332b ff.
26. *CAD* E 332b lex. section.
27. *CAD* E 333b(b).
28. *CAD* E 332b 2'.
29. *CAD* E 333b top.
30. *CAD* E 334a 2. Note that the Akkadian substantive *isru* employed in MB and NB comes to connote "collected payment" (*CAD* E 203a).

The Semantic Range of the Biblical Hebrew חלל: A Lexicographical Note X

The Biblical Hebrew חלל is considered by the majority of biblical lexicons to comprise of three or four distinct homonyms. BDB[1] had three entries: I חלל "bore, pierce" (nominal derivations, חָלָל "pierced" חַלָּה "kind of cake"; "חלון window"); II חלל (denominative verb) "to play the pipe" (noun, חָלִיל "flute, pipe"); III חלל "to pollute, defile, profane, begin" (nominal derivations, חֹל "profaneness"; חָלִילָה "profane, reprehensible"; תְּחִלָּה "beginning"). As of 1994, KB[3] follows closely BDB's assertion of the existence of three distinct homonyms.[2] As recently as 1996, DCH[3] maintains four homonyms for the root חלל as follows: I חלל "to profane" (nominal derivations,חֹל "profaneness"; חָלָל "profaned"); II חלל "to begin" (nominal derivations, תחלה "beginning"); III חָלָל "be pierced" "nominal derivations, חָלָל "slain"; מְחִלָּה "hole"); IV חלל "to play to flute" (noun, חָלִיל "flute"). While the medieval lexicographers Ibn-Janāḥ[4] and Qimḥi[5] maintain that BH has only one root חלל with extended range of meanings, nevertheless they were not explicit as to the exact semantic development of the verb from its physical-concrete to its various abstract connotations. Indeed, contrary to the modern lexicons that maintain three of four homonyms for the root חלל, we side with Ibn-Janāḥ and Qimḥi who suggest one root with various extended meanings. The purpose of the present paper is to inductively trace the logical semantic development of this single root חלל, and thereby to clarify the present confusion.

The verb חלל in its concrete-physical connotation is clearly employed to mean "to pierce, to bore a hole" as follows: חֹלְלָה יָדוֹ נָחָשׁ בָּרִחַ "His (the Lord's) hand pierced the elusive serpent" (Job 26:13); (הַמַּחְצֶבֶת רַהַב//)מְחוֹלֶלֶת תַּנִּין ("that strike Rahav//) pierced the Dragon" (Isa. 51:9); (כֻּלָּם עֲרֵלִים//) מְחֻלְלֵי חֶרֶב (all of uncircumcised//)

pierced through by the sword" (Ezek. 32:26). Indeed, the substantive חָלָל "pierced" is likewise associated with חֶרֶב in the commonly used nominal idiom חָלָל/חַלְלֵי חֶרֶב "pierced by the sword" (18 times). The lexeme is also employed in the idiomatic phrase כֻּלָּם חֲלָלִים הַנֹּפְלִים בֶּחֶרֶב "all of them pierced who had fallen by the sword" (Ezek. 32:22). More specifically, the BH *hapax* verb חָדַר to "penetrate" is employed once with חָלָל in the phrase חֶרֶב חָלָל הַגָּדוֹל הַחֹדֶרֶת לָהֶם "a sword of the great mass of the pierced that penetrates them" (Ezek. 21:19), and once more the substantive is attest in parallelism with the standard Hebrew word דָּקַר "to pierce through" e.g., וְנָפְלוּ חֲלָלִים בְּאֶרֶץ כַּשְׂדִּים//וּמְדֻקָּרִים בְּחוּצוֹתֶיהָ "let them fall pierced through in the land of Chaldea//stabbed in the streets" (Jer. 51:4). Accordingly, the root חלל which is employed in the above cases and which parallels דקר, "to pierce, bore," seems to have its original substratum physical and concrete meaning "to pierce, bore a hole,"[6] especially by means of a sword. This physical connotation of the root is clearly employed in the Late Hebrew where חֲלָלִים "empty spaces" appears in parallelism with yet another concrete noun נְקָבִים "holes, openings" e.g., בָּרוּךְ אֲשֶׁר יָצַר אֶת הָאָדָם בְּחָכְמָה וּבָרָא בוֹ נְקָבִים נְקָבִים חֲלָלִים חֲלָלִים "blessed are you who fashioned man with wisdom and created within him many opening and many cavities."[7]

The second physical connotation of חלל "to pierce, bore" is to be found in the noun חָלִיל "flute, pipe" (and its *hapax* denominative חִלֵּל "to play the flute"), a musical instrument consisting of a hollow cylinder. חָלִיל will then be the etymological and the semantic equivalent of the Akkadian hapax *ḫālilu* "piping" (e.g., *ḫālilu ša rigimšu ṭābu* "the piping flute whose voice is sweet")[8] and the more commonly employed Akkadian verb *ḫalālu* B "to pipe, wheeze," e.g., *ina irtišu ša kīma mālili qubî iḫalulu* ("he laments with his chest which wheezes like a reed pipe used for wailing").[9]

The first semantic development of the root from the physical-concrete meaning "to pierce through, bore" to its abstract transferred sense "to profane" is found in the commonly employed verb חִלֵּל (Piʿel). Consequently, though unattested the root חלל

"to pierce, bore" seems to serve as an antonym of the root שלם "whole," i.e., free from damage or defeat; unbroken, uninjured, perfect. Thus, the semantic development of חלל to its secondary abstract-transferred sense "to profane," can be explained as to violate the *whole* by injuring it, employed mainly in religious and moral context.

At the outset it should be observed that חלל may find its semantic equivalent in the verb נקב "to pierce, bore,"[10] which likewise development into its secondary meaning "to profane." The verb נקב in its physical-concrete connotation "to pierce" is employed seven times in the following cases וַיִּקֹּב חֹר בְּדַלְתּוֹ "and he bore a hole in its (the chest's) lid" (2 Kings 12:10); וּבָא בְכַפּוֹ וּנְקָבָהּ "(reed of a staff) which enters and pierces and palm of any one who leans on it" (2 Kings 18:21 = Isa. 36:6); נָקַבְתָּ בְמַטָּיו רֹאשׁ פְּרָזָו "you will pierce [his] skull with your (lit., his) bludgeon" (Hab. 3:14); מִשְׂתַּכֵּר אֶל צְרוֹר נָקוּב "he earns it for leaky (lit., pierced) purse" (Hag. 1:6); בְּמוֹקְשִׁים יִנְקָב־אָף "his nose be pierced by hooks" (Job 40:24);וּבְחוֹחַ תִּקֹּב לֶחֱיוֹ "pierce his jaw with barb" (Job 40:26).

In the religious sphere the verb חִלֵּל is commonly employed in its secondary meaning in a context of profaning the name of the Lord/God i.e., חִלֵּל שֵׁם ה'/אֱלֹהִים. This expression likewise seems to parallel the idiom נָקַב שֵׁם ה' "to profane the name of the Lord" in Lev 24:11 וַיִּקֹּב בֶּן־הָאִשָּׁה הַיִּשְׂרְאֵלִית אֶת־הַשֵּׁם וַיְקַלֵּל "and the son of the Israelite woman profaned the Name and degraded it"[11] (cf. also Lev. 24:16 [2x]). The root חלל, which is the antithesis of קֹדֶשׁ, is a *leitmotif* in Lev. 21–22. i.e., חִלֵּל אֶת שֵׁם קָדְשִׁי "to profane My holy name"[12]; חִלֵּל מִקְדָּשׁ/מִקְדַּשׁ ה' "to desecrate sanctuary/the Lord's sanctuary."[13]In the religious sphere we likewise find the following usage of חלל i.e., חִלֵּל אֶת הַשַּׁבָּת "to desecrate the Sabbath"[14] חִלֵּל חֻקֹּת "to violate (the Lord's) laws"[15]; חִלֵּל בְּרִית lit., "to break (the Lord's) pact."[16] In the moral sphere the verb is employed with the following nouns: חִלֵּל אָב/בַּת/יְצוּעַ אָב/זֶרַע/יִפְעָה/מַמְלָכָה "to desecrate, profane father[17]/daughter[18]/father's bed[19]/offspring[20]/radiance/[21] kingdom."[22]

The second semantic development of חלל from its primary physical-concrete meaning "to pierce, bore" to its abstract secondary connotation may be seen in the verb's Hiphʿil form הָחֵל "to begin, to start." As a *verbum movendi* "to begin, start"[23] exhibits the primary notion of a physical action of moving by breaking out, taking the first step by piercing a hole, an opening in the space in front, namely to make a dent in, i.e., to begin.

In summation, the physical nominal derivations from a single root חלל is as follows: חָלָל "pierced (by sword)" > "slain"[24] חַלּוֹן "empty space (in a wall)" > "window"[25]; מְחִלָּה "hole"[26]; חָלִיל "hollow cylinder" > "pipe, flute"[27] חַלָּה "a loaf of bread pierced with holes"[28]; חָלָלָה "deflowered woman" > "profaned."[29] The root חלל likewise develops to the transferred abstract nominal meaning as follows: חֹל "profaneness" (employed four times as the antonym of קֹדֶשׁ "holy, sacredness"[30]); חָלִילָה "to which is profane"[31]; תְּחִלָּה "beginning."[32]

NOTES

1. Francis Brown, S. R. Driver, Charles A. Briggs, *Hebrew and English Lexicon of the Old Testament* (Oxford, 1907), 319–20.
2. David J.A. Clines (ed.), *The Dictionary of Classical Hebrew* (Sheffield: Academic Press, 1995), 234–7;cf. also Avraham Even Shoshan, *The New Dictionary* (Vol. 2; Jerusalem, 1966), 2:7753–776 (Hebrew).
3. Ludwig Koehler and Walter Baumgartner, *The Hebrew and Aramaic Lexicon of the Old Testament Theology & Exegesis*, (Vol. 2; Grand Rapids, 1997), 145–153.
4. Yonah ibn Janāḥ, *Sepher Haschorashim*, (ed. Wildhelm Bacher; Berlin, 1896), 152–3 (Hebrew).
5. David Kimchi, *Hebraeum Bibliorum Lexicon*, (eds. Jo. H. R. Biesenthal et F. Lebrect; Berlin, 1847), s.v. חלל.
6. Note that the form תְּחֹלֵל which is employed once in associated with רוּח "wind" and which was traditionally rendered as "begins, causes," i.e., רוּחַ צָפוֹן תְּחוֹלֵל גָּשֶׁם "north wind causes, produces rain" (Prov. 25:23), was dismissed by Sigal Shelomo (*Lešonenu* 62 [1991], 183–87) as unaccepted. Since "in Israel the north wind does not herald the rain." In actuality, in Israel the wind which causes the rain come from the southwest region to north-west region. The north is the direction of stopping the rain. Accordingly, together with Vulgate, Saʿadya, Ibn-Janāḥ and others, Shelomo understand the verb תחולל in the sense of "cancellation, prevention, stopping (of the rain)." As proof Shelomo equates

חלל with Akk. *ḫalālu* "to detain, keep waiting," understanding חלל as a by-form of Akk. *kalû* = Heb. כלא (interchange of *k-ḫ*). Shelomo's thesis seems too intertwined to accept, since Heb. חלל never means to stop and since Akk. *ḫalālu* is never used with weather phenomenon. It seems better to understand תחולל in its primary sense to "bore a hole," i.e., to break, hence "the north wind will break (i.e., stop) the rain." The relationship between the Akk. *ḫalālu* A "to creep, slink," employed as *verbum movendi* and equated in the lexical texts with such similar as *bâ'u, alāku, etēqu* "to go/walk along, to walk, to cross" (*CAD* Ḫ 33b-34a) and *ḫalālu* C to confine, detain keep waiting" (*CAD* Ḫ 34b) seems to fall under the category of an *Addād*, word that has two contrary meanings. This may be, since both *ḫalālu* A and *ḫalālu* C employ the same thematic vowels a/u. Furthermore, Akk. *ḫalālu* A may be the etymological and semantic equivalent of Heb. חלל (Hiph'il, Hoph'al) where both are employed as *verbum movendi*.

7. b. *Ber*. 60b.
8. *CAD* Ḫ 42a.
9. *CAD* Ḫ 34a.
10. Note that while Heb. Employs the verb נקב only in the sense of "to pierce, bore" Akk. *naqābu* is attested in OB and SB to mean only "to deflower, to rape," e.g., *šumma awīlum amat awīlim ittaqab* "if a man deflowers another man's slave girl" (*CAD* N/328b, LE). However, while Heb. employs also the substantive נְקֵבָה "female", it is absent Akkadian. For the West Semitic *nqb* see J. Hoftigger and K. Jongeling, *Dictionary of The North-West Semitic Inscriptions* (Leiden-New York-Koln, 1995), 2:756.
11. b. *Sanh.* 56a on Lev. 24:16.
12. Cf. Lev. 20:3, 22:2, 32, Ezek. 20:39, 36:20, 22; 39:7; Am. 2:7. Cf. also Ps. 74:7. Cf. also Ezek. 7:4; Mal. 2:11.
13. Cf. Lev. 21:12, 23; Ezek. 20:39; 24:21.
14. Cf. Exod. 31:14; Isa. 56:2, 6; Ezek. 20:13, 16, 24; 23:28; Neh. 13:17, 18.
15. Cf. Ps. 89:32.
16. Cf. Mal. 2:10; Ps. 55:21; 89:35.
17. Cf. Lev. 21:9.
18. Cf. Lev. 19:29
19. Cf. Gen. 49:4; 1 Chr. 5:1
20. Cf. Lev. 21:15.
21. Cf. Ezek. 28:7.
22. Cf. Lam. 2:2.
23. The verb is employed in the Hiph'il and the Hoph'al fifty-four times.
24. See M. Z. Kaddary "חלל = Bore, -Pierce-?, *VT* 13 (1963), 486–489;

J.J. Glück, "*ḥalālîm (ḥālāl)* carrage, massacre," *RevQ* 7 (1969–71), 417–419.

25. The noun is employed thirty-one times.
26. The noun is employed only once in Isa. 2:19 i.e., מערות//מחלות "caverns// hollows."
27. The noun is employed six times.
28. The noun is employed fifteen times.
29. The noun is employed only once in Lev. 21:7, 14 in association with women that lost their virginity i.e., אלמנה "widow"; גרושה "divorced woman"; זנה "harlot." See M. Zipor, "Restrictions on Marriage for Priests (Lev. 21,7:13–14)" *Bib* 68 (1987), 259–67.
30. E.g., Lev. 10:10; Ezek. 22:26:42:20; 44:23.
31. The word is employed twenty-one times.
32. The word is employed twenty-two times.

Two Biblical Architectural Images in Light of Cuneiform Sources: A Lexicographical Note XI

For Professor Shmuel Schneider

Hebrew: כָּלִיל = Akkadian: *Kilīlu*

I

The Biblical Hebrew adjective/substantive כָּלִיל is attested 15 times. It is employed seven times in the Pentateuch,[1] twice in the Former Prophets,[2] four times in the Later Prophets,[3] and twice in the Writings.[4] כָּלִיל, which is derived from the verb כָּלִיל "complete, perfect," has basically two connotations: (1) entirety, > entire, whole, complete (5x);[5] and (2) whole-offering (5x).[6] The remaining five attestations of the lexeme (Judg. 20:40; Ezek. 16:14; 27:3; 28:12; Lam. 2:15) seem to have a more concrete and physical connotation and should be studied in light of the Akkadian etymological and semantic equivalent *kilīlu* (*CAD* K 358:1-b; *AHw* 476a).

At the outset, it should be noted that lexicons such as *BDB* (483a), *KB* (479b), and *DCH*[7] render כָּלִיל in the above five latter cases in the abstract sense, i.e., "entire, perfect (in beauty)" (Ezek. 16:14; 27:3 18:12; Lam. 2:15); "the whole (city)" (Jud. 20:40). Likewise, the majority of modern biblical commentators — such as Zimmerli,[8] Eichrodt,[9] Greenberg,[10] Allen,[11] Hillers,[12] Boling,[13] and Amit[14] — make the same rendering.

II

The Akkadian substantive *kilīlu*, which is attested from Old Akkadian (2350–2000 BCE), Old Babylonian (2950–1600 BCE), and onward, has two basic connotations: (1) "circlet, garland, headband," and (2) "battlement" (*CAD* K 358a-b; *AHw* 476a).

As to the first meaning, Akkadian *kilīlu* is equated in the synonym lexical list, *Nabnitu*, with the standard Akkadian lexeme for "a crown" *agû* (*CAD* K 358a lexical section). In Sumerian-Babylonian hymns, the lexeme is employed as follows: *[...] gilim.gilim. ma aka.zu.dé: kilīli iddû ina naškunika* "they put headdress (on your head) when you are adorned" (*CAD* K 358a lexical section). In a Middle Babylonian inventory text, we obtain the following description: *7 kilīli armati ḫurāṣi 11 GÍN [KI.LÁ]* "seven wreaths of an ornament gold weighing eleven shekels" (*CAD* K 358a 1). Akkadian personal names employ *kilīlu* in juxtaposition with names of deities: *Ilum-kilīli* "God-Is-My-Wreath" (UR III); *Irra-kilīli* "Irra-Is-My-Wreath" (OB); *Nanâ-kilīli uṣri* "Nana-Protect-My-Wreath" (LB)[15] (*CAD* K 358b d). More specifically, it is of interest to note a Neo-Assyrian letter that is written by the crown prince Sennacherib to his father Sargon II, listing various gifts received, among which we find twice the gift *1 kilīli ḫurāṣi* "one (model of a) battlemented crown of gold" (*ABL* 568:10 = *SAA,* Vol. 1: 34:10; *CAD* K 358a 1). The epigraphic information is supported by an iconographic testimonial on a relief from the reign of Sargon II, which depicts western tribute-bearers with goods, including models of battlemented crowns (figs. 1a,b). This golden *kilīlu* comes to symbolize the magnificent battlement crowning of the city wall, thereby representing the city itself. Indeed, Ešarḫaddon employed the adverb *kilīliš* "like a wreath" to describe the construction of his palace's parapeted battlement, e.g., *nēbeḫu pašqu ša ṣurri uqni ušēpišma ušalmâ kilīliš* "I had a frieze and battlements made of red and blue (enameled bricks) built like a wreath all around its crest" (*CAD* K 357b).[16] Akkadian likewise utilizes *kilīlu* as an architectural term for the battlements of stepped merlons. Accordingly, in the Babylonian wisdom literature "Fable of the Willow," — in describing the decoration of a palace — we learn that *kīma kilīli ekallu zu'unat* "the palace is decorated [with...] as if a battlement" (*CAD* K 358b 2). In the hymn to the city of Ezida, its *kilīlu* is portrayed as adorned with fine-quality gold: *kilīlšu ṣāriri ša ḫurāṣi ša liqti* "Its (Ezida's) battlements (are) of fine quality gold (even) of gold of *liqtu* quality" (*CAD* K 358b 2). More specifically, Nebuchadnezzar II, in depicting the decorations of his glorious palace in Babylon, states: *kilīli uqni rēšāša ušalmi* "I had a battlement of blue enameled bricks built around its (Babylon's) top" (*CAD* K 358b 2).

III

In light of the above cuneiform epigraphical sources, we venture to suggest that, similar to the Akkadian usage of *kilīlu*, BH כָּלִיל may likewise come to connote a physically "parapeted battlement," as well as a "crown, circlet," and not just "entire, perfect, whole" as traditionally rendered.

The notion of a parapeted battlement is applied to three cities: Gibeah, Tyre, and Jerusalem. In describing the burning of the city of Gibeah in Judg. 20:40, the narrator picturesquely depicts the flames on the top of the city's parapeted battlement as follows: והמשאת החלה לעלות מן העיר עמוד עשן ויפן בנימן אחריו והנה עלה כְלִיל הָעִיר השמימה "but when the column, the pillar of smoke began to rise from the city, the Benjaminites looked behind them, and the parapeted battlement of the city went up (in flames) to the sky." The battlement, which symbolizes the crowning beauty and splendor of both Tyre and Jerusalem, are portrayed as follows: צור את אמרת אֲנִי כְּלִילַת יֹפִי בלב ימים גבוליך בניך כָּלְלוּ יָפְיֵךְ "O Tyre you boasted I am a battlement of beauty. Your frontiers were on the high seas, your builders crowned[17] your beauty" (Ezek. 27:3–4). In portraying the destruction of Jerusalem, Lam. 2:15 reads: ספקו עליך כפים כל עברי דרך... הזאת העיר שיאמרו כְּלִילַת יֹפִי משוש לכל הארץ "clap their hands on you all who pass your way… is this the city they call parapet of beauty, joy of all the earth?"

Indeed, the second meaning of Akkadian *kilīlu*, i.e., "crown, circlet," seems to be employed in reference to both Israel and the king of Tyre, respectively. Accordingly, among various other royal gifts bestowed on Israel by the Lord for kingship, Ezekiel states: ...ותצלחי למלוכה ויצא לך שם בגוים ביפיך כי... כָּלִיל הוּא בַּהֲדָרִי אשר שמתי עליך "… you were fit for kingship you became famous among the nations for it was a crown which through my splendor I set upon you" (Ezek. 16:13–14). The rendering כָּלִיל as "a crown" was likewise a second understanding of the medieval exegete Rashi, who writes: כי כליל "קרונא" בלעז כמו "נזר" (שמות כט,ו) דמתרגמינן כלילא דבר אחר "another explanation: כִּי כָּלִיל, 'couronne' in French, like (Ex 29:6) 'crown' (נֵזֶר) which is translated כְּלִיל by Targum."[18] Similarly, Ezekiel depicts the king of Tyre as חותם תכנית מלא חכמה וּכְלִיל יֹפִי "you were the seal of perfection full of wisdom and a crown of beauty" (Ezek. 28:12).[19]

Furthermore, it should be observed that the earliest employment of כָּלִיל that clearly comes to connote "crown" is attested to in post-biblical Hebrew Dead Sea Scroll the "Rule of the Community" (1QS 4:7), e.g., שמחת עולמים בחיי נצח וּכְלִיל כבוד... עם מדת הדר באור עולמים "eternal joy in everlasting life, a crown of glory... and a garment of majesty in eternal life." Moreover, in Ben-Sira 45:12, the lexeme is employed in the description of the paraphernalia of Aaron the High Priest, e.g., וילבישהו כְּלִיל תפארת ויפארהו ב[כב]וד ועז "and He bestowed on him a glorious crown, and He glorified him with honor and might."[20] In all attestations of כָּלִיל in biblical and post-biblical Hebrew, the lexeme is always modified by הָדָר "glory" (Ezek. 16:14); יֹפִי "beauty" (Ezek. 28:12); כָּבוֹד "glory" (1QS 4:4; 1QH 9:25); תִּפְאֶרֶת "majesty" (Ben-Sira 45:8) = עֲטֶרֶת תִּפְאֶרֶת "glorious crown" (Isa. 62:3; Ezek. 16:12; 23:42; Prov. 4:9; 16:31) עֲטֶרֶת צְבִי//צְפִירַת תִּפְאָרָה "crown of beauty// diadem of glory" (Isa. 28:5) עֲטֶרֶת פָּז/זָהָב "golden crown" (Ps. 21:4/ Est 8:15) = Akk: *kilīli ḫurāṣi* "golden crown."[21]

Hebrew: מִגְדָּלוֹת/נִדְגָּלוֹת = Akkadian: *Pašqu*

I.

Songs 8:8–10 reads:

8. אחות לנו קטנה	ושדים אין לה
מה נעשה לאחותנו	ביום שידבר בה
9. אם חומה היא	נבנה עליה טירת כסף
ואם דלת היא	נצור עליה לוח ארז

10. אני חומה ושדי כַּמִּגְדָּלוֹת אז הייתי בעיניו כמוצאת שלום

Marvin Pope renders:

Our sister is young and breasts she has none
what we will do for our sister on the day she is bespoken
if she is a wall, we will build on her a silver buttress,
if she be a door, we will close her with a cedar board,
I am a wall and my breasts like towers
thus I have become in his eyes as one who finds peace.

Songs 8:8–10 is indeed a unique independent literary unit.[22] Both medieval and modern scholars are especially concerned with the interpretation of the metaphors חומה־טירה "wall-battlement" and דלת־לוח ארז "door-a cedar plank." Thus, with regard to the description of the young woman, scholars offer two alternatives whose meaning depends on the understanding of the symbolism of the metaphors. The question was therefore raised whether the parallelism דלת//חומה is synonymous or antithetical. The problem was briefly summarized by Pope as follows:

> A wall protects, preserves, and repels. A girl like a wall is thus inaccessible and impregnable. A door serves a dual function of opening, for entering, or barring entrance... A girl like a door may be either closed or open, all the time or part of the time. Thus the exegesis of this verse is divided by the door as open or closed.[23]

Consequently, Pope, for example, who is followed by Murphy,[24] understands the terms "wall" and "door" as standing in antithetical rather than synonymous parallelism. Namely, while the "wall" metaphor is understood as a symbol of chastity (she has never been known by a man and remains so), the "door" metaphor stands for promiscuity and sexual accessibility. On the other hand, Tur-Sinai,[25] followed by Gordis,[26] argues that the "wall" and the "door" are employed in synonymous parallelism, and no contrast is intended.

Our thesis maintains that the author(s) of Songs draws some

of his metaphors from various royal architectural units. He thus compares the beauty of the male's body to the various magnificent structures of the palace.[27] He likewise compares the attractiveness of the female's neck and face/nose to the luxurious Tower of David/Lebanon/Ivory.[28] More specifically, we also learned above that the female's loveliness is likened to the king's palace's beautiful cedar paneled door, which conforms to what we know about the magnificent decorative doors constructed by the various Mesopotamian kings.[29] Accordingly, both the "silver battlement" and its synonymous parallel "cedar paneled door" are indeed legitimate figures to describe the beauty, strength, and nobility of the "sister." However, the background setting of both images — "we shall build upon it a battlement of silver" and "I am a wall — my breasts are like *migdālôt*" — were not sufficiently explained. Gordis maintains that טירה is a figure drawn from military operations connected with a siege. He further suggests that the use of "cedar" and "silver" may hint at the gifts with which the suitors hope to overcome her resistance.[30] Pope, who understands verses 9–10 as antithetical parallelism, asserts that "it seems more likely that the silver buttress and cedar board refer to formidable and valuable devices, real or imaginary, for protection of cherished virginity, a kind of chastity belt."[31] Further, commentators who interpret טירה as a protective buttress, something to defend the woman, find the reference to its construction of "silver" difficult to explain. Ginsburg suggests that the "silver turret" refers to the prized silver crown worn in various ways by Levantine women: a married woman affixed it to the right side of her head, a widow to the left, and a virgin to the crown of her head.[32] Other scholars interpret טירת כסף as an adornment such as: a silver crown, a bridal crown, or a high bride price.

In order to better understand the author's choice of metaphors ("wall-battlement"; "I am a wall — my breasts are like *migdālôt*") as well as their symbolic significance, one should study these architectural terms in the light of their ancient Near Eastern epigraphical and iconographical parallels.

II

Akkadian employs the architectural terms *gabadibbû* and *samītu*, both words equated in the lexical lists with *dūru* "inner city wall" (*CAD* D 192a lexical section). Likewise, Akkadian also employs the terms *pašqu*, *naburrû*, and *kilīlu* to connote as a metonym "battlement."[33] However, while the Akkadian loan word *gabadibbû* (Sum. *gaba* "breast"; + *dib* "fasten") means "a parapet" (*CAD* G 1a lexical section) — a narrow wall on the edge of the city-wall serving to protect the defenders fighting from behind it — Akkadian *samītu/kilīlu*, on the other hand, has come to express the idea of a "battlemented parapet" (*CAD* S 117a). Furthermore, in the ancient Near East, battlements were primarily constructed for defensive military purposes. However, they were also used decoratively for the beautification of the city wall. Likewise, battlemented parapets "proclaimed the protective power and probably often the sanctity of the building which they crowned."[34] The ornamentation of the parapets and the battlements with various precious materials is well attested in cuneiform literature. Thus, Sennacherib, recounting his architectural accomplishments, boasts that *ina agurri uqnî ussimma sillu nēbeḫi u gimir pašqīšin* "I decorated their corbels, friezes, and all their battlemented merlons with bricks glazed (the color of) obsidian and lapis lazuli" (*CAD* N/II 144a 2); *nēbeḫi samēt Ešarra in a agurri abnē ma'diš ussim* "He (Sennacherib) greatly embellished the friezes of the battlemented parapet of Ešarra with glazed bricks" (*CAD* N/II 144a 2). Esarhaddon depicts the decoration of his palace as follows: *siḫirti ekalli šātu nēbēḫu pašqu ša ṣurri uqnî ušēpišma ušalmạ kilīliš* "I had a frieze and battlements of obsidian and lapis lazuli (colored bricks), made all around that palace, surrounding (it) like a wreath" (*CAD* N/II 144b top).[35]

Similar to the *samītu* and the *pašqu*, "the battlement" and "the merlons," the *gabadibbû* "the parapet" was likewise embellished, this time with *kaspu* "silver" — e.g., *ultu uššiša adi gabadibbiša kaspa ušamalli* "I lavished silver (on the building) from its foundation to its parapet" (*CAD* G 1a b). Here the Akkadian phrase *gabadibbâ kaspa šumllû* is indeed the parallel of the Hebrew sentence בנה טירת כסף "to build/lavish a silver battlement."

Iconographical evidence further proves that battlemented crowns, a symbol of a magnificent city, were worn by goddesses and queens alike. This symbol finds its iconographic evidence first in Anatolia (13th century BCE), and remains a source of inspiration in the Late Roman period. Thus, the battlemented crown first makes its appearance (1250–1200 BCE) at the rock sanctuary in Yazilikaya (from the time of Tudkhaliya IV), worn on the head of three female deities (fig. 2).[36]As noted by Porada, the *kilīlu* is likewise worn by an Elamite queen in a rock relief and by Naqsh-i Rustem from the Neo-Elamite period (ninth-seventh centuries BCE).[37] In Neo-Assyrian iconography, the *kilīlu* "the battlemented crown," designated also as "a city crown," is worn by two distinguished queens: Naqia-Zakuti, the wife of Sennacherib and the mother of Esarhaddon (680–669 BCE,)[38] and Libbalisarrat, wife of Assurbanipal (669–630 BCE). The latter queen wears it twice: once on a fragment of a limestone stele from Aššur,[39] and once more in the royal garden scene at Kuyunjik (fig. 4).[40]

The battlement representing the symbol of a "city crown" worn by goddesses, queens, and important women migrated from the Neo-Elamite period down to the Achaemenid, Parthian, Sassanian, Greek, and Early Roman periods.[41] Similarly, as convincingly argued by S. Paul, the motif of the battlemented city crown was also found in Ugarit.[42] Thus, among the various personal possessions belonging to Aḫatmilku, queen of Ugarit, we find the following item: Sum. *1 URU kù.uru gi* = Akkadian *ālu ḫurāṣu šuqultašu 2 meat 15* "one city of gold weighing 215 (shekels),"[43] identified by Paul as a "city crown" and equated with the post-biblical rabbinic compound עיר של זהב "a city of gold" = ירושלים דדהבה "Jerusalem of gold"[44] = כתר של זהב "a crown of gold,"[45] e.g., מאי עטרות כלות? עיר של זהב "What is meant by crowns of brides? A city of gold" (b. *Sot.* 49b)[46] = Akk: *kilīlu ḫurāṣu*[47] = Heb: טירת כסף (Josh. 8:9).

In light of the above, it seems somewhat safe to assume that the author(s) of Songs was indeed cognizant of the architectural symbolism that depicts the battlement (which decorates the city wall) as a crown worn by queens. This battlemented silver crown (i.e., טירת כסף) was promised to the "sister" to wear at the time of her maturity, when she is ready for her royal marriage (i.e., ביוע שידובר בה). Being fully matured for such a royal occasion, and ready to wear the bridal battlement crown, she answers her "brothers":

III

אני חומה ושדי כַּמִּגְדָּלוֹת

"I am a wall and my breasts are like *migdālôt*"

Accordingly, a chiasm is formed unifying the exchange between brothers and the beloved:[48]

שדים (8:8b)	חומה (8:9a)
חומה (8:10a)	שדי (8:10b)

The term *migdālôt* is universally rendered as "towers." Consequently, various explanations were provided as to the nature of the comparison. Gordis, for example, asserts "that the simile does double duty. It implies that she remains impregnable to them, while her breasts are well-developed so that she is ready for love…."[49] Murphy maintains that "in comparing her breasts to 'towers'... she also gives a sharp response to their manner of describing her physical maturity. She is now indeed nubile and there seems to be a note of pride in the comparison."[50] Keel assumes that "she carries her breasts proudly, as a strong city its towers."[51] Thus, since the imagery of מגדלות was selected by the poet to describe the nature of the sister's breasts, critics understood this architectural term to connote something big and visible, hence depicting the sister's breasts as towering *mammae*.[52]

It should be observed, however, that in Songs 4:5; 7:4, the breasts of the beloved are compared to the young fawns of a gazelle. Her beautiful neck (Songs 4:4) and face/nose (Songs 7:5), however, are compared to the tower of David/Lebanon (although it is not clear whether the association of the woman's breasts refers to color or form). Nevertheless, the comparison with an animal noted for its beauty, grace, charm, and innocence is indeed proper. A more suitable simile employed by the author is the comparison of the beloved's breasts to אשכלות "clusters" and אשכלות הגפן "clusters of the vine" (Songs 7:8, 9). However, in Songs 8:10a, the likening of the sister's breasts to towering *mammae* seems somewhat grotesque and improper for a girl who just proclaimed her maturity and readiness for marriage. A different solution to the interpretation of what clearly seems to be an architectural term is to philologically study the terms מִגְדָּלוֹת/ נִדְגָּלוֹת in the light of the available epigraphical and iconographical evidence from the ancient Near East.

Among various architectural elements of the city wall, Porada has also studied the shape of the battlemented merlons as they are depicted in Egyptian and Assyrio-Hittite archaeology and iconography. Porada writes:

> Parapets first appeared in Egypt. A small ivory tower, probably a gaming piece of ivory, found at Abydos in the royal graves of the first Dynasty, has on its tops strongly projecting circular platforms which rest on round beams and has a parapet with rounded merlons. Their rounded shape was probably derived from that of the shield carried by Egyptian warriors, which may have formed the earliest protective enclosures. The shape remained characteristic of Egyptian battlements... in reliefs and paintings.[53] (Fig. 5)

This Egyptian artistic tradition of round-shaped merlons had a decisive influence on battlement forms in Hittite Asia Minor, Syria, and Palestine. Thus, for example, the headgear of the goddesses in the rock sanctuary of Yazilikaya appears to be in the form of turreted crowns (fig. 2), each tower having two rounded merlons.[54] Such rounded merlons were found also at Boghazköy (fig. 6).[55] In Mesopotamian art, on the other hand, battlements were decorated with stepped merlons.[56] It should be further observed that this ancient tradition continued as late as the Sassanian period, where one can distinguish two different types of merlons of these battlemented crowns worn by the goddess Anahita. These dentated and crenellated (fig. 7)[57] merlons' shapes are likewise fit to be compared to a woman's breast.[58] More specifically, as to the architectural elements of the battlements in Mesopotamian cities, Porada maintains that while epigraphically the Akkadian lexeme *gabadibbû* means "parapet," the structural terms *samītu/kilīlu* connote generally "parapeted battlement." Whereas the *samītu* seems to have a parapet plus battlement, the *kilīlu* probably indicates the decorative battlement alone. On the other hand, "the difference between *samītu* and *pašqu* would be that the first word includes the parapet wall, whereas *samītu* would refer to the battlements on top."[59] The *pašqu* would then depict collectively the solid portion of the parapet between two embrasures, namely the merlons, which in Egyptian art are of round shape, and which in the Neo-Assyrian reliefs show us parapets made of horizontal rows of fairly evenly spaced crenels and triangular merlons (fig. 8). Both the Egyptian round and the Mesopotamian stepped merlons indeed bear resemblance to a woman's breasts.

IV

The royal city architectural elements employed in the unique literary unit of Songs 8:8–10 may find their semantic and functional parallels in Mesopotamian building inscriptions as follows: (1) Heb.: חוֹמָה = Akk: *dūru* "city way"; (2) Heb.: טִירָה (כְּלִיל) = Akk.: *sasmītu* (*kilīlu*) "parapeted battlement"; (3) Heb.: דֶּלֶת = Akk.: *daltu* "door"; (4) לוּחַ אֶרֶז = Akk.: *dappi erīni* "cedar board."[60] Likewise, one may venture to propose that the term מִגְדָּלוֹת employed in this unique architectural description does not mean "towers" as it is universally rendered. Rather, the contextual as well as the architectural content suggests that מִגְדָּלוֹת may visually depict the more suitable constructural term "merlons." This should be the functional equivalent of the Akkadian term *pašqu*.[61]

At the outset, it should be observed that Biblical Hebrew seemingly lacks an architectural term for a "merlon." However, it seems that "merlons" as a technical terms is employed once as טְפָחוֹת in 1 Kgs. 7:9. The nominal singular form טֶפַח/טֹפַח is employed seven times to mean "a span, hand-breadth": in the Pentateuch the noun is twice rendered by Targum Onqelos, Jonathan, and Neophiti by the Aramaic noun פּוּשְׁכָּא/פֹּשַׁךְ,[62] which is the etymological as wells as the semantic equivalent of the Akkadian *pušqu* "hand-breadth" employed in Late Babylonian. More specifically, the Hebrew טְפָחוֹת[63] in 1 Kgs. 7:9 is likewise rendered by Targum Jonathan as (וּמְשַׁכְלְלָן בְּ) פּוּשְׁכַּיָא "(finish with) merlons, coping." Here the Aramaic פּוּשְׁכַּיָא rendering of טְפָחוֹת is clearly the etymological and semantic equivalent of the Akkadian architectural term *pašqu* "merlon." Accordingly, the Hebrew טְפָחוֹת, which literally connotes "merlons," is used as a metonym for "parapet" in the *hapax* idiomatic phrase וּמִמַּסָּד עַד הַטְּפָחוֹת (all these buildings) "from foundations to the parapet," and will parallel the standard Akkadian phrase *ištu uššīšu adi gabadibbîšu* "from the foundation to its parapet" (*CAD* G 1a).

Returning to our subject at hand, the "sister" confirms her maturity by repeating the word חוֹמָה used by her "brothers." To further describe her bodily signs of adolescence, she depicts the more suitable architectural term מִגְדָּלוֹת, the "merlons" (shape) of the parapeted battlement (i.e., טִירָה), which resemble a woman's breasts. Indeed, the "sister" proclaims that she is ready for her royal marriage by wearing the bridal crown, the symbol of the parapeted royal city.

Furthermore, this point of comparisons between a woman and a city is based on their common beauty. Accordingly, in Songs 6:4, the male-lover describes his beloved "as beautiful as Tirzah, as comely as Jerusalem" (יפה עת רעיתי כתרצה//נאוה כירושלם). It should be observed, however, that the thematic relationship of the verse's third clause to its first two clauses — i.e., אֲיֻמָּה כַּנִּדְגָּלוֹת "awesome" ("terrific") as *nidgālôt* — is indeed difficult and enigmatic. Both Ibn Ezra (כמחנות בעלות דגלים) and Rashbam (*espaotable com coniqiniyas*) understood the idiom as "camps with banners" and "bannered hosts." Ibn Ezra and Rashbam were followed by modern biblical translations such as *The International Version* "bannered hosts"; *The New English Bible* "bannered troops"; Keel "army with banners"; *The New Jewish Publication Society Version* "bannered hosts" (noting that "meaning of Heb. uncertain"). Pope, on the other hand, goes to great lengths to prove that *nidgālôt* are trophies of war, like the Canaanite goddess Anat's necklace of severed heads and girdle of severed hands.[64] Those critics who equate the vocable with the Akkadian verb *dagālu* "to see" render *nidgālôt* as "great sights"[65] or "visions."[66] Fox, who follows the Peshiṭta גביתא "chosen, selected," renders the word as "the most conspicuous, the most eminent."[67] However, from the above interpretations and renderings, it is not clear as to the thematic association of clause *c* to clauses *b* and *a,* which likened the beauty of the female-lover to the architecture of the cities Tirzah and Jerusalem. Accordingly, one may expect the simile employed in the last clause to modify and complete the idea portrayed in the preceding two clauses. Namely, the lexeme נִדְגָּלוֹת should be considered as a poetic architectural term symbolizing the beauty of these two cities.

In the light of the twice employed root דגל in Songs — once in its nominal form דגלו "his gaze" (Songs 2:4) and once in its verbal form דָּגוּל (Songs 5:10) "visible" (Qal passive participle) = Akk: *diglu* (*CAD* D 136a) "sight, gaze" and *dagālu* "to see" (*CAD* D 21a) — and in the light of our assertion that מִגְדָּלוֹת (Songs 8:10) comes to depict the city's most visible architectural features, we likewise suggest that נִדְגָּלוֹת in Songs 6:4 (metathesis with labial interchange) literally means "great sights, things looked upon," i.e., "merlons" — used as a metonym to describe the beautiful and awesome parapeted battlement of the city (figs. 9–12).[68]

Conclusion

The Hebrew Bible, while diverse and rich in content, is nowhere near as eclectic as the tremendous corpus of texts uncovered from the ancient Near East. Epigraphy from this period includes scores of documents, the likes of which are not found in the Bible. Economic ledgers, royal inventories, and even lists of grammatical forms are among the many types of ancient Near Eastern documents that have little or no parallel in the Bible.

Having established that Hebrew, although a Western Semitic language, is both related to and heavily influenced by Eastern Semitic Akkadian dialects, the diversity of the Akkadian corpus can be utilized for the purpose of shedding light on the Hebrew language, especially in the case of idioms and technical terminology.

The Bible bears faithful witness to the inception of Judaism and the historical evolution of the Jewish people. In this regard, the Bible is not a technical document. While measurements are certainly present — such as those of Noah's Ark, the desert Tabernacle, and Solomon's Temple — architectural descriptions and terminology are blatantly lacking. Fritz decries that "[n]o one has ever really explained why the Temple furniture and utensils are so fully described compared to the brief and ambiguous description of the Temple itself."[69]

Enter the vast collection of documents attested in the Akkadian language. A complementary symbiotic relationship exists between Akkadian and Biblical Hebrew, specifically, in this case, in the architectural realm. The words examined in this article are both metonyms in light of Akkadian in that they may express one idea for the Hebrew scholar, but they most definitely denote a separate meaning for the scholar of Akkadian. Hence, the perceived lack of architectural terminology in the Hebrew language is countervailed by the presence of such nomenclature in a closely related language, both illustrating the richness of the Hebrew language and elucidating previously generalized translations in unclear contexts.

Fig. 1. (*a*) Drawing of relief depicting Medean tribute bearers at the court of Sargon II (721–705 B.C.E.) (Botta and Flandin 1849–1850: Vol. 1, pl. 127). Note that bearers at the front and rear of the parade carry models of walled cities or mural crowns. Reprinted with permission of the Library of the Institut de France.

Fig. 1. (*b*) Details from the relief showing two distinct types of walled cities or mural crowns. By permission of Museé du Louvre, Department des Antiquités Orientales AO 19887.

Fig. 2. Drawing depicting central group of Hittite gods at Yazilikaya, Turkey, 13th century B.C.E. Female deities appear to wear battlemented crowns (Akurgal and Hirmer 1962: 10–12, pl. 19).

Fig. 3. Bronze relief celebrating the restoration of Babylon by Ešarḫaddon, seen here with his mother Naqia, seventh century B.C.E. (Parrot 1961: 118, fig. 133). By permission of Museé du Louvre, Department des Antiquités Orientales AO 20185.

Fig. 4. Mural relief of Aššurbanipal and wife Libbališarrat in garden from Kunyunjik, seventh century B.C.E. Libbališarrat wears a crenellated crown (Keel 1994: 86, fig. 133). By permission of the Trustees of the British Museum.

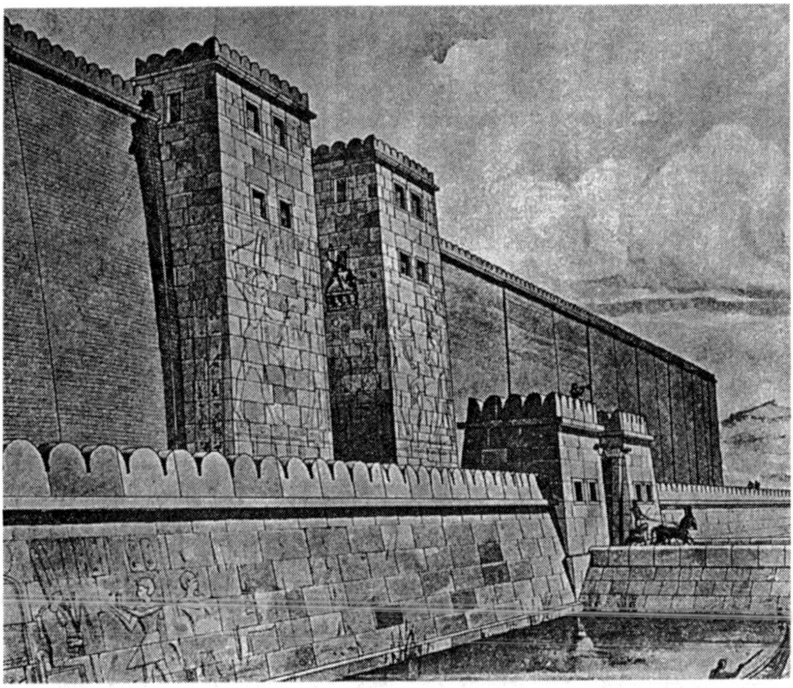

Fig. 5. Artist's impression of the walls and gate of Medinet Habu, Egypt, ca. 12th century B.C.E. (Hölscher 1910: frontispiece, pl. 1).

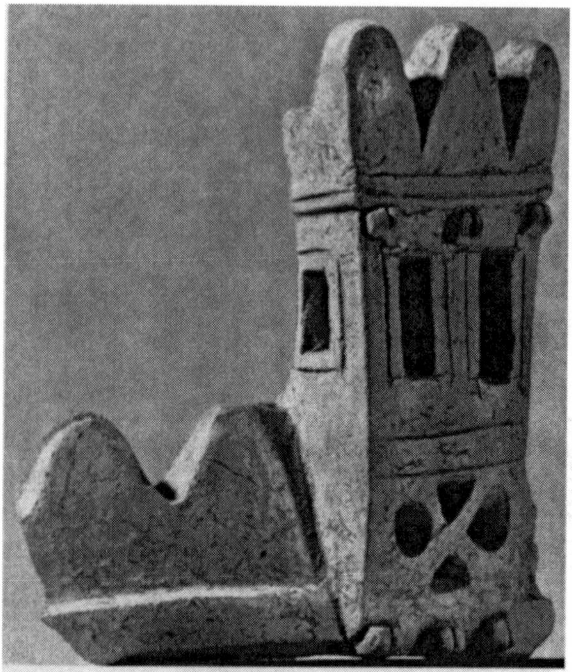

Fig. 6. Fragment of Hittite vase in the form of a battlemented wall found at Boghazköy, Turkey, ca. 15th century B.C.E. (Akurgal and Hirmer 1962: pl. 26).

Fig. 8. Types of mural crowns: dentated, crenellated, and turreted. Drawn by the author.

Fig. 7. Middle Assyrian cylinder seal impressions from Aššur depicting temples, ca. 12th century B.C.E. (Moortgat 1944: pl. 43:4a, b). By permission of the publisher, Walter de Gruyter.

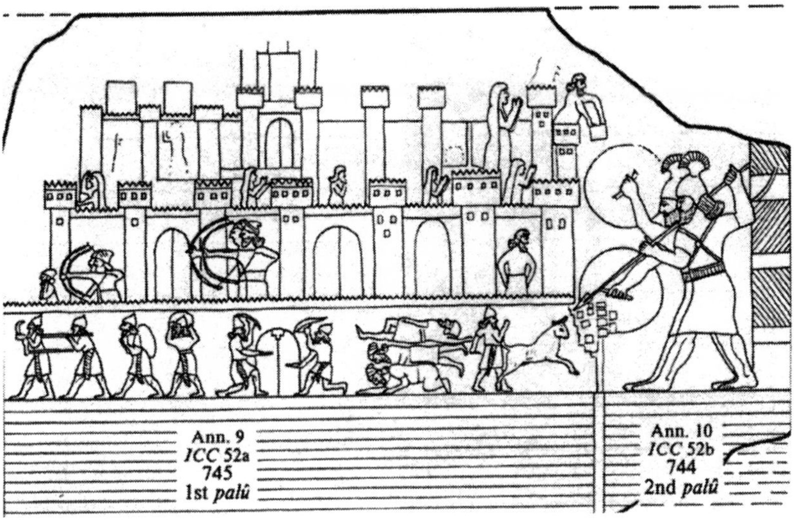

Fig. 9. Siege of what is thought to be a northern Syrian city (Tadmor 1994: fig. 11). By permission of the Trustees of the British Museum.

Fig. 10. Relief of walls from an Assyrian city from Nineveh, ca. seventh century B.C.E. (Barnett 1976: pl. 23). By permission of the Trustees of the British Museum.

Fig. 11. Artist's impression of Ishtar Gate in Babylon from the reign of Nebuchadnezzar, ca. sixth century B.C.E. (Koldewey 1918: pl. 20).

Fig. 12. Mosque in Buraida, Saudi Arabia, 10th century C.E. Photograph by author.

NOTES

1. Exod. 28:21; 39:22; Lev. 6:15,16; Num. 4:6; Deut. 13:17; 33:10.
2. Judg. 20:40; 1 Sam. 7:9.
3. Isa. 2:18; Ezek. 16:14; 27:3; 28:12.
4. Ps. 51:21; Lam. 2:15.
5. Exod. 28:31; 39:22; Num. 4:6; Deut. 13:17; Isa. 2:18.
6. Lev. 6:15, 16; Deut. 33:10; 1 Sam. 7:9; Ps. 51:21.
7. D. J. A. Clines, *The Dictionary of Classical Hebrew Vol 4: Yodh — Lamedh* (Sheffield: Sheffield Academic, 1998), 425b.
8. W. Zimmerli, *Ezekiel: A Commentary on the Book of the Prophets Ezekiel*, (eds. F. M. Cross and K. Baltzer; trans. R. E. Clements; 2 vols.; Philadelphia: Fortress Press, 1979), 325.
9. W. Eichrodt, *Ezekiel: A Commentary* (trans. C. Quin; Philadelphia: Westminster, 1970), 383, 392.
10. M. Greenberg, *Ezekiel 1–20: A New Translation with Introduction and Commentary* (AB; New York: Doubleday, 1983), 273; *Idem*, *Ezekiel 21–37: A New Translation with Introduction and Commentary* (AB; New York: Doubleday, 1997), 543.
11. L. Allen, *Ezekiel 20–48* (World Biblical Commentary 29; Dallas: Word, 1990) 224. *Idem*, *Ezekial 1–19* (WBC 28; Dallas: Word, 1994), 78, 90.
12. D. R. Hillers, *Lamentations: A New Translation with Introduction and Commentary* (AB; New York: Doubleday, 1992), 100–101.
13. R. G. Boling, *Judges* (AB; New York: Doubleday, 1975), 283.
14. Y. Amit, *Mikra Leyisra'el: Judges, Introduction and Commentary* (Jerusalem: Magnes, 1999), 306 (Heb.).
15. Note the BH feminine personal name עֲטָרָה "crown, diadem" (1 Chr. 2:26).
16. Cf. also, e.g., *kīru kal inbī u riqqî ušasḫirši kilīliš* "I (Sargon II) had it (the *bīt akītu*) surrounded like a wreath with a garden with all sorts of fruit (trees) and fragrant plants" (*CAD* K 357b).
17. Note that the verb כָּלַל is twice employed in Ezek. 27:4, 11 depicting the beauty of the city Tyre. Traditionally, the majority of the medieval and modern biblical scholars render the idiom כָּלְלוּ יָפְיֵךְ as "they (the builders) perfect, completed your beauty." Ezekiel, who dwelled in Babylonia (ca. 593–571 B.C.E.), seems to be cognizant of the technical architectural relevance of כָּלִיל, as is described, for instance, by Nebuchadnezzar concerning his palace in Babylon (*CAD* K 358b 2). However, one may venture to suggest that Ezekiel has in mind the Akkadian verb *kullulu* "to crown, to adorn" employed in Middle Assyrian, Standard Babylonian, and Middle Assyrian, while Akkadian *kullulu* is usually employed in reference to crowning, adorning a

woman — e.g., *šinašam ukalala šina šinašam ukalala maḫrušša* "they will crown them (the women) two by two, they will crown them by two in her (Mami's) presence" (*CAD* K 518b a, Atra-Ḫasis); *ina muḫḫi birše ša ina pan DN [...] ukallalšu* "he crowns him the king with the *kulūlu*-headdress, standing on the blanket which is before Aššur" (*CAD* K 518b a). Ezekiel employs the verb כָּלַל "to crown" in reference to the city Tyre, depicting the crown like the parapeted battlement of the city.

18. Note that Targum Onqelos renders Heb נֵזֶר "crown" by כְּלִיל in such cases as Exod. 29:6; 39:30; and Lev. 8:9; 21:12.
19. The post-biblical understanding of כליל as "crown" is further corroborated by the Septuagint rendering of this verse: "Thou art a seal of resemblance and a crown (στεφανος) of beauty." I would like to thank my student Yonatan Miller who pointed me to this source.
20. Note that Ben-Sira's description of Aaron's "crown of glory" was applied to Moses in the liturgy of the Sabbath morning service, e.g., יִשְׂמַח מֹשֶׁה בְּמַתְּנַת חֶלְקוֹ כִּי עֶבֶד נֶאֱמָן קָרָאת לוֹ כְּלִיל תִּפְאֶרֶת בְּרֹאשׁוֹ נָתַתָּ "Moses was happy with the gift bestowed on him for You did call him a faithful servant, a crown of glory you placed on his head."
21. Note that Akkadian depicts the crown of the gods and kings as *agê ḫurāṣi* "golden crown" in an elaborated descrption: *agê quarnī ṣīrāti agê bēlūti simat ilūti ša šalummati malāti ša uqnî u ḫurāṣi ina qaqqadišu lu aškunuma ina rēš agîšu NA4... lu aškunuma NA4... ina UGU agî[šu] lu uza'inu[ma]* "I set upon his (Marduk's) head a crown with mighty horns, a lordly crown befitting a god, full of splendor, of lapis lazuli and gold, on the very top of his crown I put (various precious) stones, and I also studded the outer surface of the crown with (various precious) stones" (*CAD* A/I 154a 1).
22. C. J. Exum. "A Literary and Structural Analysis of the Song of Songs," *Zeitschrift für Alttestamentliche Wissenschaft* 85 (1973), 75. See also M. T. Elliott, "The Literary Unit of the Canticle," *Europäische Hochschulschriften, Reihe* 23 (1989), 201–205.
23. M. H. Pope, *Song of Songs: A New Translation with Introduction and Commentary* (AB; New York: Doubleday, 1977), 679–80.
24. R. E. Murphy, *The Song of Songs: A Commentary on the Book of Canticles or Song of Songs* (ed. S. D. McBride; Minneapolis: Fortress, 1990), 192b-193a.
25. N. H. Tur-Sinai, *The Language and the Book* (2 Vols.; Jerusalem: Bialik Institute, 1954), 2:367–368 (Heb.).
26. R. Gordis, *The Songs of Songs: A Study, Modern Translation, and Commentary* (New York: JTS, 1954), 97.
27. Cf. e.g., Songs 5:14–15.
28. Cf., e.g., Songs 4:4; 7:4–5.

29. E.g., *dalāti erīni ša kakkabānnišina kaspum u ḫurāṣu* "I hung cedar doors whose 'stars' were of silver and gold" (*CAD* D 54b 2, *Šamši-Adad I*); *dalāti šurmēni ṣīrāti ša ina petî u târi ereš ṭābu mēsir sippari namri ušerkisma urattâ bābīsin* "I put brilliant copper mountings on tall doors leaves made of cypresses which (emit) a sweet smell when they open and close, and fix them on their (palaces') gates" (*CAD* D: 54b 2', Sennacherib); *dalāti iṣṣ ša ekallāti... kaspa ebba ušalbiš... dalātišina dalāti lulīmu ša erīni eššiš ešmarâ uḫḫiz* "the wooden doors of the temples I had covered in shining silver...I rebuilt their doors with cedar as *lulīmu*-doors and plated them with *ešmarû*-silver" (*CAD* D 54b-55a, Nebuchadnezzar II and *passim*).
30. Gordis, *Song of Songs*, 98.
31. Pope, *Song of Songs*, 680–681.
32. C. D. Ginzberg, *The Song of Songs and Coheleth (Commonly Called the Book of Ecclesiastes)* (trans. C. D. Ginzberg, New York: KTAV, 1970), 189.
33. E. Porada, "Battlements in the Military Architecture and in the Symbolism of the ancient Near East." In *Essays in the History of Architecture Presented to Rudolph Wittkower* (eds. D. Fraser, H. Hibbard, and M. J. Lewine; London: Phaidon, 1967), 11.
34. Ibid. 11.
35. See R. Borger *Die Inschriften Asarhaddons. Königs von Assyrien.* Archiv für Orientforschung, *Beinheft* 9 (Osnabrück: Biblo, 1967), 62 VI 24–25.
36. See K. Bittel "Die Felsbilder von Yazilikaya" *Istanbuler Forschungen* 5 (Bamberg: Druck der Buch — und kunstdruckerei Bamberger tagblatt, 1934), pl. 12; K. Bittel, R. Naumann, and H. Otto, "Yazilikaya Architektur, Felsbilder, Inschrifen un Kleinfunde." *Wissenschaftliche Veröffentlichungen der Deuteschen Orient-Gesellschaft* 61. (1941), 116–18, fig. 46; and E. Akurgal, *Späthethitische Bildkunst* (Ankara: Archeologisches Institut def Universitaet Ankara, 1949), 10–12.
37. E. Porada, *The Art of Ancient Iran: Pre-Islamic Cultures* (New York: Crown, 1965), 66–67, fig. 42; 234, n. 6.
38. Ibid. Fig 3. See also A. Parrot, *The Arts of Assyria* (trans. S. Gilbert and J. Emmons; New York: Golden, 1961), 118:33.
39. H. Frankfort, *The Art and Architecture of the Ancient Orient* (Pelican History of Art 27; Harmondsworth, Middlesex: Penguin, 1954), pl. 114. See J. Börker-Klähn, "Altvorderasiatische Bildstelen und Vergleichbare Felsreliefs" *Baghadader Forschungen* 4. (1982), pl. 227.
40. R. D. Barnett, *Sculptures from the North Palace of Assurebanipal at Nineveh (668–627 B.C.E.)* (London: British Museum, 1976), pl. 65.

41. L. van den Berghe, "La décoverte d'une sculpture rupestre à d'Ārābgird," *Iranica Antiqua* 13 (1978), 135–147.
42. S. M. Paul, "Jerusalem — A City of Gold," *IEJ* 17 (1967), 259–63.
43. J. Nougayrol, *Le Palais royal d'Ugarit*, Vol. 3: *Textes accadiens et hourrites des archives est, oust et centrales*. 2 vols. (Mission de Ras Shamra; Paris: Klincksieck, 1955), 182–186 pl. 51.
44. E.g., מאי עיר של זהב? רבה בר בר חנה א"ר יונחן ירושלים דדהבה כדעבד ליה רבי עקיבא לדביתהו "what is meant by a 'city of gold'? Rabba b. Hannah said in R. Yohanan's name: 'a Jerusalem of gold such as R. 'Aqiva made for his wife'" (b. *Šabb.* 59a-b). See also the remarks of Hoffner (1969) who bolsters Paul's thesis, invoking additional epigraphical evidence supporting the assertion that the item in question is indeed a mural crown.
45. E.g., אמרו לא מת עד שיישן של מטות של זהב שעשה כתר של זהב לאשתו... "they say that [R. 'Aqiva] did not die before he slept on beds of gold and until he made a crown of gold for his wife (*Avot de-Rabbi Nathan*, Version B, ch. 12 = S. Schechter *Avoth de-Rabbi Nathan* [New York: Feldheim, 1967], 29–30).
46. Cf. also Maimonides, *Mishneh Torah*, Laws of Shabbat 19:6.
47. Cf. n. 13.
48. M. T. Elliott, "The Literary Unit of the Canticle," 203.
49. R. Gordis, *The Songs of Songs,* 98.
50. R. E. Murphy, *The Song of Songs,* 193b.
51. O. Keel, *The Songs of Songs: A Continental Commentary* (trans. F. W. Gaiser; Minneapolis: Fortress, 1994), 279.
52. M. Pope, *Song of Songs*, 683.
53. E. Porada, "Battlements," 1b.
54. Cf. n. 18.
55. E. Akurgal and M. Hirmer, *The Art of the Hittites* (trans. C. McNab; New York: Abrams, 1962) pl. 26. See also E. Porada, "Battlements," fig. 3.
56. Ibid. 4–6. See also S. Bodenstein, "Morgan Seal 625," *JANES* 1:2 (1969), 5–13.
57. L. van den Berghe, "La décoverte d'une sculpture rupestre à d'Ārābgird," *Iranica Antiqua* 13 (1978), 144 (cf. Berghe 1978: 135–47).
58. Ibid., 144.
59. E. Porada, "Battlements," 7–8.
60. E.g., *4 ṭimmē siparri ša šeššašuna anāku ballu ṣiruššu ulzizma ina dappi erīni ša kaspa* (wr. *KI.SAG*) *litbušu ušatriṣa ṣulūšu* "four pillars of bronze (that had been alloyed with one-sixth part of tin I (Sennacherib) erected upon it (the pedestal) and laid over it (the construction) as roofing cedar boards plated with silver" (*CAD* D 106a a). Note that the semantic and the etymological equivalent of Hebrew

לוח is the Akkadian noun *lē'u* "(wooden) board," used for decorating, e.g., *ina muḫḫi dalāte ša li'āni ša erê ina muḫḫi ellûni* "concerning the doors upon which copper sheets are to be mounted" (*CAD* L 159b c); *dalāti ša bīt Sîn... ša lē'āni ša kaspi elluni raṣpa* "the doors of the temple of Sin (Šamaš and Ningal) on which silver boards are to be mounted have been put together" (*CAD* L 159b c).

61. E. Porada, "Battlements," 10a.
62. M. Jastrow, *A Dictionary of the Targumim, the Talmud Babli and Yerushalmi, and the Midrashic Literature* (2 vols.; New York: Pardes, 1950) 1149a. See also Hoftijzer and Jongeling, *Dictionary of Northwest Semitic Inscriptions* (Leiden: Brill, 1995), 946.
63. G. Barkay, "The *Megerah* and the *Tephahot,*" *Shnaton: An Annual for Biblical and Ancient Near Eastern Studies* 11 (1997), 32–45. (Heb.).
64. M. Pope, *Song of Songs*, 560–561.
65. R. Gordis, *The Song of Songs,* 90–91.
66. R. E. Murphy, *The Song of Songs*, 175.
67. M. V. Fox, *The Song of Songs and the Ancient Egyptian Love Songs* (Madison: University of Wisconsin, 1985), 152.
68. Hebrew *migdāl*, tower, is traditionally derived from the verb *gdl*, "to grow up, become great." However, in light of the Akkadian *madgaltu* (Middle Assyrian [1500–1000 B.C.E.], Neo-Assyrian [1000–600 B.C.E.]; *CAD* M/I 16a), which is derived from the verb *dagālu*, "to look, to observe" (*CAD* D 21a), Hebrew *migdāl* (metathesis) should be likewise related to the verb *dgl* "to see" (Songs 5:10, Ps. 20:6). It seems that the original root *dgl* is attested in the noun *nidgalot* in Songs 6:4,10. *Nidgalot* will then be the etymological and semantic equivalent of Hebrew *migdalot* with a dissimilation of the labials.
69. V. Fritz, "Temple Architecture: What can Archaeology Tell Us about Solomon's Temple?" *BAR* 13 (1987), 38–49.

Biblical Essays

ʿAzazel The Prince of the Steppe: A Comparative Study

I

Two scapegoats were dispatched on the Day of Atonement during the ritual purification ceremony (Lev. 16). The first was sacrificed for the Lord; the second was sent free (שלח, Piʿel) to ʿAzazel — to the open country bearing all the sins of the people.

While it seems clear המדברה "to the open country/steppe" and אל ארץ גזרה "to a cut off land" (from human habitation) modify עזאזל, the identification and etymological origin of ʿAzazel has been the subject of much debate from the post-biblical period onwards. Jewish and non-Jewish scholars, from the medieval period until the modern times, argued the meaning of the term and are unable to form a unified opinion as to the precise mythological nature of ʿAzazel and its philological affinities. Thus, while the NJPS translation[1] transliterates the vocable, the NEB[2] renders the noun as "precipice." Similarly, the two other philological treatments differ with regard to the etymological origin of the word. G.R. Driver renders it as "rugged rocks"[3] (a name of the place where the goat was led). B. Levine,[4] although following R. de Vaux's[5] thesis that ʿAzazel is a supernatural being connected with demons, admits that the interpretation of the noun is unknown.

This paper will attempt to deal with ʿAzazel primarily from the philological point of view, while not excluding the cultural, mythological, and ritualistic texts involved. We will arrive at a solution only after inductive study conducted by gathering and analyzing the accumulative evidences of the contextually relevant material.

While it was the biblical custom to send the scapegoat free "to the open country/to cut-off land," in the Second Temple, for reasons unknown, some details of the ritualistic procedures concerning the scapegoat were altered. In m. *Yoma* 6:4–6 we read:

> מיקירי ירושלים היו מלוין אותו עד סוכה הראשונה עשר סוכות מירו־
> שלים ועד צוק... מה היה עושה חולק לשון של זהורית חציו קשר בסלע
> וחציו קשר בין שתי קרניו ודחפו לאחוריו והוא מתגלגל ויורד ולא היה
> מגיע לחצי ההר עד שנעשה אברים אברים

> Certain of the eminent people of Jerusalem used to go with him (the priest) to the first booth. There were ten booths from Jerusalem to the steep cliff... what did he (the priest) do, he divided the thread of crimson wool and tied on half to the rock and the other half between its horns and he pushed it (the goat) from behind; and it went rolling down, and before it had reached half way down the hill it was dismembered.

The biblical account states that the goat was set to roam about free in the steppe until it dies. The Mishnaic story differs. The goat is to be brought to the top of the cliff, tied, and pushed from the cliff until dismembered. It is clear that the Mishnaic methodical adaptation of killing the animal was done to make sure of the animals death, and thus obviate its returning alive and bringing the iniquities back into the city.

This Mishnaic ritualistic procedure (i.e., pushing the goat from the צוק "cliff,") led the rabbis of the Talmud to explain the term ʿAzazel as a "rough and difficult place," basing it on a Midrashic interpretation of the Biblical ארץ גזרה.

(1) b. *Yoma* 67b:

> תנו רבנן עזאזל שיהיה עז וקשה יכול בישוב ת"ל במדבר ומנין שבצוק
> ת"ל גזירה תניא אידך עזאזל קשה שבהרים וכך הוא אומר ואת אילי
> הארץ לקח

> Our Rabbis thought: ʿAzazel it should be hard and rough. One might have assumed that it is to be in inhabited land, therefore our text read "in the wilderness." But whence do we know that (is to be) in a mountain peak (i.e., צוק)? Therefore the text read "cut off"; thus also does it say; "And the mighty of the land he took away."

(2) b. *Yoma* 67b:

דבר אחר אין גזירה אלא דבר המתגזר ויורד

"Another explanation: *Gezerah* means something that cuts itself and goes down."

The Talmudic interpretation of ארץ גזרה clearly demonstrates a deliberate attempt to reason and explain the Mishnaic custom of pushing the scapegoat from the "cliff." Such is also the rendering of Targum Pseudo-Jonathan on Lev. 16:10 באתר תקיף וקשה דבמדברא דצוק דהוא בית חרורי "A rough and a difficult place, which is in the desert of the cliff that it is Bet Harori," as well as the explanation employed in Midrash *Sifra* (Aḥare Mot) 2:8 למקום הקשה שבהרים "to the rough place which is on the mountains." Similarly, the tradition to justify the Talmudic interpretation that ʿAzazel is a rough and difficult place (a location name) continued. Some of the medieval exegetes,[6] looking for a more accurate philological foundation of the term ʿAzazel, based their etymology on the Arabic language. Saʿadya, in his commentary to the Pentateuch,[7] renders the term לג׳בל עזאז "to a hill of a rough ground." A more detailed discussion of the term is found in his book *The Book of Beliefs and Opinions.* There, battling the heretic Ḥiwwi al-Balchi[8] — who argues that ʿAzazel is a demon — Saʿadya states:

והתשיעי הקרבן אשר היו מקריבים לעזאזל ביום הכפורים כ̇ כבר נדמה לבני אדם שהוא שם שד ואומר כי עזאזל שם הר כמו שאמר במקום אחר (מ"ב י"ד ז) הוא הכה את אדום בגיא מלח עשרת אלפים ותפש את הסלע במלחמה ויקרא שמה יקתאל עד היום וכן יבנאל וירואל וירפאל הכל מקומות

The ninth (problem) the sacrifice that they (the Israelites) used to offer to ʿAzazel on the Day of Atonement. To certain people this name sounded like that of a demon. Our reply is that ʿAzazel was the name of a mountain as it was said in another place (II Kings 14:7) "He defeated ten thousand Edomites in the Valley of Salt and captures the rock; he gave it the name of Joktheel, which it still

> bears." Similarly, Jabneel, Irpeel, and Jeruel were all of them localities.[9]

Saʿadya's statement attempts to both refute the belief held by some that the Israelites were offering to demons, and rationalize the Mishnaic ritualistic procedure. Similarly, Ibn-Jahāḥ equates עזאזל with the Arabic עזאזה stating that: ומן העין הזה אמרו לארץ קשה עזאזל האלף והלמד נוספות בו "And from this matter they call a rough land ʿAzazel, where the Alef and the Lamed are added to it."[10] Not without philological difficulties, G. R. Driver adopts Saʿadya's and Ibn Janāḥ's Arabic etymological equation. He further argues that in the word עזאזל, the א is not an essential element of the root, and an addition of a formative ל as in Hebrew ערפל-עריף/כרמל-כרם, thus Arabic *ʿazâzu(n)* "rough ground" — *ʿazazilu* (broken plural) "jagged cliff/precipice."[11]

The second theory is that ʿAzazel is a name of a demon inhabiting the desert. This view, seeing in ʿAzazel a supernatural power, is the dominant opinion expressed in the Midrashic literature from the early post Biblical period until the very late Midrashim.[12] The oldest source for the story of ʿAzazel is found in the Ethiopic book of Enoch.[13] There, ʿAzazel (or ʿAzel), numbered the tenth in the list of the fallen angels, is represented to be the source of all evil and corruption, identified with that of the Mishnah.[14] Likewise, it is noteworthy that the Talmud has a second different interpretation of the term. Referring to the legend of the two fallen angels in b. *Yoma* 67b we read: תנא דבי ישמעאל עזאזל שמכפר על מעשה עוזא ועזאל "The school of R. Ishmael thought: ʿAzazel (it was so called) because it obtains the atonement for the affairs of ʿUza and ʿAzel." Based on Midrash *Deut. Rabba* 11 (end) Rashi comments:

> עוזא ועזאל מלאכי חבלה שירדו לארץ בימי נעמה אחות תובל קין ועליהם נאמר ויראו בני האלהים את בנות האדם (בר׳ ו) כלומר על העריות מכפר

> ʿUza and ʿAzel are demonic angels who came down to the earth in the days of Naʿama, the sister of Tubal Cain;

> of them it is said the sons of God saw the daughters of men, (Gen. 6) that is to say (ʿAzazel) atones for the sins of incest.

In the late Midrash, *Pirqe de-Rabbi Eliezer* 46, ʿAzazel is identified with שטן or סמאל "the devil."[15] In another late Midrash, referring to the two fallen angels שמחז(א)י and עזאזל, ʿAzazel, the demonic seducer, is clearly equated with that of Lev. 16:

> ...עזאזל לא חזר בתשובה ועדין עומד בקלקולו להסית בני אדם לדבר עבירה... ולכן היו ישראל מקריבין קרבנות ביום הכפורים גורל אחד לה' שיכפר על ישראל וגורל אחד לעזאזל שיסבול עונותיהן של ישראל והוא עזאזל שבתורה

> But ʿAzazel persisted, obdurately in his sin of leading mankind astray... For this reason two he-goats were sacrificed on the Day of Atonement, the one for the Lord, that He pardoned the sins of Israel, the other for ʿAzazel, that he bear the sins of Israel and this is ʿAzazel of the Torah.[16]

This tradition, understanding ʿAzazel as a supernatural demonic being, was likewise advocated by both medieval commentators: the rationalist Ibn-Ezra and the mysticist Ramban respectively. Ibn-Ezra states:

> ויאמר רב שמואל אף על פי שכתוב בשעיר חטאת שהוא לשם גם השעיר המשתלח הוא לשם ואין צריך, כיהמשתלח איננו קרבן כי לא ישחט. ואם יכלת להבין הסוד שאחר מלת עזאזל תדע סודו וסוד שמו כי יש לו חברים במקרא ואני אגלה לך קצת הסוד ברמז בן שלשים ושלש תדענו.

> Rabbi Samuel said "Although it is (only) with reference to the goat of the sin-offering that is written (explicitly) that it was for the Lord, the goat which was sent away (to ʿAzazel) was also for the Lord. But there is no need for this (comment). For the goat which was sent away was not an offering since it was not slaughtered. Now if you can understand the secret of the word after ʿAzazel, you will know its secret (that of ʿAzazel) and the

> secret of its name, since it has parallels in the Scripture. And I will reveal to you part of the secret by hint: when you will be (or, understand) thirty-three,[17] you will know it.

Ibn-Ezra's enigmatic style points out that ʿAzazel (modified by המדברה "unto the wilderness") is a שד "demon," and that the scapegoat for the demon. ʿAzazel is not to be considered as a sacrifice, but rather to be sent free to the desert bearing all the sins of the people. Ramban, on the other hand, while agreeing with Ibn-Ezra that ʿAzazel is some sort of a demon, nevertheless follows the late pseudepigraphical Midrash, maintaining that the goat was offered as a "present/bribe" (i.e., שחד) to the Satan. Describing the characteristics of ʿAzazel, he writes:

> והנה התורה אסרה לגמרי קבלת אלהותם וכל עבודה להם. אבל צוה הקב"ה ביום הכפורים שנשלח שעיר במדבר לשר המושל במקומות החרבן והוא הראוי לו מפני שהוא בעליו ומאצילות כחו יבא חורב ושממון, כי הוא העילה לכוכבי החרב והדמים והמלחמות והמריבות והפצעים והמכות והפירוד והחרבן... ובחלקו עוד השידין הנקראים מזיקים בלשון רבותינו ובלשון הכתוב שעירין.

> Now the Torah has absolutely forbidden to accept them as deities, or to worship them in any manner. However, the Holy One, blessed be He, commands us that on the Day of Atonement we should let loose a goat in the wilderness, so that "prince" which rules over wastelands, and this (goat) is fitting for it. Because he is its master, and destruction and waste emanate from his power, which in turn is the cause of the stars of the sword, wars quarrels, wounds, plagues, division and destruction… Also in his portion are the devils called "destroyers" in the language of our Rabbis, and in the language of our Scripture "satyrs (demons)."[18]

II

These legends describing ʿAzazel as a demon, though post-biblical and late, may well go back to a very ancient source. U. Cassuto, in his reconstruction of the biblical epic of creation, noted that rabbinic and midrashic literature revived the ancient mythological motif of God's war against the monsters of the sea, otherwise not attested to in the Hebrew Bible.[19] Likewise, S. Lieberman has pointed out that the rabbis of the Talmud were well familiar with the demonic world from ancient literature.[20] Indeed, many mythological/legendary elements, as well as legal terminologies found in post-biblical literature, are rooted in antiquity, specifically in the ancient Near Eastern tradition.[21] It is thus the aim of the present paper to philologically study the biblical-midrashic demon ʿAzazel in the light of its West and East Semitic magical/ritualistic background. We will ultimately arrive at the proper etymological/semantic meaning of ʿAzazel, as well as the mythological function of this enigmatic word.

At the outset, it should be noted that the comparison of the ritualistic ceremony dispatching the goat (as a substitutionary element) with the cuneiform and other magical texts (i.e., *šurpu/maqlû*) was previously noted by various scholars.[22] The latest and the most recent comparative treatment from the point of view of the ritualistic structure, as well as the relationship between the actual dispatch and the remaining aspects of the ritual (i.e., sacrifice, the atonement with the blood of the sacrifice), were studies conducted by B. Levine.[23] He utilized the more appropriate Akkadian series *utukkû lemutti* "Evil spirits"[24] as the basic inscriptions for understanding the ritual of the Day of Atonement. Indeed, these Akkadian magical, ritualistic, and incantation texts will enable us to better conceive the true demonic nature of ʿAzazel.

Turning to these Akkadian texts dealing with demons, we learn that demons, the source of all evil, destruction, desolation, iniquities, sins, diseases, and sicknesses, are the children of the netherworld: *Namtaru māru narām Enlil... ilitti Ereškigal eliš igṣuṣūma šapliš karra iddû šunu binût arallî šunu* "Namtar beloved son of Enil the offspring of Ereškigal above they (the demons) raged (lit., bared their fangs), below they have put; mourning garment, they are creatures of the netherworld";[25] *ša riḫūt Anim reḫū mārū ilitti erṣetim šunu* "They are begotten of the sperm of Anu, sons who are the offspring of the netherworld."[26] Their natural habitation is thus in the "crevices" (i.e., *nigiṣṣu* = *ḫurru* "hole")[27]/"desolated places" (i.e., *nidūtu*) of the netherworld: *ina nigiṣṣi erṣeti itanaḫlallū ina nidūti erṣeti ittenī'illū* "They (the demons) are always creeping in the subterranean crevices, amid the desolated places of the netherworld they always lie":[28] *ina nigiṣṣi erṣeti ittanaššabū ina nidūti irti ittenibbu* "They always dwell in the subterranean crevices, amid the desolated places of the bosom (of the netherworld)."[29] Demons were believed to come out from the netherworld (e.g., *utukkû lemnu alû lemnu eṭemmu lemnu galû ištu erṣetim ittaṣûšunu*)[30] through a crack/hole in the ground. From the Gilgameš Epic, we learn that Enkidu's spirit came forth from the netherworld (conceived by the Mesopotamian to be a short distance below the face of the ground),[31] from a hole: *qarradu eṭlu Nergal luman takkap erṣetim iptêma utukkû ša Enkidu kī zaqīqi ultu erṣetim ittaṣâ* "As soon as the hero Nergal opened a hole in the netherworld, the ghost of Enkidu came forth from the netherworld, like a breath of wind."[32] Furthermore, demons causing all sorts of calamities come up from the netherworld through a crack in the ground. Their arrival is equated to that plants: *aḫḫāzu kīma urqīti ṣēri ipeṣṣi... nīš dadmē ušamraṣū zumuršinā uṣarrapū* "The *aḫḫāzu* demon leaves the ground like a grass... make the people living in the cities sick, make their bodies burn."[33] A more elaborated description of demons springing throughout a crack from the netherworld and attacking mankind is found in the Babylonian Job: *ultu irat erṣetim išīḫa di'i šūlu lemnu ītaṣâ apsûššu utukku l[ā ni]i ūṣâ ultu ēkur* "Headache (demon) has sprung up from the bosom of the netherworld, Evil Cough has come forth from its subterranean deep, the Irresistible Ghost has come out from the netherworld."[34]

Coming up from the netherworld to the world of the living, demons and other powers of hostility most commonly dwell in a place that is the "steppeland" (Sumerian *EDIN* = Akkadian *ṣēru*) e.g., *utukkû lemnu eṭemmu ša ina ṣērim šūpû* "The evil demon, the ghost which is dominant (lit., visible) in the steppe."[35] The verbs employed to describe the movement of demons in the steppeland are: *alāku/šâṭu/ṣâdu/dâlu/rapādu/nagāṣu/nasarbaṭṭu* "to talk about/rove/about/whirl/hover/roam about," e.g., *Namtar ša ina ṣērim kīma zaqīqi ittanašrabiṭṭu* "Namtar who is in the steppe, like a ghost roams around";[36] *lū eṭemmu murtappidu lū eṭemmu muttaggišu lū eṭemmu ša ina ṣēri nadû* "whether it be a roving ghost, or a roaming ghost or a ghost (of a man) whose (body) was cast in the steppeland."[37]

As pointed out by K. Tallqvist, the common Sumerian term *EDIN* (= Akkadian *ṣēru)* "steppe," is also to be understood as one of the symbolic designations of the netherworld. This is employed in the Tammuz liturgical texts.[38] Istar, lamenting Tammuz and shut up in the netherworld, cries: *...edin-na sag-gá-gá lil edin nigin edin nigin šeš-mu edin nigin edin a-ra-li edin nigin šeš-mu edin nigin* "In the steppe overpowered by storm, in the steppe enclosed, my brother, in the steppe enclosed. In the steppe of the netherworld, in the steppe enclosed, my brother, in the steppe enclosed."[39] Similarly, alongside *ṣēru* "steppe," Akkadian likewise employs the idiom *erēb šamši* as another symbolic attribute for the netherworld. Conceived by the Mesopotamian to be situated in the west, the descent then might be considered as a desert journey toward the west.[40] K. Tallqvist further indicates that the substantives *ḫurbū (ḫurbātu)/namû (namūtu)/kīdi/tillānu/karmu*, usually denoting "ruins/waste/desolation," comes also to connote the "netherworld" itself.[41] Suffice it to call attention to the following two examples: *eṭemmu aḫû ina ḫurbāti iṣbas[su]* "The ghost of a stranger seized him in the waste places"[42]; *ana eṭemmi murtappidu ša pāqida lā īšû ana eṭem ḫurbī nadūti tapqidanni ana ṣēri kīdi u namê tapqidanni* "To a roaming ghost who has no one to care for, to a ghost of deserted and wasted places you hand me over, you hand me over to the steppe, open country and desolated places."[43]

From the cuneiform incantation, magical, and *pūḫu* ("substitute") ritual texts, we further learn that demons and other supernatural powers bearing diseases, destruction, and death are to be chased away from the land of the living back to their natural birth place/habitation — the netherworld, the primary source of all evil and disasters. Accordingly, Marduk, known for his anti-demonic powers, addresses the demons as follows:

liddinkūnuši Meslajntaea (ana) erṣet lā târi
lipqidkūnuši ana sibit atê [ša] Ereškigal
lipqidkūnuši ana Namtar sukkal erṣetim ša bāb k[amū]ti ukallû
liṣērebkūnuši ab[ūl erṣeti] rabīti
ana qātē gallē rabūti lim[a]llīkūnuši
Nedu Nedugal erṣetim b[āb]kūnu liṣbat
liddinkūnuši ana Ningiṣzida guzal[ê] erṣetim rapšati
Anunnaki ilāni rabūti likmūkūnuši

May Meslamtaea hand you over to the land of no return
may he commit you to the seven doorkeepers [of] Ereskigal
may he commit you to Namtar, vizier of the underworld who keeps (guard at) the Gate of the captive (gods)
may he cause you to enter the ga[te of] the great [underworld]
may he hand you over to the great devils
may Nedu head doorkeeper of the underworld hold the gate against you
may he give you over to Ningiszida, herald of the vast netherworld
may the Anunnaki the great gods bind you.[44]

Likewise, the Babylonian Job, restored back to his previous state of health, claims that Marduk was responsible for driving away sicknesses and other demonic powers back to their original localities: *ana irat erṣetim ūbi[l di'a] uštērid apsûššu šūlû lem[nu] [utuk]kû lā ni'i utir ekurriš* "He (Marduk) took the Headache demon to the bosom of the netherworld, he sent down the Evil Cough to its subterranean deep, the Irresistible Ghost he returned to the underworld."[45] Indeed, sicknesses and diseases were grasped by the Babylonians to be an evil matter. Therefore, they must be driven back to the source of all evil. This idea is clearly defined in the following *utukkû lemutti* text, where the illness is transferred from the body of the sick to the slaughtered *mašḫultuppû* goat. This goat was then dispatched to the open country, i.e., the netherworld: *ina zumur amēli muttaliki tebi pīka elli sīri liqqabi mimma lemnu [tebi uṣt] ana ašri Ereškigalli mašak mašḫultuppî [ina zumur amēli muttal]liki ublamma ina rebēti ina sūqi rapšati idīma mimma lemnu ana erṣetim li[tūr…]* "Let your pure and exalted mouth say, 'from the body of the sufferer go away. O all evil, arise and depart to the place of Ereškigal, take away the skin of the scapegoat from the body of the sufferer, into the carrefour, into the wide street (i.e., under world) throw (it), so that all evil return to the netherworld.'"[46]

Furthermore, alongside *ana erṣeti/erṣet lā târi/apsû/ekurru/ Ereškigal* "to the netherworld/land of no return/subterranean deep/underworld/Ereskigal (etc.)," we likewise learn that demons and other powers of hostility are to be driven away to their designated localities, symbolic of the netherworld *āšib namê ana namêka atlak* "dweller of desolated places go to your ruins";[47] *līṣīma māmīt ina ṣēri liḫliq eṭemmi aḫî līmurma lištappidū namê* "may the spell go out (from the patient) and may vanish in the steppe may it meet a strong ghost and may they roam the desolated places."[48]

So too, the scapegoat/figurine being a substitutionary element bearing the diseases is also dispatched to the *ṣēru* "steppe" and to *erēb šamši* "the west." Both nouns are used as a symbolic designation of the netherworld, respectively. It is thus noteworthy that the slaughtered *mašḫultuppû* goat and the *ṣalmu* are to "be shut/buried" (*peḫû/qebēru*) "in a hole/pit" (*ḫurru/būrtu*) in the steppe at the west. This is the very same hole that all powers of hostility, disease, and evil come forth: *ina ūmi šalšim ūmi [šulmi] ina erēb šamši ina ṣēri būrtu tepettēma qitebiršu* (for *teqebberšu*!) "On the third day, a propitious day, you dig (lit., open) a pit at the setting of the sun (i.e., west) at the steppe you shall bury it (the goat)";[49] *utammēka Šamaš ina rabêšu ina zumri annanna apil annanna lū teriq lū tenessi lū tataltak taqabbīma ṣalma šuʾâtu ina ḫurri ša erēb šamši tepeḫḫīšūma amēlu šuʾâtu adi balaṭisu mīti lā immar* "I conjure you away by Šamaš in his setting, from the body of so and so the son of so and so keep off; go away, depart (so) you shall say, that figurine in a hole at the west you shall bury (lit., close) it, so that man as long as he lives shall not see the dead ghost."[50]

III

Turning back to the problem at hand, we notice that in the post-biblical Ethiopic Book of Enoch, the demonic fallen angel, ʿAzazel, is being disposed of in a similar way that demons and other hostile powers are treated in the above Akkadian magical and incantation texts. In the Book of Enoch, ʿAzazel is the origin of all evil and corruption: ראית את אשר עזזאל למד את כל החמס על הארץ... "You (God) saw what ʿAzazel had done, who had thought all unrighteousness on earth";[51] ותשחת כל הארץ בלמד מעשי עזזאל וכתבת עליו את כל החטא "And the whole earth has been corrupted through the works that were thought by ʿAzazel: to him ascribe all sin."[52]

In order to get rid of all iniquities and corruption and to purify the land, God commands the angel Rapael to exterminate ʿAzazel, the source of it, in the following manner:

> אסר את עזזאל ידיו ורגליו והשלכתו אל החשך ועשית פתח אל המדבר אשר בדודאל והשלכתו שמה! ושמת עליו סלעים קשים וחדים וכסיתו בחשך וישב שם עד עולם וכסית את פניו לבל יראה אור
>
> Bind ʿAzazel hand and foot, and cast him onto the darkness: make an opening in the desert, which is in Dudael, and cast him therein. And place upon him rough and jagged rocks, and cover him with darkness, and let him dwell there forever, and cover his face that he may not see light;[53]

ואשאל... למי מכינים עת הכלבים האלה: ויאמר אלי את אלה מכינים לצבאות עזאזל לקחת אותם ולהשליכם אל תחתית כל הענש וכסו את לחייהם באבנים חדות כאשר צוה אדון הרוחות

> And I asked… "For whom are these chains being prepared?" And he said to me: "These are being prepared for the hosts of ʿAzazel, so that they may take them and cast them into the abyss of complete condemnation," and they shall cover their jaws with rough stones as the Lord of Spirits commanded.[54]

ʿAzazel is to be taken to the desert and shut in a hole to be casted in the netherworld forever. Accordingly, the literal/mythological correspondences between the above Akkadian incantation/magical texts and those of the Book of Enoch may be summarized as follows:

1. Darkness as a description of the netherworld:
   Akkadian: *nūra lā amāru*[55]
   Enoch: בל ראה אור
2. To bind/tie the demon (evil gods)
   Akkadian: *kamû*[56]
   Enoch: אסר
3. To cast/drive the demon to the netherworld (lit., darkness)
   a) Akkadian: *ina ekleti/eṭūti (nadû)*[57]
   Enoch: השלך אל חשך
   b) Akkadian: *ina šaplīti/erṣeti šaplīti (nadû)*[58]
   Enoch: השלך אל תחתית
4. To imprison/shut up the demon in the netherworld (lit., grave):
   Akkadian: *ina qabrim kalû*[59]
   Enoch: כלא בתחתית
5. To dispatch the demon/substituionary elements to the steppeland — to dig/open a hole therein:
   Akkadian: *ina ṣēri — būrtu/ḫurru petû*[60]
   Enoch: עשה פתח אל המדבר

More specifically, alongside *ṣēru* "steppeland," Akkadian also employs the substantive *mudabiru* to mean not only "an open country," but also to denote a chaotic place, characteristic of the netherworld. That is exactly ʿAzazel in Enoch. The *mašḫultuppû* goat bearing the disease is being placed in "a hole" (Akkadian *ḫuptu)* "in the open country" (i.e., *ana mudabiri* = Enoch אל המדבר) to remain there forever: *ina šērim immeru lammu haṭṭu kāsu ana mudabiri ubbulū... immera iṭabbahū... kursināti paniāti [ina] ḫuḫarāti irakkusū [ḫ]upta iḫappi[ū] dišpu u šamnē ina libbi itabbukū duraʾ ibattaqū ina libbi ḫupti išakkanū* "In the morning they (the porters) shall carry the billy-goat, the bough, the staff, and the cup into the waste-land... They shall slaughter the billy-goat... they shall tie the; front legs with snares. They shall dig a pit and pour honey and oil into it. They shall hack off the forelegs and then put them into the pit."[61]

In the Book of Enoch, the reference to מדבר as a land hostile to human, an arid and dry country, a desolated place where demons and other hostile powers freely roam around, a land of death and no return, a place symbolic of the netherworld,[62] is unmistakable. To such a physical/symbolic locale, the scapegoat bearing the sins of Israel is to be dispatched on the Day of Atonement. Accordingly, in the light of the Akkadian magical/incantation texts involving a formulaic prescription against demons/diseases, one may venture to assume that the story employed in the Book of Enoch may well go back to an antique source. Though legendary, it seems to preserve an original and a more full account of the actual/physical dispatch. That is also to suggest that the scapegoat in Lev. 16 was taken by the porter to the open country/desert, not just to freely roam about until natural death occurs, but also killed (not for sacrifice), bound, and placed in a hole and covered therein. Not unlike the Mishnaic procedure, this elaborate process was formed to prevent its returning back alive to the city.

This assumption may further gain some ground noting that alongside the biblical/Enoch מדבר (= Akkadian *ṣēru/mudabiru)*, the scapegoat is dispatched to ארץ גזרה. The employment of this specific and unique idiom in sequential order with לעזאזל and המדברה expresses a totality of the same idea. It is not without a philological and contextual foundation. It should be observed that ארץ גזרה was freely rendered by the Targumim (Onqelos, Jonathan) as ארע לא יתבא "an uninhabited land," and אתר צדיא "a desolated place." Both considered the idiom as a synonymous parallel for מדבר, respectively. Such is also the understanding of the medieval commentators with regard to this idiomatic expression.

The biblical verb גזר "to cut" is attested fifteen times. Similar to its synonym כרת, at least in four cases (only in Niphʿal) it denotes "to be cut off from the world of the living (i.e., to die)." It is further interesting that the verb גזר (Niphʿal) is always employed in contexts involving the netherworld.[63] It is likewise significant that alongside the cuneiform idioms *erṣetu qablītu/šaplītu/rapšatu/katimtu/nisātu/rūqtu* "a middle/lower/vast/covered/faraway/distant land," expressions symbolic of the netherworld,[64] Akkadian further employs the term *ašm parsu* "a cut off (i.e., secluded/forbidden) place," which also yields the netherworld itself:

[u]tukkû lemnu ṣî ana nisāti
[a]lu lemnu atlak ana namê
[man]zazka ašru parsu
šubatka bītu nadû ḫarbū

O evil demon, go forth to distant places
O evil *alu* demon, go unto the ruins
Your post is a cut off (secluded) place
a ruined desolated house is your home.[65]

Here, Akkadian *ašru parsu*, employed in sequential order with *nisātu/namû/bītu nadû/ḫarbū*, is unmistakably the exact semantic equivalent of the Hebrew idiomatic *hapax* ארץ גזרה "a cut off place (from human habitation)" used also in Lev. 16 as a symbolic designation of the netherworld.

IV

The steppe/desert referring to a chaotic location symbolic of the netherworld, where demons freely roam around, is precisely also the natural domain of Môt, the god of death and Hades, the god of all that lacks life and vitality. ʿAnat, in search of her brother Baʿal, meets Môt. The latter describes his wandering as follows:

> *an itlk waṣd kl ǵ r lkbd arṣ kl ǵ bʾ lkbd šdm npš ḫsrt bn nšm npš hmlt arṣ mǵt lnʿmy arṣ dbr ysmt šd šḥlmmt* "I indeed have gone and roam about every mountain to the bosom of the netherworld, every hill to the middle of the underworld. Lifebreath was wanting among men, lifebreath among earth's masses. I came to the pleasance of the steppe-land, the beauty of the steppe of the cress (field) of Môt."[66]

The similarity in phraseology between the above Ugaritic text and those Akkadian inscriptions describing the netherworld by the use of symbolic designations seems obvious. Accordingly, parallel to Môt, Tammuz too is portrayed to descend to the netherworld in the same manner, e.g., *illak išīt ana irat erṣeti[m] Šamaš irtabbišu ana erṣetim mītūti* "He walks, he roams about into the bosom of the netherworld, the sun sets for him into the land of the dead."[67] It should be observed that in describing the movement of demons/dead ghosts, the Akkadian verbs *alāku-šâṭu* "to walk about — to roam," corresponds to Ugaritic *ylk* (infixed *t) — ṣwd*[68] and Hebrew שוט-התהלך[69] referring to Satan's wandering in Job 1:7; 2:2. Additionally, alongside *irat kigalli/kabit arallî/libbi erṣetim,*[70] Akkadian also employs the more common expression *irat erṣetim (//erṣetim mītūti)* to mean "the bosom of the netherworld."[71] This idiom is the semantic equivalent of the Ugaritic *kbd arṣ//kbd šdm*[72] and the Hebrew[73] בטן שאול, respectively. The use of Ugaritic *ǵr//gbʿ*, which commonly means "mountain//hill" in the above specific context, seems parallel to Akkadian *šadû/ḫuršānu* employed in Mesopotamian mythology to connote "the cosmic mountain of the netherworld."[74]

Furthermore, in agreement with the usage of Akkadian *ṣēru* (= Hebrew מדבר), Ugaritic *arṣ dbr/šd šḫlmmt*[75] "steppe-land the steppe[76] of the cress[77] (field) of Môt" may likewise refer to a chaotic location symbolic of the netherworld, the natural domain of Môt.[78]

V

Further, in Akkadian magical/incantation and other related texts, demons inflicting diseases and death are described by the following adjectives: *ezzu/šamru/nadru/gaṣṣu/gašpu/dannu* "fierce furious/raging/ferocious/overbearing/savage:" *gallê šamrūti ana erṣet lā târi aṭarrad kakkēya ezzūti elīšunu ušazzaza* "I shall drive the raging demons to the netherworld, I will array my furious weapons against them";[79] *šiptu ezzēta šamrāta(m) nadrāta(m) gaṣṣāta(m) gašpāta(m) dannāta pašqatā(m) lemnēta abāta(m) ša lā Ea mannu unāḫka* "incantation you (demon) are fierce, furious, raging, ferocious, overbearing, savage, hard, evil, violent, who but Ea could appease you."[80] In describing the brute force applied by demons onto humans, death is symbolized by fury and wrath in the following passage: *gallû eṭēra ul idû ana nīšī nadrū akil šīri mušaznin damē šātû ušalaāti* "Demons who know not to save, who rage against people, devour flesh, shed blood, drink (blood) from the veins."[81] It is likewise noteworthy that Akkadian expresses the notion of raging demons by the more physical verb *gaṣāṣu* "to gnash the teeth" i.e., "to rage" e.g., *igṣuṣ kīma ūmu melammašu ša[dû iktum]* "he raged (lit., gnashed his teeth) like an *ūmu* demon, his awe inspiring aura covered the mountains."[82] It is also significant that the adjective *gaṣṣu* "ferocious" is equated in the lexical list with *mūtu* "death" (personified).[83] Similarly is the case in Songs 8:6 where the substantives עזה//קשה "fierce//overbearing" are applied to מות// שאול "death (personified)//netherworld." Accordingly, as pointed out by U. Cassuto, in Songs 8:6 and in other "verses in which the word מות occurs will show that, in several cases, this word does not denote the abstract concept of death, but is used as the personal name of a specific being, a kind of personification of death very similar to the Canaanite Môt."[84] U. Cassuto further calls our attention to the fact that "occasionally in the Ugaritic texts, the vocable *ʿz* 'fierce' is used as an epithet of Môt."[85] This usage of *ʿz* describing Môt seems to be confirmed only from the non-poetic Ugaritic letter of Iwirizarri,[86] which reads *w yd ilm p kmtm ʿz mid*.... H.L. Ginsberg and G.Maisler render: "Indeed the love of the gods is here like death very fierce (terrible, mighty)."[87] Significant is also the fact that the element *ʿz* in describing the god Môt is undoubtedly contained in the Biblical theophoric name[88] עזמות (= LXX *azmot*) and the geographical location[89] בית עזמות, respectively. The meaning is "Môt is fierce." This specific usage seems to confirm that the Ancient Israelites were familiar with Môt's attribute as a fierce god.

Similarly, in our opinion, to be viewed alongside the biblical עזמות is the term עזאזל, likewise containing two distinct elements עזז and אל to be rendered "a fierce god." The spelling of this word as employed in the MT seems to be a scribal metathesis deliberately altered to conceal the true demonic nature of this supernatural being. The inner-shift of the א is supported by the facts that the Samaritan Bible, in one out of three cases, spells the word עזזאל. Additionally, an interpretation on the legend of the fallen angels from Qumran cave four[90] twice reads עזזאל. Furthermore, the Pešiṭta renders the word three times עזזאיל. Additionally, Targum Ps.-J. on Gen. 6:4 refers to the two fallen angels as שמחזאי ועוזיאל while in the late Midrash, עזאל is clearly interchanged with עזאזל[91]. It seems thus that the identity of /עזזאל עוזיאל/עזאל/עזזאיל with עזאזל is amply certain.[92]

In the light of the above observations, we propose to specifically identify the biblical עזאזל > עזז אל with Môt the Canaanite god of the netherworld. This name, therefore, is nothing but another epithet of Môt, conceived to be a fierce god. Because of the monotheistic consciousness of the Israelites, the biblical עזאזל/מות was reduced from the status of a god to that of a devil, an angel of death. Like the Ugaritic Môt, the biblical עזאזל/מות was depicted as a demonic creature, who characteristically, as

Ramban portrayed him, personifies all evil: destruction, desolation, wars, bloodshed, wounds, plagues, diseases, and sicknesses. He is the foremost and the ultimate ruler of the netherworld. Similar to Nergal, he was conceived to be *šar ṣēri* "the king of the steppe."[93]

From all that has been said, it stands to reason that in Lev. 16, Hebrew המדברה = Akkadian *ana ṣēri/mudabiri*, and ארץ גזרה = Akkadian *ašru parsu*, are words used as a symbolic designation of the netherworld. The scapegoat, exactly as the *mašḫultuppu* goat, *ṣalmu* "figurine," and demons bearing diseases, was likewise dispatched לעזאזל "to the fierce god" (= Akkadian *ana erṣeti/erṣet lā târi/Namtar ašri Ereškigali* and the like) an epithet of Môt. This may also signify the location of his domain, the netherworld itself.

NOTES

1. *NJPS* 211.
2. *NEB*127.
3. G. R. Driver, "Three Technical Terms in the Pentateuch," *JCS* 2 (1956), 97–98.
4. B. Levine "Kippurim," *Eretz Israel* 9 (1969), 94 n. 42 (Heb.).
5. R. de Vaux, Les sacrifices de l'Ancien Testament, (Paris: Gabalda, 1964), 88–91.
6. Note that Qimḥi, following LXX, Symmacus, and the Vulgate understands the word to stand for עז אזל "a goat that departs," i.e., scapegoat.
7. J.D. Qupah, *Sa'adia's Commentary on the Pentateuch* (1963), 101 (Heb.).
8. J. Rosenthal, *Ḥiwi al-Balkhi: a Comparative Study* (Philadelphia: Dropsie College for Hebrew and Cognate Learning, 1949), 20 n. 83.
9. S. Rosenblatt, *The Book of Beliefs and Opinions of Sa'adia* (New Haven: Yale University Press, 1948), 178.
10. Jonah Ibn Janaḥ, *Sepher Haschorashim* (ed.Wilhelm Bacher; Berlin, 1896), 362 (Heb.).
11. G. R. Driver, *JSC* 2 (1956), 98.
12. For a full discussion of the term 'Azazel in the Midrashim see L. Ginzberg, *Legends of the Jews* (7 vols. Philadelphia: The Jewish Publication Society of America, 1954), 1:25, 126, 148–151; 3:472; 5:123, 170–171, 230, 311; 6: 124, 291.

13. R. H. Charles, *The Apocrypha and Pseudepigrapha of the Old Testament in English* (Oxford, The Clarendon Press, 1964), 193–196, 220, 235.
14. For the proper identification of the desert of *Dudael* (in the Book of Enoch) with the Mishnaic *Haddûdû*, referring to the modern *bêt-Ḥudêdûm*, a desert location about twelve miles to the east of Jerusalem, see A. Geiger, *Juel Zeitschr* (1864); H. Schick, *ZDPV* 3 (1867), 214–219.
15. For the identification of ʿAzazel with Satan or Sammel, see L. Zunz, *Gesammelte Schriften* I (1876), 236.
16. *Yalqut Shim ʿoni* (ed. Y. Shiloni, Jerusalem: Mosad Harav Kook, 1973), 1:155.
17. Count thirty-three starting from Lev 16:9 = Lev 17:7.
18. *Ramban's Commentary on the Pentateuch* (ed. H. D. Chavel; Jerusalem: Mosad Harav Kook, 1969), 1:89.
19. U. Cassuto, "Songs of Ascent in Israel," *Keneset* 8 (1944), 121–142. (Heb.).
20. S. Lieberman, *Greek in Jewish Palestine* (Jerusalem: Biyalik Institute, 1962), 73–86.
21. Cf. especially S. Lieberman, *Hellenism in Jewish Palestine*, (New York: JTS, 1994), 75ff; Y. Muffs, *Studies in the Aramaic Legal Papyri from Elephantine* (New York: Ktav Publishing House, 1973); *Idem* "Joy and Love as Metaphorical Expressions of Willingness and Spontaneity in Cuneiform, Ancient Hebrew, and Related Literatures," in *Christianity, Judaism, and Other Greco-Roman Cults for Morton Smith at Sixty* (ed. J. Neusner; Leiden: Brill, 1975), 1–36.
22. Cf. especially J. G. Frazer, *The Golden Bough* (New York: Macmillian, 1958), 509–559. See also W. F. Albright, *From Stone Age to Christianity; Monotheism and the Historical Process* (Baltimore: John Hopkins Press, 1957), 329; F. Blome, *Die Opfermaterial in Babylonien und Israel* (Romae: Apud Pont. Institutum Biblicum, 1934), 104–5. R. de Vaux, *Le Sacrifice*, 88–91.
23. B. Levine, "Kippurim" *Eretz Yisrael* 9 (1969), 88:95.
24. R. C. Tompson, *The Devils and Evil Spirits of Babylonia: being Babylonian and Assyrian incantations against the demons, ghouls, vampires, hobglobins, ghosts, and kindred evil spirits, which attack mankind* (New York: AMS Press, 1976).
25. *CT* 16 12:5–11.
26. Ibid. 19–22.
27. Cf. *CAD* Ḫ 252a (Lexical Section).
28. *CT* 16 44:103–4.
29. Ibid. 90–98.
30. Ibid. 17 41:1–4. Cf. also *ištu bīt ekurri ittaṣûni šunu... utukkû lemnu*

ša ṣerim amēlu balṭu inarru "They (the demons) came forth from the netherworld... the evil (*utukkû)* demon which murders the healthy man in the steppeland," *CT* 16, 1:25–28; *lū eṭemmu ša ištu erṣetim illâ* "a ghost who comes up from the netherworld," *CT* 16 10 IV:42–43.

31. A. Heidel, *The Gilgamesh Epic and Old Testament Parallels* (Chicago: University of Chicago Press, 1963), 170.
32. Gilg. XII 78–80 = 82–84.
33. Šurpu VII: 5–10; Cf. also *e'īlu kīma urqīti ina ṣeri aṣī[ma]* "the *e'elu* demon comes forth from the plain like grass," 5R 50 ii: 29–30; *itti urqitim erṣetim ipeṣṣi lu'tum* "Decay cleaves the ground together with the grass," *BWL* 42,57.
34. *BWL* 40:52–54.
35. *CT* 16, 32, 156–157.
36. *CT* 17, 29:5–7.
37. *LKA* 84, 23–24.
38. K. Tallqvist, "Sumerisch-Akkadische Namen der Totenwelt" *Studia Orientalia* 4 (1934), 17–22 (Hereafter cites as Totenwelt).
39. P. M. Witzel, "Analecta" *Orientalia* 10 (1935), 318, 327–30.
40. Though with some reservation, see A. Halder, *The Notation of the Desert in Sumero-Acccadian and West Semitic Religions* (1950), 13.
41. Totenwelt 22–23.
42. *KAR* 184, r. 11.
43. Malqû IV:21–23. For Hebrew חרבות (= Akkadian *ḫurbū/ḫurbātu*) ארץ תחתיות//יורדי בור referring of the netherworld, cf. Ez 26:20.
44. *AfO* 19 (1959): 117, 123–130.
45. *BWL* 53, 56–59.
46. O. R. Gurney, "Babylonian Prophylactic Figures and Their Rituals," *Annals of Archeology and Anthropology* 22 (1935), 86, 129–137.
47. *CT* 16, 28, 58.
48. *BRM* 4, 18, 22–24.
49. TuL, 83, 85. Cf. also *būrtu ana erēb šamšI tepette...*, *Orientalia* (NS) 24 (1955), 246.
50. TuL 134 (= *Orientalia* [NS] 24 [1955], 258). Cf. also *ina ḫurri erēb ipḫû PBS* 10/2, 18, 33.
51. 1 Enoch 9:6. Cf. also ibid. 13:2. For our purpose we use Kahan *Apocrypha* (vol. 1; Jerusalem, 1970) for the Hebrew translation of the passages above.
52. Ibid. 10:8.
53. Ibid. 10:4–5.
54. Ibid. 54:4–6.
55. *CT* 15, 45:9 (Decent of Ishtar); Gilg. VII col. IV line 39; *AMT* 88, 2:3–4.

56. E.g., *katmāt asakku marṣu alê kabti ša amēlūti* "She (Lamaštu) who fetters the dangerous asakku-demon, the severe *alû* ghost who (attacks) mankind," *ASKT* 95–95, 64–65; *ilū kamūtū ištu qabrim ittaṣûni* "the captives gods came out from the grave." *CT* 17 37:1–2.
57. For Akkadian *eklētu/eṭūtu* = Hebrew צלמות/חשך (Job 17:13; 38:17; cf. 1 Sam. 2:9; Ps. 88:7, 143:3; Lam. 3:6.) meaning not only "darkness, gloom," but also the netherworld itself. See M. Held, "Pits and Pitfalls in Akkadian and Biblical Hebrew," *JANES* 5 (1973): 173 n.53. Note while the expression *ina ekleti/eṭūti nadû* seems not to be attested in Akkadian, Enoch השלך אל חשך "to cast to the netherworld (lit. darkness)," may well find its functional equivalent with Akkadian *ana šuttati nadû* (S. Langdon, Etana, 26:5–6; *KAR* 46:24)/*ina pī karāšI nadū* (*OECT* 6, 44–45; *AfO* 19, 1960, 59:153.) and Hebrew השלך אל/ב קבר, (Jer. 26:23, 2 Kings 13:21) respectively. Cf. also הדף אל חשך (Job 18:18).
58. For Akkadian *šaplīti erṣeti šaplīti* = Hebrew ארץ תחתית (Ez. 31:14, 16, 18)/ארץ תחתיות (Ps. 63:10)/שאול תחתיה תחתית (Deut. 32:22; Ps. 86:13) see K Talqvist, Totenwelt, 11–12.
59. E.g. *ša ina ekleti kīma birqi ittanabriqū ina ekleti qirib qabrim liklûšu* "Let them shut them (the demons) who flash though the darkness like lighting, up in the darkness of the grave" (*CT* 17, 36:86–87). For the usage of Hebrew כלא referring to grave/netherworld cf. Ps. 88:10.
60. TuL 83:5; *Orientalia* (NS) 24 (1955), 246, 17.
61. TuL 74–75, 10–26.
62. For the usage of desert/open country as a symbolic designation for the netherworld, see R. Martin-Achard, *De la mort a la resurrection d'apres l'Ancient Testament,* 1956. (English translation: *From Death to Life*, 1960, 44ff.); J. Pedersen, *Israel: Its Life and Culture* (4 vols.; Copenhagen: S. L. Møller, 1927) 470ff.; K. Tallqvist, *Totenwelt*, 17–22; A Haldar, *The Notion of the Desert in Sumero-Accadian and West Semitic Religions* (Uppsala: Lundequistska bokhandeln; Leipzig: O. Harrassowitz, 1950), 12ff; N. J. Tromp, "Primitive Conceptions of Death and the Nether World in the Old Testament," *Biblica et Orientalia* 21 (1969), 129–133. It is noteworthy that in Jer. 2:31 the employment of מדבר in parallelism with ארץ מאפליה "a land of darkness" (otherwise unattested) is by no means different in meaning than ארץ חשך וצלמות (Job 10:21–22), where both come to denote the netherworld itself (cf. n.57). Likewise, this seems to be the case in Jer. 2:6, where the sequence ציה וצלמות "desolation-darkness" (otherwise unattested) appears in parallelism with ערבה ושוחת "wilderness — pit/nether world" (also unattested). Further, while M. Held, "Pits and Pitfalls in Akkadian and Biblical Hebrew," 175 n.18 admits that the sequence

ערבה ושוחת "is difficult and by no means ideal terrain for emendations," he nevertheless proposes to emend שוחה "pit" to שואה "waste, ruin." To our mind, from the parallelism מדבר — ארץ מאפליה "desert — land of darkness;" ציה — צלמות "waste land — darkness;" one cannot help feeling that Jeremiah's employment of שוחה (= Akk. *ḫaštu/šuttatu*) "pit (netherworld)" //ערבה "wilderness," is an intentional deviation from the regular parallelism to ערבה, purposely done to transmit the idea of desert-netherworld. Be it as it may, even the substantive שואה (= Akk. *kīdu/namû ḫarbu* cf. n.42–43) "desolation, waste" may also come to denote the netherworld itself, as can be seen from the pair שואה — תחתיות ארץ in Ps. 63:10.

63. Isa. 53:8; Ezek. 37:11; Ps. 88:6; Lam. 3:54.
64. See K. Tallqvist, *Totenwelt*, 10, 12, 14, 16, 17, 33.
65. *CT* 16, 29:94–100. Not that the expression *ašru parsu* seems to be employed only in ritual and incantation texts, e.g. *šiddū tašaddad zidubdubbû tattnamdi gumaḫḫa ana ašri parsi tušazzat* "you draw the curtains, set out heaps of flour, you place the choice bull in secluded (lit. cut off) place," F. Thureau-Dangin, *Rituels Accadiens,* (Osbarück: Zeller, 1975), 24, 27–28; Ibid. 54. n. 68; cf. also *Orientalia* (NS) 36 (1967), 25.
66. *1AB* II 15–20; *I AB* 4:26–29.
67. P. M. Witzel, *Analecta Orientalia* 10 (1935), 230.
68. For this pair cf. also I AB 4:26; 55:16; 67–68; BH: 34.
69. For the possible attestation of the הלך — שוט cf. Ps. 91:6, where the MT ישוד is to be read ישוט.
70. K. Tallqvist, *Totenwelt*, 6; cf. also *YOS* 1 38 I 39–40; E. Ebeling, Parfumrez pl. 49 s.
71. Cf. *BWL* 52 r. 5 (Ludlul); *VAB* IV, 60 i 36; ibid. 118 iii 18. For other references see *CAD* I/j, 186b/187a.
72. For the Ugaritic pairs *kbd//irt*; *kbd//lb* cf. IIID, r. 18–19; *VAB* II: 25–26.
73. Jon. 2:3.
74. H. Zimmern, *Zum babylonischen Neujahrfest*, 1918, 3 n. 2; K. Tallqvist, *Totenwelt*, 23–24.
75. For the Ugaritic pair cf. I AB VI: 6–7. For the pair *dbr//šd šḥlmmt* cf. I AB V 18–19. Note that Ugaritic *arṣ dbr* equals the Hebrew ארץ מדבר (Prov. 21:19).
76. For the Ugaritic pair *šd//mdbr* "Steppe//open country" cf. *IK* 103–106 (= 192–194); SS 67–68 = Akkadian *ṣēru//šadû* see A. Heidel, "A Special Usage of the Akkadian Term *šadû*," *JNES* 7 (1949), 233–235.
77. Because the parallel clause *arṣ dbr* "steppe land" (the appropriate dwelling place of Môt), is seems best to analyze the word *šḥlmmt* as comprising of two components, (a) *šḥlm* and (b) *mt* "the cress(land)

of Môt." It should be noted that while J. C. de Moor, (*The seasons Patterns in the Ugaritic Myth of Baʿlu* [Kevelaer, Butzon & Bercker, 1971] 186–187) agrees with R. Dussand (*RHR* 3, 1935, 44, n. 1) that *šḥl* is related to Arabic *sāḥil* "shore, coast," rendering the world "the coast plain of the realm of death." Etymologically (better fitting the context) it seems more suitable to reconsider M. R. Lehmann's (*VT*, 3 [1953], 367, n.3) observation completed ignored by de Moor that Ugaritic *šḥlm* means "cress," to be equated with the Late Hebrew שחלים. Though M. R. Lehmann analyzes the form as a dual, in light of Akkadian (from Old Akkadian and on) *saḫlû* (*AHw* 1009/1010), Old Aramaic שחלין (Sefire IA 36) it seems better to take the form as a pl. *tantum*, to mean "cress/weeds" identified by I. Löw (Aramäische Pflanzennamen, 1881, 396) as *lepidium sativum*, a plant grown on desolated land, the proper dwelling place of Môt.

78. T. H. Gaster, *Thespis*, 1961 125, 132 n. 19–22: "The name *Hadramaut* (Hebrew חצרמות) for arid stretches of South Arabia reflects, of course, the same usage."
79. *CT* 16, 14, IV: 23–27.
80. *TuL* 143:8–10.
81. *IV R*, No 1:34 (= J. Ballenrucher, *Nergal*, 25.)
82. *RA* 48 (1954), 147 37.
83. *LBAT* 2, 2 265; ibid. 3 IV 4 = *CAD* G, 54a (Lexical section).
84. U. Cassuto, "Baal and Mot in Ugaritic Texts," *IEJ* 12 (1962), 83 n. 23.
85. Ibid.
86. C. H. Gordon, *UT* 54 11–14.
87. *JPOS* 14 (1934), 243; 15 (1935), 181–184.
88. 2 Sam. 23:31 = (1 Chr. 11:31); Ezra 2:23–24; 1 Chr. 8:36, 9:42, 12:3, 27:25.
89. Neh. 7:28, 12:29. For the theophoric name עזמות "Môt is fierce," see W. F. Albright, *JPOS*, 1921, 55 n.1; *AASOR* 4 (1922–23), 156–157; H. Bauer, "Die Gottheiten von Ras Schamra," *ZAW* (1933), 94-96; G. R. Driver, *PEQ* (1944–45), 13–14.
90. J. M. Allegro, *Qumran Cave* 4 (1968), 78.
91. *Yalqut Sim'oni* (ed. Y. Shiloni; Jerusalem: Mosad Harav Kook, 1973), I, 156 n.5.
92. L. Ginzberg, *The Legends of the Jews*, 4:152, 5:170.
93. K. Tallqvist, *Totenwelt*, 21 n. 5–6.

The Historicity of 2 Kings 19:24 (= Isaiah 37:25): The Problem of Ye'ōrê Māṣôr

To Esther and Joseph Tawil

'ṣ ḥyym hy' lmḥzyqym bh wtmkyh m'šr
(Prov. 3:18)

The text of 2 Kings 19:24[1] (= Isa. 37:25) reads as follows:

'ny qrty wštyty mym zrym
w'ḥrb bkp p'my kl y'wry mṣwr

Scholars who have dealt with this verse encounter two textual problems, a philological one and a historical-geographical one. Philologically, the expression *mym zrym*[2] used in 2 Kings 19:24 (Isa. 37:25 has only *mym*) has been understood by the majority of modern commentators to connote "waters of foreign lands,"[3] "waters of strangers,"[4] or "foreign waters."[5] These were, presumably, the new wells constructed in a country without water to supply the needs of Sennacherib's army.[6] The second and more crucial textual problem arises from the historical-geographical enigma resulting from the use in this verse of the word *Māṣôr*.

Practically all modern commentators and translators have identified *ye'ōrê māṣôr*, "the rivers of *Māṣôr*," with the Nile, maintaining that *māṣôr* is a variant for *Miṣrayim*, "Egypt."[7] This theory was initially advocated by David Qimḥi, who based his interpretation on the parallel expression *ye'ōr(ê) miṣrayim* (Isa. 7:18; Amos 8:8; 9:5), "the river(s) of Egypt."[8] As Calderone rightly pointed out: "not a single ancient version is acquainted with this uncommon equivalent for *Miṣrayim*."[9] Most scholars have related *Māṣôr* to the root *ṣrr* or *ṣwr* meaning "to press together, enclose, surround." Not satisfied with the widely accepted identification of *Māṣôr* with *Miṣrayim*, Calderone, in his treatment of this problem, suggests it is another example of the enclictic *mem* with the *nomen regens* of the construct chain. He renders the expression *ye'ōrê-m ṣûr*, "the mountain stream,"[10] and thus derives his interpretation from the noun *ṣûr*, "mountain/ rock." Koehler and Baumgartner, ignoring the possible identification of *Māṣôr* with *Miṣrayim*, maintain that it is rather *Muṣri* in Arabia.[11] While their interpretation of biblical *Māṣôr* as a specific geographical site seems logical, their identification appears historically problematic. There are no references to an independent Arabian *Muṣri* in Neo-Assyrian texts.[12]

The accepted identification of *Māṣôr* with *Miṣrayim* generates both an orthographical and a historical problem. The orthographical problem arises from the identification because the interchange of *Māṣôr* with *Miṣrayim* is relatively rare in the Bible. Considering the fact that the Akkadian word for Egypt is *Muṣri/Miṣri* (Amarna *Miṣṣari*), and that numerous attestations of *Miṣrayim* exist in the Bible, one would expect to find this interchange more frequently. However, it occurs only five times in the Bible: twice in Isaiah (19:6; 37:25 = 2 Kings 19:24) and twice in Micah (7:12), Isaiah's contemporary eighth-century prophet. It is never again interchanged with *Miṣrayim*. The historical problem arises with identifying *Māṣôr* with *Miṣrayim*, since Sennacherib never invaded Egypt; rather, his son Esarhaddon conquered it in 671 BCE.

The purposes of this paper is to place the biblical *Māṣôr* in its appropriate geographical location, and thereby authenticate the historical validity of 2 Kings 19:24 (= Isa. 37:25). It should be noted that Sennacherib's impiety and arrogance against the Lord is recounted by Isaiah in a direct quotation (2 Kings 19:23b-24). The Rabshakeh boasts that his master's army is invincible; that he has climbed the heights of Lebanon; that he reached its remotest parts, hewing down its loftiest cedars, its best cypresses; that he has dug and drunk waters; and that he has dried up all the water pools (streams) of *Māṣôr*. Clearly, Isaiah's use of the phrase "Through your envoys you have blasphemed my Lord declaring" (2 Kings 19:23) is a direct reference to the Rabshakeh's words. For some reason, however, they were not included in his famous speech delivered in front of the walls of Jerusalem (2 Kings 18:19–25; 27–35; 19:10–14). Rather, they were recollected and quoted by Isaiah in his prophetic oracle against Assyria. In 2 Kings 18:33–35 and 19:11–13 the Rabshakeh relates his master's royal feats in foreign policy:

> Had any of the gods of the nations ever delivered his land out of the hand of the king of Assyria? Where are the gods of Hamath, and of Arpad? Where are the gods of Hena, and Ivvah? Have they delivered Samaria out of my hands? Among all the gods of the nations is there one who saved his land from me that the Lord should deliver Jerusalem out of my hand?

In 2 Kings 19:24 (= Isa. 37:25), however, the Rabshakeh proudly declares Sennacherib's accomplishments in domestic policy. The source of 2 Kings 19:24 (= Isa. 37:25) emphasizes one of Sennacherib's major domestic royal achievements: the magnificent networks of water conduits that he constructed for his new capital, Nineveh. The history of Sennacherib's grand irrigation system for supplying water to Nineveh was described in detail by T. Jacobsen and S. Lloyd in *Sennacherib's Aqueduct at Jerwan.*[13] For the present discussion, however, it will suffice to outline the historical development of this royal achievement. Two years after Sennacherib's accession to the throne in 703 BCE, he declared the construction of the irrigation network, the Kisiri Canal, as one of his first domestic accomplishments. The account can be translated as follows:

> To make the orchards luxurious, from the border of the town Kisiri to the plan about Nineveh, through the mountains and hills (?), with iron pickaxe I had a canal cut straight. For a distance of [1 ½ *beru*] I cause to flow there (i.e., in the canal) everlasting waters from the Khosr. Inside those orchards I made them run in irrigation ditches.[14]

According to Jacobsen and Lloyd, this canal, which drew water from the Khosr River, began ten miles up the Khosr from Nineveh.[15] Written in 702 BCE, the first irrigation account, dealing with the Kisiri Canal, indicated that the water supply proved quite satisfactory for some time. Between 700 and 694 BCE, however, it became necessary to increase the water supply to Nineveh. Sennacherib, in the record of his domestic improvements and new accomplishments, "The Palace Without Rival," written in 694 BCE, repeats the complaint made in his earliest record[16] that the kings, his predecessors, neglected the welfare of Nineveh and its water supply:

> But none among them (my predecessors) had turned his thought not brought his mind to widen the city area (lit., abode) to build a wall, to lay out streets, or to dig a canal (and) to set out orchards.... But I, Sennacherib, the king of the universe, king of Assyria, gave my thought and brought my mind to accomplish this work according to the command of the gods.[17]

Surely he accomplished what he had set out to do. After giving us a detailed account of his building projects in a general fashion, and the construction of his "palace without rival" more specifically, some lines further on in the inscription repeat the irrigation record dealing with the Kisiri Canal.[18] From the inscription, we learn that Sennacherib himself went out with great difficulty on an important expedition to look for possible new sources of water in order to increase the water supply of Nineveh. After much hardship, new water sources were discovered. This second irrigation account dates to 694 BCE and reads as follows:

> To explore the waters which are at the foot of the Mount Muṣri, a mountain, I took the road and climbed up with great difficulty (and) came to the city of Elmunakinne. At the head of the cities of Dur-Istar, Shibaniba, and Sulu I saw streams and enlarged their narrow sources and changed (them) into spring-fed pools. To (give) these

> waters a course (through) the steep mountains, I cut through the difficult places with pickaxes and directed their outflow on the plain of Nineveh. I strengthened their channels, heaping up (their banks) mountain high, and secured those waters within them. As something extra I added them to the Khosr's water forever.[19]

Sennacherib's third chronicle concerning his irrigation network is recorded in the Bavian inscription written in 690 BCE. This inscription creates a vast and elaborate picture of his new irrigation undertaking, which was in both its type and its dimensions unique in the history of the ancient Near East. Apart from the Mount Muṣri operation, the Bavian inscription described the following undertakings: 1) the excavation of eighteen canals joined to the Khosr; 2) the canalization of the lower part of the Khosr from Kisir to Nineveh; 3) the irrigation of Nineveh and the planning of parks and orchards; 4) the construction of a new canal from Mount Tas.[20] From the Bavian inscription we further learn that Sennacherib's personal interest in technology surpassed that of any of his predecessors. Boastful of his celebrated irrigation system, he even accuses the local inhabitants, who turn their eyes heavenward for showers of rain, of being ignorant of artificial methods of irrigation. The opening section of the Bavian inscription reads as follows:

> ... its fields, which through lack of water had fallen into neglect (lit., ruin) and... while its people, ignorant of artificial irrigation, turned their eyes heavenward for showers of rain... (these fields) I watered; and from the villages of... eighteen canals I dug (and) directed their course into the Khosr River. From the border of the town of Kisiri to the midst of Nineveh I dug a canal; those waters I caused to flow therein. Sennacherib's canal I called its name....[21]

To complete this picture of Sennacherib's irrigation efforts, we should include the account of the aqueduct at Jerwan. Copies of this text were found in many places at the site. According to Jacobsen and Lloyd, this account was intended for the glorification of Sennacherib's achievement. The standard inscription B at Jerwan reads as follows:

> Sennacherib, king of the world, king of Assyria (says): "For a long distance, adding it to the waters of the twain Ḫazur River — (namely) the waters of the river Pulpullia (and) the waters of the town Gammayara, (and) the waters of the springs of the mountains to the right and left at its sides, I caused a canal to be dug to the meadows of Nineveh. Over deep-cut ravines I spanned (lit., caused to step) a bridge of white stone blocks. Those waters I caused to pass over upon it."[22]

In one of Sennacherib's last historical records, "The Temple of the New Year's Festival" (i.e., *bīt Akīti*), he describes himself as the creator of irrigation networks *par excellence*. Although this self-description might be read as only a literary cliché, in Sennacherib's case, his actual achievements justify this depiction:

> ... who digs canals, opens wells, runs irrigation-ditches,... who furnishes water for irrigation to Assyria's meadows, engineering (lit., digging) and construction such as none has seen in Assyria in days of olds, none had known of those (kings) who preceded, none made.[23]

This astounding succession of hydraulic engineering and incomparable irrigation networks (703–690 BCE) by which Sennacherib transformed the barren environment of his new capital, Nineveh, into a garden of almost paradisiacal fertility, was *ana tabrât kiššat nišê*, "to the astonishment of all nations."[24] Thus we can safely assume that such unparalleled records of achievement might find their proper echoes in 2 Kings 19:24. The Rabshakeh, proud of his master's great domestic accomplishments, finds it suitable to mention Sennacherib's much-praised irrigation undertaking. More specifically, 2 Kings 19:24 (= Isa. 37:25): *ʾny qrty wštyty mym zrym wʾḥrb bkp pʿmy kl yʾwry mṣwr*, refers historically to Sennacherib's second outstanding irrigation account: the Mount Muṣri operation, dating to the year 694 BCE.

Regardless of prevailing theories dealing with the historical and geographical location of *Māṣôr*, we would like to suggest the identification of the biblical *Māṣôr* in 2 Kings 19:24 (= Isa. 37:25) with the more appropriate Mesopotamian geographical site *šadê Muṣri*, "Mount Muṣri." The Akkadian *namba'ū*, "water springs (/streams)"[25] that Sennacherib "found" (Akk.: *āmur*) at "the foot of Mt. Muṣri" are the historical and the geographical equivalent of the biblical *ye'ōrê Māṣôr*, "the water pools/streams of (Mount) *Māṣôr*," located northeast of Nineveh. Even though the water springs/streams at the foot of Mount Muṣri are already known from the inscriptions of Sargon to be upstream from Nineveh: e.g., "at that time I built a city by the water springs (/ streams) which at the foot of Mount Muṣri, a mountain upstream from Nineveh, *Dūr-Šarrukîn* I named it,"[26] Sennacherib was the first one to utilize these springs for the irrigation of Nineveh. It should be observed that the land of Muṣri was conquered by the Assyrians in the twelfth century BCE. When the people of Muṣri later revolted, the land was recaptured by Aššurdan II. When Muṣri appears again in the Sargonid period, the region is already an integral part of Assyria proper.[27] During Sargon's and Sennacherib's reigns, however, which overlap Isaiah's and Micah's time, the reference seems to be to the mountain *šadî Muṣri*, "Mount Muṣri." Thus, according to Jacobsen and Lloyd, Mount Muṣri is known as the modern mountains of Jebel Bashiqah.[28] Excavations at Tel Billah near Bashiqa has established beyond a doubt that this tell covers the ancient city of Shibaniba. Therefore, we may expect to find the towns Elmanakinne, Dūr-Ištar, Sulu, and Shibaniba, which are mentioned in Sennacherib's second irrigation chronicle — the Mount Muṣri operation — in the vicinity of Tell Billah. Furthermore, according to Jacobsen and Lloyd, we know that Dūr-Ištar and Sulu, unlike Shibaniba, were situated on the mountain streams at the foot of Mount Muṣri, which carries water all year round.

The historical-geographical account of Sennacherib's second

irrigation chronicle dating from 694-BCE — the Mount Muṣri operation as recorded in 2 Kings 19:24 (= Isa. 37:25) — may be rendered as follows:

> I have dug[29] and drunk flowing[30] waters;
> I have drained[31] with the soles of my feet[32] all the streams[33] of (Mount) *Māṣôr*.[34]

In the light of this suggested identification of the Hebrew *Māṣôr* in 2 Kings 19:24 (= Isa. 37:25) with the Mesopotamian geographical site (š*adê*) Muṣri, "(Mount) *Muṣur*," we would like to touch briefly upon the crucial historical problem of Sennacherib's campaign(s) in Biblical Israel. The account of the Assyrian invasion against Hezekiah in 2 Kings 18:13 to 19:37 (= Isa. 36–37) presents a difficult problem. Does our account contain the record of one military campaign or two? As Brevard S. Childs pointed out: "few problems within the Old Testament have evoked such steady streams of monographs and articles as has the account of the Assyrian invasion of Palestine. It has become a classic issue on which each new generation of biblical scholars seems constrained to test its mettle."[35] Indeed, an impasse appears to have been reached. The historical evidence required to understand the actual historical sequence of events appears to be unavailable. John Bright, in the second edition of his *A History of Israel*, likewise admits that "without any consensus having been arrived at (concerning this historical problem), it is probable that none will be, short of the discovery of fresh extra-biblical evidence — say, Sennacherib's official annals for approximately the last decade of his reign (if such ever existed)."[36] Presently, our goal is not to enter into the details of this complex debate. Rather, we wish to summarize the biblical accounts and the two major interpretative theories concerning these accounts. We will then provide our own point of view on the topic.

The biblical account is comprised of three distinguishable parts:[37]

1. Account A: 2 Kings 18:13–16: (lacking in Isaiah):

Sennacherib invades Judah and captures all the fortified cities. Hezekiah, convinced of the great Assyrian threat, does not resist and sends an offer of submission to Sennacherib, who was fighting at Lachish at that time. Sennacherib, accepting Hezekiah's surrender, imposes a heavy tribute upon him. The biblical account essentially agrees with the main features of Sennacherib's third campaign in Biblical Israel in 701 BCE as recorded in his annals.

2. Account B1: 2 Kings 18:17–19:9a. 36f (= Isa. 36:1 ff.): this account contains the story of the mission of the Rabshakeh to Jerusalem. It elaborately discusses the fruitless efforts of the Rabshakeh to convince Hezekiah's ministers to surrender. Hezekiah depends on Isaiah's prophecy of salvation and does not surrender. The Rabshakeh returns to Sennacherib whom he finds fighting in Libnah.
3. Account B2: 2 Kings 19:9b-35 (= Isa. 37:9b-36): this record includes the second expedition sent by Sennacherib to Hezekiah. After hearing about the approach of the Egyptian king Tirhakah and his army, Sennacherib sends threatening letters to Jerusalem. When Hezekiah seeks Isaiah's advice, Isaiah assured Hezekiah that Jerusalem would be saved and that the Assyrian army would be defeated. Isaiah's prophecy is fulfilled: Sennacherib lost 185,000 soldiers in one night. His defeat forces him to return to Nineveh.

Scholars attempting to reconstruct the above accounts produced the following two basic theories: a) the theory of one campaign[38] and b) the theory of two campaigns.[39] The theory of one campaign proceeds as follows: Sennacherib invaded Biblical Israel only once and was successful in repressing the revolts in Phoenicia and the southern coastal cities. These victories convinced Hezekiah that resistance was hopeless. He therefore sued for peace. Sennacherib imposed heavy tribute upon him but left Jerusalem unharmed. Afterwards, Sennacherib, perhaps because of the approach of the new Egyptian force under Tirhakah (2 Kings 19:9), regretted his leniency and changed his mind. This threat caused Sennacherib to fear that Hezekiah would cause trouble at his rear. Sennacherib, therefore, demanded complete capitulation and surrender of the city. Hezekiah, supported by Isaiah's prophecy of salvation, refused to comply. Then quite suddenly, either because his army had been afflicted by disease, or because he was needed at home, Sennacherib was forced to withdraw, leaving the city intact.

Scholars maintaining the theory of two campaigns, however, suggest that 2 Kings has telescoped the account of the two campaigns into one narrative. The first campaign is the one in 701 BCE (2 Kings 18:13–16; lacking in Isaiah), and the second is in the year 689/688 BCE. This theory fully explains the 2 Kings references to Tirhakah. Bright proposes the following reconstruction: while Sennacherib was engaged in subduing Babylon after his defeat by the Babylonians and Elamites in 691 BCE, a further rebellion flared in the west, backed by Tirhakah, into which Hezekiah was drawn. Since Sennacherib disposed of Babylon in 689 BCE, he possibly moved against Biblical Israel in 688 BCE. It was then that the Assyrians suffered an unexpected setback and the dramatic deliverance of Jerusalem took place.

According to the advocates of the two-campaign theory, the one-campaign theory suffers from one major historical flaw: the Egyptian king Tirhakah (Egyptian: Tirhaqa) cannot have ruled Egypt during Sennacherib's third campaign in the year 701 BCE. As argued by Horn,[40] the date of Tirhakah's coronation is certainly in 690–689 BCE, eleven or twelve years after Sennacherib's invasion of Biblical Israel. On the other hand, Tadmor,[41] an advocate of the one-campaign theory, proposes the following argument encompassing both the Assyrian and biblical points of view: a) Sennacherib had no further interest in the west after his campaign in 701 BCE, since he was concentrating on the transformation of Nineveh into his new capital; and b) the late prophetic story of source 2 (2 Kings 18:13; 18:17–19:37; Isa. 36–37) telescopes events (a practice used in Babylonian chronicles). For example,

Sennacherib's assassination is presented as following immediately after his return to Nineveh from Judah, while in fact it took place twenty-one years later. The mention of Tirhakah may be a result of the same process, according to which the name of a well-known king who had repeatedly fought against Assyria supplanted that of a less-known Nubian who was the adversary of Sennacherib. According to Tadmor, this late prophetic story, probably written in the second half of the seventh century, dates to fifty years after the event.

The Mount Muṣri operation, Sennacherib's second irrigation complex, is recorded and dated in the month of Ab in the eponymy of Ilu-ittīya, the governor of Damascus, in the summer of 694 BCE.[42] This prism contains two military campaigns against Cilicia, one in 698 and then again 695 BCE. The concluding section — which occupies nearly half of the text of the cylinder — contains an amplification of Sennacherib's building achievements described in the earlier prisms, as well as an elaboration of his new accomplishments that took place during the six years that elapsed from the time of the writing of the "Rassam Cylinder,"[43] dated in the *līmu* of Metunu in 700 BCE. Between 700 and 694 BCE, Sennacherib records one irrigation undertaking, i.e., the Mount Muṣri operation. Thus, after briefly referring to the canal that he constructed from Kisiri in 703 BCE (col. viii 22–30), Sennacherib recounts the need for new water sources, which he finally drew from the springs/streams at the foot of Mount Muṣri (col. viii 31–49). We can reasonably infer that since this prism was written in 694 BCE, and since the Mount Muṣri operation definitely took place between 700 and 694 BCE (probably towards the end of this period), that the Rabshakeh's boastful reference to Sennacherib's Mount Muṣri irrigation network as recorded in 2 Kings 19:24 could not have occurred prior to 700 BCE. Thus, the Mount Muṣri operation could have been mentioned by the Rabshakeh only following 694 BCE, probably during the second invasion in 689/688 BCE. Accordingly, if our identification of the biblical *yeʾōrê Māṣôr* with the Mesopotamian *nambaʾē ša (šēpe)* Muṣri, "the water springs/streams (at the foot) of (Mount)

Muṣri," is correct, the mention of the Mount Muṣri operation by the Rabshakeh in 2 Kings 19:24 may strengthen the historicity of account B2 (2 Kings 19b-35), and may be further evidence for those who advocate the theory of Sennacherib's second campaign against Hezekiah in the year 689/688 BCE. On the other hand, for scholars who consider the second account as a late prophetic story that telescopes events, 2 Kings 19:24 (= Isa. 37:25) and the Mount Muṣri operation should obviously be construed as follows: the magnificent system of Mount Muṣri was known to the writer or the compiler after its completion (around 684 BCE). He then (many years after the event) recorded this monumental construction by skillfully telescoping it in the Rabshakeh's speech, written with the intention of maximizing the importance of Sennacherib's glorified domestic royal accomplishment of transforming the barren area of Nineveh into a paradise on earth.

Finally, something should be said concerning the use of *Māṣôr* in Mic. 7:12. The verse reads:

> *ywm hwʾ wʿdyk ybwʾ lmny ʾšwr*
> *wʿry mṣwr wlmny mṣwr wʿd nhr*
> *wym mym whr hhr.*

The majority of modern biblical critics have long held the view that Micah 7, particularly vv. 7–20, are to be attributed to the post-exilic period.[44] The section is assumed to have been added to Micah's original oracles at the time when the book was edited. This assumption seems to be based primarily on the theory that a prophet would seriously weaken the force of his prophecy of doom if he immediately followed that prophecy with a prophecy of promise. In the light of this theory, the oracle of promise in Mic. 7:11–12 is considered by those critics to be a prediction of the restoration day of those who had seen the exiled from Jerusalem in 586 BCE. The oracle is, therefore, assigned to the first half of the fifth century. Scholars who oppose the above view maintain that this theory is difficult on the following grounds: a) it disregards the importance of the northern kingdom and its downfall (in 722 BCE) in the religious thought of Israel; and b) it ignores the lack of textual evidence for assigning the oracle after the Judean exile.[45] Furthermore, these scholars assert that Micah does not mention Jerusalem in chap. 7; they point out that the mention of Assyria, Carmel, Bashan, and Gilead in vv. 12 and 14 refers to the historical and geographical horizon of the northern kingdom.

Our purposes in broaching this issue is merely to point out the possibility that the historical background of the restoration motif in Mic. 7:12 is not the fall of Jerusalem, but rather the fall of Samaria. Accordingly, if my suggested identification of the Assyrian *Muṣru* with Hebrew *Māṣôr* (in 2 Kings 19:24 = Isa. 37:25) is correct, Micah, not unlike Isaiah, also refers to the same Assyrian geographical site. That is to say that Micah in his restoration prophecy describes the anticipated triumphal return of the dispersed Israelites from all the regions to which they were carried by the Assyrian king Sargon (720 BCE). According to Micah, they will come streaming from *wym mym*, "from sea to sea," i.e., from the Great Sea (Mediterranean) to the Lower Sea (Persian Gulf); from *whr hhr*, "from mountain to mountain," i.e., from the Taurus mountain region (in the west) to the Zagros mountain region (in the east). Geographically, while the general territorial appellation "from sea to sea, from mountain to mountain,"[46] would cover the peripheral borders of the Assyrian empire, Micah, Isaiah's contemporary, also uses the more specific historical-geographical location: *lmny ʾšwr wʿry mṣwr wlmny mṣwr wʿd nhr*, "from Assyria and the cities of *Māṣôr*, and from *Māṣôr* (the mountain region in the northeast) to the river (the Euphrates in the south)," which covers the heartland of the Assyrian empire,[47] to the place where (according to 2 Kings 17:6; 18:11) the exiles of Samaria were led. Thus, in Mic. 7:12, the identification of *ʿry mṣwr*, "the cities of *Māṣôr*," with the same four towns mentioned in Sennacherib's Mount Muṣri irrigation operation (694 BCE) is historically and geographically justifiable. Therefore, the *ʿry mṣwr* are better identified with Elamunakinne, Dūr-Ištar, Šibaniba, and Sulu — all situated at the foot of the Mount Muṣur[48] — instead of the more generally accepted Egypt or Tyre.[49] Thus, in addition to the biblical Ḫalaḫ, Ḫabor, Gozan in 2 Kings 17:6,[50] one may now also add Micah's "cities of *Māṣôr*" as another resettlement location for Samaria's exiles.

NOTES

1. Concerning text critical problems and preferred readings in 2 Kings 18–19 (= Isa. 36–37), see the summary discussion of Brevard S. Childs, *Isaiah and the Assyrian Crisis: Studies in Biblical Theology*, (2d ser. vol. 3 Illinois: Naperville, 1967), 3:137–40.
2. For a complete discussion of this expression, see n. 30 below.
3. *The New English Bible*, (New York: Oxford University Press, 1970), 409 [hereafter *NEB*].
4. *The Prophets*, (Philadelphia: The Jewish Publication Society of America 1978), 328 [hereafter *NJPS*].
5. *The Interpreter's Bible: the Holy Scriptures in the King James and Revised standard versions with general articles and introduction, exegesis, exposition for each book of the Bible*, (vol. 3; New York: Abingon Press, 1954), 3:301.
6. Edward J. Kissane, *The Book of Isaiah*, (vol. 2; Dublin: Browne and Nolan Limited, 1943), 2:399.
7. See James A. Montgomery, *A Critical and Exegetical Commentary on the Books of Kings* (ed. Henry S. Gehman; Edinburgh: T. & T. Clark, 1951), 504. See also S. Ahituv, "*maṣôr*" *Encyclopedia Biblica*,(S. Sukenik and M. Cassuto; Jerusalem: Biyalik Institute, 1968), 5:235 (Hebrew); *NEB* 409; *NJPS*, 328.
8. David Qimḥi, *The Commentary of David Kimhi on Isaiah* (ed. Louis Finkelstein, New York: AMS Press, 1966), 11–12.
9. Paul J. Calderone, "The Rivers of *Māṣôr*," *Biblica* 42 (1961), 423.
10. Ibid., 423–32. Calderone's argument (ibid., 428. n. 1) that in all five attestations of *Māṣôr* the *mem* is to be considered enclictic seems difficult to accept.
11. *Lexicon in Veteris Testamenti Libros* (Leiden: E.J. Brill 1958), 557. For other opinions expressed as to the meaning of *Māṣôr*, see Calderone, "Rivers," 323–24.
12. Hayim Tadmor, "The Campaign of Sargon II of Assur: A Chronological-Historical Study," *JCS* 12 (1958), 77 n. 178.
13. Thorkild Jacobsen and Senton Lloyd, *Sennacherib's Aqueduct at Jerwan*, (OIP 24; Chicago, Illinois: University of Chicago Press, 1935), 31–43 [hereafter OIP 24].
14. David D. Luckenbill, *The Annals of Sennacherib*, OIP 2 (Chicago,

Illinois: University of Chicago Press, 1924), 98, lines 89–90 [hereafter OIP 2; the translations given are not necessarily those of Luckenbill].

15. OIP 24, 33.
16. OIP 2, 94, lines 66–70.
17. Ibid., 103, lines 38–50.
18. Ibid., 114, lines 25–30.
19. Ibid., 114–15, lines 31–42.
20. For a discussion, see OIP 24, 36–38.
21. OIP 2, 79, lines 6–12.
22. For a complete discussion, see OIP 24, 19–27.
23. OIP 2, 135–36, lines 11–17.
24. Ibid., 111, line 50. Although this statement was made by Sennacherib referring to his outstanding palaces, he could have also applied it to his grand irrigation networks as well.
25. Akkadian *nambaʾu* (*AHw*, 726b) is employed from Middle Babylonian onwards to connote "spring of water/seepage," e.g., *nambaʾī uptalliša ana babāli kuppu*, "water springs (holes) were drilled in order to produce catchwaters" (*En. Eliš* V 58). In Neo-Assyrian, *nambaʾu* is employed in Sargon's (Lyon, *Sargon*, 42:39) and Sennacherib's (OIP 2, p. 114, line 34) inscriptions, specifically referring to the water springs located at the foot of Mount *Muṣri*. Furthermore, Akkadian *nambaʾu* is the etymological equivalent of Hebrew *mbwʿ* (cf. Delitzsch, *HWB*, 442) attested three times in Deutero-Isaiah and Ecclesiastes, i.e., *mbwʿ*// *bwr*, "water spring/water-hole" (Ecc. 12:6); *ʾgm*//*mbwʿy mym*, "pond/ water springs" (Isa. 35:7); Hebrew *bwʿy mym* (Isa. 49:10) is the exact etymological semantic equivalent of Akkadian *nambaʾu ša mê*, "water seepage" (Streck. *Asb*, 74, ix, line 31). In short, Hebrew *yeʾōrê Māṣôr* as employed in 2 Kings 19:24 (= Isa. 37:25) is best identified with the Akkadian *nambaʾē ša (šēpe) Muṣri*, "the water springs/streams at the foot of (mount) *Muṣri*" (Lynn, *Sargon*, p. 42, line 39).
26. Lyon, *Sargon*, 49, line 39, Mount Muṣri is attested three more times in Sargon's inscriptions, e.g., "According to my wish at the foot of *Muṣri*, a mountain, I built a city: Dūr-Šarrukên I named it," (Lyon, *Sargon*, 54, lines 9–13; cf. also ibid., 56, lines 7–11; Lyons, *Sargon*, 74, lines 9–10). For a full discussion of *māt Muṣri*, "the region of *Muṣri*," B. Landsberger and T. Bauer "Zu neuveroffentlichen Geschicjtsquellen der Zeit von Asarhaddon bis Nabonid," *ZA* 37 (1927): 75–76; P. Garelli, *Dictionaire de la Bible*, suppl., vol. 5 (Paris, 1957), 1468b-1470. For a discussion of the Old Aramaic *mṣr* in *Sefîre* IA:5, see Joseph A. Fitzmyer, *The Aramaic Inscriptions of Sefîre*, Biblica et Orientalia, no. 19 (Rome: Editrice Pontificio Istituto Biblico, 1967), 29–31. Fitzmyer, who follows Dupont-Sommer, assumes that *Sefîre mṣr* is a country in

southern Anatolia or in northern Syria. This suggestion was argued by Tadmor in Hayim Tadmor, "Notes on the Opening Lines of the Sefîre Treaty," in *S. Yevin Festschrift*, (Jerusalem: Bialik Institute, 1970), 388–89 (Hebrew), who equates Sefîre's use of *mṣr* with Akkadian *miṣru*, "border."

27. See Tadmor, "Que and Muṣri," *IEJ* 11 (1961), 146.
28. OIP 24, 35–36. For a general discussion concerning the identification of Muṣri, see also Tadmor, "Que and Muṣri," 143–50.
29. The verb *qrty* (derived from the root *qwr*) as employed in 2 Kings 19:24 (= Isa. 37:25) is rendered by Tg. Ps. J. as *ʾnʾ hwyt ḥpyr* "I have dug." Although the meaning of the Hebrew seems uncertain (*NJPS*, 328), contextually the majority of scholars follow the Targum's rendering "to dig." In this specific irrigation context, however, Hebrew *qwr* seems to be the functional equivalent of Akkadian *ḫerû* commonly employed in reference to digging canals/wells for irrigation purposes (*CAD* Ḫ 175; *AHw* 341b).
30. The expression *mym zrym*, which traditionally is rendered as "foreign waters/waters of stranger/waters of foreign lands" (see above, 195), is used once more in Jer. 18:14 in sequence with *qrym*, "cold," and *nwzlym*, "flowing." Tg. Ps.-J. renders the Jeremiah expression as *my mṭr nḥtyn*, "rain waters which come down." This rendering assumes *zwrmym*, "running/pouring," for the MT *zrym*. For a discussion, see L.A. Snijders "The Meaning of *zr* in the Old Testament: An Exegetical Study," *Oudtestamentlische Studien* 10 (1954), 48–51; cf. also Wilhelm Rudolph, *Jeremia*, (Handbuch zum Aten Testament, vol. 12; Tubingen: Mohr Siebeck, 1968), 120. Contextually, the accepted rendering "foreign waters/water of foreigner" seems difficult. If our identification of the biblical *Māṣôr* with (Mount) *Muṣri* in Mesopotamia and not with Egypt is correct, the Mount Muṣri region in the time of Sargon-Sennacherib was already an integral part of Assyria proper and not considered foreign territory (see above). Accordingly, it seems preferable to assume the reading *my-m zrm* (enclitic *mem*), "flowing waters/a torrent of waters," a stream of water flowing with great velocity or an abundant or tumultuous flow, fitting well the context of 2 Kings 19:24. This assumption may gain some ground when noting that Akkadian uses the following expression to connote flowing/running waters in contexts involving irrigation works. A few examples will suffice: *mê nuḫušti*, "abundant waters," "he conceived the idea of opening the springs of its arable land into catchwaters and irrigation everywhere, with abundant water as a huge waves of the (annual) inundation" (Lyon, *Sargon*, p. 34, lines 36–37); "The outlet of the river... opened by itself and let through an abundant supply of water" (OIP 2, 81, lines

30–31. Sennacherib). Note also the following expressions for "flowing/abundant/everlasting waters": *mê ḫegalli* (e.g., LIH 95, col. I:19 951, line 19)/*mê kuzbi* (e.g., M. Civil, "'The Message of LÚ-DINGIR-RA to His Mother' and a group of Akkado-Hittite 'Proverbs.'" *JNES* 23 [1964]: 2, line 38)/*mê duššūti* (e.g., *TCL* 3 + *KAH* 2 141, line 221)/*mê dārûti* (OIP 2, P. 98, line 90, Sennacherib). Furthermore, in cuneiform texts concerning irrigation networks, the reference is always to digging canals/conduits in order to carry flowing/abundant water. This could be illustrated, for example, from Sargon's irrigation system as Ulḫu: "he (Ursâ) dug a main canal which carried flowing waters, and... waters of abundance he caused to flow like the Euprates" (J. Laessøe, "The Irrigation System at Ulḫu, 8th Century B.C.," *JCS* [1951]:21). Accordingly, in 2 Kings 19:24, Sennacherib apparently refers to digging (Heb.: *qwr.* Akk.: *ḫerû*) water (canal) (Heb: *mym.* Akk.: *palgu*) which carried (Heb.: *ʾaḥrib.* Akk.:*bābil*) flowing waters (Heb.: *my-m zrm.* Akk.: *mê šurdūti*) from the water springs (Heb.:*yʾwry.* Akk.: *nambaʾē*) situated at the foot of (Mount) Muṣri (Heb.: *mṣwr.* Akk.: *Muṣri*) to his capital Nineveh.

31. Lit., "I have dried up." Contextually, our rendering of Heb. *wʾḥryb* as "I have drained" (cf. the sequence *dll-ḥrb*, "ebb/dry up" in Isa. 19:6) takes into consideration the sense of decreasing, lessening, reducing, and bringing low the water streams of *Maṣor* with the intention to cause the water to flow out from its source. Note further that in 2 King 19:23–24, alongside the verbs *ʿlyty*, "I have attended"; *qrty*, "I have dug"; *štyty*, "I have drunk," together with the LXX we should also read *waʾkrt*, "I have cut down"; *waʾḥryb*, "I have drained (lit., "dried up"), both with *waw* consecutive. The use of the perfect in 2 Kings 19:23–24 will then be comparable with the perfect of the narrative typically employed in the Assyrian annals.

32. The Heb. idiom *bkp pʿmy,* which literally means "with the sole of my feet," and which poetically seems to express the notion of endless efforts, may historically refer to Sennacherib's Mount Muṣur operation. That is to say that Sennacherib declares boastfully that in spite of the great geographical difficulties (Akk.: *šupšuqiš*), he and his men were able to scale the mountain on foot (Akk.: *attallak*) and reach and utilize the streams which were situated at the foot of Mount Muṣur (OIP 24, 114, lines 31–32; cf. ibid., 6).

33. Note that Heb. *yeʾōr(ê)* (an Egyptian loan word) is used in the Bible mainly either in reference to the Nile or to the water streams/pools of the Nile. In Job 28:10, however, *yeʾōrîm* simply means (mountain) "streams." In 2 Kings 19:24 (= Isa. 37:25), *yeʾōrê* may have a more general meaning, such as flowing waters, either in pools or in streams.

Therefore, it seems best to adapt S.D. Luzzato's (*Il Proffeta Isaia* [Padua, 1867], 150) interpretation that states that the reference is not to the actual rivers of Egypt. Rather, the prophet calls all great rivers by the name of the Nile because it is big. Note also the use of Heb. *yeʾōr* in Dan. 12:5–6 in reference to the Euphrates.

34. The use of *yeʾōrê māṣôr* in Isa. 19:6 is orthographically puzzling. The chapter is an oracle against Egypt. It is intriguing to find the form *miṣrayim* employed twenty-seven times in chap. 19, but *māṣôr* only once.
35. Childs, *Isaiah and the Assyrian Crises*, 11.
36. John Bright, *A History of Israel*, (Philadelphia: Westminster Press, 1972), 296.
37. For a full discussion with extensive bibliography, see Childs, *Isaiah*, 69–103.
38. For a discussion and listing of the literature concerning the one-campaign view, see Bright, *History of Israel*, 296–308; see esp. 296, n. 1.
39. For a discussion and listing of selected bibliography, see ibid., 297, n. 4.
40. S. H. Horn, "Did Sennacherib Campaign Once or Twice Against Hezekiah?" *Andrews University Seminar Studies* 4 (1966), 1–28; see esp. 3–11.
41. Hayim Tadmor, "Judah from the Fall of Samaria to the Fall of Jerusalem" in *A History of the Jewish People*, (ed. H. H. Ben-Sasson; Cambridge, Mass: Harvard University Press, 1976), 143–145; Kenneth A. Kitchen, *The Third Intermediate Period in Egypt (1100–650 B.C.)*, (Warminster, England: Aris and Phillips 1986), 154–72 and 383–86.
42. OIP 2, p. 116, line 88.
43. For a description of Sennacherib's improvements in Nineveh, see *CT*, vol. 26, pp. 16 ff.
44. For a discussion of Mic. 7: 11–12, consult the major commentaries and introductions; see also James L. Mays, *Micah*, (The Old Testament Library; Philadelphia: Westminster Press, 1976), 160–62.
45. Yehezkel Kaufmann, *The Religion of Israel*, (Jerusalem: Mossad Bialik, 1967), 3: 278 (Hebrew); J. Licht, *Encyclopaedia Biblica*, 4:886 (Hebrew); E. Hammershaimb, *Some Aspects of Old Testament Prophecy from Isaiah to Malachi*, (Copenhagen: Teologiske Skirfter, 1966) 41–42; B. Reicke, "Liturgical Traditions in Mic. 7," *Harvard Theological Review* 60 (1967), 349–67; see esp. pp. 363–64.
46. The majority of commentators and translators read: *wmym ʿd ym wmhr ʿd hr*. Moreover, it is worthwhile noting that the general geographical appellation "sea and mountain" are likewise employed in the neo-Assyrian policy of deportation. Esarhaddon states proudly that

he ordered the people who dwelt on the sea-shore (i.e., west) to be resettled in the mountain regions (i.e., east) and those who dwelt in the mountain region to be resettled on the seashore: *ša tāmti ana šadî ana tāmti ašahšumu aqhi* (R. Borger, *Die Inschriften Asarhaddons Konigs von Assyrien*, AfO Beiheit 9, p. 58, line 20.)

47. From the Neo-Assyrian annals that deal with the Assyrian deportation, we learn that out of fifty-nine cases, which are approximately eighty-five percent of the known cases, the heartland of Assyria was the main resettlement location. For a discussion, cf. Bustenay Oded, *Mass Deportations and deportees in the Neo-Assyrian Empire* (Wiesbaden: Reichert, 1979), 27 ff. More specifically, with regard to the fall of Samaria and the resettlement of its people, Sargon declares clearly that the resettlement took place in Assyria (i.e., Assyria proper): "The rest of them (the Samarians) I settled in the midst of Assyria. The city of Samaria I resettled and made it greater than before"; see Tadmor, "The Campaigns of Sargon II of Assur," *JCS* 12 (1958), 34.
48. OIP 2, p. 114, lines 31–33. Note also that these cities are mentioned once again by Sennacherib cf. OIP 2, 79, line 9). For a complete discussion, see OIP 24, 39–40.
49. For a discussion, see Calderone, "rovers," 430–432. Additional evidence against Egypt or Tyre may be gleaned from the fact that there is no historical evidence that the exiles of Samaria were ever deported to these two places.
50. These were the northern Mesopotamian regions where the exiles of Samaria were transported. For evidence of North-Israelite deportees in Mesopotamia, see William F. Albright, "An Ostracon from Calah and the North-Israelite Diaspora," *BASOR* 149 (1958), 33–36. Note that Tadmor expressed the opinion that the Mesopotamian places that are mentioned in 2 Kings 19:12 may likewise constitute an additional resettlement location of Samaria's exiles; see Tadmor, "On the History of Samaria in the Biblical Period," *Eretz Shomron* (ed. Yosef Abriram, Jerusalem: Society for the Study of Israel and its Antiquity, 1973), 71 (Hebrew).

Amos' Oracles against the Nations: A New Interpretation

לאבי יוסף,

כִּי יְשָׁרִים יִשְׁכְּנוּ אָרֶץ
וּתְמִימִים יִוָּתְרוּ בָהּ
(משלי ב:כ"א)

Shalom Paul, in his commentary on Amos, reviews the difficult problems concerning the sequential ordering of Amos' oracles against the nations (Amos 1:2–2:16) as follows:

> Commentators on the Book of Amos have had to come to grips with the historical, chronological, and literary problems of the first six oracles against the nations of Aram, Philistia, Tyre, Edom, Ammon, and Moab. Are the historical events alluded to here contemporaneous with the prophet Amos, or do they represent heinous crimes of the past, that is, are they pre- Jeroboam II? Are the oracles against Tyre, Edom, and Judah original or secondary? If secondary, are they exilic or post-exilic? Were these prophecies originally independent, self-contained units, or were they from the very outset a single literary unit?... Are the first six oracles against the foreign nations ordered in any recognizably logical fashion?[1]

Indeed, Andersen and Freedman, in their Anchor Bible commentary, maintain that the "order and arrangement of the nations probably defy rational analysis except for the one point, on which all interpreters seem to be agreed, that Israel should come last."[2] The purpose of the present paper is to briefly summarize the various theories and propose our own interpretation.

There are nine theories concerning the logic behind the prophet's ordering of the nations. A) The *ritualistic theory* (Bentzen):[3]

The sequential order of Amos' eight prophecies was modeled on the cultic patter. This resembles and draws analogy from the ritual behind Egyptian Execration texts (19–18 cent. BCE), in which the neighboring nations appear in a fixed sequential order ending with Egypt. B) *The geographical theory* (Marti):[4] The sequential order of the oracles is self-understood to be naturally geographic. Amos opens with a prophecy against Damascus (north) and ends with Moab (south). C) *The ethnological-genealogical theory* (Riedel):[5] This theory asserts that for Amos, Israel, which stands at the climax of the series, is the closest nation to the prophet. Israel's brother, Judah, follows. Judah is then followed by the cousins Moab, Ammon, Edom. Farther is Tyre, with the most distant being Philistia and Aram. D) *The psychological theory* (Weiser):[6] This theory maintains that the order reflects the degree of forceful enmity as perceived by Israel. Accordingly, the Arameans and the Philistines should stand at the top of the list. E) *The covenant festival theory* (Reventlow):[7] He posits that behind Amos 1–2 is a cursing-ritual associated with a festival proclaiming the covenant. F) *The military theory* (Wellhausen):[8] The sequential order of the nations was arranged in accordance with Assyria's military plan as envisaged by Amos. G) *The mixed motifs theory* (Wolff):[9] Wolff maintains that the nations are arranged in authentic groups according to different criteria: Aram and Philistia are mentioned first since they are the ancient enemies of Israel, followed by Ammon and Moab which are neighbors and blood related. H) *The political theory* (Kaufmann):[10] Kaufmann proposed that the order of the nations was to be understood as an alternating listing of the enemies of Israel and Judah respectively.

Concerning the above main theories, Paul comments:

> These important insights, however, did not lead to any further understanding of the overall literary patter Amos employed in his presentation of the oracles. The question may still be posed: Why does Philistia come immediately

> after Aram, and why is it followed by Tyre, which is succeeded, in turn, by Edom, Ammon, and Moab?

Paul then advances his own theory: I) *The literary theory*:[11] This theory maintains that:

> An internal literary order can be discerned that weaves the various units into a coherent whole. Each link in this chain of oracles can be shown to be tied to one another by an indissoluble bond characterized by the well-known literary mnemonic device of concatenation of similar catchwords, phrases, or ideas shared only by the two contiguous units.

Further, apart from the difficult question concerning the logical process behind Amos' sequential order of the nations, the authenticity of some of the oracles was likewise questioned. More specifically, the general argument brought forth against the authenticity of the oracles against Tyre, Edom, Judah (and also Philistia), is that they deviate from the structural outline of the other prophecies. This, therefore, reveals the hands of late editors.[12]

The composition of Amos 1:2–2:16 is indeed a literary masterpiece from both contextual and structural points of view. These 30 verses, when broken into various distinct units, reveal the manner in which Amos' powerful message is conveyed within an extremely constrained literary discipline. Although various scholars doubt the authorship of one oracle or another, nevertheless, from the intricate literary arrangement of the oracles, Amos 1:2–2:16 seems to exhibit one integrate and original entity.[13] This assumption will be further strengthened when we advance our own thesis as to the reasoning behind Amos' ordering of the oracles against the nations. The composition of Amos 1:2–2:16 contains numerous internal rhetorical devices and external compositional constructions that seem to unify the various units into a convincing whole: 1) *parallelismus memborum*[14] — negative parallelism.[15] 2) *An opening messenger formula — kw ʾmr yhwh*

"Thus said the Lord," which introduces each oracle against the eight nations followed by: 3) *preposition introductory literary element* — *ʿl+wʿl+ʿl* "For + and for + because," introducing either a simple or a complex sentence followed by a subject pronoun. 4) *The graded numerical sequence* — (the climactic number) commonly referred to as X/X +1/*šlšh -ʾrbʿh* "three-four."[16] This stylistic phenomenon not only distinguishes these prophetical components (in Amos 1:3- 2:16), but also unites them. Together they express a totality. 5) *Idiomatic reduplication* — an internal literary order weaves the various units into a coherent whole. These oracles are tied to one another by well-known, "literary mnemonic device of concatenation of similar catchwords, phrases, or ideas shared by the two contiguous units."[17] 6) *Concluding messenger formula* — at the end of each oracle, i.e., *ʾmr yhwh* "Said the Lord."

Furthermore, as a literary aesthete, Amos clearly shows a great fondness for expressing himself in 7) *Patterns that comprise heptad*,[18] namely, using the number seven as a symbolic figure representing totality, completion, and climax. This phenomenon is employed by Amos more than ten times — four of which are attested to in our own short unit (Amos 1:2–2:16): a) Seven divine speech formulas (Amos 1:3, 6, 11, 13; 2:1, 4, 6). b) Israel's seven transgressions (Amos 2:6c-8). c) The Lord's seven goodnesses (Amos 2:9–11). d) The realization of the impending seven catastrophes (Amos 2:14–16).

The following architectural literary device is employed by Amos in yet another structural figure of speech. It serves as a long range connection, linking and unifying the whole. Namely, 8) *Ascending staircase parallelism*,[19] where seven items are listed followed by a climactic statement. In this pattern of seven-eight (or seven + one), eight functions as the paired number with seven in the ascending staircase parallelism. According to James Limburg, this seven + one numerical scheme, employed a few times by Amos, is contained in small literary units.[20] In Amos 1:2–2:16, however, the ascending staircase parallelism phenomenon is utilized intentionally by the prophet to, literarily and thematically, tie together all of these expanded units. As noted and well stated by Paul: "Amos... resorted to this alternative literary pattern" to express "finality and climactic culmination in order to take his captive northern audience by surprise. This audience of Israel, believing that Amos had reached the climax of his fulmination with his oracle against Judah, is stunned the moment he continued with the eighth oracle against them."[21] Accordingly, in contrast to those who maintain that the oracles against Tyre, Edom, and Judah are secondary and post-exilic, and in light of Amos' strict usage of the literary pattern seven-eight (7+1), we may attribute the entire unit (Amos 1:2–2:16) to the prophet himself. While this attribution links all the nations together in one literary piece, the difficult problem as to why Amos chooses the present sequential order remains unsolved. Accordingly, in order to fully comprehend Amos' reason(s) for the nations sequential ordering, one must probe into the prophet's psychological state of mind at the time he addressed his audience.[22] Consequently, if possible, the spoken nature as well as the body language of the prophetic discourse must be taken into consideration. This prophetic discourse was executed by yet another elaborate rhetorical technique — this time by the employment of the well-known chiasmus. Chiastic arrangement — involving key words — becomes the controlling structure not only for individual verses, but for strophes and entire poems in Amos. The chiastic pattern is widely employed through the entire book.[23] Apart from our own unit (i.e., Amos 1:2–2:16), the chiastic rhetorical device is employed in various patterns over twenty times: a) complete chiasmus bicola: AB//BA.[24] b) Chiasmus in tetracolon AB//BA.[25] c) Hexacola chiastic order ABC//CBA.[26] d) Large-scale chiasmus ABCD//DCBA.[27]

More specifically, in the oracles against the nations (Amos 1:2–2:16), we find the following chiastic patterns: a) Complete chiasmus bicola: (AB/BA) Amos 2:4 (*ʿl mʾsm -twrt yhwh//wḥqyw — lʾ šmrw).* b) Chiasmus in tetracolon: (AB//BA) Amos 2:11–12 (*nbyʾym-nzrym//nzyrym-nbyʾym.)* c) The ABA chiastic tricolon: Amos 1:3 *ʿl šlšh pšʿy dmśq — ʿl ʾrbʿh lʾ ʾšybnw — ʿl dwśm bḥrṣwt hbrzl ʾt hglʿd.* d) Chiasmus in a longer passage: (AB/BA) Amos 1:12–2:16.[28]

Moab	Ammon
Judah's enemy	Israel's enemy
Israel	Judah

Amos' use of the chiastic pattern, along with a plethora of other literary devices, indicates that he was, indeed, the master of the oral style of his time. More specifically, the pattern common to the oracles against the nations seems to be the creation of Amos. As so rightly noted by Mays:

> In its (the oracle's) construction he shows the capacity to assimilate forms of motifs from a variety of spheres and traditions to fashion a speech appropriate for his message which is characteristic of his prophecy... He is not bound to one background or tradition, adopting broadly from available possibilities of communications, and fashioning original moments in the history of speech.[29]

Accordingly, Amos opens the oracles against the nations (Amos 1:2–2:16) with a thunderous statement of inescapable total annihilation (Amos 1:2): "He proclaimed: The Lord roars from Zion/And thunders from Jerusalem/So that the shepherds' pastures dry up/And the summit of Carmel withers." The basic charge is leveled against all the nations. Namely, the eight nations are accused of revolting against divine will. The revolt implied in Amos 1:2–2:16 is against the Lord, the universal Lord whose sphere of influence extends over all the nations. Although all nations broke their treaty with God, there is a clear-cut distinction between the nature and essence of the transgressions of the nation and those of Judah and Israel. Thus, Paul maintains correctly that while the nature of Judah's and Israel's transgression against the Lord is religious-moral-ethical, the violations of the remaining nations are different. They "flout divine authority whenever they commit major acts of barbarity and atrocity against fellow nations. For such crimes both Judah-Israel and the nations are found guilty of revolting against the Lord of history who in turn, holds them directly accountable and execute punitive action against them."[30] In the light of these numerous transgressions, an irrevocable decision has been made by God ("I will not reverse it")[31] to destroy each of the eight nations. They all have equal standing before God; all are equally guilty and will suffer equivalent fates: they will be obliterated from the face of the earth; they will be erased from the map.

Amos, the master and inventor of various literary devices, likewise uses his impressive chiasmus, this time not as a literary ploy, but rather as an external structural symbol. Namely, the prophet use the chiasmus technique in its literal sense, i.e. chiazein, which means "to mark with the (Greek) letter *chi* (=X, i.e., a cross or crossover)." More specifically, Amos employs the Ancient Hebrew sign X=*Taw*, the last letter of the Alphabet, to clearly transmit the idea of an end, cancellation, and obliteration, i.e., crossing out; in our own case (Amos 1:2–2:16), crossing out the eight nation from the face of the map. Accordingly, our proposed solution to the reasoning behind Amos' sequential arrangement of the nations will attempt to possibly demonstrate: a) the deliberate and rational nature of his ordering, and b) his psychological state of mind in conjunction with his body movements at the time he addressed his audience with his prophecy.

Structurally, Amos begins his sequential arrangement of the nations with the northeast city of Damascus, representing Aram. He then moves to Gaza, the farthest town in the southwest, representing Philistia. He then changes direction to Tyre in the northwest, which represents Phoenicia. And finally, he travels to Bozrah, the most distant city in the southeast, representing Edom. Accordingly, by the depiction of the present ordering, Amos skillfully employs two artistic devices, a literary one and a structural one. He utilizes his favorite rhetorical device, the chiasmus, to express the notion of *merismus*, namely, an expression of totality. In our case, the mention of the representative parts of totality may be named a directional chiasmus.

(south) WEST ⟍⟋ (north) WEST
(south) EAST ⟋⟍ (north) EAST

This directional chiasmus also comes to express the notion of *merismus*, that is, the totality of the geographical area with which the prophet is concerned.

The entire geographical area that the eight nations occupy is doomed for total annihilation. Accordingly, Amos utilizes the sign *X*, the last letter of the Alphabet, to structurally cross out from the map all eight nations. Two diagonal lines dissect the map: from right to left, from Damascus to Gaza; from left to right, from Tyre to Bozrah. These diagonal lines crisscross Judah and Israel, located in the center of Amos' four corners. All the nations are doomed to a devastating destruction; they are all equally guilty. The insignia of God[32] is engraved upon them.

The sign of the twenty-second letter of the Hebrew Alphabet, *Taw*, consists of two crisscrossing diagonal lines: an *X*.[33] The word *Taw* is employed in BH three times as a noun and twice as a verb. Accordingly, the idiom *htwh tw* comes to connote, "to put a mark," i.e., to mark with a *Taw* (1 Sam. 21:14; Ezek. 9:4).[34] *Taw* = *X* was likewise utilized as a personal mark (Ezek. 9:6), a signature of an illiterate. In Job 31:35, it is employed in its broader denotation "writ": *my ytn ly šmʿ ly hn twy šdy yʿnny wspr ktb ʾyš ryby* "Oh that he would listen to me that Shaddai would answer my writ and my adversary would write a letter."[35] Furthermore, it seems likely that Amos reveals another, as yet unattested, function of the letter *X* (*Chi* = *Taw*). He utilizes the shape of X to structurally convey the notion of cancellation, erasure, effacement, and blotting out. The prophet's structure of discourse, which has a strong impact on his audience, must indeed be taken into account. As noted by Gitay, "an orator carefully plans his speech in order to reach his audience. The opening must attract the audience as raise its curiosity to listen to the rest of the discourse."[36] More specifically, Amos' intention was to strongly communicate his message not only orally by spoken prophetic discourse, but also by means of a body language that utilizes the gestures. Accordingly, one may attempt to draw the following picture.

The prophet faces his audience and thunderously opens with v. 2, which paints God's appearance as a roaring lion, thus manifesting Himself by means of lighting and thunder. The result of God's appearance produces a cataclysmic reverberation and destructive upheaval in the cosmos. This is continued by indictments of sweeping concatenation of prophetic oracles that follow one another with breathtaking incisiveness. The prophet then turns and faces the northeast raising his hands towards Damascus and prophesies against Aram (Amos 1:3–5). While his hand is still raised upwards, he turns halfway, slowly lowering his hand towards the southwest, pointing to Gaza, the most southern city of Philistia and enumerates its transgressions (Amos 1:2–8). Afterwards, he lifts his hand once more in the direction of Tyre, in the northwest, indicting Phoenicia (Amos 2:9–10). Finally the prophet moves his hand away from Tyre and lowers it down towards its end destination Bozrah, the most southern city of the southeast, representing the entire eastern area. As a result, while crisscrossing Judah and Israel, Amos clearly draws the letter *Taw* = *X*. This marks the effacement of the eight nations from the face of the map, i.e., the earth. He indeed draws two crosswise *ṣiliptu* "diagonals."[37]

If our thesis that Amos draws the letter *Taw* = *X* to express the idea of obliteration is correct, then the scholarly debate concerning the authenticity and the originality of the oracles against Tyre, Edom, and Philistia seem superfluous. That is to say, Amos intentionally selected the most southern cities, Gaza in the southwest and Bozrah in the southeast, to convey the notion of total geographical inclusion. More specifically, the depiction of Tyre and not Sidon in the northwest, and Gaza and not, for example, Ashkelon in the southwest, was likewise intentional. The prophet seems to be aware of the close correspondence in distance between Damascus and Gaza and between Tyre and Bozrah. Namely, Amos appears to be cognizant of the fact that the distance between Damascus and Gaza (approximately 172

8/10 miles as the crow flies) is almost identical to the distance between of Tyre and Bozrah (approximately 170 4/10 miles), an approximate difference of one mile.[38]

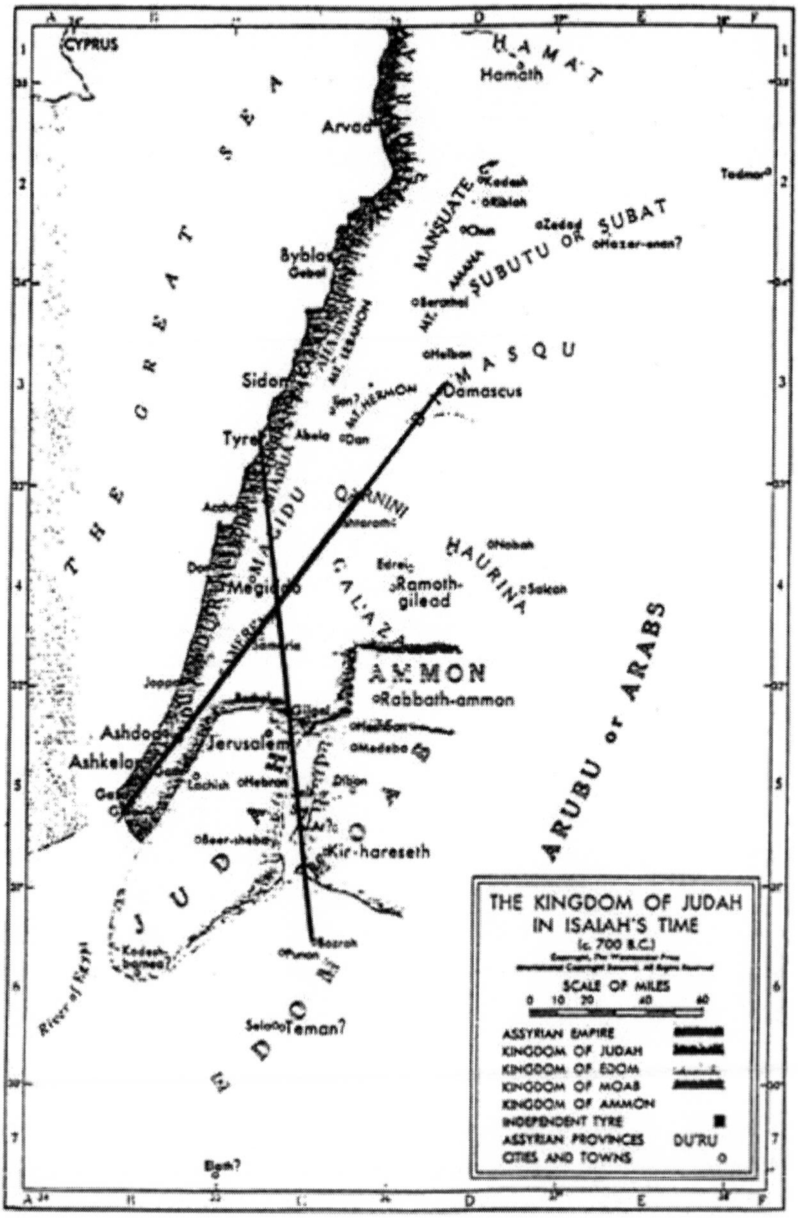

NOTES

1. See S.M. Paul, *Amos: a Commentary on the Book of Amos,* (Hermeneia; Minneapolis: Fortress Press, 1991) 11. For a full bibliography concerning Amos' oracles against the nations, see esp. Paul (ibid.); H.W. Wolff, *Dodekapropheton 2. Joel und Amos (BKAT* 14,2; Neukirchen-Vluyn: Neukirchener Verlag 1969); Joel and Amos: A commentary on the books of the Prophets Joel and Amos (tr. W. Janzen, S.D. McBride, Jr., and C.A. Muenchow; ed. S.D. McBride, Jr.; Hermeneia; Philadelphia: Fortress Press, 1977); J.L. Mays, *Amos: A Commentary* (OTL; Philadelphia: Westminster Press, 1969); F.I. Andersen and D.N. Freedman *Amos: the Anchor Bible* (Anchor Bible; New York: Doubleday, 1989); M. Weiss, *The Book of Amos* (Jerusalem: Magnes Press, 1992) vols. 1–2 (Heb.).
2. Ibid., 28.
3. A. Bentzen, "The Ritual Background of Amos I 2-ii 16," *OTS* (1950), 85–99. For critical notes on Bentzen's theory, see M. Weiss, "The Patter of Execration Texts in the Prophetic Literature," *IEJ* 19 (1969), 150–157. Cf. also Paul, Amos, 11.
4. K. Marti, "Zur Komposition von Amos 1,3–2,3," *BZAW* 33 (1918), 232–330.
5. W. Riedel, "Bemerkungen zum Buche Amos," *Altestamentliche Untersuchungen,* 1 (1902),19–36.
6. A. Weiser, *Die Profetie des Amos* (*BZAW* 53, 1929), 86–87.
7. H.G. Reventlow, *Das Amt des Propheten bei Amos (FRLANT* 80: Göttingen: Vandenhoeck & Ruprecht, 1962), 64.
8. J. Wellhausen, *Die Kleinen Propheten ubersetzt und erklart* (Berlin: Reiner, 1898; Berlin: de Gruyter 1963), 68, 75.
9. Wolff. *Amos*, 144–148.
10. Y. Kaufmann, *Toledoth Ha-Emunah Ha-Yisraelith*, (Jeruslaem: Mosad Biyalik, 1957), vol. 6, 63 (Heb.)
11. See Paul, *Amos*, 13–15 cf. also *idem,* "Amos 1:3–2:3: A Concatenous Literary Pattern," *JBL* (1971), 397–403.
12. Paul, *Amos,* 16–19.
13. Paul, *ibid.*
14. Cf. e.g. *nʾwt rwʿym/rʾš hkrml; ʾbl//ybš šʾg//ntn qwl; ṣywm//yswšlym* (Amos 1:2); *byt ḥzʾl//ʾrmnwt bn hdd* (v. 4); *ywšb//twmk šbṭ* (vv. 5, 7); *hšb yd//ʾbd* (v. 8); *trp//šmr; ʾp//ʿbrh; ʿd//nṣḥ* (v.11); *sʿr//swph; trwʿh//ym mlḥmh* (v.15); *trwʿh//qwl šwpr* (Amos 2:12); *šwpṭ/śrym; krt//hrg* (v.3); *twrh//ḥwq* (v.4); *ksp//nʿlym* (i.e., nʿlm) sliver//shoes (i.e., hidden gains); *ṣdyq//ʾbywn* (v.6); *dl//ʿnwym* (v.7); *mmʿl//ntḥt; pry//šrš; gbn//ḥsn; ʾrzym//*

ʾlwnym (v.9); *nbyʾym//nzyrym; bnym//bḥwrym* (v.11); *ql/ḥzq/gbwr* (v.14); *tpś hqšt//ql brqlym//rkb hsws* (v.15).

15. E.g. *lʾ šmr//mʾs.* Cf. also Amos v. 14 *(ṭwb//lʾ rʿ)*; 18, 20 *(ḥšk//lʾ ʿwr)*; 20 *(ʾpl//lʾ ngh)*.
16. See H.L. Ginsberg, "Towards the History of the Graded Number Sequence," in *Minḥa leDavid* (Jerusalem, 1935), 78–82 (Heb.); W.M.W Roth, "The Numerical Sequence X/X +1 in the Old Testament," *VT* 12 (1962): 300–311; *idem. Numerical Saying in the Old Testament: A Form-Critical Study* (SVT 13; Leiden: E.J. Brill, 1965); M. Weiss, "The patter of Numerical Sequence in Amos 1–2, A Re-Examination," *JBL* 86 (1967), 416–423; M. Haran, "Biblical Studies: The Literary Application of the Numerical Sequence X/X +1 and their Connections with the Patterns of Parallelism," *Tarbiẓ* 39 (1970),109- 36 (Heb.); S.E. Lowenstamm, "The Phrase 'X (or) X Plus One' in Biblical and Old Oriental Laws," *Bib* 53 (1972), 542; Y. Zakovitch, "*For Three... and for Four": The Pattern of the Numerical Sequence in the Bible* (Jerusalem: Hebrew University, 1979) (Heb.).
17. See S.M. Paul, "A Literary Reinvestigation of the Oracles against the Nations of Amos," in *De la Torah au Messie: Études d'exégese al d'herméneutique bibliques offertes á Henri Cazelles* (ed. J. Dore, P. Grelot, and M. Carrez; Paris: Desclée 1981), 189–204.
18. See Weiss, Sequence ibid., n. 16; *idem, Amos* vol. 2, 16–17; Y. Avishur, "The Forms of Repetition of Numbers indication Wholeness (3, 7, 10) — in the Bible and in Ancient Semitic Literature," *Beer-Sheva,* 1 (1973),1–55 (Heb.); J. Limburg, "Sevenfold Structure in the Book of Amos," *JBL* 106 (1987), 217–22.
19. See Paul, *Amos*, 22–23 for full discussion and bibliography.
20. *Ibid.,* n. 18.
21. Paul, *Amos,* 24.
22. Y. Gitay, "A Study of Amos's Art of Speech, A Rhetorical Analysis of Amos 3:1–15," *CBQ* 42 (1980), 293–309.
23. For a discussion on chiasmus, see the following major studies: N.W. Lund, *Chiasmus in the New Testament: A study in the form and function of chiastic structures* (Peabody, Mass: Hendrickson Publishers, 1992); Francis I. Andersen, *The Sentence in Biblical Hebrew* (The Hauge: Mouton, 1947), 119–140; *idem* "the AB:BA Word Pattern in Hebrew and Northwest Semetic with Special Reference to the Book of Job," *UF* 7 (1975), 73–88; Anthony R. Cersko, "The Chiastic Word Pattern in Hebrew," *CBQ* 38 (1976), 303–311; J.D. Waard. "The Chiastic Structure of Amos v 1–17," *VT* 17 (1977), 170–177; Anthony R. Ceresko, "The Function of Chiasmus in Hebrew Poetry," *CBQ* 40 (1978), 1–10; John.

M. Welch ed., *Chiasmus in Antiquity: Structures, Analyses, Exegesis* (Hildsesheim: Gerstenberg, 1981), cf. esp. 50–168.

24. 1) Amos 4:7 (*whmṭry -ʿl ʿyr ʾḥt//wʿl ʿyr ʾḥt-lʾ ʾmṭyr*). 2) Amos 5:2 (*nplh lʾ twsyp qwm//nṭšh-ʾyn mqymh*). 3) Amos 5:7 (*hhpkym-mšpṭ//ṣdqh-hnyḥw)*. 4) Amos 5:9 (*mblyg ʿl ʿz//ʿl mbṣr-ybʾ*). 6) Amos 6:12 (*rʾš-mšpṭ// pry ṣdq-lʿnh)*. 7) Amos 7:9 (*nšmw-bmwt yśḥq//mqdšy yśrʾl-yḥrbw*). 8) Amos 7:11 (*bḥrb ywmt-yrbʿm//yśrʾl glh yglh*). 9) Amos 9:7 *(bny kšyym-bny yśrʾl//yśrʾl-plštym/ʾrm*) 10) Amos 9:8 (*mmlkh ḥṭʾh-hšmdty// lʾ šmd ʾšmyd-byt yʿqb*). 11) Amos 9:16 (*gdrty-prṣyh//hrystyw-ʾqym*). 12) Complete chiasmus (ABC//CBA) Amos 9:6 (*hbwnh-bšmym-mʿlwtw// wʾgdtw-ʿl ʾrṣ//ysdh*).
25. 1) Amos 5:10–12 (no justice in the courts — oppressing the poor// oppressing the poor — no justice in the courts). 2) Amos 7:14–15 (*nbyʾ-bwqr/bwls šqmym//mʾḥry hṣʾn//lk hnbʾ*). 3) Amos 9:3c-4 (*ʿyny-ʾṣwh//ṣwh// ʿyny*). 4) Amos v 14–15 (*ṭwb-rʿ//rʿṭwb*).
26. Amos 5:4b-6a (ABC//CBA) *dršwny wḥyw-byt ʾl-glgl//glgl-byt ʾl-dršwny wḥyw*.
27. Amos 9:1–4 was originally identified by Lund (cf. Lund, *Chiasmus in the New Testament.*, 86–87 n. 119). Note also that as it was discovered by Waard (Waard, "The Chiastic Structure of Amos," n. 23), that the complex of this chiastic structure (i.e., ABCD//DCBA) was likewise developed by Amos (5:1–17) to include 17 verses.
28. See Zakovitch, *"For Three... and Four,"* 185 n. 16.
29. Mays, *Amos*, p. 25.
30. Ibid., 46.
31. For another interpretation, see A. R. Cersko "Janus Parallelism in Amos's Oracles against the Nations," *JBL* 113 (1994), 485–490.
32. It is of interest to know that b. *Šabb.* 55a comments on the function of the Heb. letter *Taw* as related in Ezek. 9:4 as follows: "and why *Taw*? Said Rab, *Taw* (stands for) *tiḥyê* ('you shall live'), *Taw* (stands for) *tāmût* ('you shall die'). Samuel said: the *Taw* denotes the merit of the patriarchs is exhausted (*tammāh*). R' Jonathan said: the merit of the Patriarchs will confer grace (*tāḥôn*). While Resh Lakish said: *Taw* is the end of the seal of the Holy One, blessed be He. For R' Hanina said the seal of the Hold one, blessed be He is the *emet* (truth)…."
33. See e.g., D. Diringer, *The Alphabet: A Key to the History of Mankind* (London; New York: Hutchinson's Scientific and Technical Publications, 1948), 153; G.R. Driver, *Semitic Writing From Pictograph to Alphabet* (London; New York: Oxford University Press, 1976), esp. 89 n. 3 and 192–193; Joseph Naveh, *Early History of the Alphabet: an introduction to West Semitic epigraphy and palaeography* (Jerusalem: Magnes Press, Hebrew University; Leiden: Brill, 1982), 51–76; Ada

Yardeni, *The Book of Hebrew Script: History, Palaeography, Script Styles, Calligraphy and Design*, (Jerusalem: Carta, 1997), 18–28 (Heb.).

34. Note that the letter X was used as a builders' mark, cf. S. A. Lowenshtam "Building" *Encyclopedia Bibilica* (Jerusalem: Biyalik, 1965), 2:187, fig 8, bot. (Heb.).
35. See N.H. Tur-Sinai (H. Torczyner), *The Book of Job* (Jerusalem: Mosad Rav Kook, 1967), 246–247, 447–448.
36. See Gitay "A Study of Amos's Art of Speech," 307 n.22.
37. See my article, "Hebrew *slp* Mishnaic Hebrew *ṣlp* Akkadian *ṣalāpu/ ṣullupu*: A Lexicographical Note II," *Beit Mikra* 146 (1996), 276–292.
38. See, *The Westminster Historical Atlas to the Bible* (eds. G.E. Wright and F.V. Filson. (Philadelphia: Westminster Press, 1956), 51 b-c.

Bathing in Milk (Songs 5:12): A New Look

Songs 5:12 reads:

עֵינָיו כְּיוֹנִים עַל אֲפִיקֵי מָיִם
רֹחֲצוֹת בֶּחָלָב יֹשְׁבוֹת עַל מִלֵּאת

NJPS renders:

> His eyes are like doves by watercourses,
> Bathed in milk, set by brimming pools.

In describing the beauty of the male-lover from head to toe (5:10–15), we encounter three problems in verse 12: (a) The connotation of the lexeme מִלֵּאת. (b) Depending on the interpretation of מלאת, what is then the subject of the verse? Is it the lover's eyes or the doves? (c) What does the imagery "bathing in milk" symbolize?

Marvin Pope concedes that "the meaning of this unique expression *yôšebot 'l-millē't* is uncertain."[1] Rashi, Ibn-Ezra, Rashbam, and some modern scholars[2] equated our vocable with מלאת/מלואים, employed in Ex. 25:7; 28:17; 35:9, 27, a reference to setting jewels and inlaying precious stone. Accordingly, understanding the lover's eyes to be the subject of verse 12, Rashbam comments:

> ועיניו ישבות על מלאת בתוך גלגלי העין בשוה כאבן כטבעת, לא בולטות ולא עמוקות כענין שנאמר וּמִלֵּאתָ בו מִלֻּאַת אֶבֶן וגו'

> His eyes, well-fitted in their sockets, sit flat in their sockets like a stone in a ring, neither protruding nor sunken, just as described in the verse "set in it mounted stone," etc. (Ex. 28:17).

Murphy, who follows Rudolph,[3] understands ישבות על מלאת "set in place" (lit., "sitting in fullness,") as a reference to the "firmness of the teeth set in the gums."[4] He thus inserts into his translation

"<his teeth>, washed in milk, set in place," asserting that "the insertion of 'teeth' makes the metaphor of the milk bath and fullness more intelligible."[5]

Doubting the lover's eyes as the subject of 5:12b, Fox rightly states:

> Only "like doves" belongs to the simile proper. The rest of the verse is an explanation of the picture of the doves and does not apply directly to the eyes. The attempt to relate every part of the image to the eyes quickly runs aground. If the milk is the whites of his eyes, how can his eyes bathe in them? If "eyes" here — and only here — means pupils, which may be said to bathe in the whites of the eyes, what do the pupils have in common with doves, which are neither dark nor round? And if the entire image refers back to his eyes, are they sitting by the water channels (tear ducts?) *or* bathing in milk (the whites of the eyes?), *or* sitting by a pool or bowl (sockets?). Eyes cannot do all these things, even figuratively, but doves can do them — one after another. In other words, everything after "doves" describes doves, not eyes, and what is pictured is not a static scene but a series of actions that doves can do. The doves take a life of their own.[6]

The second most common explanation of the hapax מלאת is to contextually understand the word as expressing some sort of water collection. Such is the understanding of both the LXX and the Vulgate, which translate "sitting by the fullness of water." Accordingly, Harper suggests an emendation to *mēlo hammayīm* (sitting upon) "full streams."[7] Indeed, as noted by Pope, "context appears to favor brimming pool."[8] Although the noun is considered by NJPS as "meaning of Heb. uncertain," nevertheless, they translate מלאת as "brimming pool," namely a pool full of/flooded with water. Similarly, Meek (who also considers "the meaning of the Hebrew uncertain"), while rendering ישבות על מלאת as "fitly set," seems to defend the American Translation of the Bible ("sitting by pools") by equating the Heb. מלאת with Akk. *mīlu* "flood."[9] Akk. *mīlu* (*mīl'u*), derived from the verb *malû* "full," comes to specifically connote "flooding of rivers and springs."[10] Accordingly, the Heb. *hapax* מלאת may pertain to the flooding of the"water-courses" (i.e., אפיקי מים). Further, as noted by Tur-Sinai,[11] Heb. מלאת finds its equivalent in the Late Heb. word מליתה in Midrash *Gen. Rab*. 95:

> ...שלחה אשתו (של חנניה) ואמרה לו: בתך בגרה בה והשיאה... מה עבד אזל למליתה שמע קלהן דמלוותיה אמרן בתו שלחכיניי מליי קולתיך וסוק ליך
>
> ...(Hannaniah's) wife sent to him and said: "your daughter came of age; come and get her married"... what did he do (in order to find his family?) he went to the brimming pool, he heard the water drawers when they said: "daughter (of Hannaniah son) of Hakhinai fill up your pitcher and go"....[12]

Accordingly, in the light of the parallelism אפיקי מים//חלב//מלאת, the Akk. equivalent *mīlu*, and the Late Heb. מליתה, it seems best to interpret the Heb. *hapax* מלאת as a pool flooded with water, i.e., "brimming pool," the natural resting place for the doves.

It should be further noted that while the compound אפיקי מים "watercourses" and the noun מלאת "brimming pool" fits the context of 5:12, the imagery רֹחֲצוֹת בחלב "bathing in milk," is problematic and unclear. Pope rightly states that "doves are fond of bathing and choose their abodes in regions with abundant water, but they rarely have the opportunity to bathe in milk."[13] In the light of this difficulty, he adopts the medieval exegetes' explanation that the subject of the whole verse is the lover's eyes. He thus asserts that "the bright eyes of the lover, the dark pupils encircled by milky white eyeballs, remind the poet of doves bathing in pellucid streams."[14] Fox, on the other hand, notes that "the image of doves bathing in milk is a fantasy picture, and it is hard to see what actual event could underlie it."[15] Nevertheless, Fox explains "the image emphasizes whiteness and conveys a sense of a luxury and delicacy, for milk was white, thick, and smooth. The contrast between the blackness of the boy's hair and the whiteness of his eyes is sharpened by the contrast between ravens (v.11) and doves."[16] Keel maintains that "bathing in milk also suggests fortunate circumstances, because it is possible only when milk is abundant... the milk baths indicate that the poet is talking about white doves."[17]

As noted above, the subject of the second and the third clauses of verse 12 are the doves and not the lover's eyes. Hence, similar to ישבות על מלאת "sitting on brimming pools," רחצות בחלב "washing in milk" should also refer to the doves and not (the white of) the eyes. Accordingly, a different solution is to interpret the image of "washing in milk," not literally, but rather figuratively. That is to say, the poet employs חלב "milk" to depict the whiteness of the foaming water of the brimming/flooded pool. While in BH the whiteness, brightness, and clarity of the milk is depicted as לְבֶן שִׁנַּיִם מֵחָלָב "his (Judah's) teeth are whiter than milk" (Gen. 49:12), and also (זַכּוּ [נְזִירֶיהָ] מִשֶּׁלֶג//) צַחוּ מֵחָלָב "(whiter than snow//) lighter than milk" (Lam. 4:7). חלב is not employed in BH to describe the whiteness of the foaming water.[18] Our assumption that חלב in Songs 5:12 is used as imagery to portray the foaming water of the flooded water pool, however, may gain ground when noting the usage of Akk. *šizbu* "milk" when employed in simile to describe the whiteness of the water.

In the omen series *šumma ālu (ina mêlî šakin)* "If a city (is situated on a hill)," we learn that milk seems to be figuratively employed to describe the whiteness of foaming water, (a sign of total war): *šumma mīlu šizbi ina ḫīeīt āli innamir kakku mitḫāriš iššakanū kussû kussâ idarris* "if a flood of milk appears in a moat of a town, they will prepare everywhere for war, one throne will overthrow the other."[19] Further, Akk. *šizbu* "milk" is metaphorically employed to describe the whiteness of the foaming water (a sign of rage): *šumma mû kīma šizbi peṣû uz[zat E]a* "if the water is white as milk, the ra[ge of E]a."[20] More specifically, an almost identical image in Songs is found again in the *Šumma ālu* series. The foaming water (i.e., *mû*) of the river (i.e., *nāru*) in spate (i.e., *mīlu)* is depicted as white (i.e., *peṣû*) as a milk (i.e., *šizbu*)*: šumma nāru ina mīli mûša kīma šizbi peṣû uzzat Ea* "If the water of a river in spate is as white as milk, the rage of Ea."[21]

In short, our interpretation of the idiomatic imagery "bathing in milk" is to be understood figuratively. Namely, the doves are resting on the watercourses and the flooded pool, bathing in their foaming waters that are white as milk.

NOTES

1. M. Pope, *Song of Songs: A New Commentary and Translation* (Anchor Bible; Garden City, New York: Doubleday, 1977), 538.
2. Cf. *RSV*; *KJ*; *NAB*. For a full discussion, see Pope, *Song of Songs*, 538–539. Cf. also, A. Robert et R. Toumay, *Le Cantique des Cantiques* (Paris, 1963), 214–216; Gillis Gerleman, *Ruih, Das Hohelied: BKAT*, XVII, 2–3 (Neukirchen-Vluyn: Neukrichener Verlag, 1965), 174.
3. W. Rudolph, *Das Buch Ruth. Das Hohelied, Die Khgelieder: KATXXVII/1*–3 (Gütersloth: Gerd Wohn, 1962), 158–159.
4. R. E. Murphy, *The Song of Songs* (Hermenia; Minneapolis: Fortress Press, 1990), 166.
5. Murphy, *Song of Songs,* 172.
6. M. V. Fox, *The Song of Songs and the Ancient Egyptian Love Songs* (Madison, Wis.: University of Wisconsin Press, 1985), 147–8.
7. A. Harper, *The Song of Solomon: With Introduction and Notes* (Cambridge Bible: Cambridge: University Press, 1907), 40.
8. Pope, *Song of Songs,* 539.
9. T. Meek, *The Interpreter's Bible* (12 vols.; New York, Abingdon Press 1956), 5:129.
10. *CAD* M/II, 69–72; *AHw*, 652–3.
11. N. H. Tur-Sinai, *Ha-Lashon weha-Sepher* (2 vols.; Jerusalem: Magnes, 1960), 2:379 (Heb.).
12. Ch. Albek, *Bereshit Rabba,* vol. II (Jerusalem, 1965), 1232.
13. Pope, *Song of Songs,* 538.
14. Ibid. Cf. also Robert Gordis, *The Song of Songs: A Study, Modern Translation, and Commentary* (New York: JTS, 1954), 90.
15. Fox, *Song of Songs,* 148.
16. Ibid.
17. O. Keel, *The Song of Songs: A Continental Commentary* (Minneapolis: Fortress Press, 1994), 199.
18. For the idea of foam upon the water: Heb: כקצף על פני המים (Hos. 10:7)

= Akk *kī hubbuš pān mê* "like foam on the surface of the water," see C. Cohen, "'Foam' in Hosea 10:7," *JANESCU* 2/1 (1969), 25–9.

19. *CT* 39 21:158.
20. *CT* 39 21:149.
21. *CT* 39 23:34.

Tāphat the Daughter of Solomon

לְבִתִּי טָפַת

הֲיִי לְאַלְפֵי רְבָבָה

I

Three sources, one early and two late, portray King Solomon as a great king with a large harem. While the Chronicler is completely silent as to Solomon's extraordinary harem,[1] the Deuteronomist in 1 Kings 11:1–3 recounts Solomon's marriages to his wives and concubines as follows:

> King Solomon loved many foreign women in addition to Pharaoh's daughter — Moabite, Ammonite, Edomite, Phoenician, and Hittite women... He had seven hundred royal wives and three hundred concubines....

The account of Solomon's many wives may have been alluded to in the famous verse in Ecc. 7:28: "As for what I sought further but did not find, I found only one human being in a thousand, and the one I found among so many was never a woman." So too, according to Song of Songs 6:8, Solomon's harem consisted of "sixty queens, and eighty concubines, and damsels without number." The apparent reason for Solomon's numerous marriages was summarized by Abraham Malamat as follows:

> Of all the kings of Israel and Judah, Solomon is the most renowned for his widespread use of international marriages which formed the cornerstone of his foreign policy. This style of foreign diplomacy is not unlike that practiced by the Austrian Hapsburg Dynasty (1282–1918)... Indeed, political marriages were a means of 'ratifying' peace treaties between nations in the ancient Near East.[2]

The immediate family members of Solomon's father and son are recorded by names in the books of Samuel and Chronicles.[3] But for some unknown reasons (perhaps the intentional touch of the Deuteronomistic editor), the information concerning Solomon's family members is surprisingly meager. In 1 Kings and 2 Chr., only one wife and one son are recorded by name: the queen mother (i.e., הגבירה = Akk. *ša ekalli*),[4] Solomon's first wife from his early marriage, Naama the Ammonite (1 Kgs. 14:21, 31:2 Chr. 12:13), and her son, the crown prince Rehoboam (1 Kings 11:43; 14:21; 2 Chr. 9:31).

While not mentioned by name, of all Solomon's wives, the pride of the palace at the royal court was accorded to the Queen (i.e.,אשת המלך) *par excellence*, בת פרעה "the daughter of Pharaoh." Although for some unclear reason, Donald Redford rejects out of hand the historicity of the biblical account, asserting that "the present writer personally has a little more difficulty in construing Solomon's marriage to Pharaoh's daughter as historical."[5] Redford further considers Solomon's marriage to the daughter of Pharaoh as a Deuteronomistic ploy, which "must remain themes for Midrash or fictional treatment."[6] On the other hand, among many other historians, Malamat and Kitchen[7] regard this great diplomatic marriage as a historical event, pre-Deuteronomistic and of archival nature. Malamat further states:

> The marriage of Solomon to Pharaoh's daughter appears in five different unrelated contexts in the Bible. Each of the references is of an archival nature, and supremely significant fact... that, the kings of Egypt frequently took the daughters of foreign potentates as wives, there is no other attested instance' apart from that of Solomon of a *daughter* of Pharaoh being given in marriage to a foreign ruler....[8] This fivefold repetition indicates the special importance this marriage carried in Israelite historiography and disposes of any question as to the historical veracity of the event.[9]

The records of King Solomon's rule begin with the following account: (a) "Solomon allied himself by marriage with Pharaoh, king of Egypt. He married Pharaoh's daughter and brought her to the city of David [to live there] until he had finished building his: palace..." (I Kings 3:1). In the course of the description of Solomon's royal palaces', which lasted thirteen years, we learn that, (b) "Solomon also constructed a palace like that portico for the daughter of Pharaoh, whom he had married" (I Kings 7:8). We further learn about the relationship between Solomon and his father-in-law Pharaoh Siamun:[10] (c) "Pharaoh, king of Egypt, had come and captured Gezer; he destroyed it by fire... and gave it as a dowry to his daughter, Solomon's wife" (I Kings 9:16). Solomon finally finished the construction of his palace complex as well as the palace of his wife, (i.e., אשת שלמה) daughter of Pharaoh: (d) "Pharaoh's daughter, went up from the city of David to the palace that he had built for her" (I Kings 9:24; II Chr. 8:11). Finally, among Solomon's unnamed numerous foreign wives, the daughter of Pharaoh is conspicuous: (e) "Now, King Solomon loved many foreign women, especially the daughter of Pharaoh, and Moabite, Ammonite, Edomite, Sidonian, and Hittite women" (I Kings 11:1).

The event of Solomon's diplomatic marriage to the daughter of Pharaoh superseded that of Naama, the Ammonite princess, whose diplomatic marriage was arranged by Solomon's father David, who still sat on the throne at the time of his son's marriage. Consequently, Solomon's father-in-law was Pharaoh Siamun from the rulers of the Egyptian twenty-first dynasty, who reigned between 978–959 BCE. Thus, as noted by Malamat[11] and Kitchen,[12] from the chronological biblical evidences we learn indirectly that the time of Solomon's wedding to the daughter of Pharaoh was in his first years, perhaps in the third or the fourth year of his reign. This diplomatic marriage opened a new era of detente that lasted twenty years, until the destruction of the twenty-first dynasty by Sheshonq in 945 BCE.

Furthermore, alongside the biblical mention of the queen mother Naama, her son, the crown prince, Rehoboam, as well as Solomon's chosen wife, the daughter of Pharaoh, we learn from the biblical records in 1 Kings that Solomon had additional daughters טָפַת and בָּשְׂמַת.

II

The names of the two daughters of Solomon are mentioned in a most important document that has survived from the reign of Solomon. It is preserved in the list of the twelve prefects along with the description of the regions they governed (1 Kings 4:7–19). The list is therefore of a special importance, not only for the understanding of Solomon's realm, but also for this type of geographical texts, which generally are used by biblical compilers for the description of other matters. It is generally agreed upon that the list is an archival, authentic document that the Deuteronomist himself adds nothing that we can recognize. He allows his source to speak for itself. Accordingly, the document is probably an extract from the Book of Solomon's Acts (1 Kings 11:41).[13] Solomon's purpose for this extraordinary administrative division was mainly economic. This is stated in 1 Kings 4:7: "Solomon had twelve prefects governing all Israel, who provided food for, the king and his household; each had to provide food for one month in the year."[14]

The names of the two daughters of Solomon are recorded in connection with their marriage to two of the king's prefects. Taphat married Ben-abinadab the prefect of Dor (טפת בת שלמה היתה לו לאשה. 1 Kings 4:1), and Basemath married Ahimaaz the prefect of Naphtali (גם הוא לקח את בשׂמת בת שלמה לו לאשה 1 Kings 4:15). The mere mention of these two princesses is indeed revealing: it depicts the royal status that Taphat and Basemath held in Solomon's court. Likewise, it points out the high rank that their respective husbands occupied in Solomon's administration.[15] It should be further noted that while the personal name Taphat is indeed a *hapax*, nowhere else attested in biblical and post-biblical sources, the personal name Basemath is mentioned six times — only in the book of Genesis — as the daughter of Ishmael[16] and the wife of Esau.[17] The name also occurs outside of the Hebrew

Bible, in Minaean for a woman from Gazah married to a Minaean merchant (3rd century BCE), and in a Sabean inscription for a man (i.e., Basam).[18] While the name Basemath is derived from *bośem/beśem* "sweet-smelling balm," the etymology of the PN Taphat, however, is indeed problematic.

Further, the usage and the meaning of Basemath fits well the lavish lifestyle and background setting of Solomon's reign. For, indeed, we learn that Solomon received from the Queen of Sheba בשׂמים הרבה "large quantities of spices" (1 Kings 10:10); בשׂנים לרב "a vast quantity of spices" (2 Chr. 9:9); לא בא כבשׂם ההוא עוד לרב "never again did such a vast quantity of spices arrive" (1 Kings 10:10; 2 Chr. 9:9). Solomon, likewise, received from the surrounding kings a yearly tribute of spices (1 Kings 10:25; 2 Chr. 9:24).[19] Accordingly, the lexeme בשׂם בשׂמים is employed thirty times in the Hebrew Bible, fourteen of which are attested to in connection with Solomon in 1 Kings and 2 Chr. (seven times),[20] as well as in Song of Songs (seven times).[21]

At the outset, it is generally agreed upon that Ahimaaz, the son-in-law of Solomon, seems to be the very same Ahimaaz the son of Zadok (2 Sam. 15:27, 36).[22] This is Ahimaaz the swift runner, the confidant of David, who on the advice of Hushai the Archite was sent by his father Zadok, then the priest to Jerusalem, to warn David concerning Absalom's conspiracy (2 Sam. 17:17–21). Ahimaaz was likewise the one to bring the tidings of Absalom's death to David (2 Sam. 18:19). Therefore, since we learn from the archival list of Solomon's highest officers that Ahimaaz's brother Azariah inherited the priesthood (1 Kings 4:1), it is plausible that Ahimaaz the swift runner and confidant of Solomon married the king's daughter, Basemath. He was consequently appointed to be the prefect of Naphtali, one of the most important districts in the united monarchy. The borders of Naphtali are drawn in Josh. 19:32–39. Although the text does not specify the dwelling center of Ahimaaz, the prefect of the eighth province, in all probability it is the important city Hazor, which is described in Josh. 11:10 as: "Hazor was formerly the head of all those kingdoms." Indeed, Hazor's importance as a political center is documented first in the 19th cent. BCE in the Egyptian Execration Texts. Hazor appears in the topographical lists of Pharaohs Thutmose III, Amenhotep II, and Seti I. It also appears in the Mari and Armana letters. The last reference to Hazor before the Israelite conquest is in Papyrus Anastasi I from the 13th century BCE. Nature, indeed, had determined strategic strong character for Hazor. It is in the heartland of the Galilee, the major route of trade and conquest from North by way of Damascus towards the coastal plain of Palestine and Egypt.[23] Undoubtedly:

> the province of Naphtali had its economic center in the Jordan Valley, north of the Sea of Galilee. It also housed the Solomonic fortification of the 10th century, a governor's residence, and a presumed granary of the 9th–8th centuries. These examples are vivid evidences of the strength and importance attached to this province, both in Solomonic times and during the period of the divided monarchy. Hazor, like Megiddo, was completely rebuilt by Solomon, especially as a provincial capital (1 Kings 9:15).[24]

Indeed, such an important strategic district from both a military and economic vantage could have been given only to the king's friend and loyal supporter, such as Ahimaaz the son of Zadok, the king's son-in- law. Similarly, not unlike Basemath, one ought to look for an interpretation of the PN Taphat that would fit the *Sitz im Laben* of Solomon's court. Namely, one should probe into the etymology of her name and attempt to extrapolate, if possible, any biographical details that this name may exhibit.

III

There are basically three different interpretations based on three different etymological equations. In 1928, Martin Noth[25] followed by Stamm,[26] Wagner,[27] Max Löhr,[28] as well as *KB* equates the name טָפַת with the Palestinian Aramaic noun טִפָּה "drop."

This, in turn, is derived from the Aram. verb טוף "to float, drip." Consequently, Noth considers *Ṭāpat* as an Aramaic rather than a Canaanite PN. Likewise, the *Encyclopedia Biblica*[29] suggests to derive the name from the biblical verb נטף "to drip, to flow," thus understanding the form טָפַת as an active participle fem. connoting "the one who drips/flows." There are three main difficulties with Noth's interpretation. First, one can hardly expect the Aramaic verb טוף to be employed in BH. This is clearly the case in Deut. 11:47 where Tg. Onq. renders הציף "He caused to overflow" as אטיף, where Tg. Neof. keeps the form אציף, but renders it in the margin אטיף. Additionally, the name *Ṭāpat* as understood by Noth to mean "drop" is too loose and uncommitted. It ignores the *Sitz im Laben* of this PN. Furthermore, as rightly pointed out by Layton[30] "the name would have to be revocalized with an i vowel in the first syllable. This revocalization ignores the Masoretic pointing and finds no support in the versions." The third proposed interpretation of the name *Ṭāphat* — advocated by various scholars and lately defended by Scott Layton[31] — is based on the geminate *hapax* root *ṭpp* I (Isa. 3:16), which apparently means "to skip about, trip." Consequently, it is generally assumed that the root *ṭpp* is a denominative verb from the collective noun *ṭap* "children" (Num. 14:31; Deut. 1:39). Accordingly, Layton asserts that "*Ṭāpat* is a **qall* base noun, plus *-at* feminine suffix, meaning 'young/small girl.'"[32] This interpretation poses four difficulties. First, one should expect a *dageš forte* to be inserted. Second, the meaning of one isolated lexeme (i.e., *ṭāpat*) cannot be inferred likewise from another isolated lexeme (i.e., *ṭpp*). Third, since טף is a collective noun which has no declension, one can hardly expect an *-at* fem. suffix. Fourth, this interpretation as "a young/small girl" likewise ignores the *Sitz im laben* that the PN Taphat may exhibit.

Accordingly, one ought to look for a different etymological equation and an interpretation for the PN טָפַת that would fit the background, life setting, and the life-style that spirits the atmosphere of Solomon's royal court. Namely, if possible, one should probe the etymology of the princess's name and attempt to extrapolate any biographical detail that this name may likely display. Thus, since Egypt played an enormous role in the Solomonic era,[33] especially after Solomon's marriage to the daughter of Pharaoh Siamun, one may venture to suggest that the etymological derivation of טָפַת is neither Aramaic nor Canaanite, but rather Egyptian.

It is noteworthy that although Tg. J. and the Pešiṭta keep the same consonants of the name טָפַת, the Septuagint and the Vulgate differ. While the Septuagint A reads Ταφατα, Septuagint B renders the name as Ταβληθει. Lucian, on the other hand, has Ταβααθ. The Vulgate reads the name as *Taphet*. It is also interesting to observe that the Greek spells the first consonant of טָפַת with a *t* and not with a *ṭ*. It should similarly be mentioned that while Septuagint A reads the second vowel as a, the Vulgate spells it with an e vowel.

As to the etymology and the interpretation of *Ṭāpat*, an alternative solution may lie in the Egyptian origin of this PN. This possible solution may therefore answer the question as to the background setting that the name טָפַת exhibits. From the New Kingdom (18th Dynasty) period (1550–1295 BCE), and especially in the Third Intermediate Period of the twenty-first dynasty[34] (1085–945 BCE), the Egyptian particle T3 (*TA*) served as a definite article as well as a relative pronoun feminine sing., i.e, "the one who belongs to." Accordingly, *TA* is utilized in a number of Egyptian feminine personal names, especially in the twenty-first dynasty. The Egyptian particle *TA* is employed in the biblical name תַּחְפְּנֵס, Hadad's wife and the sister of Pharaoh's wife.[35] While Kitchen[36] and Weippert[37] have independently supported the view of Grdseloff[38] that *Tahpenes* is a slightly syncopated Hebrew transcription of the Egyptian phrase — *t3-ḥ(mt)-p3-nsw* "wife of the king," i.e., "queen" (= Hittite cuneiform *daḫamunzu*),[39] Albright considers it a proper name "which may stand for the Egyptian **T3-ḥn.t-p3-(or pr)-nsw* "She Whom the King (or Palace) Protects,"[40] a yet unattested PN in Egyptian. The definite article T3 is likewise employed in the geographical name תחפנחס,[41] which is consonantly "an accurate transcription of the

Egyptian name *T3-ḫ(t)-(n.t)-p3-nḥsy* 'the fortress of Penhase,'"[42] identified with the city of Daphne in Egypt.

Consequently, one ventures to suggest that the first syllable ט of the name טָפַת may represent the Egyptian relative pronoun Tᵖ. However, it should be noted that while the Egyptian particle is written with *t*, the suggested Heb. equivalent is spelled with *ṭ*. Nevertheless, there are various cases, especially in personal, geographical, as well as professional names, that the *t* in Egyptian corresponds to *ṭ* in Hebrew and Akkadian.[43] The following clear examples are: the geographical locations tu_2 = $ʾu_3$ =*b*[44] = Heb. טוב (ארץ)[45] and Egyptian *N3j.w-t3-ḫw-t*[46] = Akk. *naṭḫu* Heb. personal name טבליהו = Egyptian *tᵌbl*[47] Heb. חרטמים[48] = Egyptian *ḥry-tm*ʾ "the one on duty"[49] = Akk. *ḫartibi.*[50] Possibly also Heb. בהט "a costly stone"[51] = Egyptian *ʾbhtj*[52]; Heb. טפחות[53] = Egyptian *tp-ḫw.t* "parapet (roof)."[54]

The second particle in Tapat's name may correspond to the Egyptian fem. noun *p.t* "heaven." The *t*, the last consonant of the name, may agree with the Egyptian fem. form case ending *t*.[55] Accordingly, while not attested to as a PN, טפת may represent the Egyptian elements *Ta-p.t*, which may be rendered as "the One (She) Who Belongs to Heaven," i.e., "the Heavenly One." If our suggested rendering is probable, then *ta-pe.t* may correspond to the Vulgate transliteration *Taphet.* Further, not unlike Basameth, Taphet's name, "she (the one) who belongs to heaven,"[56] may likewise conform well to both Solomon's spirit of universality, expansion, and wisdom, as well as the daughter of Pharaoh's Egyptian concept of cosmology. Accordingly, if our equation of טָפַת with the suggested Egyptian compound *ta-pe.t* is likely, then one may further consider the possibility that princess טָפַת is the daughter of the daughter of Pharaoh (Siamun) and Solomon.

Our suggested identification of טָפַת as the daughter of the Egyptian daughter of Pharaoh may shed some light and answer the question concerning the reason of Solomon's appointment of her husband as the prefect of the important costal district Dor. Not unlike Ahimaaz, Ben-abinadab seems likewise an integral part of the royal circle, a close confidant of the king. It has been suggested that the name Ben-abinadab ("son of Abinadab") is patronymic[57] and may be a title indicating that its bearer head a hereditary office.[58] Accordingly, Ben-abinadab, Solomon's son-in-law, may have been likewise the king's first cousin — the son of Abinadab — the second oldest brother of David.[59] Furthermore, similar to חצור in Naphtali, נָפַת דֹּאר "the wooded area[60] (region) of Dor" was significantly important. Indeed, Ephraim Stern nicknames Dor as "Ruler of the Seas,"[61] the most important costal port between the Phoenicians and the Egyptians. The earliest reference to the city appears in an inscription of Pharaoh Rameses II (13th cent. BCE). It contains a list of settlements along the *via maris* occupied by the Canaanites. The next culture to make appearance at Dor — about 1200 BCE — is that of the Sikils. The Sikils culture at Dor provides a kind of 150-year interlude between the Canaanites and their Phoenician descendants. Indeed, the most of what we know of Dor in this period is the Egyptian tale of Wen-Amon, who in his journey passes through Dor: "I reached Dor, the town of the Sikils and Beder. Its prince bought me bread, wine, and meat."[62] The period of the United Monarchy of David and Solomon (1000–925 BCE) was a time of flourishing for Dor and the Sharon coast. Both kings maintained close ties with the Phoenician cities in the north, especially Tyre. However, in Solomon's period, Dor controlled the *via maris* as well as the sea passage of the merchant marine, securing the Egyptian naval freedom of passage to Phoenicia and Asia Minor.[63] Indeed, what more appropriate city to give to Princess טפת, the suggested granddaughter of Pharaoh Siamun, than the important port city Dor, the city which rules the seas.

NOTES

1. S. Japhet, *The Ideology of the Book of Chronicles and its Place in Biblical Thought*, (Frankfurt am Main; New York: P. Lang, c1989), 350. n.296; *idem, I&II Chronicles: A* Commentary (London: SCM Press, 1973), 670–72.
2. A. Malamat, "The First Peace Treaty Between Israel and Egypt," *BAR*

5/5 (1979), 58. For further details, see Idem, "Aspects of the Foreign Policies of David and Solomon," *WES* 22 (1963), 1–17.

3. 1 Sam. 3:2–5; 5:13–17; 1 Chr. 3:1–10; 2 Chr. 11:18–21.
4. For a full discussion, see S. Arbeli, "Women in the Bible in Positions of Privilege and their Involvement in Social and Political Affairs: A Comparative Study using Ancient Near Eastern Sources," Ph.D. diss. Hebrew University (Jerusalem, 1984), 213–14; 289–308 (Heb.).
5. D. B. Redford, *Egypt, Canaan, and Israel in Ancient Times* (Princeton, N.J.: Princeton University Press, 1992), 311.
6. Ibid., 311.
7. K.A. Kitchen, *The Third Intermediate Period in Egypt* (Warminster, England: Aris & Phillips Press, 1973), 282: "The marriage-alliance by which Solomon gained a Pharaoh's daughter as a wife was in itself remarkable. As often noted, such a marriage of an Egyptian princess to a foreign potentate was unthinkable in the New Kingdom or Empire period, just a few centuries earlier."
8. A. Malamat, "Aspects of the Foreign Policies of David and Solomon," *JNES* 22 (1963), 10.
9. A. Malamat, "The First Peace Treaty Between Israel and Egypt," *BAR*, 5/5 (1979): 58–61.
10. A. Malamat, "Aspects of the Foreign," 1–17; Idem, "A Political Look at the Kingdom of David and Solomon and its Relations with Egypt" in *Studies in the Period of David and Solomon and Other Essays* (ed. Tomoo Ishida; Winona Lake: Eisenbraun, 1982), 198–200; K. Kitchen, *The Third Intermediate*, 278–83; "Solomon, Siamun, and the Double Ax" in *Magnalia Dei: The Mighty Acts of God* (eds. Frank M. Cross, Werrer E. Lawke, and Patrick D. Miller, Jr.; Garden City: Doubleday, 1976), 209–223; J.R. Bartlett, "An Adversary against Solomon, Hadad the Edomite," *ZAW* 88 (1976), 222; A. Green, "Solomon and Siamun: A Synchronism Between Early Dynastic Israel and the Twenty-First Dynasty of Egypt," *JBL* 97 (1978), 353–57; Redford, *Egypt*, 310–11.
11. Ibid., 22 (1963), 11.
12. Ibid., 280.
13. For a discussion concerning the provinces of Solomon, see especially A. Alt, "Israels Gaue unter Salomo" in *Alttestamentliche Studien Rudolf Kittel zum 60. Geburtstag dargebracht* (Leipzig, 1913), 1–19; W.F. Albright, "The Administrative Divisions of Israel and Judah," *JPOS* 5 (1925), 17–54; G. Ernest Wright, "The Provinces of Solomon," *Eretz Israel* 8 (1967), 58–68; Y. Aharoni, "The Solomonic District," *Tel-Aviv* 3 (1976), 5–15; John Bright, "The Organization and Administration of the Israelite Empire" in *Magnalia Dei: The Mighty Acts of God* (eds. Frank M. Cross, Werrer E. Lawke, and Patrick D. Miller, Jr.; Garden

City: Doubleday, 1976), 193–208; N. Na'aman, *Borders and Districts in Biblical Historiography* (Jerusalem: Simor, 1986), 167–201. Note that in a very recent article, Paul S. Ash challenges the authenticity of the list of the twelve districts, cf. *idem*, "Solomon's District List," *JSOT* 67 (1995), 67–86.

14. On the parallel between the Egyptians' and Solomon's provision system, see D.B. Redford, *Studies on the Ancient Palestinian World* (eds, J.W. Wevers and D.B. Redford. Toronto: Buffalo University of Toronto Press, 1971), 141–156.
15. See J. Gray, *I&II Kings: A Commentary* (Philadelphia: Westminster Press, 1970), 138.
16. Gen. 36:3.
17. Gen. 26:34; 35:3, 4, 10, 13, 17.
18. See *The Anchor Bible Dictionary* (New York: Doubleday, 1992), 1:623.
19. For a discussion, see especially, Kjeld Nielsen, *Incense in Ancient Israel*, Supp. to *VT* 38 (Leiden: Brill, 1986), 67, 98.
20. 1 Kings 10:2,10 (twice), 25; 2 Chr. 9:1, 9 (twice).
21. Song of Songs 4:10, 14,16; 5:1,13; 6:2; 8:14.
22. Cf. M. Cassuto, "Ahimaaz" *Encyclopedia Bibilica* (Jerusalem: Biyalik, 1965), 1:219; *The Anchor Bible Dictionary*, (New York: Doubleday, 1922), 1:116.
23. On the strategic prominence of Hazor, see especially A. Malamat, "Hazor the Head of All Those Kingdoms," *JBL* 79 (1966), 12–19; John Gray, "Hazor" *VT* 16 (1966), 26–52; Yohana Aharoni, "New Aspects of the Israelite Occupation in the North," in *Near Eastern Archaeology in the Tweintieth Century* (ed J.A. Sanders; Garden City: Doubleday, 1970), 254–67.
24. G. Ernest Wright, "The Provinces of Solomon," *Eretz Israel* 8 (1967), 66–7.
25. E.g., M. Noth, "Die Israelitischen Personennaemen" in *Rahmen der Gemeinsemitischen Namengebung.*
26. Johann Jacob Stamm, *Beitrage zur hebrdischen und altorientalischen Namenkunde* (Freiburg, 1980), 121.
27. Max Wagner, *Die Lexikalischen und grammartikalischen Aramaismen im Alttestamentlichen Hebraisch* (Berlin, 1966), 61–2.
28. Max Löhr, Die Stellung des Weibes zur Jahwe-Religion-und-Kult (Leipzig, 1908), 12.
29. M. Cassuto "Taphat" *Encyclopaedia Biblica* (1965), 3:408–9.
30. Scott C. Layton, *Archaic Features of Canaanite Personal Names in the Hebrew Bible* (Atlanta: Scholars Press, 1990), 210–11.
31. Ibid.
32. Ibid.

33. See especially W. Helck, *Zur Verwalting des Mittleren und Neuen Reichs*, (Leiden: Brill, Cologne, 1958), 61; R.J. Williams *A People Come out of Egypt* Supplement to *VT* vol. 28 (Leiden: Brill, 1975), 235–237; D.B. Redford, "Studies in Relations between Palestine and Egypt during the First Millennium B.C." in *Studies on the Ancient Palestinian World* (eds. J.W. Wevers and D.B. Redford; Toronto: University of Buffalo of Toronto Press, 1971), 141–56; Yutaka Ikeda, "Solomon's Trade in Horses and Chariots in its International: Setting," in *Studies in the Period of David and Solomon and Other Essays* (ed. Tomo Ishida; Winona Lake: Eisenbraun, 1982), 215–39; John Bright, "The Organization and Administration of the Israelite Empire" in *The Mighty Acts of God,* (eds. Frank M. Gross, Werner E. Lankc. and Patrick D. Miller. Jr;. Garden City: Doubleday, 1976), 191–208.
34. H. Ranke, *Die Agyptischen Personnannen* vol. 2 (Gluckstadt, 1935), 356f.
35. 1 Kings 11:19–20.
36. Ibid., 274 n. 183.
37. M. Weippert, "Edom: Studien und Materialien zur Geschichte der Edomiter auf' Grund schriflicher und archdologischer Quellen," PhD. Diss. (Tubingen, 1975), 298–9.
38. B. Grdseloff, *RHJE* 1 (1947), 88–90.
39. Walter Federn, "DAHAMUNZU (KBo v 6 iii 8)" *JCS* 14 (1960), 33.
40. W.F. Albright, "New Light on Early Recensions of the Hebrew Bible," *BASOR* 140 (1955), 32.
41. Jer. 2:16; 43:7, 8, 9; 44:1; 46:14; Ezek. 30:18.
42. See especially W.F. Albright, "Baal-zephon," *Festschrift Alfred Bertholot* (Tubingen, 1950), 13–14.
43. See Jan Quaegebeur, "The Egyptian equivalent of hartumim" in, *Pharaonic Egypt: The Bible and Christianity* (eds. Sara Israel it-G roll; Jerusalem: Magnes Press, 1985), 169.
44. See James E. Hoch, *Semitic Words in Egyptian Texts of the New Kingdom and Third Intermediate Period* (Princeton: Princeton University Press, 1994), 256 #524 (Thutmose III list I, 205); Thomas Schneider, *Asiatiche Personennamen in agyptichen Quellen des Neuen Reiches* (Freiburg, 1992), 231, #491.
45. Jud. 11:3, 5; 2 Sam. 10:6, 8.
46. See J. Vergote, *Grammaire Copte lb* (Louvain, 1973), 90.
47. Scheider, ibid., 231–2 #492.
48. Gen. 41:8, 24; Ex. 7:11, 22; 8:3, 14, 15; 9:11; Dan. 1:20.
49. See especially Jan Quaegebeur, ibid., 162–172; Hans Goedicke, "hartummim," *Orientalia,* 65 (1996), 24–30.
50. *CAD* H 116.

51. Esth. 1:6
52. *KB3*[3,] 111.
53. 1 Kings 7:9
54. See Manfred Gorg, "Lexikalisches zur Beschrcibung des salomonischen Palastbezirks," *Biblisch Notizen* 11 (1980), 9. n. 9.
55. A. Ennan. H Grapous *Wdtcrbuch dcr agyptichen Sprache* (Leipzig, 1926–1963), 292.
56. *Lexicon Der Ägyptologie* (Wiesbeaden, 1977), 2:1206–1213.
57. Cf. E.g., *The Anchor Bible Dictionary*, (New York; Doubleday, 1992), 1:622.
58. 1 Sam. 16:8; 17:13; 1 Chr. 2:13.
59. See Meir Ben-Dov, "נפה — A Geographical Term of Possible 'Sea People' Origin," *Tel-Aviv* 3 (1976), 70–3.
60. Ephraim Stern, *Dor, Ruler of the Seas* (Jerusalem: Israel Exploration Society, 1994).
61. For a full discussion, cf. Stern, *Ruler of the Seas*, 85–104.
62. Ibid., 104–111.
63. For a discussion, see S.Yelvin, "Did the Kingdom of Israel Have a Maritime Policy?" *JQR* 50 (1959–60), 198–207.

Paved with Love (Song of Songs 3:10d): A New Interpretation[1]

To my sisters Miryam and Ashira

Song of Songs 3:9–10 reads:

אַפִּרְיוֹן עָשָׂה לוֹ הַמֶּלֶךְ שְׁלֹמֹה
מֵעֲצֵי הַלְּבָנוֹן
עַמּוּדָיו עָשָׂה כֶסֶף רְפִידָתוֹ זָהָב
מֶרְכָּבוֹ אַרְגָּמָן
תּוֹכוֹ רָצוּף אַהֲבָה מִבְּנוֹת יְרוּשָׁלִָם

> King Solomon made him an *appiryôn* of wood from Lebanon.
>
> He made its column silver its baldachin of gold its curtain of purple.

In the description of the construction of Solomon's *appiryôn* in Song of Songs 3:9–10, the clause תוכו רצוף אהבה מבנות ירושלם is rendered by the *NJPS*, for example, as follows: "within it was decked with love by the maidens of Jerusalem."

As rightly pointed out by Pope, "interpreters have been troubled with the use here of the word love, *ʾahăḇāh*, in connection with the ornamentation of a piece of furniture."[2] Indeed, this clause created three major problems for modern biblical critics: (a) the meaning of the word אהבה in connection with the ornamentation of the *appiryôn*, and the relationship of the abstract noun אהבה "love" with the concrete verb רצוף "inlaid, paved"; (b) the topical association between Song of Songs 3:10d and 3:10 a,b,c; and (c) the role that בנות ציון played concerning the decoration of the *appiryôn*. Accordingly, the traditional rendering of the idiomatic *hapax* רצוף אהבה as "woven/invalid/decked/paved with love,"[3] or "tessellated most lovely[4]/lovingly wrought,"[5] was considered as: "unsatisfactory";[6] "does not make sense";[7] "uncertain";[8] "hard to understand"[9]; "pointless metaphor";[10] "unclear, if it is not a mistake";[11] "the clause is out of place";[12] "irregular, since it does not follow the pattern of three-four."[13] The main reason for this uncertainty stemmed from the fact that in verse 3:10 a, b, c, three specific parts of the *appiryôn* are named and three tangible materials are listed: post/silver, bolster/gold, and seat/purple stuff. Hence, the following main emendations were proposed: Graetz *hobnim* "ebony"[14] (Ezek. 27:15); Gerleman *ʾabanim* "stones";[15] Tur-Sinai הַבִּים from שֶׁנְהַבִּים "ivory" (1 Kings 10:22).[16] Driver, on the other hand, suggests to equate אהבה with the Arabic *ihab* "skin, hide, raw leather."[17] Subsequently, most modern commentators read the phrase מבנות ירושלם "by/from the maidens of Jerusalem" as "O daughters of Jerusalem," in the vocative. They assert that the מ before בנות is an enclitic מ attached to אהבה "love."[18] Various other critics, however, consider the phrase superfluous.

The majority of modern biblical critics, who assert that the compound רצוף אהבה is an unsuitable expression for the description of the *appiryôn*'s interior decoration, and consequently resort to erroneous emendations and interpretations, neglect to study this idiom in its ancient Near Eastern architectural context. At the outset, it should be observed that while the nouns מרצפת/רצפה "pavement" are employed in the Hebrew Bible eight times, always in context concerning architectural structures,[19] the *hapax* verb רצוף (Qal passive part.) is used only here in Songs 3:10d. As it will be shown below, the author of Song of Songs seems to intentionally utilize the verb רצוף with the noun אהבה.

The Heb. root רצף is the etymological and semantic equivalent of the Akk. *raṣāpu* "to arrange vertically or horizontally." Thus, for example, Akkadian employs the verb *raṣāpu* "to arrange" with *rēšu/qaqqadu/gulgullu/pagru* "head/skulls/corpse (in a pile)."[20] In architectural contexts, however, we find the verb employed as follows: *bīta/ekalla raṣāpu* "to build a house palace"[21]; *ina agurri raṣāpu*[22] to build (lit., to arrange) with the baked bricks"; *dūra ana eššūti raṣāpu* "to build newly a wall."[23] Likewise, in architectural contexts, especially in the Neo-Assyrian and Neo-Babylonian royal and building inscriptions, the various Assyrian and Babylonian kings will sum up the description of the construction of their respective temples and palaces with a general statement, e.g., *arṣip(s) ušaklil(u)*, "I have constructed, I have completed (the building)."[24] This statement will often be followed by the expression *lalâ/lulâ mullû/šumlû* "to fill with splendor/glamour/attractiveness," namely, "to fill (the place/temple) with sumptuous decorations." Akk. *lulû/lalû* (v. *ullû*),[25] which often are employed alongside *kuzbu/ulṣu*, all come to connote "sexual attractiveness/charm and vigor."

However, in contexts involving building, such as city wall, gates, temples, and palaces, *kuzbu ulṣu*,[26] and especially *lulû/lalû*,[27] refer in general terms to the beauty, rich adornment, and sumptuous decoration of these respective buildings. Accordingly, the Neo-Assyrian kings Sargon, Sennacherib, Esarhaddon, and Assurbanipal, as well as the Neo-Babylonian kings Nebuchadnezzar and Nabunā'id usually conclude their respective building activities with the sum up standard formula *ana tabrât/dagal nišê/kiššat ariṣpu ušaklilu... lulê/lalê umallû/ušamlû*. "I constructed, completed and filled (the palace/temple etc.) with sumptuous decoration to be marveled and looked at by all the people." The following few examples will suffice:

> *ina ūmešuma ultu ekalla qabal āli ša Ninua ana rimīt šarrūtiya ušaklilu ana tabrât kiššat nišē lulê umallûši.*
>
> At the time after I (Sennacherib) had completed the palace in the midst of the city of Ninveh, for my royal residence, to the astonishment of all the people I filled it with sumptuous decoration.[28]

Esarḫaddon, after the completion of his *bītānu* "summerhouse," states:

> *ekallu šu'atu ultu uššīša adi gabidbêša arṣipu ušaklilu lulê umallû*

> This palace from its foundation up to its top, I have constructed, completed, and filled it with sumptuous decoration.[29]

Nebuchadnezzar further elaborates:

> *bīta šâtim ana tabrâti ušepišma ana dagal kiššat nišê lulê ušamlîšâ balti uzzu puluḫti melammi šarūtim itâtiša saḫrama.*
>
> I built this palace for the astonishment: I filled it with sumptuous decoration for the people to look at. It (the palace's) sides were surrounded with ferocious pride, the awe-inspiring sheen of kingship.[30]

Further, it is interesting to note the verb רצף "to pave/arrange" is used with sumptuous decorations in Midrash *Esth. Rab.*: על רצפת בהט ושש "on pavement of marble, alabaster..." (Esth. 1:6) e.g., אמר רב נחמן בא וראה שלותו של אותו רשע מה הוא שהיה ביתו רצוף באבנים טובות ומרגליות בהט ושש ודר וסוחרת ר' ניסא דקיסרי אמר למרגלית שהיא אהובה על בעלה "Rabbi Nahman said: from this you may judge how great was the prosperity of that evil man, for his palace was inlaid with precious stones and pearls, marble, alabaster, molten-of pearl, and mosaics. Rabbi Nisa of Caesarea said: like a pearl of which its owner is particularly desires (i.e., fond of)."[31] As noted by the *CAD*, "the references (of *raṣāspu)* from the West[32] may be cognate with West Semitic *rṣp*[33] 'to pave' with precious stones." The *CAD* compares well especially to the passage from Ugarit, where in a letter of *GAL. GI. NA.* to his master, the king of Ugarit: PN...*algameššī lilqâ u bītātu šarri aḫika lirṣipū* "let PN take the *algamešu*- precious stones — and them pave the palaces of the king, your brother.[34]

Likewise, it is worthwhile to observe that the sequential employment of the concrete and tangible substances כסף "silver," זהב "gold," and ארגמן "purple dye" with אהבה finds its parallel in Neo-Assyrian building description. Both Esarḫaddon and his son Aššurbanipal employ the substantives *kaspu* "silver" and *ḫurāṣu* "gold" with the abstract noun *lulû* "sumptuous decorations," e.g., *Emašmaš bīt bēlet māti kaspa ḫurāṣa uz'in lulê umalli* "I (Esarḫaddon) plated Emašmaš the temple of the Lady of the land (i.e., Ištar) with silver and gold and filled it with sumptuous decorations."[35]

In light of the above Mesopotamian architectural-epigraphical material, we venture to propose that the *hapax* compound רצוף אהבה may functionally be compared to the Akkadian standard sum up formula *lalû/lulû mullû/šumlû*. Accordingly, the author of Song of Songs employs the noun אהבה not just to simply mean "love." He intentionally selects this word that lavishly depicts the essence of Song of Songs.[36] He thus deliberately utilizes the architectural term רצוף "paved, arranged" with אהבה as double entendre. It connotes "love" as well as "attractiveness, luxuriance" i.e., "sumptuous decorations" (= Akk. l*alû/lulû/kuzbu*), which artistically was executed by the choicest handicrafts of women from Jerusalem.

Accordingly, as the sequential order of the list of the special units of the *appiryôn* as employed in Song of Songs 3:9–10, we propose the following structural arrangement. The author opens with a general statement.

(a) "King Solomon built him *appiryôn* from the wood of Lebanon" (v. 9). He then continues to list the tangible architectural material, and their respective units:
(b) "Its columns/silver" (v.10a)
"Its baldachins/gold" (v. 10b)
"Its hangings/purple" (v.10c).

He finally concludes with the sum up statement:

(c) "Its interior arranged/paved with sumptuous decorations by the maidens of Jerusalem" (v.10d).

The idiomatic *hapax* expression רצוף אהבה (Song of Songs 3:10) created a major problem for modern biblical critics asserting that the expression is unsuitable for the description of the אפריון interior decoration. While various emendations were proposed, we maintain that in the light of cuneiform architectural context involving buildings such as city walls, gates, temples, and palaces, the Hebrew expression should be studied. Namely, the Neo-Assyrian and Neo-Babylonian kings will sum up the description of their palaces/temples using the expression *aṣrip ušaklil* "I have constructed I have completed." This expression is followed by yet another sum up formula *lalâ/lulâ mullû/šumlû*, which to our mind will be the functional equivalent of רצוף אהבה, to now be rendered as "paved/arranged with sumptuous decorations."

NOTES

1. See H. Tawil "Bathing in Milk (SoS 5:12): A New Look," *Beit Miqra* 151 (1997), 388–90; I would like to thank my student Jonathan Strauss for his help.
2. Marvin H. Pope, *Song of Songs* (AB 7c; Garden City, NY: Doubleday, 1977), 445.
3. *KJV.*
4. C.D. Ginsburg, *The Song of Songs* (1857. Reprint. New York: Ktav, 1970),153.
5. *RSV.*
6. Robert Gordis, *The Song of Songs: A Study, Modern Translation, and Commentary,* (New York: Jewish Theological Seminary, 1954), 84.
7. *IB* 120.
8. Roland E. Murphy, *The Song of Songs*: *Hermeneia*, (Minneapolis, MN: Augsburg, 1990), 149b.
9. Gunter Krinetzki, *Kommentar zum Hohenlied*, (Frankfurt und Bern 1981),125.
10. Michael V. Fox, *The Song of Songs and the Ancient Egyptian Love Songs*, (Madison, WI: University of Wisconsin, 1985),126.
11. Murphy, ibid., 152a.
12. Eliezer Ben Yehuda, *A Complete Dictionary of Ancient and Modern Hebrew* (New York, NY: Thoma Yoseloff, 1901), 3:6718a n.1 (Heb.).
13. Yair Zakovitch, *The Song of Songs: Mikra Leyisra'el a Bible Commentary for Israel* (Tel Aviv: Am Oved, 1992), 84 (Heb.).
14. H. H. Graetz, *Schir Ha-Schirim oder das Salomonische Hohelied* (Vienna, 1871).
15. G. Gerleman, *Ruth, Das Hohelied* (*BKAT* 18; Neukirchen-Vlyuyn, 1965), 139–40. Gerleman's emendation was likewise accepted by Fox cf. ibid n. 9.
16. N.H. Tur Sinai "Shir Hashirim Asher Lishelomo," in *Halashon*

Vehasefer, Vol. 2 (Jerusalem, 1951), 356:8 (Heb.), followed by G. Krinetzki, *Kommentar zum Hohenlied: Bildsprache und theologische Boschaft* (*BBET* 16; Frankfurt am Main and Bern: Lang, 1981),125.

17. G.R. Drivier "Supposed Arabism in the Old Testament," *JBL* 55 (1936), 111.

18. Othmar Keel, *The Song of Songs: A Continental Commentary* (trans. Frederick J. Gaiser; Minneapolis: Fortress Press, 1994), 130; cf. also Pope, Murphy Fox (ibid.). Note that Keel suggests to read אהבים in the plural, rendering the word as "sense of love" or "joys of love," understanding that the interior of the *appiryôn* was decorated with "erotic motifs" (Keel, ibid., 134).

19. 2 Kings 16:17 (i.e., מַרְצֶפֶת אֲבָנִים "pavement of stones"). Cf. also רִצְפָּה Ezek. 40:17 (twice); 40:18 (twice); 42:3; Est. 1:16 2 Chr. 7:3). Note the Akk. substantives *riṣpu* "well maintained structure" (*CAD* R 376b), as well as *riṣiptu* e.g., *riṣsiptu ziqqurati ša Kalhi* "(brick from) the relevant of the temple-tower of Calah" *CAD* ibid.

20. E.g., *qaqqadātišuna unekkis ana asīti arṣip* "I (*Aššurnāṣipal* II) cut off their heads and arranged them in a pile" (*CAD* R 186b) and *passim*.

21. E.g., *āla šuātu ana la ṣabāte u duršu la raṣāpi ina muḫḫi alṭur bītu ša agurri ina muḫḫišu arṣip* "I wrote on it that the city is not to be reoccupied nor its wall to be erected again., I erected a structure of baked brick over it" (*CAD* R 184a 1.); *ekallāti ina šiddi mātiya arṣipma* "I (Adad-nīrāri II) construced palaces throughout my land" (*CAD* R 185b).

22. E.g., *ištu uššīšu adi gabadibbīšu ina agurri arṣip* "from its foundations to its parapets I (Tiglat-Pileser I) built it up with baked bricks" (*CAD* R 184b and *passim*.).

23. E.g., *dura rabâ ša āliya... ana eššutte arṣip* "the great wall of my city... I (Tiglat-Pileser I) constructed anew" (*CAD* R 184b b' and *passim*.).

24. E.g., [*ekallu] ša* RN *abī... ēpušu [la u]šeklilu ekalla šuātu arṣip ušeklil* "the palace which my father Aššur-rēš-iši built but did not complete, I finished the construction of the palace" (*CAD* R 184b c' and *passim*.)

25. The verb *ullû* which is employed in EA and SB "to provide with beauty, happiness, pleasure" e.g., "a statue of alabaster" *ša epšētuššu ana dagāti lullâ* whose workmanship gives please to look at" (*CAD* L 252 b).

26. Referring to the beauty and rich adornment of buildings and their parts, e.g., *ina bāb [ḫi.Li.Su] maštak ṣarpānītu ša kuzbu salḫu* "(I installed a bed) in the HI.LI.SU — quarter the bed chamber of DN, which is 'sprinkled with luxury'" (*CAD* K 615a e); 12 *apsasâte ša kuzbu u ulṣu ḫitlupa baltu lalâ kummuru ṣīruššin* "twelve sphinxes which are

wrapped in exuberant luxury, laden with divine beauty and dignity" (*CAD* B 143a 2').

27. *CAD* L 51a, b-c; 242 b,b; *AHw* 530b; 562b. Note that Akk. *lalû* is a loan word from Sum. *la la*. Note also that while Akk. *lalû/lulû* is the functional equivalent of אהבה in SoS 3:10, its semantic equivalent is Akk. *râmu/ru'āmu* "love, lovemaking" (*CAD* R 136b;392a; *AHw* 951a;991a.).
28. *OIP* 2 128 vi 37–8.
29. Borger, *Esarh* 62 vi 36–7.
30. *VAB* 4 118 ii 53–55.
31. Note that Midrash *Song of Song Rabba* understood idiom the רצוף אהבה as alluding to animals' decoration engraved on the Throne of Glory: תוכו רצוף אהבה ר' ברכיה ורבי בון בשם ר' אבהו ארבע גאים הם גאה שבעופות נשר גאה שבבהמות שור נאה שבחיות אריה גאה שבכלן אדם וכלן נטלן הקב"ה וחקקן בכסא הכבוד "the Interior is inlaid with love": Rabbi Berekiah and Rabbi Bun in the name of Rabbi Abbahu said: there are four lordly creatures. The lord among the birds in the eagle: the lord among cattle is the ox; the lord among the beasts is the lion, the lord of all of them is man. The Holy One blessed be He took them and engraved them on the Throne of Glory.
32. *CAD* R 186b, note.
33. Note the El-Amarna *raṣāpu* is glossed by *banû* (Heb. בנה) "to build" e.g., *nukurtum ĭstu šadî ana yâši u raṣpātē* (gloss: *b[a-n]i-t[i]= banītī)* *bīta išten Manḫate šumši ana pani ṣābē piṭāt šarri* "there is hostility against me from the mountains; so I have built up a house, Manḫate is its name, prepare for the king's archers" (*EA* 292:28–31).
34. *Ugaritica* 7 (1978), pl. 17 *RS* 34.135:16.
35. Streck *Asb.* 150 x 47–8; Thomson, *Esarh.* pl. 14 ii 8–9.
36. Note that the while the verb אהב is employed seven times, the noun אהבה is utilized eleven times in Song of Songs.

"If the Sun Has Risen Upon Him" (Exodus 22:2): Legal Terminology in Light of Akkadian Texts from Ugarit[1]

For Gloria Silbert, Esq.

I

> If a thief is found in a tunnel and is struck so that he dies, there shall be no bloodguilt for him. If the sun has risen upon him, there shall be bloodguilt for him. He shall make restitution; if he has nothing, then he shall be sold for his theft (Exod. 22:2).

Modern biblical scholarship is united in arriving at the literal understanding of the verse "If the sun has risen upon him."[2] Nahum Sarna summarizes this approach as follows:[3]

> The particular case of a thief who is surprised in the act of breaking and entering is parenthetically injected into the law dealing with theft. The contrast between the phrases, "if the sun has arisen" and "while tunneling" shows the latter to presuppose a nighttime setting [...] His nocturnal timing creates a presumption of homicidal intent [...] hence, no bloodguilt is incurred should the intruder be killed [...] if the break-in occurred in broad daylight, however, it is not presumed to present imminent danger to life; the use of deadly force is therefore deemed to be unwarranted, and bloodguilt would ensue.

However, it is interesting that the early and medieval commentaries are deeply divided in understanding the exact meaning of this verse. First of all, one should note that while Targum Onqelos translates our verse metaphorically: "If the eye of the witnesses has fallen upon him," Targum Neofiti translates it literally: "If the sun has fallen upon him." It is important to point out that the Targum attributed to Jonathan [Pseudo-Jonathan] understands our verse as follows: "If the matter is as clear as the sun." Indeed, the divergent translations reveal deep differences in understanding the verse, a dispute whose origins are at the very least in the second century CE. The author of the *Mekhilta de-Rabbi Yishmaʿel* understood "If the sun has risen upon him" as an expression of complete certainty: "'If the sun has risen upon him' — [Rabbi Yishmaʿel said,] 'Has the sun risen upon him alone? Has it not risen upon the entire world?! Rather, just as the sun signifies that there is peace in the world, so, too, this one (the tunneling thief): if it is known that he is at peace with him (the homeowner) and he (the latter) kills him, he is culpable.'"[4] The *Mekhilta* here negates the criterion of timing, namely the distinction based on the question of whether the thief was killed during the daytime or at night, and limits the murder dealt with in the verse to circumstances in which the homicidal intent of the trespasser is known, without leaving any trace of doubt. Following the *Mekhilta*, the Babylonian Talmud elucidates: "Another *baraita* teaches: 'If the sun has risen upon him, there shall be bloodguilt for him.' Has the sun risen upon him alone? Rather, if it is as clear to you (the homeowner) as the sun that he has peace with you, do not kill him, and if not, kill him" (b. *Sanh.* 72a).[5]

In light of the above, Rashi explains the biblical verse as follows:

> This is nothing but a type of metaphor: if the matter is clear to you that he has peace with you, like the sun which [signifies] peace in the world, so is it obvious to you that he is not coming to kill, even if the homeowner (you) confronts him. For instance, if a father is tunneling to steal his son's property and it is known that the father has compassion for his son and is not coming [to deal in] capital matters, there shall be bloodguilt for him — he is

> considered like a living being and it is [an act of] murder if the homeowner (the son) kills him.

Here too, the timing of the event is not the subject of discussion — whether it took place during the daytime or at night — but rather ascertaining the goal of the trespasser is the critical issue. This is also the case with Maimonides' formulation in *Mishneh Torah*:

> If the matter was clear to the homeowner that this thief who was coming upon him would not kill him and was only coming [to deal in] monetary matters, it is forbidden to kill him, and if he killed him, he has murdered a soul, as it is said, "If the sun has risen upon him" — if the matter is clear to you like the sun that he has peace with you, do not kill him (*Hilkhot Genevah* 9:10).[6]

Arnold B. Ehrlich mockingly rejects the explanations cited above:

> The early ones with their exegesis, and Onqelos who translates after them, distorted this verse for us. Its basic meaning is [rather] in accordance with its simple sense, [namely] that in contrast to what it said before "If a thief is found in a tunnel," where one who tunnels into a house does so at night, it says here "If the sun has risen upon him" — in other words, if he is caught stealing during the day, there shall be bloodguilt for him, because one who steals during the day intends to kill anyone who confronts him.[7]

Ehrlich follows the second opinion that was widespread among medieval commentators such as R. Saʿadyah Gaʾon,[8] Ibn Ezra, Rashbam, Nahmanides, and Ḥizzequni, and the modern Jewish commentators like Shadal and Cassuto.[9] They understood the verse according to its simple sense; in other words, "If the sun has risen upon him" means during the daytime. Rabad supports this interpretation vigorously, attacking and criticizing severely Maimonides' metaphorical understanding:

> I will not refrain from expressing my opinion, [namely] that it appears to me that even though the Sages exegeted "If the sun has risen upon him" metaphorically [...] nevertheless, it does not leave its simple sense. He [the homeowner] may not kill him during the day, because a thief does not come during the day [to kill]; rather, if he can escape, he escapes and runs away and does not tarry to steal much wealth and to stand up against its owner to kill him. But a thief [who comes] at night, because he knows that the homeowner is at home, is coming either to kill or to be killed. With regard to a thief [who comes] during the day, though, the homeowner is not around, and he is coming only to escape [once he has stolen what he wants]. And I swear that this should suffice for any understanding person. (*Hassagot ha-Rabad* to *Mishneh Torah, Hilkhot Genevah* 9:10)

II

The dispute cited above attests to a significant divide between the opinions, a difference that has legal and practical ramifications. It appears that this issue can be clarified in light of parallel extra-biblical material from the ancient Near East, especially from Ugaritic writings.

First, we should consider that from different cuneiform sources we know that the patron of the sun is the sun god Šamaš, the master of righteousness and uprightness. In iconography, this fact is known from the famous stela of King Hammurabi, in which the god Šamaš gives with his right hand the ring and the staff to the renowned lawgiver Hammurabi.[10]

From an epigraphic standpoint, we have much evidence, beginning in the Ancient Babylonian Era, that a common epithet of Šamaš is *dayyānu* "judge, justice." He is the god of righteousness and uprightness in the full sense of the word: *[da]yyān kīnātim abi ekiātim* "judge of righteousness, father of orphans";[11] *Šamaš dayyānu rabû ša šamê u erṣitim* "Šamaš, the great judge of heaven and earth."[12] Šamaš is described as one who punishes based on the attribute of righteousness: *dayyāna ṣalpa mēsira tukallam* "You [Šamaš] instruct the wicked judge with regard to the jailhouse."[13] In the hymns to Šamaš he is depicted as *mušnamir* "the illuminating one," whose purpose is *pētû ekleti mušnamir erṣetim rapšātim* "he scatters darkness, he illuminates an expansive land."[14] Šamaš is *nūr kiššati* "the light of the entire populated land."[15] In addition, he seeks justice: *tašemmê tebiršināti ša ruggugu tamassi dīnšu* "he hears and interrogates them [the iniquitous], while he decrees his verdict for the unjust,"[16] and therefore *muttaḫlilu šarrāqu muṣallû ša šamaš* "the thief who prowls is the enemy of Šamaš."[17] It is also appropriate to note that among the different properties of the sun mentioned in the Amarna letters. It (the sun) serves three times to describe the well being and security of the king in the idiomatic expression *lu tīdi inūma šalim šarru kīma* *^{D}UTU-aš [=šamaš] ina šamê* "know that the king is healthy and at peace as the sun in the skies."[18] Therefore, it is possible to connect the metaphor in the Amarna letters *šalim kīma šamši* "at peace as the sun" to the statement of R. Yishma'el in the *Mekhilta*, "Just as the sun [signifies that there is] peace (in the world, so, too, this one [the tunneling thief], if it is known that he is at peace with him [the homeowner])." Both of these sources connect peace = *šalāmu* to sun = *šamšu*.

It should further be noted that in a letter that a scholar sent to King Esarhaddon, the purity of one who brings a sacrifice is compared to the radiance of the sun: "[In the month of] Nisan on the first day, (*amēlu [l]ītebib*) the man shall purify himself: he shall place the bread offering before Marduk and pour out water and fine wine from his right and his left; (*amēlu šu kīma šamaš namir*) that man shall shine as the sun."[19]

More precisely, the legal term *barur ka-shemesh* [clear as the sun], which apparently appears first in the Babylonian Talmud, comes to support and strengthen R. Yishma'el's interpretation. According to him, the biblical verse "If the sun has risen upon him" hints not at the timing of the act but, at the [homeowner's] certainty of the thief's intent. It is possible that this point can be clarified with the help of the Akkadian legal texts that were found at Ugarit.

For the purpose of elucidating this matter, it is possible to cite at least eight examples from the Akkadian texts from Ugarit that all deal with legal issues concerning the defendant's status as innocent and exempt from appearance in court.[20] The standard legal formula defines the defendant's innocence as clear as the purity of the sun: *kīma ^{D}UTU [=šamaš] zakīti zaki* "he [=the defendant] is innocent [=pure] of claims [against him] like the purity of the sun." Three examples will suffice:

I. MRS 668 RS 16.269

1	*[i]štu ūmi annî[m]*	"From this day,
2	*Niqmaddu šar Ugarit*	Niqmaddu, king of Ugarit,
3	*inadin bīt U[R]ganam mār Sakukuna*	shall give the house of U[R]ganam son of Sakukuna,
4	*eqilšu karānšu serdašu*	his field, his vineyard and olive orchard,
5	*kirāšu gabbu mimmi šumšišu*	his garden, and every other item
6	*nadin ana Gabʿanu mār LU A.RIT*	he shall give to Gabʿanu son of (?)
7	*inūma nakir Yatarmu ṭupšarru*	and when Yatarmu the scribe
8	*itti šarri bēlišu u Gab^{c}ana*	became the enemy of his master the king, Gabʿana
9	*idūkšu u inadin*	killed him and gave
10	*beka-Ištar ana šarri*	beka-Ištar to the king his master.
11	*aššum dīnišuma: bēlišu*	Because of this verdict by his master,
12	*nadin nidnūš*	this proposal was fulfilled
13	*ana Gabʿanu ana mārīšu*	for Gabʿanu and his sons.
14	*u uzakkīšu šarru bēlšu*	The king his master shall exempt him
15	*ištu šipri ekallim*	from the temple service.
16	*kīma šamši zakāti bēlu zaki*	Just as the sun is pure, so is the owner [of this property] pure.

II. MRS 16 RS 17.67

2	*[k]īma šapaš zakā[t]i zakīmi*	Just as the sun is pure, so is he pure:
3	*mamman ana ardi la ira[gum]*	no man can claim [this].
4	*u iluzakapti 20 kaspa*	Iluzakapti gave 20 pieces of silver
5	*ana qāti Milkinari*	to Milkinari
6	*mārat Arsuwana ittadin*	daughter of Arsuwana.
7	*ištênšu bēlšu uzakkīšu*	On the one hand, his master purified him,
8	*u ina šanišu Ibri-šarru rābiṣu*	but on the other hand, Ibri-šarru the agent,
9	*ana pî šibûtišu*	through his witnesses,
10	*uzakkīšu kīma šapaš zakāti zaki*	purified him. Just as the sun is pure, so is he pure.
11	*urra šeram*	In the future,
12	*mannumma ana muḫḫišu*	against him a man
13	*la iqarrub*	shall not bring a claim;
14	*aban Ibri-šarru*	the seal of Ibri-šarru
15	*Ilumilku ṭupšarru*	Ilumilku the scribe.

III. MRS 6 110 RS 16.267

1	*ištu ūmi annîm*	From this day,
2	*Amistamru mār Niqmepu*	Amistarmu son of Niqmepu,
3	*šar Ugarit*	king of Ugarit,
4	*uzakki Šayâ amatšu*	purified Šayâ, his maidservant,
5	*ištu amûti kīma šamši zaki*	from servitude. Just as the sun is pure,
6	*uzakat Šaya ištu amâti*	[so] is Šaya pure from servitude.

For our purposes, the verb *zakû* "to be pure," in other words, "free of liabilities or claims," and similarly the adjective *zakû* "pure (innocent)," are the etymological and semantic parallels of the biblical verb *zakhah* and of the adjective *zakh*, which also appear in legal contexts.[21] It is important to note that in Biblical Hebrew, *zakh* appears in synonymous parallelism with *bar* "pure": "My doctrine is pure [*zakh*]//and I am clean [*bar*] in Your eyes" (Job 11:4). In addition, even outside of legal contexts, the adjective *bar* is connected to *ḥammah* "sun," as in the idiomatic expression *barah ka-ḥammah* "pure as the sun" in the Song of Songs 6:9. If so, this biblical expression is the semantic parallel of the Akkadian legal expression from Ugarit *kīma šamši zaki/zakīti* "pure as the sun." Indeed, the fact that in the alphabetic texts from Ugarit the Akkadian legal formula *kīma šamši zaki/zakīti* is the parallel of the northwestern Semitic formula *km špš d brt* "like the sun which is pure," is enlightening. It appears that this formula appears once in a letter that Niqmaddu, king of Ugarit, wrote as a royal order:

2	*bunṯ km. špš*	From a lien, like the sun
3	*d brt. kmt.*	which is pure,[22] so is
4	*br. ṣtqšlm.*	Ṣtqšlm. pure
5	*bunṯ ʿd. ʿlm*	from a lien forever;
6	*mešmn. nqmd.*	the seal of Niqmad,
7	*mlk. ugrt*	king of Ugarit.
8	*nqmd. mlk. ugrt.*	Niqmad, king of Ugarit,
9	*ktb. spr. hnd.*	wrote this document
10	*dt. brrt. ṣtqšlm.*	on the purity [i.e. the freeing from lien] of Ṣtqšlm.,
11	*ʿbdh. hnd.*	this servant of his.
12	*w.mnkm. lyqḫ.*	And no man may take
13	*spr. mlk. hnd.*	this document of the king
14	*b yd. ṣtqšlm.*	from the hand of Ṣtqšlm.
15	*ʿd. ʿlm.*	ever.[23]

III

From the certificate cited here, in which there is a sort of royal privilege that frees *Ṣtqšlm* from a lien placed on real estate that he owns — apparently from payments — we learn that the Ugaritic legal formula *km špš d brt (kmt br ṣtqšlm bunṯ ʿd ʿlm)* "like the sun which is pure, (so is *Ṣtqšlm* pure from a lien forever)" = *kīma šamši zakāt* is the etymological and semantic parallel of the Talmudic legal formula *barur ka-shemesh*. This is a term that denotes complete certainty. It strengthens R. Yishmaʿel's understanding that the biblical sentence "If the sun has risen upon him" reflects the concept of innocence, purity, and complete certainty about the intent of the thief more than it reflects the question of the timing of the act — if it was done during the day or at night.

Based on the above, it is highly reasonable to assume that the term is a metaphor that comes to characterize R. Yishmaʿel's mode of interpretation of the present verse. It does not need to be understood in a figurative manner. Rather, the opposite is more logical: it appears that R. Yishmaʿel's explanation is well rooted in the simple understanding of the verse. It seems that he understands the verse "If the sun has risen upon him" in its legal sense, namely denoting pure intent; the sun is connected with righteousness, peace, and purity of heart. Therefore, it is likely that the phrase *zareḥah ha-shemesh* "the sun has risen," which appears in a legal context in Exod. 22:2, can serve as the biblical formulaic equivalent of the Akkadian legal expression (from Ugarit) *(kīma) šamši zaki/zakât*, the alphabetic Ugaritic term *(km) špš d brt*, the biblical (poetic) idiom *barah ka-ḥammah*, and the Tannaitic phrase *barur ka-shemesh*.

NOTES

1. This article is a translation from H. Tawil, "'If the Sun Has Risen Upon Him' (Exodus 22:2): Legal Terminology in Light of Akkadian Texts from Ugarit" *Lešonenu* 69 (2008), 30–8.
2. *The Interpreter's Bible* (12 vols.; New York: Abingdon Press, 1952), 1:1002; M. Noth, *Exodus: A Commentary* (Philadelphia: Westminster Press, 1962), 183; J. P. Hyatt, *Exodus* (*New Century Bible*; Grand Rapids: Eerdmans, 1980), 237; J. I. Durham, *Exodus* (*Word Biblical Commentary* III; Waco, Texas: Word Books, 1987), 325; C. Houtman, *Exodus* (*Historical Commentary on the Old Testament* III; Lueven:

Peeters, 1993), 190; R. Rothenbusch, *Die Kasuistische Rechtssammlung im Bundesbuch (Ex 21,2 — 11.18 — 22,16)* (*AOAT*, 259), Münster 2000, 343.

3. N. M. Sarna, *The JPS Torah Commentary, Exodus* (Philadelphia: JPS, 1991), 130.
4. *Mekhilta de-R. Yishmaʿel, Mishpatim* 13 (Horowitz and Rabin edition), 293.
5. See also y. *Ket.* 4:4 [28c]; *Sifre Devarim*, par. 237 (Finkelstein edition, 269).
6. See also B. Jacob, *Exodus* (trans. W. Jacob in association with Y. Elman; Hoboken, N.J., 1992), 667–668.
7. A. B. Ehrlich, *Miqra ki-Peshuto* (2 vols.; New York, 1969), 1:179.
8. See Y. Ratshavi, *Perushe Rav Saʿadyah Ga'on le-Sefer Shemot* (Jerusalem 5758 [1998]), 121.
9. *Perush Shadal ʿal Hamishah Hummeshe Torah* (Tel Aviv, 5756 [1996]), 349–350; M. D. Cassuto, *Perush ʿal Sefer Shemot* (Jerusalem, 5709 [1949]), 197. See also D. Henshke, "Ha-ba ba-mahteret — le-yahaso shel ha-midrash la-peshat," *Megadim* 7 (5749 [1989]), 9–15.
10. J. B. Pritchard, *The Ancient Near East in Pictures* (ANEP) (Princeton: Princeton University Press, 1969), nos. 246, 515.
11. *CAD* D 32b 3'; cf.: *šāpit ilī u awīlūtim* "the judge of gods and man" (*CAD* Š1 458b).
12. *CAD* D 32b 3'.
13. *CAD* D 32a 1; cf.: *bēl kitti u mēšari (šamaš)* "the god of truth and righteousness" (K. Tallqvist, *Akkadische Götterepitheta* (Leipzig, 1938), 47, 106–106, cf. 456; N. Sarna, "Psalms and the Near Eastern Sun-God Literature," *Fourth World Congress of Jewish Studies* (Jerusalem, 1967), 171–175.
14. *BWL* 136:177.
15. *BWL* 128:34.
16. *BWL* 134:127.
17. *BWL* 134:143.
18. *CAD* Š1 336a; *EA* 162:78–79; to this formulation of the Amarna writings, cf. *EA* 99:21–24.
19. *ABL* 1396:8 = S. Parpola, *Letters from Assyrian Scholars of the Kings Esarhaddon and Assurbanipal* (Kevelaer: Butzon & Bercker, 1970), no. 71.
20. *CAD* Š/1 336a b.
21. See Prov. 6:11; Ps. 51:6; Job 33:9.
22. G. del Olmo Lete and J. Sanmartin, *A Dictionary of the Ugaritic Language in the Alphabetic Tradition* (Leiden-Boston: Brill, 2003), 1:239, s.v. b-r(-r).

23. Ch. Virolleaud, *Le Palais Royal D'Ugarit*, II, (Paris: Impr. nationale, 1957), text 15.125:1–15; see also W. F. Albright, "Specimens of Late Ugaritic Prose," *BASOR* 150 (1958), 37 line 10; S. A. Loewenstamm, "Teqstim hadashim bi-leshon 'ugarit," *Tarbiz* 28 (1958), 246.

The Lion and the Birds: Isaiah 31:4–5 in the light of Neo-Assyrian Royal Inscriptions

To my dear student Mordechai Siev

יְהִי כְבוֹד תַּלְמִידְךָ חָבִיב עָלֶיךָ כְּשֶׁלָּךְ
(M. *ʾAvot* 4:15)

Isaiah 31:4–5 reads:

ד. כִּי כֹה אָמַר־יְהוָה אֵלַי כַּאֲשֶׁר יֶהְגֶּה הָאַרְיֵה וְהַכְּפִיר עַל־טַרְפּוֹ
אֲשֶׁר יִקָּרֵא עָלָיו מְלֹא רֹעִים, מִקּוֹלָם לֹא יֵחָת, וּמֵהֲמוֹנָם לֹא יַעֲנֶה;
כֵּן, יֵרֵד יְהוָה צְבָאוֹת, לִצְבֹּא עַל־הַר־צִיּוֹן, וְעַל־גִּבְעָתָהּ.
ה. כְּצִפֳּרִים עָפוֹת – כֵּן יָגֵן יְהוָה צְבָאוֹת, עַל־יְרוּשָׁלָם;
גָּנוֹן וְהִצִּיל, פָּסֹחַ וְהִמְלִיט

NJPS renders:

4. For thus the Lord has said to me: As a lion- a great beast- growls over his prey and, when the shepherds gather in force against him, is not dismayed by their cries nor cowed by their noise, so the Lord of Hosts will descend to make war against the mount and the hill of Zion
5. Like the birds that fly, even so the Lord of Hosts shield Jerusalem, shielding and saving, protecting and rescuing

In his commentary on Isaiah, Clements states that Isaiah 31:4–5 has "occasioned not a little difficulty to commentators."[1] These difficulties are closely linked to the alleged unusual and perplexing combination of the two animal similes: one relating to a lion (v. 4) and the other relating to birds (v. 5). Similarly, as noted by Childs, "It has been argued that vv. 1–3 are 'authentic' to Isaiah and reflect a primary Isaianic tradition, apart from some minor expansion. However, vv. 4–5 are thought to be hopelessly incoherent. Verse 4 speaks of a divine intent to destroy Zion, whereas v. 5 expresses the exact opposite position in proclaiming Yahweh's protection."[2] Summarized well by Childs, there are basically three different understandings by commentators as to the unity of vv. 4 and 5.

a. The traditional interpretation (AV, RSV, NEB) translates the verb לִצְבֹּא עַל in positive fashion, 'to fight for,' and sees the action of Yahweh in v. 4 to be part of the same protective action as v. 5.
b. Other commentators suggest either to delete portions of the text in order to remove the tension (Duhm, Scott) or claim that parts of vv. 4 and 5 have been lost (Eichrodt). Several propose that the sequence of the verses be reordered in order to eliminate the problem (Procksch).
c. Most recently a redactional solution has been confidently defended (Vermeylen, Barth, Clements). Accordingly, at a later date a redactor retrojected from the events of 701 the hope for a reversal of Jerusalem's fortunes, thus changing an original negative oracle (v. 4) into a positive omen (v.5).[3]

Childs objects to the first interpretation, noting: "the Hebrew verb with its preposition is used consistently in a negative sense, 'to fight against' (cf. Num 31:7; Isa 29:7; Zech 14:12)." Moreover, Childs likewise maintains: "the image of the attacking lion seems out of place as a protective symbol."[4] With regard to the second interpretation, Childs states: "the great variety of these emendations only illustrates the high level of subjectivity involved."[5] As for the third interpretation, Childs rejects the redactional approach, particularly the solution offered by Clements, who retains v. 4 as genuinely Isaianic, but assigns vv.5 and 8–9 to a seventh-century Josianic redactor.

Childs, who takes v.4 in a negative sense, understands v. 5 as a later stage in the development of the tradition, which reinterprets and transforms v. 4 into a word of promise. Agreeing with his earlier treatment of this problem,[6] Childs continues to hold the position that "first of all, I would like still to insist that the translation of the verb in v. 4 demands a negative connotation, 'to fight against' (cf. NJPS)."[7] Cheryl Exum,[8] while asserting that "it appears that the verses (4–5) are composite from a form-critical as well as a literary perspective," supports Childs, who maintains "persuasively" that v. 5 represents a later addition. However, in regards to the question of the threat or promise that v. 4 may exhibit, Exum suggests that the verse perhaps portrays both![9] Following Exum's interpretation as "quite convincing," G. Eidevall ascertains that "the utterance in v. 4 can be seen as potentially, or even intentionally, ambiguous."[10] Eidevall likewise maintains that "taken in isolation from the simile in v.5, it reads more naturally as a threat. But the juxtaposition of the two similes forces us to read also the first one as a promise."[11]

An alternative, but rather philologically and metaphorically unsound interpretation, is W.L. Barre's understanding that "there is some evidence to indicate that the passage is a unity and thus that the two similes belong together. In their original intent, both are negative."[12] Accordingly, Barre asserts that in light of "*yērēd...ʿal* in the lions simile, the meaning of *yāgēn...ʿal* in Isa. 31:5 is evident. It means 'to (descend and) light upon'." Namely, Barre, on the basis of Aramaic and Syriac, offers us a new meaning of BH *gnn ʿl*: "to descend, come, to rest upon"[13] and not "to protect." Hence, according to Barre, God is portrayed in v. 5 like flying birds (of prey) who will descend and light upon Jerusalem. As for the last four words of v. 5, Barre considers them as "an editorial addition."[14] Barre's interpretation is completely unacceptable, failing to show that a) Heb. *gnn ʿl* means "to descend upon", b) God is never likened to or presented in the Hebrew Bible in the image of "a predatory bird", and c) considering the last four verbs of v.5 (*gānôn whiṣṣil pāsōaḥ whimlîṭ*) as editorial additions is clearly done in order to enhance Barre's doubtful interpretation.

In regards to the lion simile (v. 4), corroborated by various modern commentators, the lion simile is clearly negative, namely, God will come down as a lion or a young lion pounces upon its prey to fight against Mount Zion and against its hill. On the other hand, those scholars who see the lion image as positive hold that the image here is of a lion that protects its prey from those who seek to take it away. "The lion will not allow anyone to steal from him what belongs to him."[15] These scholars compare this behavior to the Lord's determination to defend the city, which belongs to him.

As to the flying birds simile (v. 5), more than one commentator has observed that "the flying birds" is hardly a transparent figure of protection. As noted by Exum, "though the precise meaning of the fluttering birds vehicle may be questioned, the series of protective images which accompanies it (*gānôn whiṣṣil pāsōaḥ whimlîṭ*) makes its defensive symbolism indisputable and emphatic."[16] The simile of the "flying birds" was basically understood in the following four ways: a) as birds of prey defending their prey; b) as birds of prey who will descend and attack Jerusalem; c) as mother birds protecting their young in the nest; d) as frightened birds fleeing danger.

Completely ignored by the aforementioned modern biblical scholars, medieval Jewish exegetes regards Isa 31:4–5 as one inseparable unit, understanding both the lion and "flying birds" similes as positive oracles, an Isaianic salvation prophecy defending Jerusalem from the Assyrian threat.

As for the insistence of Childs that צבא על in Isa 31:4 means "to fight against" i.e., the Lord comes down to fight against Judah, Tg. J understood it as: לְמִשְׁרֵי עַל (טורא דציון ועל רמתה), "to rest upon (Mount Zion and its hill)," to make war against the Assyrian attackers. Similarly, Qimḥi notes כי האל ירד עליה לצבא צבא כנגד צבא מחנה אשור, "for the Lord will descend upon it to fight against the army of the Assyrian camp." Likewise, Joseph Kara states: על מחנה אשור (the Lord will descend…to fight) "against the Assyrian camp." By the "flying birds" simile, the majority of the Jewish medieval exegetes, such as Ibn-Ezra, Joseph Kara, and Isaiah of Miteran, are of the opinion that the birds are flying and protecting their young in the nest. On the other hand, Qimḥi, quoting his father, states: המשיל מלאך ה׳ אשר הכה מחנהו לאריה בגבורתו ולצפרים עפות במהירותו, (my father) "compared the messenger of the Lord that smote the Assyrian camp to a lion in his might and to flying birds in his quickness."

Modern biblical scholarship is in agreement that the historical setting of Isaiah 31 falls in the same general period of 705–701 BCE, leading up to the invasion of Sennacherib[17]; while excluding Isa 31:5, Isa 31:4, however, should almost certainly be placed at the same time, that of the threat to Jerusalem from the army of Sennacherib. To our mind, Isa 31:5 likewise echoes the Assyrian threat and should not be considered a late addition as the majority of modern biblical scholars ascertain.

Accordingly, the purpose of the present article is to show that Isa 31:4–5 is one inseparable unit. These two similes, which gave modern biblical scholarship difficulties as an "unusual and perplexing combination of animal metaphors,"[18] may be clarified in the light of Assyrian royal inscriptions, especially those of Sennacherib.

In 1969, the Semitist H.W.F. Saggs, in his inaugural lecture "Assyriology and the Study of the Old Testament,"[19] delivered at University College Cardiff, observed that:

> the prophet Isaiah himself, in whose time Assyrian imperial power and cultural influence were at their height, showed a keen interest in the affairs and even certain features of the culture of Assyria, which he hailed as God's instrument, directed against a godless nation. His interests appear to have extended beyond Theology to Comparative Semitic Philology, for we find the prophet making a pun based on cross-correspondences between Hebrew and Akkadian vocabulary. 'Are not', he credits the Assyrian empire with saying, 'my commanders all kings?' (Isa 10:8). The literal answer to this rhetorical question was- as Isaiah well knew- that they were not. Isaiah was showing his linguistic erudition, in that the

> Akkadian word for 'king' was, in the Assyrian dialect of Isaiah's time, a homophone of the Hebrew word for 'commander'; so that to call an Assyrian field-commander by his proper title in Hebrew was to call him a king in his own language.

In 1979, Chaim Cohen in his article "Neo-Assyrian Elements in the First Speech of the Biblical Rab-Šāqê,"[20] isolated various elements that have parallels in Neo-Assyrian annals. In 1982, Peter Machinist, in an extensive article entitled "Assyria and its Image in the First Isaiah,"[21] noted some six specific examples where the Assyrian royal inscription phraseology is echoed in Isaiah, when describing the fierce Assyrian army. Likewise, in 1982, Hayim Tawil, in his article "The Historicity of 2 Kings 19:24 (= Isaiah 37:25): The Problem of *Ye'ōrê Māṣôr*,"[22] pointed out that Isaiah was likewise familiar with Sennacherib's domestic affairs. In 1999, in his book "Sennacherib's Campaign to Judah,"[23] William Gallagher observed various other Assyrian-Isaianic parallels. Shawn Aster published two articles (2007 and 2009)[24] demonstrating some parallels indicating that Isaiah was familiar with both the ideas found in Neo-Assyrian royal inscriptions and the stereotypical phrases and characteristic language found in them.

In the light of the above Assyrian-Isaianic highly specific parallels, one may proceed to analyze Isa 31:4–5. Indeed, these two verses will prove that Isaiah is employing the motif of the reverse or replacement theology.

It is well known that in their annals, the Assyrian kings compare themselves to a raging lion, which symbolizes might, great strength, and boldness. Aššurnāṣirpal II boasts that he is *labbāku u zikrāku*, "I am a lion and a warrior."[25] Esarhaddon describes himself as *labbu nadru mutīr gimil abī ālidišu,* "a raging lion, who avenges his own father"[26] (i.e., Sennacherib). More specifically, in the Neo-Assyrian annals, in a warfare context, the adverbs *labbiš* and *kīma labbi*, "like a lion" are used to portray Sargon, who marches proudly against his enemies, like a raging terror-laden lion: *ina uggat libbiya ummānāt aššur gapšāti adkēma labbiš anadirma ana kavad mātāti šâtima aštakan panīya* "In the anger of my heart I set in motion the mighty armies of Aššur, and, raging like a lion, set out to conquer those lands."[27] In his campaign against Unantu, Sargon boasts: *kīma labbi nadri ša puluḫtu ramû etelliš attalakma*, "I marched (through Urartu) proudly, like a raging, terror-laden lion."[28] Likewise, Sennacherib in his annals portrays himself as *labbiš ammadirma allabie abūbiš*, "I became rampant like a lion, raging like a storm."[29]

Indeed, Jeremiah (Jer 4:7) describes the threat of the invader Nebuchadnezzar as follows: עָלָה אַרְיֵה מִסֻּבְּכוֹ, וּמַשְׁחִית גּוֹיִם נָסַע יָצָא מִמְּקֹמוֹ לָשׂוּם אַרְצֵךְ לְשַׁמָּה..., "The lion comes up from its thicket, the destroyer of the nation has set out, has departed from his place, to make your land a desolation...." More specifically, in portraying the Assyrian invasion into Judah, Sennacherib is likened by Isaiah to a terror-laden lion as follows: שְׁאָגָה לוֹ כַּלָּבִיא יִשְׁאַג כַּכְּפִירִים וְיִנְהֹם וְיֹאחֵז טֶרֶף וְיַפְלִיט וְאֵין מַצִּיל. "His (Sennacherib) roaring is like a lion's, his roar like a great beast, when he growls and seizes his prey, he carries it off and none can recover it" (Isa 5:29).[30]

It is well known that, metaphorically, the Lord is depicted as roaring (i.e. thundering) like a lion.[31] However, in the reverse or replacement theology motif, the Lord and not the Assyrian king is portrayed as a lion, attacking the enemies of Judah. This motif is evident when Hosea (11:10) depicts the Lord as a lion who saves his nation: אַחֲרֵי יְהוָה יֵלְכוּ כְּאַרְיֵה יִשְׁאָג כִּי־הוּא יִשְׁאַג וְיֶחֶרְדוּ בָנִים מִיָּם. "The lion will roar like a lion, and they shall march behind him when he roars, his children shall come fluttering out of the west." In Isa 31:4, the prophet likewise metaphorically portrays the Lord as a lion who descends upon Mount Zion to fight against King Sennacherib and to free Judah from the Assyrian siege.

Though modern biblical scholarship regards Isa 31:5 as later editorial insertion, it fails to understand the metaphorical relationship of "the lion" and "the flying birds." However, in light of the following proposed new interpretation, based upon the Neo-Assyrian inscriptions, especially those of Sennacherib, v. 5 will become clearer and the unity of vv. 4–5 will become evident.

The simile "flying like a bird" occurs a number of times in the Assyrian royal inscriptions.[32] Akkadian employs the verb *naprušu/naparšudu* "to fly," employed a number of times with the idiom *kīma iṣṣūri/iṣṣūrāti*, "like birds." Indeed, numerous Assyrian kings report that their enemies, in order to save their lives and escape to freedom, flew away like birds, i.e. *kī/kīma iṣṣūri/iṣṣūriš naparšudu*, "flying like birds" (in order to see freedom). Tiglath-Pileser I states: *ana šūzub napšātēšum ilānīšuru iššana gisallāt šaqûti kīma iṣṣūri ipparšū* "In order to save themselves they (the enemies) took their gods and flew off to the highest mountain peaks like birds."[33] Likewise, Sargon boasts that his enemies *ana qereb birāti šuʾātina kīma iṣṣūri ipparšu*, "flew like birds into those fortresses."[34]Indeed the Akkadian simile *kī/kīma iṣṣūri/iṣṣūriš naparšudu* is the semantic equivalent of Isaiah's כצפורים עפות, "like flying birds."

More specifically, the bird is also utilized twice in the neo-Assyrian annals to invoke the image of incarceration (i.e., *esēru*), especially in reference to the besieged cities. Tiglat Pileser III recounts the siege of Rezin of Damascus as follows: *ālišu akṣurma kīma iṣṣur quppi esiršu* "…I set up around his city, like a bird in a cage I shut him up."[35] This simile is also used by Sennacherib in the well celebrated case describing the siege of Jerusalem during his campaign against Hezekiah (2 Kings 18:14–16) in 701: *šâšu kī kīma iṣṣūr quppi qereb ursalimma/u āl šarrūtīšu ēsiršu* "Himself, like a bird in a cage, in his royal city, Jerusalem, I shut him up."[36]

As noted by Peter Machinist, the author of First Isaiah was familiar with both the ideas found in the Neo-Assyrian royal inscriptions and the characteristic language found in them. Accordingly, Machinist supposed: "Isaiah's knowledge of Assyria was gained not merely from actual experience of the Assyrians in Palestine, but from official literature, especially of the court."[37]

Consequently, the prophet Isaiah seems deeply familiar with Sennacherib's boastful statement, confining Hezekiah and, for that matter, Jerusalem's dwellers *kīma iṣṣur quppi* "like a bird in a cage." Isaiah in v. 5 employed once again the motif of the reverse or replacement theology. Namely, Hezekiah will not be confined 'like a bird' in a cage, rather Hezekiah and, for that matter, the city's dwellers will be free as flying birds (כצפורים עפות), protected by the Lord. Hence, Isaiah's employment of the four verbs (v. 5) גָּנוֹן וְהִצִּיל פָּסֹחַ וְהִמְלִיט, "protecting and saving, sparing and rescuing," is not a late editorial addition. Rather, the prophet seems to intentionally employ these four verbs, reflecting the four expressions of redemption from the Egyptian bondage: וְהוֹצֵאתִי, וְהִצַּלְתִּי, וְגָאַלְתִּי, וְלָקַחְתִּי "(and I will) free, deliver, redeem, take out." Indeed, this was the understanding of the usage of the verb פָּסֹחַ (v. 5) in the Mekhilta of Rabbi Ishmael[38]:

> ומה ת"ל וראיתי את הדם אלא בשכר מצוה שאתם עושים אני נגלה וחס עליכם שנאמר ופסחתי עליכם אין פסיחה אלא חייס שנאמר כצפרים עפות כן יגן שנאמר כצפרים עפות כן יגן ה' צבאות על ירושלים גנון והציל פסוח והמליט.
>
> What is the purpose of 'and when I see the blood'? It is only this: as a reward for your performing this duty, I shall reveal myself and protect you, as it is said: Passing over merely means protecting, as it is said: 'As birds hovering' so the Lord of hosts protects Jerusalem, protecting and saving, sparing and rescuing.

NOTES

1. R. E. Clements, *Isaiah 1–39* (Grand Rapids: Eerdmans, 1980), 256.
2. B. S. Childs, *Isaiah*, (Louisville: Westminster John Knox Press, 2001), 231.
3. Ibid., 232–233.
4. Ibid., 233.
5. Ibid.
6. B. S. Childs, *Isaiah and the Assyrian Crisis* (London: S.C.M. Press, 1967), 58.
7. Childs, *Isaiah,* 233.
8. J. C. Exum, "Of Broken Pots, Fluttering Birds and Visions in the Night: Extended Simile and Poetic Technique in Isaiah," CBQ 43 (1981), 337.

9. Ibid., 338.
10. G. Eidevall "Lions and Birds as Literature. Some Notes on Isaiah 31 and Hosea 11," *SJOT* 7 (1993), 79.
11. *Ibid.*, 82.
12. M. L. Barre, "Of Lions and Birds: A Note on Isaiah 31.4" in Among the Prophets: Language, Image, and Structure in the Prophetic Writings (eds. D. Clines and P. Davies; JSOTSup 144; Sheffield: JSOT press, 1993), 57.
13. Ibid., 58.
14. Ibid., 59.
15. Exum, "Of Broken Pots," 338.
16. Ibid.
17. Childs, *Isaiah and the Assyrian Crisis*, 58; *Idem*, *Isaiah*, 232–233.
18. Eidevall, "Lions and Birds," 79.
19. H. W. F. Saggs, *Assyriology and the study of the Old Testament: an inaugural lecture delivered at University College, Cardiff, Tuesday December 3rd, 1968* (Cardiff: University of Wales Press, 1969), 1–27.
20. C. Cohen, "Neo-Assyrian Elements in the First Speech of the Biblical Rab-šaqê," *IOS* 9 (1979), 32–48.
21. P. Machinist, "Assyria and Its Image in the First Isaiah," *JAOS* 103 (1983), 719–37.
22. H. Tawil, The Historicity of 2 Kings 19:24 (= Isaiah 37:25): The Problem of *Ye'ōrê Māṣôr*," *JNES* 41 (1982), 195–206.
23. W. R. Gallagher, *Sennacherib's Campaign to Judah: New Studies* (Leiden: Brill, 1999).
24. S. Z. Aster, "The Image of Assyria in Isaiah 2:5–22: The Campaign Motif Reversed," *JAOS* 127 (2007). 249–278; *idem.* What Sennacherib Said, and What the Prophet Heard: On the Use of Assyrian Sources in the Prophetic Narrative of the Campaign of 701 BCE," *Snaton* 19 (2009), 105–124. (Heb.)
25. *CAD* L 25a 2'.
26. *CAD Ibid.*
27. *CAD* L 236 a). cf. Also the idiom *kīma labbi/nēši nayāru* "to roar like a lion."
28. *CAD* L 24b b).
29. CAD L 23b a) Note also e.g. *labbiš annadirma iṣṣarḫ kabattī* "I (Esarhaddon) became as angry as a lion, my mood became furious" (*CAD* ibid.). See D. Marcus, "Animal Similes in Assyrian Royal Inscriptions," *Orientalia* 46 (1977), 87–88; S. Vargon, "The Descriptions of the Coming of the Enemy in Isaiah 5:26–30," *Beit Mikra* 159 (1999), 299–301. (Heb.).
30. Cf. also Joel 1:6; Nah 2:12.

31. See B. Strawn, "What is Stronger than a Lion? Leonine Image and Metaphor in the Hebrew Bible and the Ancient Near East," *Orbis Biblicus et Orientalis* (2005), 58–63.
32. Marcus, "Animal Similes," 97–98.
33. *CAD* I/j 211b e).
34. *CAD* I/j 212a.
35. *CAD* ibid.
36. *CAD* ibid.
37. Machinist, "Assyria and its Image," 79.
38. J. Z. Lauterbach, *Mekhilta of Rabbi Ishmael* (Philadelphia: JPS, 1933), 56.

Northwest Semitic Inscriptions

A Note on the Aḥiram Inscription

In the first line of the Aḥiram inscription (*KAI*, No. 1:1) mentions of the construction of Aḥiram's sarcophagus by his son. It contains the enigmatic phrase כשתה בעלם. In 1926, Albright,[1] followed by Harris,[2] rendered the phrase "as a place of sleeping in the otherworld." He derived שתה from Akkadian *šittu*, Hebrew שנה, "sleep," and בעלם from the Late Hebrew expression בעלם הבא. Twenty-one years later, Albright, following Dussaid,[3] rendered it "as his ab(o)de in eternity,"[4] assuming an omission of a ב, i.e., *kšth>kš(b)th*. He compared the usage of ישב with עולם to the Biblical Hebrew phrase מכון לשבתך עולמים,[5] "your everlasting dwelling place," translating בעלם "in eternity." In his translation of the Aḥiram inscription, Rosenthal[6] adopts Albright's *kaš(ib) tih(u)*, but his rendering, "as his eternal <dwelling> place," glosses over the difficult usage of the proposition ב.

Albright's interpretation is open to questions for several reasons. First, although the verb ישב is attested in Biblical Hebrew in connection with burial places, e.g., הישבים בקברים ובנצורים ילינו[7] "who dwell in the tombs, who lodge in the niches," there the prophet refers not to the dead, but to the living who occupy burial places. Also, the analogy drawn by Albright to מכון לשבתך עולמים is inappropriate. ישב is employed in the context of the divine abode rather than one involving a place of human burial. In short, the verb ישב is not employed to express burial either in Biblical Hebrew or in Phoenician.

Second, Albright's emendation of *šth>š(b)th* overlooks the attested usage of שית and its semantic equivalents in contexts clearly involving burial. Biblical Hebrew employs both the verb שות and its poetic counterpart שפת in such contexts. For example:[8] כצאן לשאול שתו "like sheep they are placed(!) into Sheol";[9] שתני בבור תחתיות "you placed me in the nethermost pit"; ולעפר מות תשפתני[10] "you put me in the grave of (lit. the dust of) death." Ugaritic employs the verb *šyt* with *ḥrt*, "hollows, holes," e.g., *abky waqbrnh ašt bḥrt ilm arṣ*[11] "I weep and place it in the hollows of the earth-ghosts." Similarly, the verb שים is attested in Phoenician alongside the substantive קבר, e.g.,[12] אש (ש)ם לקבר זה, "that placed in this grave." It would seem best to follow those scholars[13] who construe the form שתה as the 3 per. masc. perfect of שית with the 3 per. masc. sing. accumulative suffix, and render שתהכ "when he put him."

Third, Albright's rendering of בעלם, "in eternity,"[14] is problematic since Northwest Semitic never employs the preposition ב with the substantive עלם. So too, Akkadian **ina dār/dārāti/dārīti* seems not to be attested.[15]

The problem is avoided when the ב of בעלם is interpreted as something other than the preposition "in." The most likely alternative to the latter is in viewing בעלם as an abbreviation of בת עלם, "in[16] the house of eternity." It should be recalled that the omission of the ת in the word בית, "house," is attested in Old Aramaic[17] בי טב, "a good house," in Egyptian Aramaic[18] אתי ארק בי I זילי "there is the land of one house belonging to me," and[19] כאיש גנב זי שתר בי "like a thief who demolishes a house." In Jewish Aramaic, בי is the regular construct of בית in such cases as בי רבנן, "college,"[20] בי אבא, "a house of the father," and[21] בי קבורא, "cemetery."

More striking is the abbreviation of בית in the expression[22] בי עלמא, "cemetery." The identical euphemism, בת עלם, is attested in Punic with the meaning "tomb," e.g., חדר בת עלם קבר נ[פעל],[23] "a niche in a tomb, a grave has been made," as well as in Palmyrene inscriptions, e.g.,[24] עלם דנא עבר מתני... "this house of eternity has been made by Matani...." In Biblical Hebrew, one finds[25] כי הולך אדם אל בית עולמו "because man goes to his house of eternity." This usage continues and is commonly attested in Late Hebrew.

As long noted, Egyptian employs the euphemistic expression *ṅiwt ntt nḥḥ*,[26] "the city of eternity." To be viewed alongside this usage is the Akkadian *šubat dārāti/dārât*, "the dwelling place of eternity," attested as follows: (a) *ēkal ṣalāli kimaḫ tapšuḫti šubat dārâti*[27] "a palace of sleeping, a resting tomb, a dwelling place of eternity;" and (b) *ēkal tapšuḫti šubat dārât*[28] "a palace of repose, a dwelling place of eternity." It should be noted that both of those references are drawn from inscriptions appearing on bricks from the royal sepulcher at Assur. Thus, Akkadian *šubat dārâti/dārât*, "a dwelling place of eternity," rendered as "Garb" by von Soden,[29] is the exact semantic equivalent of Northwest Semitic בית עולם or, as it appears in the Aḥiram inscription, בעלם.

NOTES

1. W. F. Albright, "The End of the Sarcophagus Text of Aḥiram," *JPOS* 6 (1926), 79.
2. Z. Harris, *A Grammar of the Phoenician Language* (New Haven: American Oriental Scoiety, 1936), 107.
3. Dussaid, "Les Inscriptions phéniciennes du tombeau d' Aḥiram, roi de Byblos," *Syria* 5 (1924), 136.
4. W. F. Albright, "The Phoenician Inscriptions of the Tenth Century B.C. from Byblos," *JAOS* 67 (1947), 155, n. 19.
5. I Kings 8:13 = II Chr. 6:2.
6. *ANET*[3] 661b.
7. Isa. 65:4.
8. Ps. 49:15.
9. Ps. 88:7.
10. Ps. 22:16 Note that the Targum renders עפר מות as בית קבורתא.
11. *ID*:112, 126, 141; cf. 1**AB*,5:5; *IAB*, 1:16–18.
12. A. M. Honeyman, "The Phoenician Inscriptions of the Cyprus Museum," *Iraq* 6 (1939), 107.
13. C. Torrey, "The Aḥiram Inscription from Byblos," *JAOS* 45 (1925): 270; M. Montet, "*Byblos et l'Egypte* (Paris, 1928–29), 238, n. l; J. Friedrich, "Zur Einleitungsformel der ältesten phönizischen Inschriften aus Byblos," *Mélanges syriens* (Paris, 1939), 43. See most recently H. Donner and W. Röllig, *Kanaanäische und aramäiche Inschriften* (Wiesbaden, 1968) (hereafter *KAI*), Band II, 2–3.
14. So, too, J. Friedrich, *op. cit.*, p. 43, renders the phrase בעלם כשתה "when he put him in eternity (= the tomb)." The rendering "in eternity" is also adopted in *KAI* II, p. 2.
15. Note that *ina dārīti* (*EA* 147:48) is considered an error for *ana dārīti* by *CAD* D 115.
16. The preposition ב need not appear orthographically when it precedes a word beginning with the same letter; cf. e.g., Gen. 24:23. The phenomenon also occurs in Ugaritic, e.g., *bty (for *bbty)* in *IK:205; IK, 1:14–15 bḥyk abn nšmḥ blmtk* (for **bblmtk*) *ngln;* ibid., II. 98–99. See further

H.L. Ginsberg, "The North-Canaanite Myth of Anath and Aqhat: II," *BASOR* 98 (1945), 16, n. 27, and 20, n. 46; U. Cassuto, *The Goddess Anath* (Jerusalem: Magnes Press, 1953), 39. Clearly, the examples are too numerous to be explained on the basis of haplography. Note that Torrey (*op. cit.*, p. 272) considered עלם the abbreviated form of בת עלם, anticipating, somewhat, the suggestion offered above. However, he retained ב as the preposition, rather than as an abbreviation of בת.

17. *KAI*, No. 216:16 (Bīr- Rākib). In this example, and in those which follow, the abbreviation בי׳ for בית, "house," reflects the indication of the diphthong by *yod*. In Byblian Phoenician, the diphthong is not preserved. In the Aḥiram inscription ב may stand for בת, "house."
18. A. Cowley, *Aramaic Papyri of the Fifth Century B.C.* (reprint: 1967), No. 9:3.
19. Ibid., *Aḥiqar*, 125.
20. See M. Jastrow, *Dictionary* (2 vols.; New York: Peabody, 1950), 158b for other examples.
21. Targum on Job 7:9.
22. T. Nöldeke, "Syrische Inschriften," *ZA* 21 (1908), 158.
23. *CIS*: 124; also N. Slouschz, *The Thesaurus of the Phoenician Inscriptions* (Tel-Aviv: Mossad Biyalik, 1942), 126, No. 109.
24. G. Cooke, *A Text-Book of North-Semitic Inscription* (Oxford: Clarendon Press, 1903), 307:1; cf. ibid., 308:1, 339:6.
25. Ecc. 12:5. See H. L. Ginsberg, *Koheleth* (Jerusalem, 1961), 132.
26. Montet, *op. cit.*, p. 238, n. l.
27. *OIP* 2, 151, No. 14:3.
28. Ibid., No. 13:2.
29. *AHw*, 164; contrast the rendering "to dwell there forever" in *CAD* D 111.

The End of the Hadad Inscription in the Light of Akkadian[1]

The end of the Hadad inscription (*KAI* no. 214:33–34) reads as follows: או תחק עליה או תאלב אש זר [ל]הרגה. Although most of the words are clear, the passage as a whole has been troublesome to scholars. The problem centers around the antecedent of the prepositional phrase עליה and the infinitival phrase [ל]הרגה. These two phrases were rendered by Cooke,[2] followed by Donner-Röllig,[3] as "concerning him" and "to kill him," respectively. Thus, the antecedent has been construed as a future descendant of Panammuwa who might either be defamed or killed. The traditional translation of the above passage reads as follows: "or shall write concerning him, or teach a stranger to kill him."

An alternative to this interpretation takes as the antecedent of the third person pronoun not a descendant, but rather the memorial stele itself.[4] This suggestion gains in probability when we note that Mesopotamian royal inscriptions, boundary stones, and some votive inscriptions, etc., may conclude with (a) prohibitions against alteration or destruction of the object, and (b) a series of curses.

Our main concern at present, however, is the list of prohibitions. The conventional prohibitions may be grouped as follows: (1) not to erase the name of the king or the gods from the stele and/or reinscribe it with other names;[5] (2) not to hide/bury, cover in the dust/ground/earth, place where (it) cannot be seen;[6] not to bring (it) into a darker place;[7] not to bring it into a place where (it) cannot be seen;[8] not to enclose (it) within a wall;[9] not to hide (it);[10] not to cast (it) down/throw into a river/well/water/fire;[11] not to topple/alter/remove (it) by force from its location;[12] not to steal (it).[13]

Similarly, it is apparent that in Northwest Semitic inscriptions (i.e., Azitawadda, Sefîre) the scribes are equally concerned with the above dual prohibition against erasure or mutilation of the inscription:

Azitawadda:

(a) ...אם אדם אש אדם שמ אש ימח שם אזתוד בשעד זה ושת שם

or any ordinary man, who shall erase the name of Azitawadda from this gate and put down (= write) his own name.[14]

(b) אם אף יחמד אית הקרת ז ויסע השער ז אש פעל אזתוד

if he covets this city and removes this gate which Azitawadda constructed....[15]

Sefîre:

(a) [ומן י]אמר להלדת ספריא [א]לן

and whoever will give orders to efface these inscriptions.[16]

(b) ו[י]אמר אהאבד ספר [י] א

and will say 'I shall destroy the inscriptions.'[17]

So, too, it stands to reason to divide the lines in the Hadad inscription into two sections: (1) או תחק עליה; (2) [ל]הרגה או תאלב אש זר. The former, rendered by Cooke and Donner-Röllig as "you shall write concerning him," would seem to imply either defamation of, or conspiracy against, the king's heir. If such were the case, however, one would expect the author to employ an idiom such as אמר כרצי "to slander"[18] or מלל על "to plot, conspire." Indeed, such an idiom in a similar context is attested in the Sefîre inscriptions: וי[מל]ל [ע]לי "and will plot against me";[19] and וימלל מלן לחית לעלי "and plot evil against me."[20] Accordingly, it seems best to assume that חקק על means "to inscribe on" in our context. This equates this expression with the following Akkadian-Hebrew idioms denoting "to inscribe on (a stele, statue, etc.)": Akkadian *šaṭāru eli/ina muḫḫi/ina qereb/ina libbi/ina ṣēri*[21] = Hebrew כתב/חקק על.[22] This assumption gains in probability when one notes that from

Old Akkadian onwards we find attested the formula *šumī pašāṭu/šupšuṭu — šumšu šaṭāru/šušṭuru/šakānu* "to erase/order to erase my name — to write/order to write his name." The earliest form of this formula is attested in a Narām-Sîn inscription: *u awīlam nakaram ukallamūma šumšume pišiṭma šumī šuku[n] iqabbiu* "or instructs a stranger and orders (him): 'erase his name and put down my name.'"[23] In Old Babylonian we find this formula employed in the royal inscription of Tākil-Ilišu of Malgium,[24] in the foundation inscription of Yaḫdunlim,[25] and in the epilogue to the Code of Ḫammurabi.[26] From the Kassite period onwards this formula is well attested in the *kudurrus*,[27] as well as in Assyrian royal inscriptions.[28]

Both Hadad's scribe and the Phoenician scribe of Azitawadda do not employ the classical Akkadian formula *šumī pašāṭu — šumšu šaṭāru* in its entirety.[29] Nevertheless, Hadad's scribe's usage of חקק על in this context seems to indicate an awareness of the formulaic ending in cuneiform royal inscriptions.

Moreover, the Old Aramaic idiom אלב אש זר[30] employed at the end of the inscription points betrays structural and semantic Akkadian influences. Donner-Röllig renders the verb אלב "lernen/lehren," treating it as Qal.[31] It is preferable to seek here the intensive conjugation of אלב, which normally denotes "to teach." It will become clear, moreover, that conventional usage favors a stronger nuance, i.e. "to instigate, to incite."

A glance at the closing statements of standard Akkadian royal inscriptions will suffice to make it clear that Donner-Röllig fails to grasp the particular usage of the verb אלב in our context. In addition to the curse against a willful violator of the prohibitions, a well-known feature of these inscriptions is a clause extending the curse to the would-be accomplice.

Thus, Akkadian employs the following verbs to indicate the instigation of another: *kullumu*, "to instruct" (lit., "show"),[32] *wu''uru* "to order, to commission,"[33] and *qabû* "to order."[34]

A more common way to convey the above idea is by using the Akkadian *aḫāzu*, which in the *Š* conjugation normally denotes "to teach, to educate." It is also frequently found with the meaning "to incite, to instigate (to do something)."[35] Thus, the Akkadian *aḫāzu* in the causative conjugation is the exact semantic equivalent of the Old Aramaic אלב in the intensive stem.

Further, from Old Akkadian royal inscriptions onwards, the accomplice hired to damage the monument may belong to any of the following categories: *nakrum* (*nakarum*) "stranger"; *ajjābum* "enemy"; *awīlum lemnum* "evil man"; *lā pāliḫ ili* "irreverent person"; *saklum* "fool"; *lā nāṭilum* "one without intelligence"; *lā mūdûm* "witless" (lit., "not knowing"); *nuʿûm* "imbecile";[36] *sakkum* (*sukkukum*) "deaf man"; *samûm* "undependable person"; *isḫappum* "rogue";[37] *(ša) bīt kīli* "prisoner";[38] *lišānu nakirtu* "foreigner"; *awīlūtum šikin napišti* "any human being."[39] Another way to describe the accomplice is by the Akkadian terms *aḫûm* "stranger" and *šanûm* "someone else."[40] These, of course, are the exact semantic equivalents of our Old Aramaic אש זר. The following few examples will suffice in order to demonstrate the usage of the Akkadian formula "to incite/instigate a stranger/someone else" = Old Aramaic אלב אש זר (a) OB: *aššum errētim šinātì šanīamma uštāḫiz* "if he has instigated someone else on account of these curses";[41] (b) MB: *lū aššum errēti šinātina nakara aḫâ ajjāba lemna lišana nakirta... ušaḫḫaz* "If he instigates a hostile stranger, an evil enemy, a foreigner on account of these curses";[42] (c) NA: *aššum izzirti šinātina nakra aḫâ ajjāba lemna lū bīt kīli lū amēlūta šikin napišti... ušaḫḫazu* "if he instigates a hostile stranger, an evil enemy, a prisoner, or any human being on account of these curses."[43] Moreover, it is worthwhile to compare our formula אלב אש זר "to instigate a stranger" to the one employed in the Sefîre inscription: ויזחל הא מן לד ספר[י]א מן בתי אלהיא ויאמר לזי לידע... ו[י]אמר לד [ספ]ריא אלן מן בתי [א]להיא "should that (man) be frightened from effacing the inscription from the bethels and command an idiot....and (then) order him 'efface these inscriptions from the bethels.'"[44] Thus, both the Hadad and the Sefîre inscriptions demonstrate a striking example of Akkadian influence on Old Aramaic. Both faithfully adhere to the cuneiform tradition while drawing their respective terminologies from different sources within that tradition. Thus:

(a) Hadad אלב = Akk. *šūḫuzu*
Sefîre אמר = Akk. *qabû*
(b) Hadad אש זר = Akk. *aḫu/šanû*
Sefîre זי לידע = Akk. *lā mūdû*

Furthermore, although Cooke, followed by Donner-Röllig, renders [ל]הרגה "to kill him" — the reference being to Panammuwa's heir — one may prefer Müller's rendering "to destroy it," referring to the memorial stele erected rather than the heir.[45]

Müller's suggestion gains in probability when we note that in the cuneiform royal inscriptions and boundary stones the Akkadian idiom *šanâ/aḫâ šūḫuzu* "to incite a stranger/someone else" (old Aramaic אלב אש זר) is frequently used in conjunction with the destruction and mutilation of a stele.[46]

The following examples will demonstrate the structure of the Akkadian phrase under consideration: (a) *lū bārâ lū mamma šanû ṣalmu šuātu ḫulliq ša pīšu lā epāše iqabbâššu* "Whether he orders a diviner or anyone else saying what he should not say: 'destroy this stele'";[47] (b) *šanâmma ušaḫḫazūma... narâ annâ ina abni ubbatu* "(if) he instigates someone else and he destroys this stele with a stone."[48] Thus, the Akkadian phrases *lū mamma šanâ/šanâmma... qabû/šūḫuzu — ḫulluqu/ubbutu* "to instruct/instigate anybody else — to destroy," may be the functional and structural equivalent of the Old Aramaic phrase אלב אש זר [ל]הרג "to instigate someone else to destroy (lit., to kill)."

Similarly, most Northwest Semitic royal inscriptions are concluded with a brief warning to avoid the destruction of a stele/statue/inscription: Kilamuwa: שחת/נזק ספר "to destroy/demolish the inscription";[49] Zākir: הגע נצבא "to cast down the stele";[50] Zākir-Nērab הנס נצבא/צלמא מן אשרה "to remove (by force) the stele/statue from its location";[51] Sefîre: האבד/הלד ספר "to destroy/efface an inscription";[52] Tēmā: חבל סותא "to destroy a stele."[53]

It should be noted that the Canaanite verb הרג is employed seven times in Old Aramaic, all occurrences being restricted to the dialect of Samʾal.[54] Of these, only in the four cases attested in Panammuwa II does it clearly denote "to kill."

Further, the semantic equivalent of the Canaanite הרג is Akkadian *dâku*, which usually denotes "to kill, slay," but may also mean "to destroy, to break (a tablet)." This usage is attested in only Old Assyrian. It corresponds to the Old Babylonian, Middle and Neo-Assyrian use of the verb *ḫepû* "to break, destroy (a tablet)."[55] Though not attested in conjunction with a *ṣalmu* or *narû*, Akkadian *dâku* in this derived meaning may shed some light upon the otherwise unique usage of הרג in our inscription. The use of the verb "to kill" with respect to destroying a physical object may be related to a broader pattern of figurative usage, not unlike ערף in Biblical Hebrew.[56]

In the light of the above evidence, the Hadad passage או תחק עליה או תאלב אש זר is to be translated as follows: "or shall inscribe on it, or instigate someone else to destroy it."

NOTES

1. This paper is based on the writer's Ph.D. dissertation entitled "Idioms in Old Aramaic Royal Inscriptions in the Light of Akkadian," submitted to Columbia University, May 1971.

   Abbreviations for Akkadian sources are those employed in the *Chicago Assyrian Dictionary*. Abbreviations of Northwest Semitic sources are those listed in volume 2 of H. Donner-W. Röllig's *Kanaanäische und Aramäische Inschriften*, (2 vols.; Wiesbaden: Harrassowitz, 1968), hereafter cited as *KAI*.
2. *NSI*, P. 163.
3. *KAI* 2, P. 216.
4. See D. H. Müller, *The Contemporary Review* 65 (1894), 573.
5. For a discussion of this prohibition, see below, notes 24–26.
6. E.g. *VAS* 1 37 v. 29 (*ina eperi temēru*); *BBSt.*, 35:36 (*ina eqel lā amāri temēru*); ibid., 45:12 (*ina erṣeti/ašar lā amāri temēru*); ibid., 17:46–47 (*ina eperi šutmuru*); *AOB* 1 24 v. 18–20 (*ina eperim qebērum*); *KAH* 1 3 r. 14 (*ina eperi kuttumu*); *BBSt.*, p. 28:20 (*ina erṣeti qebēru*).
7. E.g., *BBSt.*, 28 iii 7–8 (*ana bīt ekleti šūrubu*).
8. E.g., ibid., line 7 (*ašar lā amāri šūrubu*); ibid., 22:7 (*ašar lā amāri šuškunu*); ibid., 78-21-22 (*ašar lā amāri šakānu*).
9. E.g., *MDP* 2 pl. 22 v. 54 (*ina igāri peḫû*).
10. E.g., VAS 1 36:1; ibid., 37:31 (puzra šūḫuzu/šūtāḫuzu).<FNE> not to burn (it) in fire;

11. E.g., *BBSt.*, p. 17:44; ibid., p. 35:36 (*ina išāti šūkulu*); ibid., p. 41–11 (*ina išāti qalû*); *VAS* 1 36 iv 21 (*ina išāti qamû*); 1R 70 iii 4 (*ina išāti šarāpu*).
12. E.g., *BBSt.*, 7:21–22 (*ana mê nadû*); ibid., 22:2–3 (*ana mê/išāti nadû*); ibid., 28:18–19 (*ana mê/išāti šuddû*); ibid., 41:10–11; ibid., 69 v. 1–2 (*ana nāri nadû//ana būrti nasāku*).
13. For a discussion of these prohibitions and related materials, see below, notes 50 and 51.
14. Note that although this warning is not commonly employed, it is attested in the statue of Idrimi: *mannummê ṣalmīya anninâti išarriqu* "whoever steals these statues of mine" (S. Smith, *The Statue of Idri-mi* [London: British Institute of Archeology in Ankara, 1949], 22, line 92). Akkadian *ṣalma šarāqu* may be equated with the Punic expression גנב אבן/מתנת, e.g., *CIS* 1 3783:5–6; ibid., 3784:1–2. For a translation and discussion of these Punic texts see S. Gervitz, "West-Semitic Curses and the Problem of the Origines of Hebrew Law," *VT* 11 (1961), 151.
15. *KAI* 26 iii 12–14; Gervitz, "West-Semitic Curses," 142–143.
16. Ibid., lines 14–16.
17. Ibid., 223c:1–2; cf. also ibid., 222c:18–19.
18. Ibid., 223c:3–4.
19. *KAI* 269:2 וכרצי איש לא אמרת "you have not denounced anyone." For a full discussion of the Old Aramaic אמר כרצי (= Amarna *karṣi qabû*) = Akkadian *karṣi akālu* = Biblical Aramaic אכל קרצין, see M. Held, "A Faithful Lover in an Old Babylonian Dialogue," *JCS* 15 (1961), 12b.
20. *KAI* 224:1. The Sefîre idiom מלל על cannot simply mean "to speak against"; contrast F. Rosenthal, "Notes on the Third Aramaic Inscription from Sefîre-Sûjûn" *BASOR* 158 (1960), 28; idem, *ANET*, 3d ed.. 660b; J. Fitzmyer, *The Aramaic Inscriptions of Sefîre* (Roma: Editrice Pontificio Istituto Biblico 1967), 97, 104–5 (hereafter cited as Sefîre). Rather, this expression has a more specific nuance, i.e. "to plot, to conspire against." To clarify the background of this idiom, as well as its specific connotation, one may compare our expression with Akkadian *ana/ina muḫḫi dabābu* "to plot, to conspire against," an idiom which is the exact semantic equivalent of the Old Aramaic מלל על: *ūmussu ana muḫḫi dâkiya u ḫulluqiya idabbub* "all the time he plots to murder me and do away with me" (*ABL* 716 r. 3). Similarly, it is interesting to note that the Sefîre phrase וי[מלל] [ע]לי או על ברי... הסכר תהסכרהם בידי... "...and will plot against me or against my son...hand them over to me" (*KAI* 224:1–2), finds its counterpart in Akkadian in a similar context: *ša ina muḫḫika idbubu gabbišunu ina qā[tēka] ašakkan* "I shall hand over to you all those who plotted against you" (*ABL* 965:8).
21. *KAI* 224:2. Note that the idiom מלל מלן לחית לעלי... cannot be translated

literally "to utter evil words against" as proposed by Fitzmeyer (*Sefîre*, 97) nor can it be restored to לעלי [לו] תי as supported by Dupont-Sommer and followed by Donner-Röllig (*KAI* 2, P. 226). As pointed out by Fitzmeyer (*Sefîre*, 105) the form of the compound preposition על + ל is attested at least three times in the Aramaic texts of Qumran. Further, it seems that this compound preposition is the exact semantic equivalent of the Akkadian *ana*/*ina* (= ל); *muḫḫI* (= על) "to plot, conspire against PN" (see above, n. 19). Moreover, observe that the Akkadian expression *amat lemutti qabû/dabābu* "to plot, conspire against" (lit., "to speak evil words"; see, e.g., Knudtzon *Gebete*, 236:6ff.) is semantically equal to the Sefîre idiom מלל מלן לחית.

22. E.g., *AKA* 288:98–99 (*ina libbi aštur*); *OIP* 2 27:9 (*ṣēruššu ušašṭir*); *3R* 7 1:26 (*ina qerebšu alṭur*); Streck *Asb.* 14:13 (*ina muḫḫi aštur*).
23. Note that the Samalian scribe employs the Canaanite verb חקק attested only in Hebrew (כתב//in Isa. 10:1; 30:8; Job 19:23) and in Phoenician (*CIS* 1 51:2), as against כתב in Zākir (*KAI* 202b:14–15; cf. also ibid., 233:9, 12; 245:1) and רשם employed in Sefîre (*KAI* 223c:3), Biblical Aramaic (Dan. 6:10), and in later Aramaic dialects.
24. H. Hirsch, *AfO* 20 77 I 16–23.
25. *AfO* 12 365 22–24: *ša šumī šaṭram ipaššiṭūma šumšu išaṭṭaru* "whoever erases my inscribed name and writes down his (own) name."
26. *Syria* 32 16 v. 2–5: *(ša) šumī šaṭram ipaššiṭu u ušapšaṭu šumšu lā šaṭram išaṭṭaru u ušašṭaru* "whoever erases my name or orders to erase it, inscribes his own name not previously inscribed or orders to write it down."
27. *CH* 26:33–35:*šumī šaṭram ipšiṭma šumšu ištaṭar*.
28. E.g., King, *BBSt.*, p. 6:18; ibid., p. 35:33 and others.
29. Note especially Adad-Nīrāri III (810–783 B.C.), the contemporary of Panammuwa I; see Unger *Reliefstele*, 12:18.
30. *KAI* 26 iii 13–14: אש ימח שם אזתוד... ושת שם "(whoever) shall erase the name of Azitawadda…and put down his (own) name." M. Held has recently dealt with this formula in a paper entitled "Azitawadda in the Light of Old Babylonian Royal Inscriptions," presented before the American Oriental Society in New York, 1969.
31. In Aramaic this word is normally spelled with *p*; see *KAI* 2, pp. 219 and 223 for a full discussion.
32. *KAI* 2, p. 223.
33. H. Hirsch *AfO* 20 77 16–18; for *kullumu*(*m*) "to show > to teach, instruct," see, e.g., *CH* 25:84–87.
34. E.g., *AOB* 1 64 44–46; King, *BBSt.*, 35: 34–35; ibid., 40:9; ibid., 48:1–2.
35. Hirsch, *AfO* 20 77 16–18; *AKA* 251:7–78.
36. See *CAD* A/1 181: *AHw.*, 19B.

37. E.g., King, *BBSt.*, p. 40:9.
38. E.g., ibid., 78:19.
39. *AKA* 250:69.
40. Ibid., lines 69–70.
41. E.g., King, *BBSt.*, p. 28:10, *VAS* I 37 v. 25.
42. *CH* 26:36–38; cf. *Syria* 32 16 v. 6–7: *u aššum errētim šanīam ušaḫḫazu.*
43. *AOB* I 64 43–46 (Adad-Nīrāri).
44. *AKA* 250: 67–71 (Aššurnaṣirpal II).
45. *KAI* 223c:6–10. For a full discussion of this curse formula, see K. R. Veenhof, *BiOr* 20 (1963), 142ff.
46. Müller, *The Contemporary Review* 65 (1894), 573.
47. Hinke, *Kudurru*, 48–49, §§5–6.
48. *AKA* 251:77–79.
49. King, *BBSt.*, pp. 40–41:8ff. Cf. also *ina abni naqāru*, ibid., 35:35.
50. *KAI* 24:15.
51. Ibid., 202b:16; note that following Lidzbarski (*Eph.* 3 10), Donner-Röllig (*KAI* 2, p. 210; cf. also recently, R. Degen, *Altaramäische Grammatik* [Wiesbaden: Kommissionsverlag Steiner, 1969], 76) derive from the Old Aramaic verb הגע as Haph'el from גוע rendered as "verenden, verscheiden." This rendering must be rejected on the following accounts: (a) Biblical Hebrew גוע "to perish, die" refers only to human beings, and (b) the verb is never attested in the Hiph'il as already pointed out by Torrey (*JAOS* 35 [1916–1917], 363; cf. also Dupont-Sommer, *Handbook*, I/2, p. 5a), it is more to the point to consider our Old Aramaic form as a Haph'el from נגע. Hebrew employs this verb in the Hiph'il no less than four times in contexts involving the destruction of a city wall (השח//הגיע Isa. 25:12), citadel (השח//השפיל//הגיע ibid., 26:5), fortress (הרס//הגיע Lam. 2:2) and wall (הרס//הגיע, Ezek. 13:14). This equation proposed by the writer two years ago in his Ph.D. dissertation, is not also advocated by Z. Ben Ḥayyim (*Lešonénu* 35 [1971], 252) who rightly considers הגע נצבא as a shortened expression for הגע נצבא עד ארק. Further, it is worth noting that הגע(//הרס) attested in Ezek. 13:14 is rendered by the Targum as רמא "to throw, cast down." This calls to mind the usage of the Akkadian verbs *nadû/(šuddû)/nasāku* "to throw, cast down" in contexts involving a destruction of an *uṣurtu* "carved figure" (e.g. *CH* 25:73–74); *tuppu* "tablet" (e.g., *BBSt.* 7:21–22); *abnu* "boundary stone" (e.g., ibid., 22:2–3) as well as *narû* "stele" (e.g., ibid., 65 v 1–2).
52. *KAI* 202b:20–21 (Zākir); ibid., 225:6–8 (Nērab). Note that in both Zākir and Nērab, Donner-Röllig (*KAI* 2, p. 210; ibid., p. 275; cf. also Degen, *Altaramäische Grammatik*, 76) following Nöldeke (*ZA* 21 383) derive הנס as a Haph'el from נוס "fliehen" rendering our הנס

as "fortschschleppen." Both the etymology and rendering must be rejected, and to be preferred is J. Barth's suggestion (*OLZ* 12 11; cf. also I. Löw, ibid., pp. 115–116) which equates our vocable with Aramaic אנס, the latter being the Targum's equation of Hebrew גזל "to take away by force." Indeed, from context as well as from the prepositional phrase "from its location," it is clear that our הנס = אנס must be rendered "to remove." It should also be noted that our idiom הנס... מן אשרה is the exact semantic equivalent of the Akkadian idioms *ina ašrišu nukkuru* (e.g., King, *BBSt.*, p. 22:2–3) and *ištu ašrišu dekû* (e.g., *MDP* 2 pl. 22 v. 40) respectively, both meaning "to remove from its location." Thus, Old Aramaic (a) מן אשרה = Akkadian *ina/ištu ašrišu*, while Old Aramaic (b) הנס (= אנס) = Akkadian *nukkuru/dekû*.

53. *KAI* 223c:4, 6, 9; cf. also Gevirtz, "West Semitic Curses," 144.
54. *KAI* 228:13.
55. Ibid., 214:26, 33, 34; 215:3 (twice), 5, 7. Note the problematic הרג attested in Sefîre (*KAI* 222a: 24). For a full discussion of this enigmatic verb see Fitzmyer, *Sefîre*, 43–44.
56. See *CAD* D 41, meaning 3; note also that *dâku* is equated with *ḫepû* in the lexical texts (ibid., 35b).
57. Note that the verb ערף, usually denoting "to break the neck of an animal," is employed in Hos. 10:2 in a context involving the destruction of an altar.

Some Literary Elements in the Opening Sections of the Hadad, Zākir, and the Nērab II Inscriptions in the Light of East and West Semitic Royal Inscriptions[1]

To Moshe Held, Teacher and Friend

The corpus of Old Aramaic royal inscriptions has been scrutinized in the past from several distinct perspectives. Some scholars have dealt exclusively with problems of orthography, while others have restricted their study to morphological features. A third group of scholars have concentrated on lexicographical problems, but have conducted their investigation along the very limited line of inquiry afforded by the study of etymology. Little[2] or no emphasis has been placed upon the systematic isolation of the various idioms, formulae, and other literary elements employed in these inscriptions, nor upon elucidation of the stylistic and philological affinities, which they exhibit.

More specifically, close study of those literary elements employed by Akkadian scribes in the composition of inscriptions with the same genre as the Old Aramaic material will reveal mutually elucidating correspondences between the two languages. So too, consideration of equally pertinent Canaanite material helps supply a more complete picture of scribal rhetoric in the ancient Semitic world.

The paper here proposed will attempt to subject to a comparative analysis various idioms or formulae attested in the Old Aramaic royal inscriptions, stressing the importance of usage over the more common approach of strictly etymological considerations. To this end, correspondences between Old Aramaic and their counterparts in Akkadian and North-West Semitic dialects will be arrived at only after inductive study of the contextually relevant material. This study will attempt to analyze the introductory statements of Hadad, Zākir, and Nērab II inscriptions having this purpose in mind.

I. Hadad (*KAI* 214:1–4)

The opening section of the Hadad inscription (lines 1–4) read as follows:

1. אנך[3] פנמו בר קרל מלך יאדי זי מקמת נצב[4] זן להדד בעלמי
2. קמו עמי אלהו הדד ואל ורשף ורכבאל ושמש ונתן בידי הדד ואל
3. ורכבאל ושמש ורשף חטר חלבבה וקם עמי רשף פמז אחז
4. ביד [י...] הא פלח .. ומז אשא [ל מ] ן אלהי יתנו לי ושנם חויו

Within this introductory statement the following themes will be discussed: 1. The early bestowal of divine favor upon the king; 2. Bestowal of divine aid; 3. The king's divinely bestowed legitimacy; 2. Divine fulfillment of the king's request; 5. Divine bestowal of longevity.

1. The Early Bestowal of Divine Favor Upon the King: בעלמי

Donner-Röllig render line 1 as follows: *"der I hdiese Statue dem Hadad für meine Fortdauer errichtet babe."*[5] Following Nöldeke[6] they still assume that the vocable בעלמי is to be derived from the substantive עלם "Ewigkeit, Fortdauer." To support their argument they cite the problematic Phoneician phrase כשת[ה] בעלם (Aḥiram, *KAI* 1:1) rendered by them as follows: "heir hat er ihn für die Ewigkeit hingesetzt."[7] On the other hand, Cooke (although in doubt),[8] followed by Poebel,[9] and Jean-Hoftijzer[10] propose to translate the word בעלמי "in my youth."

A glance at the cuneiform royal-hymnic lexicon will suffice to make it abundantly clear that Cooke's proposal is well established. At the outset, it should be noted that Akkadian, as well as Biblical Hebrew, employs various expressions denoting the notion of the distant past where some of these idioms are characteristic of the royal and hymnic literary genre.[11] Our main concern at present, however, is to examine the Old Aramaic expression בעלמי in light of the more general motif of the early bestowal of divine favor upon the king, well attested in Akkadian royal inscriptions.

Among several other expressions, Akkadian employs the following:

a. *ištu/ultu ṣeḫēri* (*ṣuḫri*);
b. *ištu/ultu ūmī ṣeḫēri*;
c. *ištu/ultu/ina meṣḫerūti*;
d. *ina ṣeḫrūti*.

The following passages demonstrate the usage of these idoms in contexts similar to that of the Hadad inscription, that is, in depicting the king as a recipient of divine favor even from his youth:

a) *rēʾû(m) kēnu migir ilī rabûti ša ultu ṣeḫērišu Aššur Šamaš... ana šarrūti māt Aššur ibbû zikiršu* "The legitimate shepherd, the favorite of the great gods, whom Aššur, Šamaš... designated from his childhood for the kingship of Assyria."[12]
b) *ištu meṣḫerūtiya išariš ṣabtanni* "He (Marduk) has provided for me fully from my youth."[13]
c) *šarru ša ina ṣeḫrūtišu Aššur šar Igigi uttûšūma* (for *ūtûšuma*!) *malkūt lā šanān umallû qātuššu* "The king whom Aššur the king of the Igigi selected from his youth, and an unrivaled kingship entrusted into his hands."[14]

It is apparent that Akkadian *ina ṣeḫrūti* (*ištu ṣeḫrūti*) "since childhood," is the exact semantic equivalent of Old Aramaic בעלמי,[15] an expression drawn from the royal hymnic lexicon attested in Akkadian, Hebrew, and in Phoenician[16] as well. Accordingly, it seems safe to assume the vocable בעלמי "since my childhood (youth)" introduces a new theme, referring to a bestowal of divine favor upon the king even from his youth. Thus in contrast to the rendering of Donner-Röllig, our line should be translated as follows: "From (since) my youth (childhood) the gods[17] Hadad and

El and Resef and Rakib-El and Šamaš supported me (lit., stood by me)." The interdialectical distribution of the above idiom is as follows: Akkadian *ištu/ultu/ina ṣeḫrūti/ṣeḫēri/meṣḫerūti*; Phoenician: למנערם; Hebrew: מנער/מעלימים; Old Aramaic[18]: בעלמי.

2. Bestowal of Divine Aid: קום עם

Another correspondence between Akkadian-Biblical Hebrew royal and hymnic literature and Old Aramaic inscriptions is the motif of the divine aid. To denote this idea Akkadian employs various idioms:

a) *imna/ida alāku* = *ina imni*[19]*/idi alāku*[20] "to aid/protect" (lit., to go at the right/side);
b) *qāta ṣabātu (aḫazu)*[21]*/tarāṣu*[22]*nadānu*[23]*/šakānu*[24] "to hold/grasp/extend/give/set a hand" (i.e., to aid, to assist);
c) *rēṣūta*[25]*/tappûta alāku*[26] "to go to help/to give assistance"'
d) the verbs *tukkulu/rêṣu* "to support/to help."[27]

Another way of expressing divine assistance is by the use of Akkadian a) *ida/aḫa/imna i/uzuzzu* "to stand at the right side/right" (i.e., to assist), b) *uzuzzu itti* "to side with." The latter idiom is the exact semantic equivalent of our Old Aramaic קום עם. The following few examples will illustrate the Akkadian phrase under consideration:

a) *[ilū] sibittu ilū rabûtu ša idi šarri pāliḫšun izzazzū* "The seven [gods], the great gods who assist the king their worshiper."[28]
b) *ittīka lizzizzū ilū šūt Enlil ittīka lizzizzū ilū šūt Ekur* "May the gods those of Enlil assist you; may the gods those of the Ekur aid you."[29]

Similarly, Biblical Hebrew expresses the notion of the divine aid by the following idiomatic expressions: a) עמד לימין/הושע "to stand at the right (i.e., to assist) to save," attested in Ps. 109:42. Here Hebrew עמד לימין is the semantic equivalent of the Akkadian *ina imni/imna uzuzzu.* b) קום ל//התיצב ל "to assist" (lit: to stand with), attested in Ps 94:16. Further, it should be noted that the biblical *hapax*[30] עמד את rendered by Targum Onqelos as קום עם is the exact semantic equivalent of Akkadian *i/uzuzzu itti*.

Of interest is the use of the idiom, *naṣābu itti* in the Amarna letters with obvious North-West Semitic coloring: *šar Ḫazūra ītezib karšu* (for *karassu!*) *u ittaṣa [b] itti Ḫabiri* "The king of Ḫaṣōr or deserted his army camp and sided with the Ḫabiru."[31]

Furthermore, the Old Aramaic[32] idiom קום עם is attested elsewhere. Thus, in the Aramaic papyri from Elephantine, the Aramaic version of the Behistun inscription reads as follows: [אלה גבר] יא זי קמן עמי הוו "These are the men who supported me."[33] The Aramaic tradition with regard to this poetic idiom is carried to later Aramaic dialects. In Palestinian Aramaic we encounter the following expressions: a) מקיים עם "to protect": עד אימתי את מקיים עם אילין יהודאי "Until when do you protect these Jews?"[34] b) בשר ודם יש לו פטרון.. אמר להן אני מקיים עליו: מקיים על "A mortal has a patron…he said to them I shall protect him."[35] C) עמד על: שפלוני פטרונו עומד עליו "That his patron such-and-such protects him."[36]

In Samaritan Aramaic the following phrases are employed in the hymnic literature: a) קעם עם יעקב לגו נחל יבקה "The one who helped Jacob at the river Yabok,"[37] b) דאת קעם עם סגודיך "That you (God) aid your worshipers."[38] In short, it is worthwhile noting that the scribe of the Hadad inscription adheres faithfully to the poetic style of the royal-hymnic inscriptions. That is, he prefers to employ the poetic idiom, קום עם "to stand with" instead of the regular Aramaic verb סעד "to help," attested twice in the dialect of Samal.[39]

The interdialectical distribution of the above idiom is as follows: Akkadian: *i/uzuzzu itti*; Amarna: *naṣābu itti*; Hebrew: קם/עמד/התיצב ל/את; Old Aramaic: קום עם.

3. The King's Divinely Bestowed Legitimacy: נתן חטר (חלבבה) ביד

From the Akkadian parallels cited above it seems that the inclusion in the Hadad inscription of such motifs as the early divine selection as king, and the personalized divine aid, conform to establish stylistic conventions of cuneiform royal inscriptions. So too, the traditions of this genre motivated the scribe of the Hadad inscription to include specific reference to the king's divinely ordained legitimacy. This motif is expressed figuratively by depicting the king as having received the royal scepter directly from the patron deities.

This motif is traceable to well-known Sumerian prototypes.[40] Similarly, in the Akkadian royal inscriptions we find the concept of the divinely bestowed scepter as follows:

a) *ḫaṭṭa išarta ina qāti RN mullû* "To entrust a legitimate scepter into the hand of RN."[41]
b) *ḫaṭṭa išarta/ušpara kīna ina qāti/retti RN šutmuḫu* "To cause the hand of RN to hold the legitimate scepter/the just staff."[42]
c) *ḫaṭṭa išarta šarāku//šibirra kīna qâpu* "To bestow the legitimate scepter to entrust the just staff."[43]

Our Old Aramaic expression RN תנן חטר חלבבה ביד finds an even closer semantic parallel in the Akkadian formula: *ḫaṭṭi šarrūti/išarti ina qāti/retti RN nadānu* "To give a royal/just scepter into the hand of RN."[44]

This close correspondence between the Old Aramaic and Akkadian formulae may shed some light on the meaning of the problematic חלבבה, a vocable found only in the Hadad inscription.[45] That is, חלבבה should properly be the semantic equivalent of one of those terms modifying *ḫaṭṭu* in the Akkadian formulae. Although the etymology of the word is unknown,[46] context seems to indicate that חטר חלבבה may denote "a scepter of kingship/dominion."[47] Our supposition gains in probability when we take into consideration the interdialectal distribution of the following phrases involving "scepter" in contexts mentioning symbols of royalty.

Thus the distribution is as follows: Akkadian: *ḫaṭṭi šarrūti*; Ugaritic: *ḫṭ mṯpṭ*[48]; Phoenician: חטר משפט[49]; Hebrew: שבט מלכות[50]; Old Aramaic: חטר חלבבה.

4. Divine Fulfillment of the King's Request: שאל מן- נתן

Another correspondence between Akkadian, Hebrew, and Old Aramaic royal hymnic literature are the following motifs: a) to fulfill the king's request, b) to grant the king an enduring life. As for the first motif, Old Aramaic expresses the notion of the god's beneficence by employing the formulaic sequence שאל־נתן "to ask- to grant." The identical sequence is employed negatively in the curse-formula of lines 22–23: לה הדד ומז ישאל אל יתן "And whatsoever he shall ask may Hadad not grant him." To be viewed alongside this formula is the Old Aramaic expression שאל־יתר "to request-to grant in abundance": ומה אשאל מן אלהי מת! יתר לי "And what I shall ask from the gods... may they grant me in abundance."[51]

The above formula is frequently attested in Biblical Hebrew, thus in the royal and hymnic Psalms we encounter the following expressions:

a) נתן/מלא־שאלא/משאלא "to grant/fulfill- request"[52]
b) נתן־ירשה- "to grant- wish[53]"
c) תאות לב/ארשת שפתים־נתן/בל מנע "The heart's desire/the request — to grant/not to withhold"[54]

Similarly, to be viewed alongside the above Hebrew expressions are the following two formulaic idioms employed in royal Psalms: שאל ממני... ואתנה "Ask of me... and I shall grant"[55] as well as חיים שאל ממך נתתה לו ארך ימים עולם ועד "Life he asked of you, you granted (it) to him, length of days for ever and ever."[56]

Ugaritic employs the roots *ʾrs-ytn/šlḥ* "to ask — grant/ bestow": *irš ḥym watnk blmt wašlḥk* "Ask for life and I will grant (it) to you, for not dying and I will bestow (it) upon you."[57]

The formulaic sequence cited above would seem to argue for assigning the Old Aramaic formula to a North-West Semitic provenance.

In cuneiform royal and hymnic inscriptions the sequence *erēšu — nadānu* "to ask- to grant" is by no means a common feature but nevertheless is attested in several cases:

a) *išti Anim hāwiriša tēteršaššum dārīam balāṭam arkam mādātim šanātim balāṭim ana Ammiditana tušatlim Ištar tattadin* "She requested from Anu, her spouse, a lasting long life for him, many years of life, to Ammiditana he has granted, Ištar has given."[58]
b) *qibīamma ša terrišanni luddikku* (for *luddikkum*!) "Tell me, and I will grant you what you desire of me."[59]
c) *anāku ana DN eterriš DN liddinnu* "I implore Ahuramazada, may Ahuramazda grant (it to me)."[60]

In short, the interdialectal distribution of this formula is as follows: Akkadian: *erēšu-nadānu*; Ugartitic: *ʾrš- ytn*; Hebrew: נתן-שאל; Old Aramaic: נתן-שאל.

5. Divine Bestowal of Longevity: שנם חוי

Problematic indeed is the above expression. Note that even the most recent treatment of our inscription leaves this phrase untranslated.[61] A solution to this problem, however, is suggested by a structural analysis of the opening section of our inscription, the first four lines of which constitute a single unit. Within this introductory section, the following literary elements appear in sequence:

a) בעלמי, Akkadian: *ina ṣeḫrūti* (The early bestowal of divine favor)
b) קום עם, Akkadian: *i/uzuzzu itti* (the divine assistance)
c) RN נתן חטר חלבבה ביד, Akkadian: *ḫaṭṭi šarrūti ina qātī RN nadānu* (the king's divinely ordained legitimacy)
d) שאל-נתן, Ugaritic: *ʾrš-ytn* (request-granting, commonly employed in West Semitic, but not excluded from Akkadian i.e., *erēšu-nadānu*.) One should consider the idiom ושנם חויו as a logical, stylistically appropriate continuation of the above sequence of elements.

It is significant that the motif of divine beneficence to the royal-hymnic genre invariably involves bestowal of longevity. Thus the sequence "to ask- to grant" appears most often with the direct object "life":

> Hebrew: חיים שאל ממך נתתה לו ארך ימים עולם ועד (Ps. 21:5)[62]
> Ugaritic: *irš ḥym watnk blmt wašlḥk* (*II D*, 6:26–28).
> Akkadian: *išti Anim... tēteršaššum... šanātim balāṭim ana RN... Ištar tattadin* (*RA* 22 p. 173, r. 45–48).

Moreover a formula mentioning divinely bestowed longevity is one of the stereotyped elements in Akkadian, Ugaritic, Phoenician, and Hebrew royal and hymnic literature:

a) Akkadian: *ūmī/šanāti/balāṭa* "to prolong days/years/life,"[63] Hebrew[64]: הארך ימים, Phoenician[65]: יאר ימת/שנת, Old Aramaic[66]: הארך יומין.
b) Akkadian: *balāṭa/ūmī arkūtī nadānu/šarāku/qâšu/šakānu* "to give/bestow/grant/establish life/long days."[67] Phoenician[68] and Egyptian Aramaic[69]: נתן/יתן חיים.
c) Akkadian: *ūmī/šanāta uṣṣubu/pu* "to add days/years,[70] Hebrew: הוסף שנים.
d) Akkadian: *ūmī/šanāti (w)utturu/šumû'du* "to increase days/years,"[71] Hebrew: הרבה ימים.[72]
e) Akkadian; *balāṭa šebû/šubbû* " to be satiated/to satiate with life"[73] Hebrew שבע/השבע[74] ימים.[75]
f) Akkadian: *bulluṭu* "to keep alive,"[76] Hebrew: החיה/חיה, Ugaritic: (Pi'el),[77] Phoenician: חו (Pi'el).[78]

Accordingly, contextually it seems best to render our Old Aramaic expression ושנם חויו[79] as "And they (the gods) kept (me) alive for years." The latter being the functional equivalent of the Akkadian formula *bulluṭu ana dāriātim/dāriš* "to keep (one) alive forever."[80]

Finally, a word should be said with regard to the grammatical form of the vocable חויו. Namely, if the rendering proposed above is correct, one may analyze חויו as 3 pers. masc. pl. Pi'el perfect of *ḥyy* "to keep alive." Further, it is worthwhile noting that although the D conjugation of the verb *ḥyy* is attested neither in Old nor in Biblical and Royal Aramaic, nevertheless it is employed in Ugaritic, Phoenician, and Biblical Hebrew. Ugaritic and

Phoenician go hand in hand, in that both employ the Piʿel of *ḥyy*, where a *w* is placed in the second position against *y* in Hebrew. Thus, in Phoenician the following forms are attested: חוי[81] (perfect), תחו,[82] and יחוו[83] (imperfect). Ugaritic: *aḥwy*,[84] *aḥw*,[85] *yḥwy*[86] (imperfect). In the G on the other hand, Ugaritic retains the *y* in the second position: e.g., *ḥyt*,[87] *ḥy*.[88] Accordingly, חויו in the Old Aramaic dialect from Zinjirly seems to be under Canaanite influence, retaining its various morphological peculiarities.

II. Zākir (*KAI* 202A:1–4a)

The opening section of the Zākir inscription (lines 1–4a) reads as follows:

1. [נ]צבא זי שם זכר מלך [ח] מת ולעש לאלור [בחזרך][89]
2. [א]נה זכר מלך חמת ולעש אש ענה אנה ו[קרא
3. נ]י בעלשמין וקם עמי והמלכני בעלשמ[ין על
4. ח]זרך

Within this introductory passage two themes will be discussed: 1. Piety of the king; and 2. Divine selection of the king in order to rule the land of GN.

1. Piety of the King: אש ענה

This idiomatic expression has been understood by students of the Zākir inscription in different ways. C.C. Torrey[90] in his detailed study of this inscription proposes to restore the lacuna in lines 2–3a ו[שמע אל]י. Thus, construing ענה as 'an active or passive participle,' and אש as the relative pronoun, he renders the whole line as follows: "I am Zakar, king of Hamazth and Laas, whom, whenever I am in distress, Baalšamaim hears and supports."

Albright[91] follows Torrey's rendering of אש as the relative pronoun but his restoration of lines 2–3a differs. He bases his restoration on the Biblical Aramaic idiom ענה ואמר "Speak, take up a conversation." Accordingly, he proposes the following rendering: "I am Zakir, king of Ḫamat and Luʾaš, who speaks (as follows): 'my god is Ba'al-šamem and Ba'al-šamem stood beside me.'"

Both Torrey's and Albright's rendering of אש as the relative pronoun must be rejected. While it is true that many Canaanite features are employed in Zākir, nevertheless the relative pronoun in Zākir[92] as in old Aramaic in general is זי. Nowhere in Old, Biblical, or Elephantine[93] Aramaic is the Canaanite[94] אש/אשר employed. Further, it will become clear that both renderings must also be rejected on stylistic grounds.

The first to propose the solution currently accepted by a majority of scholars appears to have been Dussaud.[95] Although his rendering of אש ענה as "*un homme pieux*" was dismissed by Albright as being a "very improbable,"[96] and is still italicized in Donner-Röllig's most recent translation, it seems worthwhile to examine carefully this suggestion in the light of cuneiform and North-West Semitic royal inscription.

A study of the cuneiform royal lexicon reveals that Dussaud's rendering is well founded. Akkadian as well as Phoenician/Biblical Hebrew employs various expressions denoting the notion of the king's/man's piety towards his god, and that these idioms are characteristic of the royal-hymnic literary genre. Thus, in the opening section of many royal inscriptions from the Old Babylonian period onwards we observe that the king ascribes to himself the following attributes: *na'du* "obedient,"[97] *kanšu,*[98]/(*ḫanšu-ḫaššu*) "submissive,"[99] *šaḫṭu* "pious,"[100] *muštēmiqu* "suppliant,"[101] *pāliḫu* "reverent,"[102] *pāliḫ ili* "reverer of god,"[103] *šemû* "obedient," *šēmî ili* "obedient to the god(s),[104] *ardu/(rēšu)* "worshiper (lit., slave),"[105] *mutnennû* "continuously prayerful."[106]

Another way to express the above religious characteristics is by the use of the Akkadian adjective *(w)ašrum* "humble," attested already in Old Babylonian royal inscriptions:

a) OB (Ḫammurapi): ...*wašrum muštēmiqum... šēmî Šamaš* "... The humble, suppliant... the obedient of Šamaš."[107]
b) MA (Aššur-uballiṭ I): ...*ašru na'du muṭīb bēlišu* "... The humble, obedient, the one who pleases his lord."[108]

c) NA (Esarḫaddon): *rēšu mutnennû ašru kanšu pāliḫ ilūtišunu rabīti* "The worshiper (lit., slave), continuously prayerful, humble submissive, who reveres their great divine power."[109]

Here, Akkadian *(w)ašrum* appears to be the exact semantic equivalent of the Old Aramaic ענה "humble," where both are utilized in the opening section of royal inscriptions.

Further, the listing of religious or moral attributes in the opening section of an inscription is clearly illustrated in the inscription of Panammuwa II: ב[צד]ק אבה פלטוה אלהו יאדי מן שחתה "On account of the righteousness of his father the god(s) of Ya'udi delivered him from a calamity."[110] So, too, in the opening section of the Nērab II inscription Agbar the priest of Sahar in Nērab states: בצדקתי קדמוה שמני שם טב "On account of my righteousness towards him he made me famous."[111]

Similarly, in both Phoenician building and royal inscriptions the king calls himself צדק/ישר "righteous/upright" evidently referring to his piety towards his gods: כמלך צדק ומלך ישר לפן אל גבל קדשם [הא] "... For he is a righteous king and upright king towards the holy gods of Byblos."[112] So too, in the opening statement of the Azitawadda inscription, the king describes himself as follows: אנך אזתוד הברך בעל עבד בעל "I am Azitawadda the blessed (steward?) of Baʿal, the worshiper (lit., servant) of Baʿal."[113] Similar in function is the following passage attested in the Middle Aramaic Ḫatrian dialect: צלמא די אתלו מלכא .. פלח אלהא בריך אלהא "The statue which ʾAtlw the king... the reverent of god the blessed of god... has set?"[114] The Ḫatrian idiom פלח אלהא is both the exact semantic and etymological equivalent of Akkadian *pāliḫ ili* and should be viewed alongside Hebrew ירא ה'/אלהים employed in describing the religious piety of king or man.

Further, among the various expressions denoting the piety of king- man towards his God, Hebrew employs the adjective[115] ענו = Old Aramaic ענה = Akkadian *(w)ašrum* "humble." Thus, it should be noted that when דלים//ענוי ארץ,[116] אביון//ענוי ארץ,[117] אביונים// ענוי ארץ,[118] are in synonymous parallelism, ענוי ארץ may denote a status of poverty. On the other hand, it is clear that when Biblical Hebrew employs ענו/ענוים in parallelism with חסידים;[119] דרשי ה'[120] and ענוה[121] with צדק[122] and יראת ה',[123] ענו there denoted religious piety. The latter is evident when we bear in mind that in Biblical hymnic literatures ענו is the antonym of חטאים[124] and רשעים.[125]

Returning to our idiom, Halevy[126] followed by Montgomery[127] and Dupont-Sommer,[128] regard the Old Aramaic idiom אש ענה "not merely as an expression of piety in order to stress the all-powerful help of his god but also, it seems, as an allusion to his humble origin."[129]

From the usages illustrated above, however, it seems that the scribe of Zākir inscription is not interested in giving us a biographical detail, but merely employs a stereotyped expression in a chain of formulaic features typical of royal inscriptions.

2. Divine Selection of the King: ו[ ]י

Students of the inscription differ with regard to the filling of the lacuna. Thus, a number of restorations were proposed; Dussaud[130] ו[הכבדנ]י Montgomery[131] ו[יעדרנ]י; Torrey[132] ו[שמע אל]י; Albright[133] ו[אמר אל]י; Rosenthal[134] "helped me," evidently ו[סעדנ]י; Greenfield[135] ו[חצלנ]י, while Donner-Röllig leave the lacuna unrestored.

More probable are the restorations suggested by Havley[136] ו[הרמנ]י, "elevated me," Gressmann[137] "Es erwählte mich *Beʿel-shamain*" evidently restoring ו[בחרנ]י. Similarly, Dupont-Sommer's proposed restoration[138] ו[קראנ]י, rendered as "mais Baʿal-Shamain mʾa [appelé],"[139] is worthy of consideration. Although his rendering of ו[קראנ]י as "mʾa [appelé]" is inadequate, it will become clear that idiomatic usage favors the rendering "to single out, designate" (for a specific task).[140]

Related material from Akkadian royal inscriptions seems to point out that Dupont-Sommer's restoration has much validity. Akkadian employs various idioms expressing the motif of the king's designation/selection by a divine being, idioms such as: *(w)atû* "to select, recognize,"[141] *ullû/rēša(m) ullû* "to elevate."[142]

A more common way to express the king's divine selection

attested from Old Babylonian onwards, is by the use of Akkadian: *šumšu/zikiršu/nibīssu/zakār šumišu nabû/zakāru* "to designate/ single out" (lit., to call by name) = Hebrew[143] קרא/זכר בשם. The following examples will suffice to demonstrate the usage of a sequence of elements similar to that of the Zākir inscription:

a) OB: *inūma Ea u Damkīna ana rēʾût GN šumī ibbû* "When Ea and Damkina designated me to rule (lit., shepherd) Malgium.[144]
b) MA: *Tukulti-apil-Ešarra... rēʾî naʾdi ša ina kēni libbikunu tūtâšu... ana šarrūt māt DN rabîš tukinnûšu* "RN the obedient shepherd whom you (the gods) in your steadfast heart have selected... for the kingship of the land of DN greatly you established him."[145]
c) NA: *rēʾûm kēnu... ša ultu ṣeḫērišu Aššur Šamaš... ana šarrūti māt Aššur ibbû zikiršu* "(Esarḫaddon) the faithful shepherd... whom Aššur, Šamaš... designated from his youth for the kingship of Assyria."[146]

The sequence of the Akkadian idioms *rēʾû nadu/kēnu* "obedient/faithful shepherd" *šuma(m)/zikra nabû/(w)atû* "to designate by name/to select" are comparable to the order of elements in Zākir אש ענה "A humble man," ו[קראנ]י בעלשמין, "So, Baʿal-Šamên designated me." Moreover, significant, is the fact that the literary elements a) *rēʾû nadu/kēnu* b) *šuma(m)/zikra nabû/(w)atû* in the examples cited above, are juxtaposed with *ana šarrūti/rēʾût GN* "for kingship/rulership of GN."[147] This sequential order is structurally similar to that employed in Zākir where the idioms a) אש ענה b) ו[קראנ]י c) וקם עמי attested to in sequence with d) GN והמלכני על.[148] Similarly, it may be noted in passing that the sequence of ו[קראנ]י בעלשמין and וקם עמי is to be compared to such similar Hebrew idioms in Ps. 3:4; Isa. 42:6 where the motif of the divine designation is juxtaposed with the divine assistance. Observe also that biblical קרא (without שם) "to designate, select" (for a specific task), is employed with אמץ, עזה, תמך all denoting assistance, as in Isa. 41:9–10 and Isa. 42:6. The sequence of motifs in Isa. 42:6 corresponds to that of Zākir ו[קראנ]י and וקם עמי "designated me, assisted me" (lit., stood with me), where the prototype of the Old Aramaic idiom denoting divine aid is Akkadian *uzuzzu itti* "to aid" (lit., to stand with).[149]

III. Nerab II (*KAI* 226:2b-5)

The introductory statement of the Nerab II inscription (lines 2b-5) reads as follows:

2. ... בצדקתי קדמוה[150]
3. שמני שם טב והארך יומי
4. ביום מתת פמי לאתאחז מן מלן
5. ובעיני מחזה אנה בני רבע בכונ
6. י

Within the above pronouncement the following motifs will be analyzed: 1) Divine bestowal of fame; 2) Endurance of mental faculties; and 3) Longevity.

1. Divine Bestowal of Fame: שום שם טב

Biblical Hebrew שים שם/נתן, Biblical Aramaic שום/יהב, שם, Phoenician שת שם, and its Akkadian semantic equivalent *šuma šakānu/nadānu* share at least two different meanings: a) "to give/establish a name[151] — to designate"[152]; b) "to make famous." It is the latter meaning which is our prime concern at present.

The motif of the king's divinely bestowed fame as expressed in Old Aramaic by the idiom שום שם טב is well attested in cuneiform royal inscriptions. To express the notion of "fame," Akkadian employs from Old Babylonian onwards various idiomatic expressions utilizing the vocables *šumu/zikru* "name/fame," a) *šuma šutēšuru* "to make famous" (lit., to cause a name to prosper);[153] b) *šuma/zikra/zikir šumi šurbû* "to make a name famous" (lit., great),[154] here Akkadian *zikir šumi šūṣû* corresponds to the biblical expression[155] גדל שם; c) *zikir šumi šūṣû* "to make famous" (lit: to cause a name to go out).[156] The latter is semantically equal to the Hebrew idiom יצא שם (in Qal) employed in a very similar context.[157]

More specifically, Akkadian also employs the expression *šuma/zikir šumi šakānu* "to establish fame," e.g., *šumišu ištakanu lē'ûssu uweddi* "He (Yaḫdunlim) established his fame (lit., name),[158] and made known his power." It is evident that Akkadian *šuma šakānu*[159] is the semantic equivalent of our Old Aramaic שום שם and Biblical Hebrew שים שם attests contexts indicating "fame": ושמתים לתהלה ולשם "I will establish for praise and renown."[160]

Closely associated is Hebrew[161] עשה שם "to make/become famous" which should be viewed alongside the expressions a)[162] עולם עשה שם b)[163] נתן שם עולם to establish, bestow an everlasting fame," employed only in Deutero-Isaiah. These idioms, being the semantic equivalent of Akkadian *šuma dārâ šakānu,*[164] may supply an additional example the phraseology of Deutero-Isaiah reflects that of Neo-Babylonian inscriptions.[165]

Returning to our passage, the Old Aramaic expression שמני שם טב, should be viewed alongside the following idioms attested in cuneiform royal inscriptions:

a) *šumam rabêm šakānu* "to establish a great fame": *kīma aḫūka šumam rabêm ištaknu u attā i[na mātika] šumam rabêm ši[tkan]* "Even your brother who acquired great fame for himself, so you acquire for yourself renown in your land."[166] Here Akkadian *šumam rabêm šakānu* is semantically equal to the Hebrew expression שום שם גדולות.[167]

b) *šuma kabta šakānu* "to establish glorious fame": *ilū rabûtu... šume kabtu zikri ṣīra eli napḫar bēlē ma'diš iskunū'inni* "The great god established for me a glorious name, exalted fame, superior to all the other rulers.[168] In this passage Akkadian *zikru ṣīru (//šumu kabtu) šakānu* seems to be the functional equivalent of the Hebrew *hapax* עשה שם תפארת "to acquire glorious fame."[169]

c) *šuma damqa šakānu* "to establish fame" (lit: "a good

name"): *šumī damqa... in pī nišī lū aškun* "I made my renown a by word among the people."[170]

Thus the Old Aramaic idiom שם שם טב is the exact semantic equivalent of Akkadian *šuma damqa šakānu*. More specifically, as pointed out by B. Landsberger,[171] our Old Aramaic expression שמני שם טב corresponds exactly to the Neo-Babylonian phrase *šuma ṭāba iškunanni* attested in the Ḫarran inscription of Nabonidus: *rēšiya ullīma šuma ṭāba ina māti iškunanni*[172] "He (Sin) singled me out (lit., elevated my head) and made me famous (lit., established for me a good name)[173] in the land."

2. Endurance of Mental Faculties: פמי לאתאחז מן מלן

By this expression Agbar[174] priest of Nerab, describes his physical state at the time of his death. In descriptions of old age, well-being or disability is expressed in terms of the main parts of the body, a) the hands and the legs, b) the ears, c) the eyes, d) the mouth. A complete description of the four parts can be seen, for example, in a Sumerian prayer where the scribe portrays his physical pain and mental suffering: "My hand is 'gone' for writing, my mouth is inadequate for dialogue; I am not old, (yet) my hearing is heavy, my glace cross-eyed."[175] So too, in the Egyptian instruction of the vizier Ptah-hotep the agony involved in achieving old age is painted as follows: "O sovereign, my lord! Oldness has come; old age has descended... The eyes are weak, the ears are deaf... and the mouth is silent and cannot speak."[176] Similarly, Biblical Hebrew describes advanced age in the well-known allegorical passage in Qoh. 12:3–4, where the author is concerned with the following four parts of the body: a) שמרי הבית "the hands"; אנשי החיל "the legs"; b) טחנות "the teeth; c) הראות בארבות "the eyes"; d) דלתים "the ears." Furthermore, it is significant to note that in the royal inscription of Nabonidus from Ḫarran Adad-guppi describes her physical-mental health as follows: a) *niṭil īnīya namrirma*; b) *šūturāk ḫasīsī;* c) *qāti u šēpē šalimma;* d) *nussuqā amātūʾa* "My eyesight is fine, my hearing excellent; my hands and feet are sound, my words well chosen."[177]

In Nerab II the description of well-being is limited solely to the faculty of speech, i.e., פמי לאתאחז מן מלן "My mouth was not closed to words," which conveys in a negative way Agbar's ability to express himself. Adad-guppi expresses the same idea in a positive manner, i.e., *nussuqā amātūa* "well-chosen are my words." It is of interest to note that in the Ḫarran inscription of Nabonidus the element of retaining a healthy mental-physical condition (i.e., *nussuqā amātūa*) is followed by mention of the god's bestowal of fame (i.e., *šumu ṭābu šakānu*), just as the idiom שם שם טב is followed by the expression פמי לאתאחז מן מלן in Nerab II.[178]

Our main interest, however, is to examine the above Old Aramaic expression in the light of Akkadian and Biblical Hebrew idioms denoting impairment of speech. In Akkadian medical texts symptoms of speech difficulties are expressed in the following ways *atmâ naparkû* "to deprive (lit., stop, block) of ability to speak (lit., speech)."[179] Similarly, in medical texts, Akkadian *dān* "heavy," is employed to express disability of speech as follows: a) *pâšu ana dabābi dān* "his mouth is (too) heavy for speech";[180] b) *pâšu ana amāti dān* "his mouth is (too) heavy to (utter) words."[181] To be viewed alongside *dannu* is Akkadian *kabātu/kabtu* "to be heavy, heavy," which is employed to denote physical symptoms of parts of the body, e.g., said of his feet: *šēpā kabtā*;[182] said of the ears (hearing, understanding) *uznā kabtā*[183] (= Sumerian *GEŠTU DUGUD*[184]) = Hebrew כבד/הכבד אזן[185], said of the eyes: *īnā kabtā*[186] = Hebrew[187] כבד עין. Further, Akkadian employs also the idiom *kabātu ša pî* "to be heavy with the mouth"[188] in medical texts in contexts involving speech difficulties. The latter evokes the Biblical idioms[189] כבדי לשון (//עמקי שפה). On the other hand Hebrew עמקי שפה (rendered by the Targum Onq. as[190] עמקי ממלל) corresponds to Akkadian *dān* "heavy," (lit., strong) employed with *dabābu* "to speak," and *amātu* "words." Moreover, Akkadian *pû kabtu*, which also corresponds to Hebrew (וכבד לשון) כבד פה,[191] rendered by Targum Onq. as (עמיק לישן) יקיר ממלל; Targum Ps.-Jon. (וחגיר ממלל) חגיר פום; Targum Jerus. (וקשי ממלל) חגיר פום. Thus the usage of עמק and קשה in the Targumim equals that of Akkadian *dannu*. Less apparent, however, is the rendering of חגיר for Heb. כבד in Ps.-Jon. This usage is more readily understood when it is borne in mind that the Targum's חגיר referring to mouth (i.e., פום) is the semantic as well as the etymological equivalent of Akkadian *egēru* "to twist, to be or become twisted,"[192] said also of a speech defect.

Alongside *egēru* Akkadian employs also the verb *kaṣāru* "to tie, bind" (referring to the tongue). Thus in the medical texts a defect of speech is expressed by the idiom *lišānšu kaṣrat* "his tongue is tied."[193] Similarly, to denote inability to speak, Akkadian utilizes the verb *kuttumu* "to close (lit., to cover)," employed with the words *šaptā* "lips"[194] and *pû* "mouth."[195]

Returning to the expression פמי לאתאחז מן מלן it should be noted that as previously pointed out[196] Old Aramaic אחז (= אחד) "to seize" also denotes "to close." Likewise, Lieberman calls attention to the fact that in Palestinian Talmud a similar development occurs with the Aramaic verb צור denoting both "to seize" as well as "to close," also employed with פום "mouth": כאינש דצייר פומהון דשהדיא דלא ישהדון "Like a man who crosses the mouth of the witnesses that they shalt not testify."[197]

More specifically, our Old Aramaic פמי לאתאחז מן מלן may also be viewed alongside the usage of Akkadian *ṣabātu*, which like North-West Semitic אחז/אחד denotes "to seize." Both Akkadian *ṣabātu* and the substantive *ṣibtu* are employed with *lišānu* "tongue" and *pû* "mouth" to denote inability to speak, exactly as אחז is employed with פום in our inscription:

a) *atmê pîya ittaṣb[at]//uznā'a amiru lamâni* "The words of my mouth (i.e., my speech) are obstructed (lit., seized)// my ears are stopped with ear wax."[198]
b) *pûšu ṣubbutma dabāba lā ile'e* "His mouth is obstructed (lit., seized), so that he cannot speak."[199] Further, note the usage of the Akkadian idiom *ṣibit pî* (Sumerian: *KA.DIB. BI.DA kadibbidû* in Akkadian[200]) "seizure of the mouth," attested in the following curse formula: *šīmat lā naṭāli sakāk uzni u ṣibit pî ana ṣât ūmī lišīmūšu* "May they (the

gods) assign for him a fate of blindness, deafness, and dumbness (lit., seizure of the mouth) forever.[201]

If our association of the Old Aramaic idiom אחז פום with Akkadian *pâ ṣabātu/ṣibit pị* is maintained, the Nērab II passage may be rendered as follows: "my mouth was not afflicted by seizure (preventing) speech (lit., 'from words')."

3. Longevity: חזה בני רבע

The motif of the divine bestowal of longevity in Nērab II is expressed in two ways: a) הארך יומין "to prolong days", b) חזה בני רבע "to see the children of the fourth generation." The former expression is commonly attested in cuneiform royal inscriptions, where among many other idiomatic expressions Akkadian employs *ūmī/šanāti/balāṭa urruku/šūruku* "to prolong (one's) days/years/life."[202] The Old Aramaic idiom חזה בני רבע expressing Agbar's attainment of long life, is well attested in Hebrew. The general sense of the idiom is expressed in Prov. 17:6, where the author portrays the glory of reaching old age as follows: עטרת זקנים בני בנים "Grandchildren are the crown of the elderly." Further, the key word denoting the relationship to the younger generation is expressed by Hebrew ראה "to see" (= Old Aramaic חזה), attested no fewer than four times: Ps. 128:6 ראה בנים לבניך "Live to see the children of your children," Isa. 53:10 יראה זרע יאריך ימים "He shall see his offspring enjoy long life." Even closer in phraseology to our idiom are Gen. 50:23: וירא יוסף לאפרים בני שלשים "Joseph lived to see Ephraim's children to the third generation"; and Job 42:16 וירא את בניו ואת בני בניו ארבעה דרות "and he (Job) saw his sons and grandsons to four generations."

Though the idea of future generation expressing longevity is not at all common in cuneiform literature,[203] it is not entirely absent. Thus Akkadian expresses the motif of reaching old age by the widening of the family: *awīlūtam illak bīta urappaš* "He will grow old (and) enlarge the family."[204]

Akkadian also expresses the idea of the old man being contemporary with his posterity by the verb *amāru* to see (= Hebrew

ראה; Old Aramaic חזה) *awīlum awīlūtam illak mār mārišu immar* "The man will attain old age, he will see his grandchildren."[205]

In a Neo-Assyrian text we find a greeting formula in which the bestowal of longevity is likewise expressed by the use of the verb *amāru* "to see": *šarru bēlī mār mārēšu ina burkēšu lintuḫu paršumāte ina ziqnīšunu līmur* "May the king my lord hold his grandchildren in his lab; and may he (live to) see the gray hair in their beards."[206]

An even more striking parallel to the Old Aramaic expression חזה בני רבע is afforded by the inscription of Nabonidus, in which the queen mother describes the divine bestowal of longevity as follows: *mārī mārī mārī mārīya adi rebê līpīta āmur* "I saw even my great-great-grandchildren up to the fourth generation all in a state of good health."[207] Thus the Neo-Babylonian expression *adi rebê līpīya āmur* "my grandchildren up to the fourth generation I saw," is the semantic equivalent of Hebrew ראה בני שלשים and Old Aramaic חזה בני רבע, where:

Akkadian: *līpū*= West Semitic בנים (בני)
Akkadian: *rebû*= West Semitic רבעים/רבע
Akkadian: *amāru*= West Semitic ראה/חזה

This correspondence in phraseology between Nērab II and the inscription of Nabondius, as well as those cited above, should not be viewed in isolation. Rather, it should be noted that those motifs which the two inscriptions share and which expressed in similar terms, also appear in the same sequential order. The correspondences between Nērab II and the inscription of Nabonidus may be summarized as follows

I. Piety of the king:
Nabonidus: *ilūta palāḫu*[208]
Agbar: בצדקתי קדמוה

II. Divine bestowal of fame:
Nabonidus: *šuma ṭāba šakānu*[209]
Agbar: שום שם טב

III. Divine bestowal of longevity:
Nabonidus: *ūmī arkūti uṣṣub/pu*[210]
Agbar: הארך יומין

IV. Endurance of mental-physical faculties:
Nabonidus: *nussuqā amātūʾa* (etc.)[211]
Agbar: פמי לאתאחז מן מלן[212]

V. Seeing the fourth generation:
Nabonidus: *mārī mārī mārī adi rebê līpīya amāru*[213]
Agbar: חזה בני רבע

It is significant that this last idiomatic expression seems to find its Akkadian parallel only in the Nabonidus inscription from Ḫarran and, consequently, the notion of seeing one's posterity to the fourth generation would seem to have a specifically North-West Semitic provenance.

NOTES

1. Abbreviations of Akkadian sources are those employed in the *Chicago Assyrian Dictionary.* Abbreviations for North-West Semitic material are those employed in H. Donner- W. Rölling, *Kanaanäische und aramäisch Inschriften, Bd.* II (Wiesbaden 1968). The substance of this study is based on part of the writer's Ph.D. dissertation, "Idioms in Old Aramaic Royal Inscriptions in the Light of Akkadian," submitted in May 1971, to Colombia University, written under the supervision of Professor M. Held.
2. See particularly the following two articles: H.L. Ginsberg, "Psalms and Inscriptions of Petition and Acknowledgment", *Louis Ginzberg Jubilee* (vol. 1; New York 1945), 1:159–71; S. Gevritz, "West Semitic Curses and the Problem of the origins of Hebrew Law," *VT* 11 (1961), 137–58.
3. For the pronoun אנך in Samalian instead of אנה or אנא see H.L. Ginsberg, *ASJL* 50 (1933), 2.
4. On the absence of the emphatic state of the noun in Samalian, see Ginsberg, ibid. 2, n. 7; idem, *JAOS* 62 (1942), 235–236; idem, *Louis Ginzberg Jubilee,* 1:159, n. 3. Note that Old Aramaic expresses the stereotyped formula (a) to erect, (b) to set up a stele, as follows: (a) הקם נצב/נצבא (*KAI* 214:14); (b) שים נצב/נצבא (*KAI* 201:1, Bir-Hadad; ibid., 202A:1, Zākir; ibid., 215:20. Panammuwa). For the formula "to erect a

statue", Old Aramaic employs (צלמתא) הקם צלמא (*KAI* 239: 1–2; ibid., 248:1–2). The Akkadian counterparts to these formulas are: (a) "to erect a stele" *narâ šuzuzzu* (e.g., *RA* 11 [1914] 93:15. *Manzāz narêm OIP* II, 84:55, *narû* + *ṣalmu*);] (b) "to set up a stele" narâ šakānu (e.g., *AOB* I, p. 24, IV:13–18 Šamši-Adad I). Erection/setting up of a statue is expressed as follows: (a) *ṣalma šuzuzzu* (e.g., *AKA*, p. 290:104–105); (b) *ṣalma zaqāp* (e.g., *KAH* II, N 113, 1:7 = זקף קמה cf. Targum on Gn 31,45); (c) *ṣalma kunnu* (e.g., *VAB* IV, p. 232:36 ff.); (d) *ṣalma nadû* (e.g., *AKA*, p. 346, 11:135 = Heb. ירה מצבא Gen. 31:51). Most interesting is the use of the formula in Mari which seems to contain West Semitic coloring, i.e. *ṣalma šūlû: šanat Zimrilim ṣalmašu ana Adad ša Ḫalab ušēlû* "Year in which Zimri -Lim dedicated (lit., raised up) his own statue to Adad of Ḫalab" (Studia Mariana. 57. n. 20; ibid., 21). The same formula is also attested in both poetic (*II D*, 1:27, ibid., 2:6, *nṣb skn*) and non-poetic (*UT* 69:1–2, *šʿly skn*) Ugaritic texts. In short, the interdialectical distribution of the above formulas is a s follows: I. "to erect a stele": Akkadian: *narâ šakānu/(šuzuzzu)*; Ugaritic *šʿly skn/nṣb skn;* Phoenician: טנע מצבת/מטנא; Hebrew: הרם/הקם מצבא Old Aramaic: הקם נצב/נצבא. II. ""to erect a statue", Akkadian: *ṣalma šuzuzzu (zaqāpu)*; Mari: *ṣalma šūlû*; Phoenician: טנא סמל; Hebrew: הקם/העמד פסל; Old Aramaic: הקם צלם.

5. *KAI* II (1964), 214.
6. *ZDMG* 47 (1893), 98.
7. *Op. cit*., p. 217. For a different interpretation of this Phoenician phrase see the writer's article "A Note on the Aḥiram Inscription", *The Journal of the Ancient Near Eastern Society of Columbia University)* (= ANES) III/I (1970–1), 33–36.
8. *NSI* (1903), 164–165.
9. *AS* 3 (1932), 43, n. 3.
10. *DISO*, 214.
11. Note idioms such as Akkadian *ištu/ultu ūmī ṣât(i)* "since the days of yore" (e.g., *RA* 33 [1936] 51, II 12–14), *ištu/ultu/ina labiri/labirti* "from of old" (e.g., Ungnad,, *BB*, n. 262:1) = Hebrew: מני קדם (Ps. 78:2), מקדם (Isa. 45:21; 46:10; Mich. 5:1; Hab. 1:12; Ps. 77:6, 12; Ps. 77:6, 12; 143:5). Akkadian *ina labār/labāri ūmī* "from ancient times" (e.g., *VAB* IV, 248:30) = Hebrew 2) מימי קדם Kgs 19:25 = Isa. 37:26; Mich.7:20; Lam. 1:7, 2:17). In Mari on the other hand, *ištu aqdāmi* (e.g., *ARM* X, 80:17–20) is the exact cognate of Hebrew מקדם. Further it is interesting to note that the following expression used rarely in Old Akkadian and in the peripheral dialects (i.e., Amarna, Ugarit). Old Akkadian employs the idiom *ištum dār* "since all times" (e.g., Gelb, *MAD* III, 106), Amarna and Ugarit: *ištu/ultu dārīti* "from old" (e.g., *EA*

88:44–45) = Hebrew מעולם (Isa. 42:14; Ps. 119:52); Amarna *ištu dārīt ūmī* "from time immemorial" (e.g., *EA* 116:55–56) = Hebrew מימי עולם (Mic. 5:1). Amarna *ištu ūmī ša abbūstišu* "since the days of his fathers" (e.g., 74:6–8) = Hebrew למימי אבתיכם (Mal. 3:7).

12. Borger, *Esarḫ*, 39:4 ff.
13. *VAB* IV, 214:19 (= *AnSt* 8 [1958] 46:5). Cf. also *šarru šaḫṭu ša ultu ūmē ṣeḫrišu* (for *ṣeḫērišu*!) *belūssunu putuqqu* "The humble king who has revered their (the gods') lordship since childhood" (Borger, *Esarḫ*, 39:4 ff). For a similar idea cf. Hebrew ועבדך ירא את ה' מנערי (I Kgs. 18:12). Note also that the exact semantic equivalent of Akkadian *ūmī ṣeḫēri* is in the Hebrew expression ימי נעורים (Hos. 2:17).
14. *KB* I, 188 b: 2–5. Cf. also H. Lewy *JNES* 11 (1952): 264 n. 5. Pamammuwa's declaration is paralleled by that of his contemporary Adad-Nīrāri III (810–783 BCE).
15. See N. Sarna, "The Interchange of the Preposition Beth and Min in Biblical Hebrew," *JBL* 78 (1959), 310–316.
16. E.g., למנעריי "from his youth" (*KAI* 24:12, Kilammuwa).
17. For the *ū* ending indicating the nominative case of the masculine plural nouns, see Ginzberg, *AJSL* 50 (1933), 2.
18. The noun עלים "a child" is attested in Sefîre (*KAI* 222A:22).
19. E.g., *YOS* 9, n. 35, II: 79–80 *in imnika nillak* (OB, Samsuiluna). It may be observed that only Deutero-Isaiah employs the idiom מוליך לימין (Isa. 63:12). מוליך לימין corresponds to the Akkadian *šūluku ana idi*, and the passage in Isaiah should be compared to NB *melammū birbirrūka... ana šalāli māt nakriya šūlik(k)i idāa*, "Let the splendor of your luminosity aid me to plunder the land of my enemy" (*VAB* IV, 260:39–40).
20. E.g., Borger, *Esarḫ*, 43:62 *idāka nittallak*.
21. For the Akkadian idioms *qāta ṣabātu* (*aḫāzu*) "to help, assist," see the references in *CAD* Ṣ 31ff; ibid., A/I, p. 179a = Hebrew החזק/אחז יד/ביד ימין (Gen. 19:16; Isa. 41:13; 45:1; Ps. 73:23; Jub. 8:20) = Ugaritic: *aḫd yd* (*II D*, I:31–32; ibid., 2:5–6; 19–20)/Cf. Also the Akkadian pair *qāta ṣabātu//redû* "to hold by the hand/to lead" (*Gilg.* II:31–32) = Hebrew: נהל//החזק ביד (Isa. 51:18).
22. For Akkadian *qāta tarāṣu* "to stretch out the hand, to protect," (said of divinity) see A. L. Oppenheim, "Idiomatic Accadian" (*JAOS* 61 [1941], 268, 270) = Hebrew: שלח יד attested in Ps. 138:7; 14:7; 2 Sam. 22:17 = Ps. 18:17 (i.e., ישלח ממרום, for ישלח <ידו> ממרום) cf. *JBL* 72 (1953): 26, n. 44.
23. Oppenheim, *art. cit.*, 270, n. 109.
24. Ibid., 268.
25. E.g., *rēṣut awīlim ilum illak* "The god will assist the man" (*YOS*, 10 n. 42 II:55–56), Hebrew employs חוש לעזרה attested only in Psalms

(e.g., Ps. 22:20; 38:23; 40:14; 70:2). Compare Akkadian *ḫīšamma idāni izizma tukultani lū attā* "Hasten hither and come to our aid for you are our trust" (*OIP* II, 42:36–37). For the Akkadian sequence *ḫâšu-alāku* and the Hebrew הלך-חוש, see Held, *JBL* 84 (1965), 277 n. 26.

26. E.g., *Zababa… u Ištar… tappūti illikūna* "DN_1 and DN_2 came to my help" (*RA* 8 [1911] 66:27ff.).
27. Streck, *Ašb*, 100:31–32 (*tukkulu*); Lambert, *BWL*, 46:12 (*rêṣu//qāta ṣabātu*).
28. *AfO* 20 (1963) 88:2.
29. Ebeling, *Handerhebung*, 26:30–31. Note also the expression *ina idi uzuzzzu* "to assist" in *BIN* 7, 32:7.
30. Num. 1:5.
31. *EA* 48:41–43 (Abi-Milki).
32. The references for the verb קום provided by B. Uffenheimer (*Leshnenu* 30 [1966]: 165) are not accurate. Our idiom is קום עם, not just קום. Moreover, his example from Ps. 74:23, i.e. קמיך//צרריך, has the opposite meaning: "your adversaries."
33. Cowley, *AP*, 254:59
34. For a full discussion of this idiom see S. Leiberman, *Tarbitz* 3 (1932): 455 n. 5.
35. Idem, *Greek in Jewish Palestine* (New York, 1942), 64–66.
36. Ibid., 64.
37. See Z. Ben Ḥayyim, עברית וארמית נוסח שומרון, Vol. III/II (Jerusalem, 1967) 17),73–74.
38. Ibid., 203:8; cf. also, ibid., 244:6.
39. *KAI* 214L15, 21.
40. See E Dhorme, *La religion assyro-bablyonienne* (Paris 1910) 150 ff.; R. Labat, *Le caractere religieux de la royauté assyro-babylonienne* (Paris 1939) 40ff.; H. Frankfort, *Kingship and the Gods* (Chicago 1948), 238–40; 245–46.
41. E.g., King, *BBst*, 123 III:8–10; *KAH*, II, n 84:8.
42. E.g., *VAB* IV, 122:45, ibid., 280, VII:16–29.
43. Ibid., 216 I:29–32; 226:20–21.
44. E.g., *OIP* II, 117:5–6; *VAB* IV 128:19–20 (*ḫaṭṭa išarta nadānu*); *ABL* no. 1369, r. 6 (*ḫaṭṭa šarrūti nadānu*).
45. *KAI* 214:9, 10, 13, 19
46. For the different options see *DISO*, 88.
47. Poebel, *AS* 3, 46 n.6, comes to a similar conclusion.
48. *Lyhpk ksa mlkk//lyṯbr ḫṭ mṯpṭk* (*I AB*, 6;28–29 = *III AB*, C:17–18).
49. KAI 1:2 (Aḥiram): חטר משפטה//כסא מלך. Contrast J.C. Greenfield (*Near eastern Studies in honor of W.F. Albright* [ed. H. Goedicke, Baltimore 1971] 256). Phoenician חטר משפט as well as Ugaritic *ḫṭ mṯpṭ* are not the

parallel idioms of Akkadian *ḫaṭṭi išarti*, Hebrew שבט מישור. "scepter of justice." From the parallelism with *ksa mlk* as well as from the inter-dialectal distribution discussed above, Phoenician חטר משפט; Ugaritic *ḫṭ mṯpṭ* denote "scepter of dominion," as translated by H.L. Ginsberg in *ANET*, 141b.

50. Ps. 45:7 (a royal hymn).
51. *KAI* 214:12–13 (Hadad).
52. Cf. e.g., Ps. 20:5–6; 37:4; 106:15.
53. Cf. e.g., Ps. 61:6.
54. Cf. e.g., Ps. 21:3.
55. Ps. 2:8. Note that Dahhood's reading of the MT *mimmennī* "from me" as *māmōnī* "wealth of me" (*Psalms* I, 12), is not without difficulties. The idiom שאל מ/מן is attested again in a royal hymn (Ps. 21:5) and is frequently employed in the sequence שאל מ־נתן (cf. above). Moreover, although Late Hebrew ממון = Aramaic ממונא goes back to Akkadian *mimmû,* it is nowhere attested in Biblical Hebrew.
56. Ps. 21:5.
57. *II D,* 6:26–28, cf. also ibid., 17–18.
58. *RA* 22 (1925) 173, r. 45–48 (OB hymn to Ištar).
59. Langdon, *Etana,* 41:7.
60. See *KAI* II, 215; *DISO*, 84, 314. Cf. also Cooke, *NSI*, 161, 166.
61. See *KAI II*, 215; *DISO*, 84, 314. Cf. also Cooke, *NSI*, 161, 166.
62. Cf. also Ps. 61:6–7: 2 Chr. 1:11–12.
63. E.g., *CH*, 26:101 ff. (*ūm balāṭim šūruku[m]*); *VAB* IV, 78, no. 1, III:43–45 (*ūmī urruku*).
64. Deut. 5:30, i.e. חיה//הארך ימים; cf. also Deut. 5:16; 6:2; 11:9; 1 Kgs. 3:14 and others.
65. E.g., יארך בעל שמם... ימת יחמלך ושנתו "May Ba'al-Šamêm... prolong the days and the years of Yeḥimilk" (*KAI* 4:3–5); cf. also ibid., 5:2; 6:2–3; 7:4–5, and *KAI* 10:9 = Deut. 5:30.
66. *KAI* 226:3 (Nērab II); note also that in the Behistun inscription the idiom ויומיך יארכון is employed, where the Akkadian version has *ūmēka [lūr]ik* Cowley, *AP*, 253:58; 257:58 (*VAB* III, 69,66:107).
67. E.g., *YOS* 9, no. 35:148–154 (*balāṭam qâšum//šarāku[m]*) *PBS* 7, no. 133, 1:11–12 (*ūmī arkūtim šarāku[m]*).
68. *KAI* 26, III:4–6, e.g. לתתי בעל כרנתריש... לעזתודא ארך ימים ורב שנת; cf. also *KAI* 48:4.
69. E.g., וחין אריכן ינתן לך (Cowley, *AP* 30:3 = 31:2–3).
70. E.g., *VAB* IV, 292, II:23–34 *ūmū arkūtu šanāti ṭūb libbi uṣṣipam* = Ps. 61:7 ימים על ימי מלך תוסיף שנותיו כמו דר ודור.
71. E.g., *AKA*, 160:3–4 (*arāk ūmī šumûd*); *MDP* 10, 11, III:7 (*ūmī urruku šanāti [w]utturu*).

72. Deut. 11:21 Prov. 4:10; 9:11.
73. E.g., Ebleling, *Handerhebung*, 38:38: Streck, *Ašb*, 208:31 (*balāṭa šebû*).
74. E.g., ארך ימים אשביעהו (Ps. 91:16).
75. Compare the formula *lišbūki šībūt[a]* "May they (the gods) satiate you with old age," *Ugaritica* V, 147 f. RS 20. 178:10.
76. E.g., *VAB* IV, p. 292:27–30.
77. E.g., *II D*, 6:32–33.
78. *KAI* 10:9; cf. also ibid., 12:4.
79. In Samalian dialect one can hardly expect a *mem* case ending for the pl. masc. nouns. As pointed out to me by H.L. Ginsberg, perhaps the *mem* here is to be considered as an adverbial *mem*.
80. Greeting formula in Old Bablyonian letters (see *CAD* D 111).
81. *KAI* 4:2 (Yeḥimilk).
82. *KAI* 10:9 (Yeḥawwmilk).
83. Ibid., 12:4.
84. *II D*, 6:32; *III D, 4:27*.
85. *I D*: 16.
86. *II D*, 6:30 *kbʿl kyḥwy yʿšr* "And Baal when he gives life gives a feast." For the interpretation and translation see Albright, *BASOR* 94 (1944), 33 and Ginsberg *ANET*, 151b; contrast Gordon (*Ugaritic and Minoan Crete,* 127) and Driver (*CML*, 55a).
87. *II AB*, 4–5:42 = *VAB*, E:39. Problematic indeed is *ḥwt* in *IV AB*, 2:20. The latter may be a greeting formula to be compared with Arabic *taḥiyytum*.
88. *I AB*, 3:2, 8, 20.
89. For the present restoration, cf. C.C. Torrey, *JAOS* 35 (1916/1917): 357, followed by Dupont-Sommer, *An Aramaic Handbook*, part 1/1 (Wiesbaden, 1967), 1. Other proposed restorations are: Dussaud (*RAr* IVᵉ, série, 11 [1908,] 233) [באשרה], Rosenthal (*ANET*, 655b) ["his god"], Donner-Röllig (*KAI* II, 106), [מראה]. The restoration proposed by Rosenthal, Donner-Röllig does not follow the expected order מראה אלור, as in למראה למלקרת I (*KAI* 201:3–4) and לאבה לפנמו (*KAI* 215:1). Therefore, Torrey's restoration is preferable.
90. Op. cit., 357–358.
91. *JPOS* 6 (1926), 86–87. Cf. also the rendering proposed by H. Gressman, *AOT* (1926), 443 ("A man from 'Ana I am").
92. Cf., e.g., Zākir (KAI 202A:1, 16).
93. For a full discussion of the relative pronoun in Imperial Aramaic, cf. M.Z. I Caddari, *Proceedings of the International Conference on Semitic Studies* (Jerusalem, 1969), 102–115.
94. The expression אשר ידי attested in Zākir (*KAI* 202B:15b), should be

also restored in lines 16b-17a, as sustained by numerous scholars. Students of the Zākir inscription differ with regard to the meaning of אשר. Lidzbarski (*Eph* 3 [1909–1915], 10) renders the word "inscription," Dussaud (*RAr* IVe série, 11 [1908], 233 n. 1) followed by Degen (*Altaramäische Grammatik* [Wisebaden, 1969], 45), equates it with the standard Old Aramaic אתר = אשר "place," while Donner-Röllig (*KAI* III, 29b) list it under the entry אשר II rendered as "Werk." On the other hand, Torrey (*JAOS* 35 [1915], 355) construes אשר in line 15b as the Canaanite relative pronoun. Torrey's rendering must be rejected, since in Old Biblical or Elephantine Aramaic, the relative אשר is never attested. Contextually, the sense of our expression is "achievements," and both Rosenthal (*ANET*[3], 251:8–81) and Dupont-Sommer (*Handbook*, part I/2, 2a) translate it accordingly. That our text refers to "achievements," is evident from a comparison with Akkadian royal inscriptions. There the scribes employ a separate warning against altering, erasing, or destroying the list of accomplishments achieved by the king: *u ša manma amat lemutti iḫassasamma ana epšētiya u ṣalmiya uma'iru* "Or whoever shall plan an evil plot against me and orders (it) against (the list of) my accomplishments or (against) my statue," (*AKA*, 251:8–82); *ša epšēt qātīya unakkarūma bunnannêya usaḫḫû* "Whoever changes (the list of) my accomplishments, alters my likeness" (Lyon, *Sargon*, 46:103; ibid., 38:76). In the Zākir passage the two clauses concerning a) the casting down (the list of) the achievements (i.e. הגע אשר יד lines 16–17), b) the casting down of the stele (i.e. הגע נצבא lines 18–19) are functionally equal to the pair of warnings concerning *epšētu/epšēt qātī* "(list of) accomplishments," and *ṣalmu/bunnannû,* "statue/image" in above Akkadian passages. Further the use of the verb כתב with אשר יד in Zākir, serves to confirm the rendering "achievements." In addition, Akkadian expresses the notion of "accomplishments" by idioms formed with *qātu* "hand": *epšēt/epēš/lipit qāti šaṭāru* "to inscribe achievements/deeds/accomplishments" (on a stele) (e.g., *OIP* II, 154:11–13; Borger, *Esraḫ*, 28:13–17.) This usage is reflected in our אשר ידי. Moreover, the sequence of a) erecting a stele before the god(s) and b) inscribing the royal achievements upon it as preserved in the Zākir, i.e., [ו]שמת קדם [אלור] נצבא זנה וכ[תבת ב]ה אית אשר ידי, corresponds to the Akkadian passage *6 narê... u ṣalam šarrūtiya maḫaršun ulziz mimma liptāt qātīya... ṣēruššu(n) ušašṭir* "I erected 6 steles... and my roayal statue before them (the gods) and whatever of my achievements, I inscribed thereon" (*OIP* II, 84:55–56). Here Akkadian a) *narâ/(ṣalma) maḫar DN šuzuzzu* equals Old Aramaic שמת קדם *DN* נצבא b) *liptāt qātī ṣēruššu(n) šušṭuru* equals Old Aramaic וכ[תבת ב]ה אית אשר ידי. In short, whatever the etymology of אשר may be, from the comparative

Akkadian material cited above, the expression אשר ידי would logically seem to denote "accomplishments." That is, Old Aramaic אשר ידי is the functional equivalent of any of the following Akkadian expressions: *epēš (epšēt)/lipit (liptāt) qātī*.

95. Op. cit., 234, n. 1.
96. Albright, op. cit., 87.
97. *KAI* II, p. 204. *AHw,* 428b.
98. Ibid., 438b.
99. *CAD* Ḫ 81–82. E.g., *ilu rēmenû zāqip ḫašši* "Merciful god who raises up the submissive." The Akkadian idiom *zāqip ḫašši* is the semantic equivalent of Hebrew זוקף כפופים (//אוהב צדיקים in Ps. 146:8//סומך נופלים Ps. 145:14), while Hebrew סומך נופלים is the functional equivalent of Akkadian *ṣābit qāt maqti/naski* "the one who assists (lit., who holds the hand of) the fallen." *CAD* Ṣ 31 ff.
100. See *CAD* A 455 ff.
101. *AHw*, 686b.
102. Ibid., 813a.
103. E.g., *CH*, col. I:31.
104. Cf., e.g., *YOS*, 9, 35:91.
105. *CAD* A 250b.
106. *AHw*, 688b.
107. *CH*, col. II:18 ff.
108. *AOB*, 38, No. 2:3.
109. Borger, *Esarḫ*, 12, I:16–18.
110. *KAI* 215:1–2. The expression פלט מן שחתה, denoting in Panammuwa II the notion of divine deliverance, may be compared with Akkadian *ina pušqi šūzubu* (e.g., Ebeling, *Handerhebung,* 122b:6)/*ina pušqi-šapšaqi eṭēru* (e.g., *En. el.* VI:126, 150)/*ina pušqi šalāpu (Šurpu,* IV:40)/*ina pušqi gamālu* (*Maqlû* II:12) = Hebrew הצל/חלץ/מלט מצרה/ ממצוקה "to save/rescue from hardship/trouble" (e.g., Ps. 34:18). More specifically, our Old Aramaic expression should be equated with the Akkadian idioms a) (*ina qabri bulluṭu)//ina karašê eṭēru* "(to save from the grave)//to spare from disaster" (Lambert, *BWL,* 58:35–36); b) *ina ḫašti šulû/ina pî karašê eṭēru* "to bring up from a pit//to save from the brink of a catastrophe" (*Šupru* IV:43–44) = Hebrew העלה משחת (Jonah 2:7)/פדה/גאל משחת (e.g., Ps. 103:4; Jub. 33:38). Thus, as pointed out by M. Held (*The Fourth World Congress of Jewish Studies*, Jerusalem, 1969) Akkadian *ḫaštu* equated in the commentary on *Šurpu* IV:43 with *šuttatu* semantically equals Hebrew שוחה/שחת "pit/grave" and should be kept apart from its homonym II שחת "net" = Akk. *šētu.* Likewise, one may consider Old Aramaic שחתה as the semantic and etymological counterpart of Akkadian *ḫašt,* Hebrew

שחת, thus rendering פלט מן שחתה "to save from disaster (lit: pit)." The majority of scholars (i.e., Cooke, *NIS*, 175; Donner-Röllig, *KAI* II, 225) propose to analyze the substantive שחתה as fem. sg. With3 per. masc. sg. Suffix -ה rendered "his destruction." In view of Akkadain *ina ḫašti*/karašê Hebrew משחת/משאול "from disaster (lit., pit)," we propose to compare the form of שחתה with the עזרתה "help" (Ps. 44:27; 63:8; 94:17)/ישועתה "salvation" (Jon. 2:10; Ps. 3:3; 80:3)/עולתה "injustice" (Ezek. 28:15; Hos. 10:13; Ps. 92:16; 125:3)/צרתה "trouble" (Ps. 120:1). All of these forms are fem. sg. abs. with two feminine markers -ת and -ה.

111. *KAI* 226:2–3.
112. *KAI* 4:6–7, cf. also *KAI* 10:9, כי מלך צדק הוא.
113. *KAI* 26, A:1.
114. *KAI* 243:1–2.
115. Note that the verb *ʿny*" "to humble," is attested in West Semitic inscriptions, cf., e.g., Azitawadda (*KAI* 26, A:18,19); Meša (*KAI* 181:5). Further, as pointed out recently by M. Held (*El* 9 [1969]72, n. 15), the same verb may be attested in Ugaritic in *III AB* B:35; cf. ibid., line 28.
116. Isa. 11:4.
117. Amos 8:4.
118. Jb. 24:4. For the reading ענוי ארץ//דלים in Am. 2:7, cf. Ginsberg, *El* 3 (1954), 83.
119. Ps. 149:4–5.
120. Ps. 22:27.
121. Note that ענוה is attested in royal Psalms expressing religious and moral qualities of the king, cf., e.g., רכב על דבר אמת וענוה Ps. 45:5. In Ps. 132:1, e.g., זכור ה' לדוד את כל ענותו is rendered by the Septuagint and the Syriac as ענותו "his humility." The latter rendering was recently rejected by M. Weinfeld, *JAOS* 99 (1970), 187a, where he proposes to render ענותו as "submissiveness" or "devotion."
122. Zech. 2:3.
123. Prov. 22:4. For a full discussion of the term יראת ה', see R.H. Pfeiffer, *El* 3 (1954), 59–62.
124. Ps. 25:8–9.
125. Ps. 37:10–11; 147:6.
126. See *RS* 16 (1908), 256, 358, 364, where he equates Old Aramaic ענה with Hebrew עני "poor."
127. *JBL* 28 (1909) 59.
128. *Les Araméens* (Paris 1949) 46–47.
129. *Handbook*, part I/1, n. 2.
130. *RAr* IV série, 11 (1908) 234, n. 2.

131. *JBL* 28 (1909) 59.
132. *JAOS* 35 (1916/17) 357–358.
133. *JPOS* 6 (1926) 86–87.
134. *ANET*, p. 655b.
135. *Lešonénu*, 27–28 (1964) 312.
136. *RS* 16 (1908) 363–364.
137. *AOT*, 443.
138. *Handbook*, I/1, 1.
139. *Les Araméens*, 46.
140. Note that the verb קרא utilized in the Hadad inscription (*KAI* 214:13) has also the specific denotation "to choose/single out." That is, the expressions קרני לבנא "He (Hadad) singled me out to build," may be equated with Akkadian *ša Marduk... ana zanān maḫāzī u uddušu ešrēti šumšu kīniš izkuru ana šarrūti* "Whom Marduk... had duly singled me out for the kingship in order to provide for the cult centers and to renovate the sanctuaries" (*VAB* IV, 234 1:13–15) = Hebrew: ראה עתה כי ה' בחר בך לבנות בית למקדש (1Chr. 28:10).
141. See *CAD* A 519 ff.
142. See *CAD* E 125ff.
143. For a discussion of the Hebrew idioms זכר בשם/קרא in Deutero-Isaiah and their Akkadian counterparts, see S. Paul, *JAOS 88* (1968), 181–182.
144. *AfO* 12 (1937/39) 364:5–8 (Tākil-Ilišu).
145. *AKA*, 30, col. I:18–23.
146. Borger, *Esarḫ*, 35:5 ff.
147. Cf. also E. Weidner, *Die Inschriften Tukulti-Ninurtas I und seiner Nachfolger* (Graz 1959) = *AfO*, Beiheft 12, 51:1–3; Borger, *Esraḫ*, 115 Text 82:7–10; *VAB* 7, Vol. 2 11:1–5; ibid. 252–254:1–6 (Aššurbanipal).
148. Cf. also ב בחר...על ישראל להיות מלך... 1 Chr. 28:4–5.
149. For a full discussion of this idiomatic expression, see *supra*, 4–7.
150. Cf. *supra*, 14–17.
151. For Hebrew שים שם "to name", cf. e.g. Judges 8:31; 1 Kings 17:34; Dan. 1:7; Neh. 9:7. Biblical Aramaic יהב/שום שם, e.g. Dan. 5:12. Phoenician שת שם, cf. e.g. Azitawadda *(KAI* 26 II:9–10, 17–18)
152. This meaning is not differing (in function) from the Hebrew idioms קרא/זכר (ב)שם and its Akkadian semantic equivalents *šuma/zikra nabû/zakāru*; cf. *supra*, 17–19.
153. E.g., *šarri ša tarammūma... tuštešser šumšu* "You (Marduk) make famous... the king whom you love" (*VAB* IV p. 122:56–59).
154. E.g., *ēnu Aššur... ušarbâ zikir šumiya* "When Aššur... made my fame great" (Borger, *Esarḫ*, 98:30–32); cf. also *zikir šumi šurruḫu* "to make fame supreme" (Streck, *ASb*, 92 I 9).
155. Gen. 12:2; 1 Chr. 17,24. Note also that Akkadian *zikra šupû* "to

proclaim fame" (referring to the gods, e.g., *lušāpi zikiršu lušarbi šumšu* "Let me proclaim his fame, let me make his name famous." *BA* 5 652 n. 16:7) is the functional equivalent of the Hebrew idiom הודיע שם in Isa. 64:1.

156. E.g., *ša... zikir šumišu ušeṣṣû ana rēšāti* "(Sargon) whose fame (the gods) extend (lit., cause to go out) to the outmost" (Lyon, *Sargon*, 30:3).

157. 2 Chr. 26:15; cf. also Ez. 16:14; 1 Chr. 14:17. Note also that Hebrew הלך שם (2 Chr. 26:8) = הלך שמע (Esth. 9:4) denotes "to be famous."

158. *Syria* 32 (1955), 14, Col. II:20–21. The idiom *awīl šumi* "famous man" in Mari (e.g. *ARM* I 90:22) corresponds to אנשי שם (Gen. 6:4); קריאי מועד//אנשי שם (Num. 16:2) as well as 1) אנשי שמות Chr. 5:24; 12:30–31) S. Gebritz's (*VT* 11 [1961] 142, n.4) equation of *awīl šumi* with Phoenician אדם שם attested in Azitawadda (*KAI* 26, III: 12–13; IV:1) was recently rejected by M. Held ("Azitawadda in the Light of Old Babylonian Royal Inscriptions," a paper presented before the American Oriental Society in New York, 1968) who argues convincingly that Phoenician אדם שם being a part of a longer formula, i.e. ואם מלך במלכם ורזן ברזנם אם אדם אש אדם שם is in the shadow of Old Babylonian royal inscription and should be rendered as follows: "If there be a king among the kings (= any king), or a viceroy (territorial governor) among viceroys (= any viceroy), or any ordinary (living) man (= any citizen)."

159. Cf. also *amur šarri bēliya šakan šumšu ana mūṣī šamšI u erbi šamši* "Behold the king my lord has made himself famous everywhere" (lit., "at the rising and the setting of the sun"), *EA* 288:5–7, and *amur šarri šakan šumšu ina māt Urusalim ana dāriš* "Behold the king made himself famous in the land of Jerusalem" (*EA* 287: 60–61).

160. Zec. 3:19–20.

161. Gen. 11:4.

162. Isa. 63:12.

163. Ibid., 56, 5.

164. E.g., *zikir šumika liššakin ana ūmī dārūti* "May your fame be established forever" (*VAB* IV, p. 68:41; Nabopolassar); *šumam dārīam ša šarrūtiya lū aštakkan* "I keep establishing everlasting fame for my kingship" ibid., II:14–16; Nebuchadrezzar). Akkadian *šumam dārīam* (Hebrew שם עולם) *šakānu* (= Hebrew עשה/נתן), is attested already in Old Babylonian period e.g. [*š*]*umam dārīam* [*š*]*a šarrūtiya lū aškun* "I established everlasting fame for my kingship" (*AfO* 12 [1937–9], 364–5:19–21; Tākil Ilišu).

165. See Paul's thesis, "Deutero-Isaiah and Cuneiform Royal Inscriptions" *JAOS* 88 (1968), 180–186.

166. *ARM* I, 69, r. 14–16.
167. 1 Chr. 17:21.
168. 3*R* 7 I:4 (Salm. III).
169. Isa. 63:14.
170. *PBS* 7,133, 32:75 ff. cf. I. J. Gelb, *JNES* 7 (1948), 270 (Ḫammurabi). Akkadian *šuma/zikra dummuqu* "to establish a good reputation" (*CAD,* D, 626) is the semantic equivalent of הטיב שם (e.g., 1 Kgs. 1:47).
171. Halil Edhem, *Hatira Kitabi* I (Ankara 1947), 140–141.
172. *AnSt* 8 (1958), 48:24; *VAB* IV, 290 ff: 21–22.
173. The interdialectal distribution of the idiom "good name" (i.e., fame) if is as follows: Akkadian *šumu damqu (ābu)*: Hebrew שם טוב; Old Aramaic שם טב; Phoenician שם נעם (e.g., *KAI* 18:6).
174. For a new proposed reading of this personal name (i.e. *Sigabbar* instead of the commonly accepted *Sagbar* "belonging to Agbar"), see S. Kaufman, *JAOS* 90 (1970), 270–271.
175. On the present translation, cf. W. W. Hallo, *JAOS* 88 (1968), 85:22_23.
176. *ANET*, 412a.
177. *AnSt* 8 (1958)m 50:29–31. = *VAB* IV, 292:30–32, e.g. *niṭlu īnē namirma šūturāk ḫasīs qātī u šēpī salimma nussuqā amātū'a.*
178. Cf. Ladnsberger, Halil Edhem, *Hatira Kitabi I,* 141.
179. E.g., *šumma uznāšu kabtāšu ṭēmšu ittakiršu atmûšu itteneprekku imât* "If his hearing (lit., ears) faded (lit., stopped), his mind is deranged and his speech continuously stopped he shall die" (R. Labat, *TDP*, 70:14; ibid., 22:42).
180. Ibid., 22:45.
181. Ibid., 22:41.
182. R.C. Thompson, *AMT*, 69:7, 8.
183. Ibid., 34:1, 20.
184. *JAOS* 88 (1968), 88:22.
185. Isa. 6:10; 59:1; Zech. 7:11.
186. E.g., Labat, *TDP,* 50:15.
187. Gen. 48:10.
188. E.g., *TDP*, 228:97: *šumma šerru...pâšu kabit būšānu iṣbassu* "If a baby's... mouth is heavy a disease of the mouth has seized it."
189. Ezek. 3:5–6.
190. Targum on Ezek. 3:5.
191. Ex. 4:10.
192. E.g., Zimmern, *BBR*, n. 83 II:7–8; cf. ibid., 82 IV:13–14. For a discussion of Akkadian *egēru* Aramaic חגר see D. Sperling, *The Journal of the Ancient Near Eastern Society of Columbia University* (= ANES), III/(1970–1), 121–128.

193. *TDP*, 232:9. Note also *lišānšu ikṣurma atmâ ul utâr* "He (the demon) has bound his (the patient's) tongue so that he is unable to reply" (*ZA* 45 [1939] 26:7–8; see M. Held, *JCS* 15 [1961] 10a).
194. E.g., *En.el.* II:89: *šaptāšunu kuttumāma qāl [iš ušbū]* "Their lips closed (lit. covered) they sat in silence."
195. E.g., Lambert, *BWL*, p. 52:24 *pîya ša uktattimu ṣabāriš aš[ṭu]* "My mouth which has blocked (lit., covered) hard to speak (lit., prattle)."
196. Cooke, *NSI*, 1190. Note that Hebrew סגר "to close" is commonly rendered by the Targum as אחד (cf., e.g., Gen. 19:6. 10; Ex. 14:3; Jos. 6:1; Isa. 22:22; 24:10). Note also that Hebrew אחז may denote "to close" in Neh. 7:3. For a possible attestation of אחז "to cover" in Ps. 77:5, cf. Y. Blau's discussion in *EI*3 (1954). 107b. Blau's equation of אחז with Akkadian *uḫḫuzu* must be rejected. Akkadian *uḫḫuzu* never means "to cover." Heb. אחז is the semantic equivalent of Akkadian *uḫḫuzu* (*CAD* A 179f.) only when it denotes "to mount an object in precious metal."
197. *Greek in Jewish Palestine* (New York 1942), 168.
198. *AfO* 19 (1950–60), 50:64–64.
199. *TDP*, 220:22; cf. Held, *BASOR* 200 (1970), 38f., n. 71. Note also the usage of Akkadian *ṣabātu* with *lišānu*, e.g. *Maqlû* III:94 "I obstructed your mouth, I seized your tongue."
200. *AHw*, p. 419.
201. *MDP* 2, pl. 23, VII:38–39.
202. For a full discussion of the divinely bestowed longevity in cuneiform and in West Semitic inscriptions cf. *supra*, 50 ff.
203. As recently pointed out by M. Held (*BASOR* 200 [1970], 34, n. 13) even "the very concept 'generation' is alien to the Akkadian lexicon."
204. F.R. Kraus, *Texte*, n. 36 II:48.
205. *YOS* 10, 44:70.
206. *ABL* 178, r. 5–9. (*CAD* Z 126a); cf. A Heidel, *AS* 13 (1940) 25 f.
207. *AnSt* 8, (1958), 50:33–34.
208. *AnSt* 8, 48:23; cf. *VAB* IV, 290:20.
209. Ibid., 48:24; cf. op. cit., 22.
210. Ibid., 25; cf. op. cit., 23–24.
211. Ibid., 50:29–32; cf. op. cit., 32.
212. Though the OA פם לאתאחז מן מלן is not the semantic correspondent of the Akkadian *nussuqā amātūa* both idioms express a very similar idea.
213. Op. cit., 50:33–34.

A Curse Concerning Crop-Consuming Insects in the Sefîre Treaty and in Akkadian: A New Interpretation

To H.L. Ginsberg On His Seventieth Birthday

כי ארך ימים ושנות חיים ושלום יוסיפו לך
(Prov. 3:2)

Sefîre IA 27–32b reads as follows:

(27) ושבע שנן יאכל ארבה ושבע שנן תאכל תולעה ושבע [שנן ים]
(28) ק תוי על אפי ארקה ואל יפק חצר וליתחזה ירק ולי [שגה]
(29) אחוה...
(30) ...וישלחן אלהן מן כל מה אכל בארפד ובעמה...
(31) ...וסס וקמל וא [... יהוו]
(32) ...עלה

J.A. Fitzmyer renders this passage as follows:

> For seven years may the locust devour, and for seven years may the worm eat, and for seven [years may] TWY come up upon the face of its land: May the grass not come forth so that no green may be seen: and may its vegetation not be [seen]: ... May the gods send every sort of devourer against Arpad and against its people! ... And may a moth and a louse and a [...][1]

Stylistically, Greenfield's restoration[2] *wyl* [*śgh*] *ʾḥwh* (= Job 8:11) is preferable to *wly* [*tḥzh*] proposed by Fitzmeyer and Donner-Röllig.[3]

I. Lines 27–28

Among the list of maledictions in Sefîre IA 212–33 are the names of wild and domesticated animals,[4] as well as crop-consuming insects. Indeed, crop-consuming pests as an agricultural threat are well attested in both Mesopotamian and biblical sources. We are all familiar with the biblical lists: *gzm/ʾrbh/ylq/ḥsyl* (Joel 1:4; 2:25) rendered by the Targum as *zḥʾ/gwbʾ/prḥʾ/šmwṭʾ*, and *ḥgb/ḥrgl/slʿm* (Lev. 11:22) rendered by Targum Pseudo-Jonathan as *krzbʾ/nypwlʾ/ršwnʾ*, all of which belong to the locust family. In the curse formula above, however, we find in sequence the *ʾrbh* "locust," *twlʿh* "worm of the field," and the problematic vocal *twy*.

Dupont-Sommer, while admitting that the meaning of this enigmatic word is uncertain, maintains that *twy* is "perhaps a name of a river causing a calamitous inundation."[5] J. Koopmans, though in doubt, proposes to equate the vocable with the Hebrew *tʾw/y* (Deut. 14:5; Isa. 51:20) "Wildschaf/Wildstier."[6] Fitzmeyer suggests an etymological connection between *twy* and Ugaritic *thw*, Arabic *tyh*, Hebrew *tôhu*, "waterless/impassible desert."[7] Ben-Ḥayyim, following closely Fitzmyer's equation and assumption that *twy* "must refer to some sort of blight," relates this word with the Syriac *twʾ/thʾ/twh*, "desert/desolation."[8]

While all the following have approached the problem solely on etymological grounds, Weinfeld assumes that contextually *twy* is an agricultural pest to be equated functionally with Hebrew *ṣlṣl* "cricket." He argues that: (a) the sequence of *twy*, *twlʿh*, *ʾrbh* in Sefîre (in reverse order) equals that of *ʾrbh, tlʿt, ṣlṣl,* in Deut. 28:38–42; and (b) the usage of Hebrew *wyʿl ʾrbh* (Exod. 10:14–15) = Sefîre [*ys*]*q twy*.[9] In addition to Weinfeld's semantic equation of Hebrew *ʿlh ʾrbh* = Old Aramaic *slq twy,* it should be noted that late Hebrew also employs the expression *ʿlh gwbʾy*: (a) *mšmt ršb"g ʿlh gwbʾy* "When Ršbg died, the locust arose and troubles increased" (b. *Sot*. 49b); and (b) *bʿwn gzl hgwbʾy ʿwlh* "As a punishment for the crime of oppression and the locust rises" (b. *Šabb*. 32b). Likewise, Akkadian employs the expression *tibūt erbi* "the rising of the locust," as well as *erbâ tebû*: [*ina šatti šiā*]*ti erbū ittebīima še'i ebūri ikkal* "[within the same year] the locust will invade (lit., will rise) and devour the barley crop."[10]

Related material from the fauna of ancient Mesopotamia tends to support Weinfeld's contention as the most logical one. The threat of crop-consuming insets played a great role in the agricultural life of the Sumero-Akkadians. Accordingly, one is not surprised to find numerous words for various kinds of locusts and other types of crop consuming insects.

The bilingual series of the *ḪAR-ra* = *ḫubullu* lists among various types of crop-consuming insects the *ZA.NA* (*maḫ/mul/bal)- UŠU* (*gal/sim/sima)*, which corresponds to Akkadian *mūnu*, rendered by Landsberger as "caterpillar."[11] So too *ZA.NA* (*maḫ/mul/-bal)* = Akkadian *mūnu* is equated with *nappillu* "caterpillar"[12] and seems to be the equivalent of Aramaic *nypwl'* rendering of the Hebrew *hapax* word *ḥrgl* (Targum Pseudo-Johnahan. on Lev. 11:12). Note that while Jastrow lists the Aramaic *npwl* "young bird" (probably derived form the Hebrew *npl* "to fall") together with *npwl'* "a species of locust,"[13] in the light of the Akkadian *nappilu* = Aramaic *npwl'*, it is best to separate the two substantives. It should be noted further that though Midrash *Sifra* (Šeminî par. 3, ch. 5) states that *ḥrgl zh npwl*, the Babylonian Talmud (b. *Ḥul.* 65b) identifies the *npwl* with the Hebrew *sl'm* employed in Lev. 11:22.

Further, *UŠU* (*/sim.ma=mūnu)* also corresponds to *ākilu*[14] = Hebrew *'kl* (Mal 3:11) = *ḥsyl* = *ākil* (Sefîre IA:30).[15] Also noteworthy is the fact that *āki[lum]* = *mubattiru* = *UḪ.DÚR. RA*,[16] where *UḪ.DÚR.RA* is equated with *tūltu*[17] =Hebrew *twl't* (Deut. 28:39) = *twl'h* (Sefîre IA:27); all of these are crop-consuming insects listed in sequential order in the lexical texts.

More specifically, *mu-ni A.ŠÃ (mūni eqli)* "caterpillar of the field," corresponds in the *ḪAR-ra* = *ḫubullu* to Akkadian *da-a-a-e* (*dayye/ṭayya*).[18] Both appear in a sequence with *tim-bu-ut A.ŠÁ* (= *timbut eqli*) "a cricket," equated with *arabû* "locust."[19] This is much like the Hebrew *ṣlṣl* "cricket" juxtaposed with *'rbh* in Deut. 28:38–42 and *'rbh* with *twy* in Sefîre IA 27–28.

We thus propose semantically and etymologically to equate

the Akkadian substantive *da-a-a-e* (= *mūni ša eqli*) with the Sefîre vocable *twy*. Both are crop-consuming insects, probably winged. Additionally, Akkadian *dayye* (= *mūni ša eqli*) corresponds also in the lexical lists to *muttaprišu*[20] rendered by von Soden as "geflugeit."[21] The shift *d>t*, as in Akkadian *dayye* = Aramaic *twy*, is also found in the following examples: (a) Akkadian *nadānu* "to give" (= Aramaic *ndn*) = Ugaritic/Hebrew/Phoenician *y/ntn* = Old Aramaic *ntn*; (b)Akkadian *abātu* "to destroy" = Ugaritic/Hebrew/Phoenician *ʾbd* = Old Aramaic *ʾbd*; (c) Akkadian *kabātu* "to be heavy" = Ugaritic/Hebrew/Phoenician *kbd* = Neo-Assyrian *kabādu*;[22] (d) Akkadian (substantive) *batqu* (in *batqa ṣabātu)* = Hebrew *bdq* (in *ḥzq bdq*) = Aramaic *bdqtʾ*.[23] Note also the shift *d>t* in Ugaritic *ṯpd/srd* = Heavy *špt/šrt* "to place/serve."[24]

II. Line 30

This line traditionally is rendered as follows: "May the gods send every sort of devourer against Arpad and against its people."[25] Aside from the syntactical problem that the word *mn* creates, such a rendering is not without difficulties. It is virtually impossible to render *mn kl mh* as "every sort of," especially when one notes that the Aramaic compound *kl mh* is aptly attested in various parts of the Sefîre inscriptions,[26] but not elsewhere preceded by *mn*. Fitzmyer, while following Dupont-Sommer's rendering "de tout espèce," admits that the use of *mn* "is peculiar." Though doubtful about the position of *mn* in the sentence, he proposes to understand it as an interrogative-indefinite pronoun.[27] This proposal was followed by Donner and Röllig[28] and Degen.[29] It should be noted that unlike the majority of Old Aramaic descriptions (e.g., *Bir-Hadad*; *Zākir*; *Hadad*; *Panammuwa*; *Bir-Rākib)*, word dividers are not used at all in the Sefîre inscriptions. Therefore, an alternative interpretation is to consider the phrase *mn kl mh* as comprising two distinct units of which the compound *kl mh* is to be treated as a single word.

It will be recalled that lines 27–28 deal with crop-consuming insects devouring the produce of the land. There we find three types of crop-consuming pests: the *ʾrbh* = Akkadian *erbû(/erēbu/aribu)*"locust"; *twlʿh* = Akkadian *tūltu* "crop-consuming worm"; and, if our proposed equation is correct, the *twy* = Akkadian *dayye* (*ṭayye*) "caterpillar." Likewise in line 30, we see in the words *mn, klmh,* and *ʾkl* three distinct substantives, all crop-consuming insects. (a) The *ʾkl (ākil)* is to be equated with the Hebrew *hapax ʾkl* "crop-consuming devourer" (= Hebrew *ḥsyl*) = Akkadian *ākilu*, referring (in the lexical texts lists and in other literary texts) mostly to crop-consuming pests (see above). (b) The Old Aramaic *mn* is to be equated with *ZA.NA/UŠU* = Akkadian *mūnu* "caterpillar" (see above). (c) The vocable *klmh* is to be interpreted as the equivalent of Sumerian *UḪ* = Akkadian *kalmatu*[30] = Aramaic *qlmtʾ* (Targum Onq. on Exod. 8:12 rendering the Hebrew *knym*) = Syriac *qalmā* "louse."

It should be noted, however, that while Akkadian *kalmatu* generally means "louse," *klmh* in our case probably refers to a crop-consuming insect since it is employed in sequence with *mn* and *ʾkl*. Therefore, *klmh* should correspond to *UḪ* (*a.šà.ga/giš SAR/še/giš. ì/zú.lum.ma*) = Akkadian *kalmat eqli/kirî/šeʾim/šamaššammê/suluppi*, "a louse/insect of the field/orchard/barley/sesame/dates."[31] Note that in light of the Akkadian *kalmatu*, Fitzmyer errs in arguing that *qml* (employed in the Sefîre IA: 31) "agreeing with the Arabic *qamlum*" is the original form.[32] On the contrary, (a) the suggested cognate *klmh*, Targum Onq. *qlmtʾ*, Babylonian Aramaic *klmy*,[33] Syriac *qalmā*, goes back to the Akkadian *kalmatu*; (b) these forms are all feminine substantives agreeing with Akkadian *kalmatu*, whereas the late metathesized *qml* is one of those feminine nouns with a masculine ending;[34] and (c) note that Sefîre *klmh*, Babylonian Aramaic *klmy* is written with *k* agreeing with the original Akkadian spelling *kalmat*. The Sefîre, Targum Onq., Syriac, and Arabic spelling with *q* is indeed secondary.

Furthermore, just as Aramaic *mn* and *ʾkl* occur together, Akkadian *mūnu* and *ākilu* appear in sequential order in both the lexical series and in a literary-astrological text: *mēnu u ākilu ina māti ibaššû* "a caterpillar and a devourer will be in the land."[35]

Just as the Aramaic *mn, klmh, ʾkl* occur in sequence in Sefîre IA: 30, they also occur in sequence in another literary-incantation text dealing with the removal of crop-consuming insects, *mēnu, ākilu*, as well as *kalmat eqli*, e.g., [*mū*]*naāki*[*la*...] *ṣāṣira sāmāna kalmat eqli ina libbi eqli šūlî*: "An incantation to remove caterpillar devourer,... cricket, red bug, vermin of the field from the field." More significant is the fact that the exact curse formula as it occurs in the Sefîre, i.e., *wyšlḥn ʾlhn mn klmn ʾkl bʾrpd wb ʿmh* "May the gods let loose caterpillar, vermin (of the field), crop-consuming devourer against Arpad and its people," is also employed in the maledictions of the Vassal-Treaties of Esarhaddon:

> *k[ī]ša erbê kalmutu mūnu ākilu ālānikunu*
> *mātkunu nagīkunu lūšakilū*
>
> May they (the gods) let vermin (of the fields), caterpillars, devourers, consume your cities, your country, and your provinces, like locusts[36]

Degen seems to err in deriving the verb *yšlḥn* as *Peʿal*.[37] The form in all probability is to be taken as *Paʿel,* as could be seen from the use of the Hebrew *šlḥ* (*piʿel*) employed with *dbr/ṣrʿh/ʾrywt/nḥšym/ṣpʿwnym/ḥyh rʿh/ʿrwb* "to let loose pestilence/plague/lions/snakes/beasts of prey, swarms of insects" (Lev. 26:25; Deut. 7:20; 2 Kings 5:2; 17:2; Jer. 8:17; Ezek. 5:17; Ps. 78:45).

III. Lines 31b-32a

Finally, a word should be said with regard to the specific meaning of the metathesized form *qml* employed in line 31. As noted above, while Akkadian *kalmatu* is generally used to mean "vermin/louse" in literary texts, its precise sense can be ascertained only by its contextual usage. This also seems to be the case in Sefîre where in line 30 *klmh* refers to "vermin of the field." *qml* in line 31, however, seems to have a different connotation. It should be observed that Akkadian *kalmatu*

(= Sumerian *UḪ*) "louse" is employed in the Gilgamesh Epic (XII: 93–94) in the sense of "moth of the clothes:" [*kīma lub*] *āri labīri kalmatu ekkal* "(my body?)… like an old garment that vermin eat (it)." Such is also the case in the Babylonian Talmud, where in one case Aramaic *klmtʾ* means "head-louse;" *viz. ʾstyyʿ mltʾ wšdr lh sryqwtʾ dmqṭlʾ klmy*: "It happened that he sent him a comb that kills head-lice" (b. *Nid.* 20b). Note that also in the lexical list Akkadian *mutqa* = *kalmat*[*u*] "a head-louse."[38] In the *ḪAR-ra* = *ḫubullu* series, *mutqu* is employed in sequence with Sumerian *uḫ.sag.du* = Akkadian *kalmat qaqqadi* "a head-louse."[39] In another case, it clearly refers to "vermin of the clothes": *mmhdwry myly wmsmrṭwṭy klmy* "from peddlers comes gossip, from rags moth" (b. *Ber.* 51b). Likewise, contextually, *qml* in line 31 seems to refer to "moth of the clothes," since it follows *ss* = Akkadian *sāsu* = Hebrew *ss* (//*ʿš*) "vermin of the clothes."

In lines 27–28, there are three crop-consuming insects: *ʾrbh, twlʿh, twy*; in line 30, we have found three other crop-pests: *mn, klmh, ʾkl*. It stands to reason that in line 31, the Aramaic scribe would employ three substantives: (a) *ss* (b) *qml*, where under (c) we propose to restore *w*ʾ[*šš*…], all referring to "moth/vermin of clothes." Our proposed restoration gains in probability noting that (a) Hebrew *ʿš* is parallel to *ss* (Isa. 51:8) and sometimes replaces it (Isa. 50:9; Hos. 5:12; Ps. 39:12; Also Sir. 42:13: *ky mbgd yṣʾ ʿš wmʾšh rʿt ʾšh*, "For out of clothes comes the moth and out of a woman comes woman's wickedness."); (b) Hebrew/Aramaic *ʿš*/*ʿš* is the etymological equivalent of Akkadian *ašāšu* = Sumerian *uḫ.Ḫa*,[40] which corresponds also in the list to *sāsu*, "moth of clothes;"[41] and (c) in the *ḪAR-ra* = *ḫubullu* series, similar to our proposed restoration (i.e. *wss wqml w*ʾ[*šš*]), we find in sequential order the same nouns:[42]

Sum: *uḫ.tu₉.ba* = Akk. *kalmat ṣubāti* (= Sefîre *qml*)
Sum: *uḫ.ḪA* = Akk. *ašāšu* (= Sefîre *ʾ[šš]*)
Sum: *uḫ.ḪA* = Akk. *sāsu* (= Sefîre *ss*)

NOTES

1. J. A. Fitzmyer, *The Aramaic Inscriptions of Sefîre* (Rome: Pontifical Biblical Institute, 1967), 14.
2. J. C. Greenfield, "Linguistic Maters in the *Sefîre* Inscription," *Lešonenu* 27–28 (1964), 303–313 (Heb.). See also Idem, "Stylistic Aspects of the Sefire Treaty Inscriptions" *Acta Orientalia* 29 (1965), 1–18.
3. H. Donner and W. Rölling, *Kanaanäische und aramäische Inschriften* (3 vols.; Wiesbaden: Harrassowitz, 1962–4), 1:41.
4. F. C. Fensham, "The Wild Ass in the Aramean Treaty between Bar-Ga'ayah and Mati'el," *JANES* 22 (1963), 185–186. See also J. C. Greenfield, "Three Notes on the Sefire Inscription," *JSS* (1966), 98–100.
5. A. Dupont-Sommer, "Ancient Aramaic Monumental Inscriptions: Glossary," in *An Aramaic Handbook* (ed. H. Rosenthal; Wiesbaden: Harrassowitz, 1967), 7.
6. J. J. Koopmans, *Aramäische Chrestomathie: ausgewählte Texte* (2 Vols.; Leiden: Nderland Instituut voor het Nabije Oosten, 1962), 51.
7. J. Fitzmyer, *The Aramaic Inscriptions*, 45–46.
8. Z. Ben-Ḥayyim, "Comments on the Inscription of Sfire" *Lešonenu* 35 (1971), 245. See also J. C. L. Gibson, *Textbook of Syrian Semitic Inscriptions II, Aramaic Inscriptions* (Oxford: Clarendon, 1975), 39.
9. M. Weinfeld, "Traces of Assyrian Treaty Formulae in Deuteronomy," *Biblica* 46 (1965), 424 n. 2.
10. *CAD* E 257b.
11. B. Landsberger, *The Fauna of Ancient Mesopotamia, Second Part. = Materialen zum sumerischen Lexikon* VIII (Rome: Pontifical Biblical Institute, 1962), 31:273a-c, 276–78.
12. Ibid., 31:273–275.
13. M. Jastrow, *A Dictionary of the Targumim, the Talmud Babli and Yerushalmi, and the Midrashic Literature* (New York: Putnam, 1886–1903), 907a.
14. B. Landsberger, *The Fauna*, 32:279.
15. For the proper identification of Hebrew *ḥsyl*, see M. Held, "Studies in Comparative Semitic Lexicography" in *Studies in Honor of Benno Landsberger on his Seventy-fifth Birthday, April 21,* (Assyriological Studies 16; Chicago: University of Chicago, 1965), 398–401.
16. B. Landsberger, *The Fauna*, 30:271.
17. Ibid., 30:271.
18. Ibid., 65:359.
19. Ibid., 65:357.
20. *CAD* D 27a.

21. W. von Soden, *Akkadisches Handwörterbuch* (Wiesbaden: Harrassowtiz, 1959), 689b.
22. D. J. Wiseman, "The Vassal-Treaties of Esarhaddon" *Iraq* 20 (1958), 53:335.
23. Ibid. 115; J. C. Greenfield, "Lexicographical Notes I," *HUCA* 29 (1958), 217–22; B. A. Levine, "Comments on Some Technical Terms of the Biblical Cult," *Lešonenu* 30 (1966), 4–11.
24. M. Held, "A Difficult Biblical Expression and its Parallel in Ugaritic," *Eretz-Israel* 3(1954), 103, n. 41.
25. J. Fitzmyer, *The Aramaic Inscriptions*, 26; D. R. Hillers, *Treaty-Curses and the Old Testament Prophets* (Rome: Pontifical Biblical Institute, 1964), 54.
26. Fitzmyer, *Aramaic Inscriptions*, 26.
27. Ibid., 48.
28. Donner and Rölling, *Kanaanäische*, 2:249.
29. R. Degen, "Altarmäische Grammatik der Inschriften des 10.-8. Jh. V. Chr." *Abhandlugen für die Kunde des Morgenlandes* 38:3 (Mainz: Deutsche Morgenländische Gesellschaft, 1969), 62.
30. B. Landsberger, *The Fauna*, 28:253; *CAD* K 86a.
31. Ibid., 256–60.
32. J. Fitzmyer, *The Aramaic Inscriptions*, 49.
33. M. Jastrow, *Dictionary*, 645a.
34. J. Fitzmyer, *The Aramaic Inscriptions*, 156.
35. *CAD* A/I 267a.
36. D. J. Wiseman, "The Vassal Treaties of Essarhadon," 73:599–600.
37. R. Degen, "Altarmäische," 69.
38. *CAD* K 86b lexical section.
39. B. Landsberger, *The Fauna*, 28–29:254–55.
40. F. Schulthess, "Aramäisches," *Zeitschfrit für Assyriologie* 24 (1910), 47–58. See also *AHw* 79b.
41. B. Landsberger, *The Fauna*, 30:268a.
42. Ibid., 30:267–68a.

Two Notes on the Treaty Terminology of the Sefîre inscriptions

1. A warning not to commit a *razzia* (Sefîre II B:7; III: 23–24)

Sefîre II B:7 reads as follows *wlḥbzthm wl'bdt 'šmhm.* The problem centers around the Sefîre verb *ḥbz*, which does not occur anywhere in Aramaic. Students who dealt with these inscriptions based their study solely on etymological grounds. Dupont-Sommer equates *ḥbz* with the Semitic verb *ḥbt* "to hit."[1] Fitzmyer dismisses Dupont-Sommer's observation on phonetic grounds and calls it "farfetched." Nevertheless, he argues that the Aramaic *ḥbz* is a cognate of the Arabic *ḥbz*, which also has the sense "to strike."[2] F. Rosenthal relates the Aramaic *ḥbz* to the Hebrew *ḥpz* "to flee in a hurry," and Arabic *ḥfz* "to push."[3] Greenfield likewise approaches the problem on etymological grounds. While not dealing with the usage of *ḥbz* in Sefîre II B:7, he does deal with the Mishnaic Hebrew *ḥbs* "to crush (the skull, etc.)" and with the Akkadian verb *ḫabāšu* "to smash (with a mace); to chop to pieces."[4]

Although from various etymological stands, all (Dupont-Summer, Fitzmyer, Greenfield) arrive at a similar meaning "to hit, strike, crash (chop)," a rendering that in our opinion can hardly fit the context. A different approach in discussing the semantic/functional equivalent of *ḥbz* (in Sefîre, II B:7; III: 24) within its proper context is called for. It should be noted that in cuneiform royal and treaty inscriptions, the theme of a sudden or irregular incursion in boarder warfare, especially one with a view to plunder, is a well known convention. Akkadian employs the verb *ekēmu* "to take away by force" in the above indicated context, e.g., *ša Aramû ina danāni ēkimūni ana ramēniya utirra* "(the cities) which (the king) of Aramu took by force, I annexed again[5]; *ālāni... ša tarṣi abīya Elamû ēkimu danāniš... akšud* "I conquered the cities that the Elamites had taken by force during the reign of my father."[6] Akkadian *ekēmu* is also employed in sequence with *ḫabātu* "to plunder, commit *razzia*": *ana dâki ḫabāti u ekēmi Muṣur illika* "I came to kill, to raid, and to take Egypt by force."[7] Indeed, Akkadian *ḫabātu* is also used in treaty contexts similar to that of the Sefîre inscription. It should, therefore, be considered as the semantic equivalent of our Old Aramaic *ḥbz* with the specific sense "to move across/commit *razzia*/incursion into an enemy territory" — not "to strike, hit, smash" as previously advocated. The following arguments may be adduced. First, exactly as in the vassal treaties of Esarhaddon, in a similar context as in Sefîre II B:7, the various vassals are warned not to commit a *razzia* against the crown prince: i.e., *ḫubtāšu lā taḫabbatani* "do not make a *razzia* against him," followed in sequence by *šumšu u zērāšu ina māti lā tuḫallaqani* "do not eradicate his name and his descendants from the land."[8] Such is also the case in Sefîre where *wlḥbzthm* "do not commit *razzia* against them (the descendants)," is juxtaposed with *wl'bdt 'šmhm* "do not eradicate their names."[9] Akkadian *ḫabātu* is well employed in treaties from the second millennium, used in a stipulation not to plunder/commit a *razzia* against one's ally: *mātāti ša ebirti Puratti ulllīti attā taḫabbat u anāku aḫabbatma mātāti ša ebirti Puratti ullīti* "if you commit a *razzia*/raid the territories on the far bank of the Euphrates, I too will commit a *razzia*/raid the territories on the far bank of the Euphrates."[10]

More specifically, in contexts concerning border arrangements, such as the treaty between Suppilulimas and Mattiwaza, we find the following passage: *u mātāti ša ebirti annīti aḫtabatma u ana miṣriya utter* "and the territories of the bank I raided and annexed (them) to my border."[11] Here Akkadian *ḫabātu* "to make an incursion" is employed in a apposition to *ana misriya utter* "I annexed to my border." For example, *wkzy ḥbtzw 'lhn byt 'by* "when (the) gods raided the estate/inheritance of my father" is juxtaposed with *wk't hšbw 'lhn šybt by [t 'by...]* "but now the gods have restored (the restoration of) my father's estate" in Sefîre

III: 24–25, a text dealing with border restoration of Tal'ayim, annexed by Bir Ga'yah.[12]

In short, while it is true that *z* in Aramaic can hardly represent *ṯ*,[13] whatever the etymological origin of the Sefîre verb may be, from the comparative Akkadian material cited above, contextually, *ḥbz* seems to be the semantic equivalent of the Aramaic *ḫabātu*, better rendered as "to commit a *razzia*/incursion (into an enemy territory),[14] rather than the accepted translation "to strike/hit/smash."

2. A warning not to plot/conspire against the king's descendants (Sefîre IB: 24–25; II B:6)

Dealing with the subject concerning (a) duty in a strife for succession to the throne, (b) plot against the suzerain's household, Sefîre III 17–18; 21 stipulates that no outsider is permitted to plot/conspire against the king's descendants. To denote this idea authors use the idiomatic expression *šlḥ lšn b*. It seems that while *šlḥ lšn b* "to plot/conspire" (lit., "to let loose the tongue") is restricted to North West Semitic idiomatic lexicon,[15] and finds its close association with the biblical expression *šlḥ ph b (hṣmd lšwn)* "to scheme,"[16] as well as with *h'rk lšwn (hrḥb ph)* "to stick out the tongue."[17] The idiom *šlḥ yd b*, employed twice in Sefîre (I B: 24–5, II B:6) in a similar context, has also this very connotation (i.e. to plot/conspire) and thus seems to find its close parallel with the Akkadian lexicon commonly employed in royal-treaty texts.

It should be observed that in Sefîre, exactly as in Biblical Hebrew, the idiomatic expression *šlḥ yd b* has at least two different connotations: (a) to harm/smite (lit., "to raise a hand against physically");[18] (b) "to plot/conspire/scheme" (mentally). It should further be noted that students of the Sefîre inscriptions fail to distinguish between the two different nuances that this idiom exhibits, rendering in both cases "to raise a hand."[19] It is our main interest at present, however, to examine the Old Aramaic expression *šlḥ yd b* in the light of Akkadian and biblical idioms denoting "to plot/conspire/scheme."

At the outset, it is noteworthy that the closely associated with the Sefîre (Hebrew) *šlḥ yd b (= šlḥ lšn/ph b)* are the biblical idioms: (a) *yrh b'ṣbʿ, qrṣ bʿyn/mll brgl//*) "to plot/scheme" (lit. "to point the finger") employed in Prov 6:12–13;[20] (b) *dbr 'wn//hsr mwth//) šlḥ 'ṣbʿ* employed in Isa 58:9: *'m tsyn mtwkk mwṭh šlḥ 'ṣbʿ wdbr 'wn,* "If you banish lawlessness from your midst, extending the finger,[21] and evil speech."

Similarly, among other various meanings, Akkadian also expresses the notion of plotting/scheming by the gesture of extending the finger, employing the verb *tarāṣu.* For example, *ana alāni šunūti isqi annî īnšu lā ittašu* (for *ittaššû*) *ubānšu ana lemutti lā ittašu* (for *ittaššû*) "shall not covet (lit., raise his eyes against) these villages and this property (and) shall not plot with evil intent (lit., point his finger)"[22]; *matīma ana ūmī dārūti... lū rē'û lu šakkanakku... ana idi lemutti uma'aru šanâmma ina lemnēti ušāḫazu* (for *ušaḫḫazu ubānišu ana lemutti itarraṣu* "forever, for everlasting days... be it a ruler or a territorial governor... (who) commissions someone else with evil intent, with evil intent instigates (him), plots, (lit. points his finger) evilly."[23] It is apparent that here the Akkadian idiom *ubāna tarāṣu*[24] is the semantic equivalent of the Hebrew expression *yrh/šlḥ 'ṣbʿ*, both employed in contexts involving the notion of plotting/scheming (to do evil).

More specifically, while Akkadian *ubāna tarāṣu* in this specific sense seems to be attested in the Old and Middle Babylonian inscriptions, the idea of plotting/scheming, in our opinion, is also conveyed by a similar gesture of extending the hand. The Akkadian *qāta (w)abālu,* commonly employed in Neo-Assyrian royal and treaty inscriptions, seems to replace the older idiom *ubāna tarāṣu.*[25] It should be further noted that the Akkadian *qāta (w)abālu* is the exact semantic equivalent of the North West Semitic *šlḥ yd.* It also seems to share at least two different connotations: "to lay a hand on" (in a physical sense), i.e., "to touch/harm"[26] and the less apparent nuance "to plot/scheme" (mentally).[27] The following few examples from Assyrian royal inscriptions will illustrate the Akkadian phrase under consideration. The murder Tukulti-Ninurta I is recorded as follows:

a. *arki amēlūti rabûti ša māt Akkadî ša karduniaš ibbalkitūma Adad-šum-uṣur ina kussî abīšu ušēšibū Tukulti-ninutra ša ana Bābili ana lemutti* [*qās*] *su ubbilū Aššur-nāṣir-apli māršu u amēlūi rabûti ša māt Aššur ibbalkitūšu*

Then the Akkadian nobles of Kardunias had rebelled and put Adad-sum-usur on his father's throne, Assur-nasir-apil, the son of Tukulti-nutra — who with evil intent had plotted against Babylon — and the nobles of Assyria rebelled againt him (Tukulti-ninurta) and removed him from his throne.[28]

b. *sīḫu bartu ana muḫḫi Aššur-aḫe-addina šar māt Aššur u Aššur-bani-apil mār šarri ša bīt redûti ippušu ušēpišu qāssu ana lemutti ina libbišun ubbal.*

Will he rebel or incite a rebellion against Esarhaddon the king of Assyria and (against) Assurbanipal the crown prince? Will he plot with the evil intent against them?[29]

Further, it is significant that Akkadian *qāta (w)abālu* in the sense of "to plot/to scheme" as employed in Assyrian royal inscriptions finds its semantic parallel in the Phoenician royal inscription of Kilamuwa. Phoenician *šlḥ yd* exhibits the more definite connotation "to plot/scheme" rather than "to stretch forth the hand," in literal-abstract sense as previously rendered.[30] Accordingly, Kilamuwa (*KAI* 24A:5–6): *kn bt ʾby bmtkt mlkm ʾdrm wkl šlḥ yd ll (ḥ)m* may be rendered as follows: "My father's dynasty was in the midst of mighty kings, everybody conspired/schemed to do battle."[31]

Similarly, to our mind, Biblical Hebrew expresses the notion of plotting/scheming also by this very gesture. The cases may be adduced. In Esth. 8:7 *ʿl ʾšr šlḥ ydw byhwdym* "For scheming against the Jews."[32] In Dan. 11:42: *wyšlḥ ydw b'rṣwt w'rṣ mṣrym l' thyh lplyṭh* "And He shall plot against the countries, and the land of Egypt shall not escape." Of considerable importance is the employment of this idiom in Ps. 55:21: *šlḥ ydw bšlmyw ḥll brytw* "He plotted against his allies he violated his covenant." In this verse, the usage of these three treaty terminologies clearly indicates that the Psalmist, being familiar with the subject, draws his idiomatic expression from the political-diplomatic lexical corpus. Where the following Hebrew-Akkadian correspondences are evident: Hebrew *šlmyw* = Akkadian *salmū*, "allies";[33] Hebrew *ḥll bryt* = Akkadian *adê (māmīta/salīma) etēqu*, "to transgress a treaty"; *šlḥ yd b* = Akkadian *qāta (w)abālu ina* "to plot/scheme against." The latter is commonly employed in the Vassal Treaties of Esarhaddon in identical context to that of Sefîre. The following few cases may well be cited:

a. A warning not to plot/rebel against the crown prince and his brothers:

> *qātēkuna ina limnēti ina libbišunuma tabbalāni ipšu bartu abutu lā ṭābtu teppašaniššūni*
>
> (If) you plot with evil intent against them, set a rebellion or unfriendly plans against them.[34]

b. A warning not to plot/rebel/incite a strife between the royal family:

> *qātēkunu ana limnēti ina libbišu tubbalāni ipšu bartu abutu lā ṭābtu lā de'iqtu teppašaniššūni ina sarrūti māt Aššur tukakkaršūni issi libbi aḫḫēšu rabû ṣehru ina kūmusu kussî māt Aššur tušaṣbatāni....*
>
> (If) you plot with evil intent against him, set a rebellion or wrong or evil against him, if you remove him from the kingship of Assyria and help one of his brothers, younger or older to take the throne of Assyria in his stead....[35]

In short, dealing with the subject concerning a strife for the succession to the throne, the idea of plotting/scheming conveyed in the Vassal Treaties of Esarhaddon by the idiom *qāta (w)abālu ina*, and in an identical context (in Sefîre III: 17–18,21), the Old Aramaic scribe expresses the very notion by the North West Semitic idiom *šlḥ lšn b*.... Where in Sefîre I B:24–25; II B:6 he seems to be familiar with Akkadian political-diplomatic lexicon, employing *šlḥ yd b* = Akkadian *qāta (w)abālu ina*.

NOTES

1. Dupont-Sommer, *An Aramaic Handbook* (2 vols.; Wiesbaden. Otto Harrasowitz. 1967), 1: 3.
2. J. Fitzmyer, *The Aramaic Inscription of Sefîre (BibOr* 19; Rome; Pontifical Biblical Institute, 1967).
3. F. Rosenthal, "Notes on the Third Inscription of Sifre-Sujim," *BASOR* 158 (1960), 30. n. 14. Note also that J. C. L. Gibson, *Textbook of Syrian Semitic Inscriptions* II (Oxford: Claredon, 1975), 56, adapts "both" (Rosenthal's and Fitzmyer's) interpretation to "give suitable meanings."
4. J. C. Greenfield, "Studies in West Semitic Inscriptions. I: Stylistic Aspects of the *Sefîre* Treaty Inscriptions," *AcOr* 29 (1965), 5, n. 12.
5. E. A. W. Budge and L. W. King, *The Annals of the Kings of Assyria* (London: The Museum, 1902), 239:44 (hereafter *AKA*).
6. *OIP* II IV:57.
7. M. Streck, *Assurbanipal und die Letzten assyrischen konige (Vorderasiatische Bibibliothek* 7; Stuck; Leipzig, 1916), 6 i 59. (hereafter Streck, *A3b*).
8. D. J. Wiseman, "The Vassal-Treaties of Esarhaddon," *Iraq* 20 (1958), 51–53:313–315 (hereafter Wiseman, *VTE*): "do not make *razzias* against him, do not defeat him, do not eradicate his name and descendants from the country..." (for the present translation, cf. E. Reiner, *ANET*[3], 537).
9. Note that the semantic equivalent of Akkadian *ḫabātu* "to raid/commit a *razzia*" is the biblical Hebrew *pšṭ* attested thirteen times, twice in Hos. 7:11; Job 1:17. The remainder are in the historical/warfare texts. It is likewise worthwhile to observe that seven of the occurrences of the Hebrew *pšṭ* "to raid" are juxtaposed with the verbs *lkd* "to capture" (Judg. 9:44; 2 Chr. 28:18): *lqḥ* "to seize" (Job 1:17) as well as with *nkh* "to defeat" (Judg. 20:37; 1 Sam. 23:37; 27:8; 2 Chr. 25:13). Here the

Hebrew sequence is similar to the Akkadian usage *ḫabātu-dīkta dâku* "to commit a *razzia* — to defeat" (e.g. Wiseman *VTE*, 51–53:313–315).

10. E. F. Weidner, "Politische Dokumente aus Kleinasien," *Boghazkoi-Studien* 8 (1923), 2:6–7 (Šuppiluliuma-Mattiwaza).
11. Ibid., 24:4; Ibid., 14:46–47.
12. Note also that in the statue of Idrimi, in the treaty portion dealing with border restoration, we find the following: *u bīta ḫalqu utêrsu* "and I (Idrimi) restored to him (Barattarna) his lost inheritance." S. Smith, *The Statue of Idrimi* (London: British Institute of Archeology, 1949), 18:56.
13. Cf. Fitzmyer, *Sefîre*, 88.
14. Cf. *CAD* H 12 (*ḫabātu* D); *AHw* 304 (*ḫabātu* III).
15. The alleged equivalent of the Aramaic *šlḥ lšn* with the Akkadian *lišān lemuttim wu'uru* proposed by D. Sperling ("The Informer and Conniver," *JANESCU* [1970],101–104) is not without difficulties:

    a. Nowhere else does Akkadian employ the expression *lišāna wu''uru* in the proposed sense "to direct the tongue, i.e., to intrigue."

    b. Contextually, we are confronted with two different subjects. In *Sefîre*, a strife for succession to the throne, in the Akkadian text, the destruction of the Kudurru.

    c. From the *narû-kudurru* and other related texts, the evidence clearly shows that traditionally (from Old Akkadian and on) an accomplice is hired to damage the object (cf. K. R. Veenhof, "An Aramaic Curse with a Sumero-Akkadian Prototype," *BO* 20 [1963], 142–144).

    d. Among other verbs (i.e. *kullumu* "to instruct"; *šūḫuzu* "to investigate"; *qabû* "to order," the verb *wu''uru* "to order, commission" is always employed to indicate the instigation of the accomplice in the *narû-kudurru* and other related texts. For a full discussion, see H. Tawil "The End of the Hadad Inscription in Light of Akkadian," *JNES* 32 (1973), 477–482. Further, Thureau-Dangin (*RA* 16 [1919], 144); *CAD* (a2, 320A; l. 128b) while rendering *lišān lemuttim* "malandrin/false witness/mischievous person," both understood the expression as referring to an agent/accomplice, commissioned to destroy the *kudurru*. In our opinion, the idiom *lišān lemuttim* stands for (*ša*) *liśān lemuttim* lit., "a person of an evil tongue," i.e., "a slanderer," exactly as *bīt kīli* listed as an accomplice in aka 250:69 stands for (*ša*) *bīt kīli* "a prisoner."
16. Ps. 50:19
17. Isa. 57:4.
18. Cf. e.g. Gen. 37:22; 1 Sam. 24:7; 26:23, for a full discussion of the Hebrew idiom *šlḥ yd*, see P. Humbert "Etendre la main" *VT* 12 (1962), 383–395 (called to my attention by Ed Greenstein). Note that while Humbert identifies around eleven different semantic usages of *šlḥ yd*

in Prov. 31:20; we propose at least four more (2 Sam. 27:17 = Ps. 18:17; 138:7; 144:2). For a full discussion of Hebrew *šlḥ yd* and Akkadian *qāta tarāṣu*, "to assist," expressing divine aid. See Hayim Tawil "Some Literary Elements in the Opening Sections of the Hadad, Zākin and Nērab Inscriptions," *Or* 43 (1974), 44, n. 21.

19. Fitzmyer, *Sefîre*, 66; Donner-Rollig, *KAI* 2, 225. Note that Rosenthal, (*BASOR* 158 [1960]), 30, N. 10) though in doubt and without elaboration, was the first to suggest *Sefîre šlḥ lšn* "may be an adaptation of the more common idiom *šlḥ yd*." From the comparative material presented in this note, his suggestion seems to be fully corroborated.
20. This verse was fully treated by M. Held in his yet unpublished article entitled "On the Language and Dating of Proverbs 1–9" (presented before the *Society of Biblical Literature*, New York, 1970). He shows that the idiom *qrṣ bʿyn* (employed in sequence with *yrh bʾṣbʿ*) is the equivalent of Akkadian *īna ṣubburu* similarly employed in context involving the notion of scheming/plotting.
21. Note A. B. Ehrlich's (*Mikrâ ki-pheshutô)* III, reprinted, New York: KTAV, [1969], 144) rendering "Schlauen Untersleif."
22. *Mémories de la Délégation en Perse*, 10 (1925), 90 III:24–27 (hereafter *MDP*).
23. W. J. Hinke, *A New Boundary Stone of Nebuchadnezzar* (Philadelphia, 1907), 148 col. III: 17–24).
24. Cf. also *ubān lemutti arkišu tarṣat* "an evil finger is pointed behind him" (*KAR* 26:3). It should be further noted that an emendation (*CAD* Ṣ 3b.) yields *ubānāti* in Ludlul: *sūqa abâma turruṣā ubānāti* (text: *uzunāti*) *errub ēkallišma iṣabburā īnāti* "when I enter the palace eyes are blinked at me" (W. G. Lambert, *Babylonian Wisdom Literature* [Oxford: Clarendon, 1960] 34:80–81). As noted by Held (ibid.), the juxtaposition of *ubāna tarăṣu* with *īna ṣubburu* is identical to the sequence (in reverse order) of the Hebrew *qrṣ bʿyn-yrh bʾṣbʿ* where both gestures seem to refer to scheming/plotting respectively. Further note that the Talmudic (b. *Yoma* 19b) paraphrase on Prov. 6:12–13: "He who reads the Shema may neither blink with his eyes, nor gesticulate with his lips, nor point with his fingers; and it has also been taught: R. Eleazer Hisma said concerning him who will read the Shema blinks with his eyes, gesticulates with his lips or points with his fingers, Scripture has said: You have not invoked me, O Jacob."
25. It is noteworthy that the Akkadian expression *ubāna tarăṣu* "to point the finger" employed in apposition with *karṣī akālu* in Middle Babylonian text (i.e., *mūtamû nullāti ākil karṣī ša arki meḫrišu ubān lemmuti itarraṣu* "He who speaks falsehood, he who calumniates, who behind his *eqhal* points an evil finger," Lambert *BWL* 119:6–8) is being

replaced in Neo-Assyrian by *aḫa wabālu* "to extend the arm." This is similarly employed in juxtaposition with *karṣi akālu* i.e. *ša aḫḫēsu māri ummišu karṣīšunu takkalani... aḫēkunu ina bitisunu tubbalani* "If you slander his brothers the sons of his mother….plot/conspire (lit., extend the arm/hand) against their households" (Wiseman, *VTE*, 170–173).

26. Cf. *CAD* (A/I 19a).
27. Note *CAD-s* (A/I 19b) rendering "to act as an enemy against/to act in a hostile way."
28. E. Weidner, "*Die Inschriften Tukulti-Ninurtas I*" (= *AfO Beiheft* 12 [1959], 41–42. No. 37:8–10.) See also A.K. Grayson, *Assyrian Royal Inscriptions I* (Wiesbaden: Harrassowitz, 1972), 134 § 874.
29. J. A. Knudtzon, *Assyrische Gebete an den Sonnengott für Statt und königliches Hausa us der Zeit Asarhaddons und Asurbanipals* (Leipzig, 1893), 238, No. 116:13–15; ibid., 11, 13–14. cf. also E. Klauber, *Politisch-Religiöse Texte aus der Sargonidenzeit* (Leipzig, 1913), 67 No. 44:20–21; ibid., reverse 118–9.
30. *KAI* 2, 31, Rosenthal, *ANET*[3] 654b.
31. Note that one need not restore *l[h]l[ḥ]m* "to fight" (Niphʿal) as proposed by Donner-Rollig (*KAI* II, 32). The verb *lḥm* "to fight" in the Qal is attested several times in Biblical Hebrew (Ps. 35:1; 56:2). Thus, together with Z. Harris (*A Grammar of the Phoenician Language*: [New Haven: American Oriental Society, 1936], 114) it is preferable to take *ll(ḥ)m* "to fight" as a Qal infinitive construct.
32. Cf. H. L. Ginsberg's rendering in *The Five Megilloth and Jonah* (Philadelphia: JPS, 1969), 104–105.
33. Cf. e.g. *itti nakriya lū nakrata itti salmīya lū salmata* "with my enemies be an enemy; with my allies be an ally" (*PRU* IV 36:11–13; ibid., 49:12–13; *Boghazköi Studien*, 8 [1923] 60:6–7, etc.). For the Akkadian expression *salīma šakānu(m)* " to make a treaty," cf. recently M. Held, "Philological Notes on the Mari Covenant Ritual" *BASOR* 200 (1970), 33, n.9.
34. Wiseman, *VTE* 37:105–107.
35. Ibid., 33:66–70; cf. also ibid., 55:365–372.

Hebrew Section

"אִם זָרְחָה הַשֶּׁמֶשׁ עָלָיו" (שמות כב, ב)
מונח משפטי לאור הטקסטים האכדיים מאוגרית

לעו"ד גלוריה סילברט

I

> אם במחתרת יִמָּצֵא הגנב והֻכָּה ומת אין לו דמים; אם זרחה השמש עליו דמים לו, שלם ישלם אם אין לו ונמכר בגנבתו. (שמ' כב א־ב).

המחקר המקראי המודרני מאוחד בהבנתו המילולית של הפסוק "אם זרחה השמש עליו".[1] נחום סרנה מסכם הבנה זו כדלהלן:[2]

> The particular case of a thief who is surprised in the act of breaking and entering is parenthetically injected into the law dealing with theft. The contrast between the phrases, "if the sun has arisen" and "while tunneling" shows the latter to presuppose a nighttime setting […] His nocturnal timing creates a presumption of homicidal intent […] hence, no bloodguilt is incurred should the intruder be killed […] if the break-in occurred in broad daylight, however, it is not presumed to present imminent danger to life; the use of deadly force is therefore deemed to be unwarranted, and bloodguilt would ensue.

ואולם מעניין הדבר שהפרשנות הקדומה ופרשנות ימי הביניים חלוקות עמוקות בפירושו המדויק של הפסוק הזה. תחילה יש לשים לב שבעוד שתרגום אונקלוס מתרגם את פסוקנו בהשאלה: "אם עינא דסהדיא נפלת עלוהי", תרגום ניאופיטי מתרגמו תרגום מילולי: "אן דנחת עלוהי שמשא". חשוב לציין שהתרגום המיוחס ליונתן מבין את פסוקנו כדלהלן: "אין בריר פתגמא כשמשא". אכן, התרגומים השונים זה מזה מגלים הבדלים עמוקים בהבנת הפסוק, שתחילתם לכל הפחות במאה השנייה לסה"נ. בעל המכילתא דרבי ישמעאל הבין "אם זרחה השמש עליו" כביטוי של ודאות מוחלטת: "'אם זרחה השמש עליו' [רבי ישמעאל אמר] וכי השמש עליו בלבד זרחה? והלא

על כל העולם כלו זרחה! אלא מה שמש שלום בעולם אף זה אם ידוע הוא שבשלום עמו והרגו זה חייב" (מכילתא דר' ישמעאל, משפטים יג [מהדורת הורוביץ ורבין, עמ' 293]). המכילתא מבטלת כאן את קריטריון העיתוי, דהיינו ההבחנה על פי השאלה אם הגנב נהרג בשעות היום או בשעות הלילה, ומגבילה את ההרג הנדון בפסוק לנסיבות אשר בהן הכוונה הרצחנית של הפולש לרשות חברו ידועה, בלי להשאיר שמץ של ספק. בעקבות המכילתא התלמוד הבבלי מבהיר: "תניא אידך 'אם זרחה השמש עליו' דמים לו. וכי השמש עליו בלבד זרחה? אלא אם ברור לך כשמש שיש לו שלום עמך, אל תהרגהו. ואם לא, הרגהו" (סנהדרין עב ע"א. וראה גם ירושלמי, כתובות ד, ד [כח ע"ג]; ספרי דברים פיס' רלז [מהדורת פינקלשטיין, עמ' 269]).

לאור מה שנאמר לעיל, רש"י מסביר את הפסוק המקראי כדלהלן: "אין זה אלא כמין משל, אם ברור לך הדבר שיש לו שלום עמך כשמש הזה שהוא שלום בעולם, כך פשוט לך שאינו בא להרוג אפילו [אם] יעמוד בעל הממון כנגדו. כגון אב החותר לגנוב ממון הבן וידוע שרחמי האב על הבן, ואינו בא על עסקי נפשות דמים לו, כחי הוא חשוב ורציחה היא אם יהרגנו בעל הבית". גם כאן שעת המעשה אינה הנושא לדיון, אם הוא התרחש בשעות היום או בשעות הלילה, אלא בירור מטרתו של הפולש. הוא הדין לניסוחו של הרמב"ם במשנה תורה: "היה הדבר ברור לבעל הבית שזה הגנב הבא עליו אינו הורגו ואינו בא אלא על עסקי ממון – אסור להורגו, ואם הרגו – הרי זה הורג נפש שנאמר: 'אם זרחה השמש עליו' – אם ברור לך הדבר כשמש שיש לו שלום עמך – אל תהרגהו" (הלכות גנבה ט, י).[3]

חוקר המקרא המודרני ארנולד ב. ארליך דוחה בלגלוג את הפירושים המובאים לעיל: "הראשונים בדרשותיהם ואונקלוס שמתרגם על פיהן, עקמו עלינו את המקרא הזה. ופשוטו כמשמעו, שכנגד מה שאמר לפניו 'אם במחתרת ימצא הגנב', שהחותר בתים עושה בלילה, אמר כאן 'אם זרחה השמש עליו', כלומר אם יתפש בגנבתו ביום דמים לו, לפי שהגונב ביום דעתו להרוג את העומד נגדו".[4] ארליך הולך בעקבות הדעה השנייה הרווחת בקרב מפרשי ימי הביניים כגון רס"ג,[5] אבן עזרא, רשב"ם, רמב"ן וחזקוני, ושמחזיקים בה המפרשים היהודיים המודרניים שד"ל וקאסוטו,[6] אשר הבינו את הפסוק כפשוטו, כלומר "אם זרחה השמש עליו" פירושו בשעות היום. בפירוש הזה תומך תמיכה נמרצת הראב"ד, התוקף ומבקר בחומרה את הבנתו המטפורית של הרמב"ם: "איני נמנע מלכתוב את דעתי, שנראה לי שאף על פי שדרשו חכמים 'אם זרחה השמש עליו' דרך משל [...] אף על פי כן אינו יוצא מידי פשוטו. ביום אינו רשאי להרגו שאין גנב בא ביום, אלא אם יכול להשמיט שומט ובורח ואינו מתעכב לגנוב ממון גדול ולעמוד על בעליו להרגו, אלא גנב בלילה, מפני שהגנב יודע שבעל הבית בבית אז בא להרוג או

ליהרג, אבל גנב ביום אין בעל הבית מצוי, ושמוטא בעלמא הוא ובחיי ראשי כל מבין די לו בזה" (השגות הראב"ד על משנה תורה, הלכות גנבה ט, י).

II

המחלוקת המובאת לעיל מעידה על הבדל מהותי בין הדעות, הבדל בעל השלכה משפטית ומעשית. נראה שסוגיה זו תוכל להתבהר לאור החומר החוץ־מקראי המקביל מן המזרח הקדמון, ובמיוחד מכְּתבי אוגרית.

ראשית עלינו לתת את הדעת שמן המקורות השונים הכתובים בכתב היתדות ידוע שהפטרון של השמש הוא אל השמש שַׁמַשׁ, אדון הצדק והיושר. באיקונוגרפיה עובדה זו ידועה מן הסטילה המפורסמת של המלך חמורבי, אשר בה האל שַׁמַשׁ מוסר בידו הימנית את הטבעת ואת המטה למחוקק המפורסם חמורבי.[7]

מבחינת האפיגרפיה, בידינו עדויות רבות החל מהתקופה הבבלית העתיקה שהכינוי השכיח של שמש הוא *dayyānu* 'דַיָּן, שופט', הוא אל הצדק והיושר במלוא מובן המילה: *da]yyān kīnātim abi ekiātim]* 'שופט צדק אבי יתומים';[8] *Šamaš dayyānu rabû ša šamê u erṣitim* 'שַׁמַשׁ השופט הגדול של השמים והארץ'.[9] שַׁמַשׁ מתואר כמי שמעניש על פי מידת הצדק: *ṣalpa dayyāna mēsira tukallam* 'אתה [שַׁמַשׁ] מורה על בית הכלא לשופט המרושע'.[10] בהמנונים לשַׁמַשׁ הוא מוצג כְּ־*mušnamir* 'המאיר', אשר תפקידו הוא *pētû ekleti mušnamir erṣetim rapšātim* 'מפזר חושך, מאיר ארץ רחבת ידיים'.[11] שַׁמַשׁ הוא *nūr kiššati* 'האור של כל הארץ המאוכלסת'.[12] נוסף על כך הוא דורש צדק: *tašemmê tebiršināti ša ruggugu tamassi dīnšu* 'שומע וחוקר אותם [את פועלי און], באשר לעַוָּל הוא חורץ את דינו',[13] ולפיכך *muttaḫlilu šarrāqu muṣallû ša šamaš* 'הגנב המשחר לטרף הוא אויבו של שַׁמַשׁ'.[14] ראוי לציין גם שבין התכונות השונות של השֶׁמש הנזכרות במכתבי עמרנה היא משמשת שלוש פעמים לתיאור שלומו וביטחונו של המלך בביטוי האידיומטי *lu tīdi inūma šalim šarru kīma* *ᴰUTU-aš [= šamaš] ina šamê* 'דע כי המלך בריא ושלם כמו השמש בשמים'.[15]לפיכך ניתן לקשור בין המטפורה במכתבי עמרנה *šalim kīma šamši* 'שָׁלֵם כמו השמש' להצהרת רבי ישמעאל במכילתא "מה שמש שלום (בעולם אף זה אם ידוע הוא שבשלום עמו)". שני המקורות קושרים שלום = *šalāmu* אל שמש = *šamšu*.

יש להעיר עוד שבמכתב ששלח מלומד אל המלך אסרחדון מושווה טוהַר מקריב הקרבן אל זוהר השמש: "[בחודש] ניסן ביום הראשון (*amēlu [l]* *ītebib*) האיש יטהר את עצמו, ייתן את קרבן הלחם לפני מרדוך וינסוך מים

וראשית שכר מימין ומשמאל (*amēlu šu kīma šamaš namir*), האיש ההוא יזרח כשמש".[16]

ליתר דיוק, הביטוי המשפטי ברור כשמש, שכנראה מופיע לראשונה בתלמוד הבבלי, בא לתמוך בפירושו של רבי ישמעאל ולחזקו. לפיו הפסוק המקראי "אם זרחה השמש עליו" רומז לא על עיתוי המעשה אלא על ודאות כוונתו של הגנב. ייתכן שנקודה זו יכולה להתבהר בעזרת הטקסטים המשפטיים האכדיים שנמצאו באוגרית.

להבהרת העניין ניתן להביא לפחות שמונה דוגמאות מן הטקסטים האכדיים מאוגרית העוסקים כולם בעניינים משפטיים ונוגעים להיותו של הנאשם חף מפשע ופטור מהעמדה לדין.[17] הנוסחה המשפטית הסטנדרטית מגדירה את חפותו של הנאשם כברורה כטוהר השמש: *kīma* ^{D}*UTU* [= *šamaš*] *zakīti zaki* 'הוא [= הנאשם] זכאי [= טהור] מתביעות כטוהר השמש'. שלוש דוגמאות תספקנה:

א. MRS 668 RS 16.269

1	*[i]štu ūmi annî[m]*	מן היום הזה
2	*Niqmaddu šar Ugarit*	נקמאדו מלך אוגרית
3	*inadin bīt U[R]ganam mār Sakukuna*	יתן את ביתו של אורגנם בן סכוכונה
4	*eqilšu karānšu serdašu*	שדהו, כרמו ופרדס זיתיו,
5	*kirāšu gabbu mimmi šumšišu*	גנו וכל דבר אחר
6	*nadin ana Gab^canu mār LU A.RIT*	יתן לגבאנו בן (?)
7	*inūma nakir Yatarmu ṭupšarru*	וכאשר יתרמו הסופר
8	*itti šarri bēlišu u Gab^cana*	נהיה לאויב אדונו המלך, גבאנה
9	*idūkšu u inadin*	יהרגו ויתן
10	*beka-Ištar ana šarri*	את בקה־אישתר למלך אדונו.
11	*aššum dīnišuma: bēlišu*	בגלל פסק דין זה של אדונו,
12	*nadin nidnūš*	הצעה זאת נעשתה
13	*ana Gab^canu ana mārīšu*	לגבאנו ולבניו.
14	*u uzakkīšu šarru bēlšu*	המלך אדונו יזכהו
15	*ištu šipri ekallim*	מעבודת ההיכל.
16	*kīma šamši zakāti bēlu zaki*	כמו שהשמש טהורה טהור בעל [הרכוש הזה].

ב. MRS 16 RS 17.67

2	*[k]īma šapaš zakā[t]i zakīmi*	כמו שהשמש טהורה הוא טהור:
3	*mamman ana ardi la ira[gum]*	איש לא יוכל לתבוע [את זה].
4	*u Iluzakapti 20 kaspa*	אילוזקפטי נתן 20 כסף
5	*ana qāti Milkinari*	לידי מילכינרי
6	*mārat Arsuwana ittadin*	בת ארסוונה.
7	*ištênšu bēlšu uzakkīšu*	מחד גיסא אדונו טיהרו
8	*u ina šanišu Ibri-šarru rābišu*	ומאידך גיסא איברי־שרו הסוכן,
9	*ana pî šibûtišu*	על פי עדיו
10	*uzakkīšu kīma šapaš zakāti zaki*	טיהרו. כמו שהשמש טהורה הוא טהור.
11	*urra šeram*	לעתיד
12	*mannumma ana muḫḫišu*	איש כנגדו
13	*la iqarrub*	לא יגיש תביעה
14	*aban Ibri-šarru*	חותמת אברי־שרו
15	*Ilumilku ṭupšarru*	אילומילכו הסופר.

ג. MRS 6 110 RS 16.267

1	*ištu ūmi annîm*	מן היום הזה
2	*Amisṭamru mār Niqmepu*	אמיסטרמו בן ניקמאפו
3	*šar Ugarit*	מלך אוגרית
4	*uzakki Šayâ amatšu*	טיהר את שיה אמתו
5	*ištu amûti kīma šamši zaki*	מעבדות. כמו שהשמש טהורה
6	*uzakat Šayâ ištu amâti*	שיה טהורה מעבדות.

לענייננו, הפועל *zakû* 'להיות טהור', כלומר חופשי מהתחייבויות או תביעות, וכן שם התואר *zakû* 'טהור (זכאי)' הם המקבילות האטימולוגיות והסמנטיות של הפועל המקראי זכה ושל שם התואר זך, המופיעים גם בהקשרים משפטיים.[18] חשוב להעיר שבעברית המקראית "זך" מופיע בתקבולת נרדפת לבר: "זך לקחי // ובר הייתי בעיניך" (איוב יא, ד). נוסף על כך גם מחוץ להקשר המשפטי נקשר שם התואר בר עם חמה בביטוי האידיומטי ברה כחמה בשיר השירים ו, ט. אם כן, ביטוי מקראי זה הוא המקבילה הסמנטית של הביטוי המשפטי האכדי מאוגרית *kīma šamši*

zaki/zakīti 'טהור כשמש'. אמנם כן, מאירת עיניים העובדה שבטקסטים
האלפבתיים מאוגרית הנוסחה המשפטית האכדית kīma šamši zaki/zakīti
היא המקבילה לנוסחה השמית הצפון מערבית km špš d brt 'כמו השמש
אשר ברה'. נראה כי נוסחה זאת מופיעה פעם אחת במכתב שכתב ניקמאדו
מלך אוגרית כפעולה מלכותית:

2	*bunṭ km. špš.*	משעבוד, כמו השמש
3	*d brt. kmt.*	שְׁבָּרה,[19] כן
4	*br. ṣṭqšlm.*	בר צטקשלם
5	*bunṭ ᶜd. ᶜlm.*	משעבוד עד עולם
6	*mešmn. nqmd.*	חותם נקמאד
7	*mlk. ugrt.*	מלך אוגרית
8	*nqmd. mlk. ugrt.*	נקמאד מלך אוגרית
9	*ktb. spr. hnd.*	כתב ספר הלזה
10	*dt. brrt. ṣqšlm.*	של בר [היינו שחרור משעבוד] צטקשלם
11	*ᶜbdh. hnd.*	עבדו הלזה.
12	*w.mnkm. lyqḥ*	ואיש אל ייקח
13	*spr. mlk. hnd.*	ספר מלך הלזה
14	*b yd. ṣṭqšlm.*	מיד צטקשלם
15	*ᶜd. ᶜlm.*	עד עולם.[20]

III

מן התעודה שהובאה כאן, שבה מעין פריווילגיה מלכותית המשחררת
את צטקשלם משעבוד המוטל על הקרקעות שהוא מחזיק בהן – כנראה
מתשלומים – אנו למדים שהנוסחה המשפטית האוגריתית km špš d brt)
kmt br ṣṭšlm bunṭ ᶜd ᶜlm) 'כמו השמש שברה (כן בר צטקשלם משעבוד
עד עולם)' = kīma šamši zakāt היא התקבולת האטימולוגית והסמנטית
של הנוסחה המשפטית התלמודית ברור כשמש. זהו מונח העוסק בוודאות
מוחלטת, והוא בא לחזק את הבנתו של רבי ישמעאל שהמשפט המקראי "אם
זרחה השמש עליו" משקף את הרעיון של זכאות, טוהר וודאות מוחלטת של
כוונת הגנב יותר ממה שהוא משקף את שאלת עיתוי המעשה – אם נעשה
ביום או בלילה.

לאור האמור לעיל, סביר למדי להניח שהמונח משל, הבא לאפיין את

שיטת פירושו של רבי ישמעאל לפסוק הנוכחי, אינו צריך להיות מובן בצורה פיגורטיבית. איפכא מסתברא, נראה כי פירושו של רבי ישמעאל מעוגן היטב בפשוטו של מקרא. נדמה שהוא תופש את הפסוק "אם זרחה השמש עליו" במשמעותו המשפטית, דהיינו כוונה טהורה, והשמש נקשרת עם צדק, שלום וטוהר הלב. על כן ייתכן שהצירוף זרחה השמש המופיע בהקשר משפטי בשמות כב, ב יכול לתפקד כנוסחה המקראית של הביטוי המשפטי האכדי (מאוגרית) *(kīma) šamši zaki/zakât*, המונח האלפביתי האוגריתי *(km) špš d brt*, הביטוי המקראי (הפואטי) "ברה כחמה" והצירוף התנאי "ברור כשמש".

הערות

* ברצוני להודות לד"ר אריה גייגר, לתלמידי עזרא מזרחי ולבן אחותי דויד יוסף ביבי על עזרתם המסורה בעריכת המאמר.

1. *The Interpreter's Bible* (12 vols.; New York: Abingdon Press, 1952), 1:1002; M. Noth, *Exodus: A Commentary* (Philadelphia: Westminster Press, 1962), 183; J. P. Hyatt, *Exodus* (*New Century Bible*; Grand Rapids: Eerdmans, 1980), 237; J. I. Durham, *Exodus* (*Word Biblical Commentary* III; Waco, Texas: Word Books, 1987), 325; C. Houtman, *Exodus* (*Historical Commentary on the Old Testament* III; Lueven: Peeters, 1993), 190; R. Rothenbusch, *Die Kasuistische Rechtssammlung im Bundesbuch (Ex 21,2 — 11.18 — 22,16)* (*AOAT*, 259), Münster 2000, 343.
2. N. M. Sarna, *The JPS Torah Commentary*, *Exodus* (Philadelphia: JPS, 1991), 130.
3. See also B. Jacob, *Exodus* (trans. W. Jacob in association with Y. Elman; Hoboken, N.J., 1992), 667–668.
4. A. B. Ehrlich, *Miqra ki-Peshuto* (2 vols.; New York, 1969), 1:179.
5. See Y. Ratshavi, *Perushe Rav Sa'adyah Ga'on le-Sefer Shemot* (Jerusalem 5758 [1998]), 121
6. *Perush Shadal 'al Hamishah Hummeshe Torah* (Tel Aviv, 5756 [1996]), 349–350; M. D. Cassuto, *Perush 'al Sefer Shemot* (Jerusalem, 5709 [1949]), 197. See also D. Henshke, "Ha-ba ba-mahteret — le-yahaso shel ha-midrash la-peshat," *Megadim* 7 (5749 [1989]), 9–1.
7. J. B. Pritchard, *The Ancient Near East in Pictures* (*ANEP*), Princeton 1969, nos. 246, 515
8. *CAD* D 32b 3^{1}; cf.: *šāpit ilī u awīlūtim* "the judge of gods and man" (*CAD* Š/I 458b).
9. *CAD* D 32b 3^{1}
10. *CAD* D 32a 1; והשווה: *(bēl kitti u mēšari (šamaš* 'אל האמת והצדק'K. Tallqvist, *Akkadische Götterepitheta*, Leipzig 1938, pp. 47, 104–106, cf. 456; N.

Sarna, "Psalms and the Near Eastern Sun-God Literature", *Fourth World Congress of Jewish Studies*, I, Jerusalem 1967, pp. 171–175

11. *BWL* 136:177
12. *BWL* 128:34
13. *BWL* 134:127
14. *BWL* 134:143
15. *CAD* Š1 336a ;EA 162:78–79 לנוסחה זו של כתבי עמרנה השווה: .EA 99:21–24
16. ABL 1396:8 = S. Parpola, *Letters from Assyrian Scholars of the Kings Esarhadion and Assurbanipal*, Kevelaer 1970, no. 71
17. *CAD* Š/I 336a b
18. ראה מי' ו, יא; תה' נא, ו: איוב לג, ט.
19. G. del Olmo Lete and J. Sanmartin, *A Dictionary of the Ugaritic Language in the Alphabetic Tradition*, Leiden-Boston 2003, I, p. 239, s.v. b-r(-r)
20. Ch. Virolleaud, *Le Palais Royal D'Ugarit*, II, Paris 1957, text 15.125:1–15; ראה גם W. F. Albright, "Specimens of Late Ugaritic Prose", *BASOR* 150 (1958), p. 37, line 10; ש"א לוינשטם, "טקסטים חדשים בלשון אוגרית", תרביץ כח (1958), עמ' 246.

הערה לכתובת אחירם

הזכרת מבנה הסארקופאגוס של אחירם בשורה הראשונה של כתובת אחרי (KAI 1:1) על ידי בנו [א]תבעל מלווה במשפט הקשה "כשתה בעלם". בשנת 1926 אולברייט[1] (וההולך בעקבותיו זליג הריס)[2] מתרגם את המשפט "As a place of sleeping in the other world". הוא מנתח את המלה "שתה" כשם-עצם ומשווה אותה אל האכדית *šittu* והעברית "שנה", ואת המלה "בעלם" הוא מסמיך לביטוי המצוי בעברית מאוחדת "בעולם הבא". עשרים ואחת שנה לאחר מכן, אולברייט, ההולך בעקבותיו של רנה דיסו,[3] מתרגם את המשפט הפניקי, "As his ab(o)de in eternity"[4] וכך הוא מניח, שהייתה השמטת האות ב; זאת אומרת כשתה כש<ב>תה. אולברייט משווה את השימוש בפועל ישב, הבא לצד המלה עלם, לפסוק המקראי "מכון לשבתך עולמים",[5] וכך הוא מתרגם את המלה "בעלם" "in eternity" פראנץ רוזנטאל[6] מאמץ את קריאתו של אולברייט, אבל תרגומו "As his eternal dwelling place" עובר בשתיקה על השימוש הקשה במלת היחס ב.

פירושו של אולברייט מניח מקום לשאלות מספר מן הטעמים הבאים: ראשית, אף על פי שהפועל ישב משמש בעברית מקראית בהקשר למקומות קבורה, "היושבים בקברים ובנצורים ילינו",[7] הרי בפסוק זה הנביא אינו מתכַּון למתים, אלא לחיים השוכנים במקומות המיועדים לקבורת מתים. נוסף לכך, האנאלוגיה של אולברייט, המסמיכה את הביטוי הפניקי לפסוק המקראי "מכון לשבתך עולמים", אינה מתאימה כלל לענייננו, מאחר שבפסוק זה השורש ישב משמש לעניין מושבו של הקב"ה, ולא לעניין מקום קבורה של בני אנוש – כעניינו בכתובת אחירם. לסיכום ניתן להיאמר, שאין משתמשים בפועל ישב לא בפניקית ולא בעברית מקראית כדי להביע עניין קבורה של בני אדם.

שנית, תיקונו של אולברייט (שתה > ש<ב>תה). מתעלם משימושו של הפועל השמי הצפוני-מערבי "שית" ושל המקביל הסמנטי שלו בתכנים ברורים, המביעים עניין קבורה. כלומר, בעברית המקראית הפועל "שית" ובמקביל הפיוטי שלו "שפת" משמשים כלהלן: א) "כצאן לשאול שַׁתּוּ";[8] ב) "שַׁתַּנִי בבור תחתיות";[9] ג) "ולעפד מות תִּשְׁפְּתֵנִי".[10] באוגריתית הפועל *šyt* מופיע מספר פעמים עם המלה *ḫrt* "חורים, מערות": *abky waqbrnh* אבכה ואקברנו אשית(נו) בחורי אלמי ארץ" *ašt bḫrt ilm arṣ*.[11] בפניקית הפועל "שים" בא עם השם קֶבֶר: אש [ש]ם לקבר זה, "אשר [ש]ם בקבר

זה".[12] הוא הדין, לדוגמה, בפועל האכדי *šakānu* (= שית), המופיע לצד המלה *kimaḫḫu* "קבר":[13] *ana kimaḫḫi šakānu* "לשים בקבר". מכאן נראה, שהדרך הטובה ביותר להבנת המלה שתה היא ללכת בעקבותיהם של אותם חוקרים,[14] הגוזרים את המלה כפועל בגוף שלישי יחיד זכר פרפקט מן השורש שית + ה, שהיא הסיומת האקוזאטיבית של גוף שלישי יחיד זכר, סיומת המאפיינת את הדיאלקט הפניקי מגבל, וכך לתרגם את המלה כשתה: "כאשר הוא (אתבעל) שת/(שם) אותו".

שלישית, תרגומו של אולברייט "בעלם"[15] "in eternity" הוא מוקשה, מאחר שבשמית צפון־מערבית לעולם אין משתמשים במלת־היחס ב עם עלם, וההוא הדין *ina dār/dārârti/dārīti** שכנראה נעדר מאוצר המלים האכדי.[16]

שאלת האות ב יכולה להיפתר, אם נחפש מוצא אחר, כלומר פתרון שאינו רואה באות ב את מלת־היחס "in" האלטרנאטיבה הסבירה ביותר היא להבין את המלה בעלם כקיצור של בת עלם "in the house of eternity".[17] וכך מצינו גם את הקיצור בי עלמא.[18] "לשון נקייה" בת עלם מצויה גם בפונית במובן "קבר": "חדר בת עלם קבר נ[פעל]" ("חדר (ב) בית עולם קבר נעשה").[19] וכן ביטוי זה מצוי מספר פעמים בכתובות תדמוריות: בת עלם דנא עבד מתני...., "בית עולם זה עשה מתני...".[20] כידוע, בעברית מקראית נמצא ביטוי זה פעם אחת: "כי הולך האדם אל בית עולמו".[21] השימוש בלשון נקייה זו רגיל ומצוי פעמים הרבה בעברית המאוחרת.

כפי שכבר הובחן, המצרית ההירוגליפית משתמשת בלשון הנקייה *Nˀiwt n nḥḥ*:[22] "The city of eternity" וכמו שכבר ציין האגיפטולוג וילסון גם הביטוי *n nḥḥ pr* "בית עולם" מצוי במצרית ההירוגליפית.[23] לצד הביטויים השונים שציינּו לעיל יש להוסיף ולהביא את שימושו של הביטוי האכדי "מושב (בית) עולם": *šubat dārâti/dārât*

א) "היכל שנה קבר מנוחה מושב עולם".[24]	*ēkal ṣalāli kimaḫ tapsuḫti šubat dārâti*
ב) "היכל מנוחה מושב עולם".[25]	*ēkal tapšuḫti šubat dārât*

יש להעיר, ששתי המובאות האכדיות האלה נמצאו חרותות על גבי לבנים בכוכי קבר מלכותיים באשור. "מושב (בית) עולם", שתרגמו פון סודן[26] *šubat dārât/ dārâti* לסיכום ניתן להיאמר, שהביטוי האכדי "Grab" הוא המקביל הסמנטי המדויק לשמית הצפונית־מערבית בית/בי עולם/עלמא, או-כמו שהוא מופיע בכתובת אחירם-בעלם.

הערות

1. W. F. Albright, "The End of the Sarcophagus Text of Aḥiram," *JPOS* 6 (1926), 79.
2. Z. Harris, *A Grammar of the Phoenician Language* (New Haven: American Oriental Society, 1936), 107.
3. Dussaid, "Les Inscriptions phéniciennes du tombeau d' Aḥiram, roi de Byblos," *Syria* 5 (1924), 136.
4. W. F. Albright, "The Phoenician Inscriptions of the Tenth Century B.C. from Byblos," *JAOS* 67 (1947), 155, n. 19.
5. I Kings 8:13 = II Chr. 6:2.
6. *ANET*[3] 661b.
7. Isa. 65:4.
8. Ps. 49:15.
9. Ps. 88:7
10. Ps. 22:16 Note that the Targum renders מות עפר as קבורתא בית.
11. *ID*:112, 126, 141; cf. 1**AB*,5:5; *IAB*, 1:16–18.
12. A. M. Honeyman, "The Phoenician Inscriptions of the Cyprus Museum," *Iraq* 6 (1939), 107.
13. E. Ebeling, *TuL, p. 58:18*
14. C. Torrey, "The Aḥiram Inscription from Byblos," *JAOS* 45 (1925): 270; M. Montet, "*Byblos et l'Egypte* (Paris, 1928–29), 238, n.l; J. Friedrich, "Zur Einleitungsformel der ältesten phönizischen Inschriften aus Byblos," *Mélanges syriens* (Paris, 1939), 43. See most recently H. Donner and W. Röllig, *Kanaanäische und aramäiche Inschriften* (Wiesbaden, 1968) (hereafter *KAI*), Band II, 2–3
15. So, too, J. Friedrich, *op. cit.,* p. 43, renders the phrase בעלם כשתה "when he put him in eternity (=the tomb)." The rendering "in eternity" is also adopted in *KAI* II, p. 2.
16. Note that *ina dārīti* (*EA* 147:48) is considered an error for *ana dārīti* by *CAD* D 115
17. The preposition ב need not appear orthographically when it precedes a word beginning with the same letter; cf. e.g., Gen. 24:23. The phenomenon also occurs in Ugaritic, e.g., *bty (for *bbty)* in *IK:205; IK, 1:14–15 bḥyk abn nšmḫ blmtk* (for **bblmtk*) *ngln*; ibid., II. 98–99. See further H.L. Ginsberg, "The North-Canaanite Myth of Anath and Aqhat: II," *BASOR* 98 (1945), 16, n. 27, and 20, n. 46; U. Cassuto, *The Goddess Anath* (Jerusalem: Magnes Press, 1953), 39. Clearly, the examples are too numerous to be explained on the basis of haplography. Note that Torrey (*op. cit*., p. 272) considered עלם the abbreviated form of עלם בת, anticipating, somewhat, the suggestion offered above. However, he retained ב as the preposition, rather than as an abbreviation of בת.

18. See *KAI*, No. 216:16 (Bīr- Rākib). In this example, and in those which follow, the abbreviation בי for בית, "house," reflects the indication of the diphthong by *yod*. In Byblian Phoenician, the diphthong is not preserved. In the Aḥiram inscription ב may stand for בת, "house."
19. T. Nöldeke, "Syrische Inschriften," *ZA* 21 (1908), 158.
20. *CIS*: 124; also N. Slouschz, *The Thesaurus of the Phoenician Inscriptions* (Tel-Aviv: Mossad Biyalik, 1942), 126, No. 109.
21. G. Cooke, *A Text-Book of North-Semitic Inscription* (Oxford: Clarendon Press, 1903), 307:1; cf. ibid., 308:1, 339:6.
22. Ecc. 12:5. See H. L. Ginsberg, *Koheleth* (Jerusalem, 1961), 132.
23. Montet, *op. cit*., p. 238, n. l.
24. J. A. Wilson, *JNES,* 3 (1944): 208a, n.1.
25. *OIP* 2, 151, No. 14:3.
26. Ibid., No. 13:2.
27. *AHw*, 164; contrast the rendering "to dwell there forever" in *CAD* D 111.

Indices

Akkadian

abātu, 314
abnu, 275 n. 51
agu, 124
aḫāzu, 269–270
aḫu, 271
aḫum, 270
ajjābum, 270
ākilu, 313–315
akītu, 180
alāku, 121 n. 6, 166, 280
amātu, 294
amāru, 296–297
āmur, 181
apālu, 111
arad-ekalli, 72
ardu, 287
arkūtū, 285
arnu, 59
ašāšu, 317
ašru parsu, 165, 169
ašrum, 287–288
attallak, 192 n. 32
atû, 289
awātim, 111
awīl šumi, 308 n. 158
awīlum lemnum, 270
ayābu, 59

bābil, 191 n. 30
balātu, 285
banû, 236 n. 33
batqu, 314
bâ'u, 121 n. 6
būrtu, 161
bŭṣu, 71

dabābu, 111, 273–274 nn. 20–21, 294
dagālu, 135, 147 n. 68
dâku, 272
daltu, 133
damāmu, 66
damqātim, 111
dannu, 111, 167, 295
dappi erīni, 133
dār, 264
dayyānu, 240
dayye, 313–315
dekû, 276 n. 52
diglu, 135
diqaru, 71
dišpu, 71
dullu, 111
dūru, 129, 133

edku, 59
egēru, 48 n. 53, 295
egru, 37
ekēmu, 322
eklētu, 172 n. 57
emēdu, 111
epšētu, 304 n. 94
eqlu, 71
erbû, 315
erēb šamši, 159–161
erēšu, 283–284

erištu, 30 n. 43
esēru, 107–113, 256
ešēru, 19–25
etēqu, 121 n. 6, 326
eṭēru, 305 n. 110
eṭūtu, 172 n. 57
ezzu, 167

gabadibbû, 129–136
gallābi, 70
gaṣāṣu, 167
gaṣṣu, 167
gašpu, 167
gazāzu, 27 n. 7
gullubi, 71
guzallu, 58

ḫabāšu, 321
ḫabātu, 322
ḫālālu, 118, 121 n. 6
ḫalāṣu, 79
ḫālilu, 118
ḫamaṣu, 29 n. 42
ḫamaṭu, 25
ḫanšu, 287
ḫarbu, 173 n. 62
ḫartibi, 223
ḫaṣṣinnu, 70
ḫaštu, 173 n. 62, 305 n. 110
ḫaṭṭi išarti, 302 n. 49
ḫaṭṭu, 282, 284
ḫerû, 190 n. 29, 191 n. 30
ḫepû, 272
ḫubullu, 313
ḫuptu, 164
ḫurāṣu, 124, 126, 131, 232
ḫurbū, 171
ḫurru, 158, 161
ḫuršānu, 166

irat erṣetim, 166
isḫappu, 58
isḫappum, 270
iṣṣūri, 256

kabāru, 101
kabātu, 101, 294, 314
kabtu, see *kabātu*
kalmatu, 316
kalu, 121 n. 6
kamaru, 72
kamû, 163
kanšu, 287
karābu, 71
kaspu, 129, 232
kaṣāru, 295
kīlu, 270
kilīlu, 123–136
kittu, 38
kudurrus, 58, 269, 328 n. 15
kulbābu, 73 n. 31
kullulu, 143 n. 17
kullumu, 269, 328 n. 15
kunnu, 299n. 4
kuttumu, 295
kuzbu, 231

lā mūdûm, 270–271
lā nāṭilum, 270
lā pāliḫ ili, 270
labbu, 254
laḫru, 71

lalû, 231, 236 n. 27
lamattu, 71, 73 n. 31
lemnētu, 59
lêmu, 76
lē'u, 147 n. 60
līmu, 185
līpū, 297
lišanu, 295
lišānu nakirtu, 270
liqtu, 124–125
lulû, 231–2, 236 n. 27

madgaltu, 147 n. 68
malû, 211
maqlû, 157
massu, 110
mašḫultuppû, 161, 164, 169
mašmašu, 76
matu, 315
mīlu, 211–213
mīl'u, 211
mimmû, 302 n. 55
miṣri, 176
mû, 212
mudabiru, 164, 169
mudû, 58
mūnu, 313–315
muṣri, 176, 187
mušnamir, 241.
muštēmiqu, 287
mutnennû, 287
mutqa, 317
muttaprišu, 314
mūtu, 167

na'asu, 75–77
nabnitu, 124
naburrû, 129
nadānu, 283–284, 291
nadru. 167
nadû, 275 n. 51
na'du, 287
nakāsu, 36
nakrum, 270
nalpattu, 70
namba'ū, 181, 189 n. 25
namba'ē, 191 n. 30
napāṣu, 91
nappillu, 313
naprušu, 256
naqābu. 121 n. 10
narû, 272, 275 n. 51, 328 n. 15
nāru, 212
nasāku, 275 n. 51
naṣābu, 281
naṭḫu, 223
nāṭilu, 58
nidūtu, 158
nigiṣṣu, 158
nīru, 111
nuḫušti, 190 n. 30
nukkuru, 276 n. 52
nukkusu, 36
nu'ûm, 270

palgu, 191 n. 30
pāliḫu, 287–288
parāru, 57
parzillu, 70
pašqu, 126–129, 133–134
peḫu, 161
peṣû, 213

pû, 295–296
pūḫu, 160
pussusu, 36

qabû, 269, 271, 328 n. 15
qalapu, 36
qalpu, 103
qatnu, 101–103
qebēru, 161
qutrinnu, 24

rabû, 101, 103
raggu, 59
râmu, 236 n. 27
rapādu, 71
raṣāpu, 230. 236 n. 33
raṣāspu, 232
rebû, 297
rêṣu, 280
rēša, 289
rēšu, 287
rē'û, 290
riṣpu, 235 n. 19
ru'āmu, 236 n. 27

sablum, 110
saḫlu, 174 n. 77
sakku, 58
sakkum, 270
saklu, 53–64
saklum, 270
salmu, 326
samītu, 129, 133
samû, 58
sasu, 317
semeru, 72
simmiltu, 71
sirpu, 69–72
sullû, 47 n. 38

ṣabātu, 94, 295–296
ṣaḥātu, 47 n. 38, 79
ṣâḫu, 47 n. 38
ṣalāpu, 33–45, 203
ṣalmu, 161, 169, 272
ṣarāḫu, 25
sasmītu, 133
ṣeḫrūti, 279, 284
ṣelû, 24
ṣēnu, 48 n. 53
ṣepēru, 69
ṣēru, 159–169 *passim*
ṣibtu, 295
ṣiḫru,101
ṣiliptu, see *ṣalāpu*
ṣiriḫtu, 24
ṣubat-, 103
ṣubburu, 329 nn. 20, 24
ṣullu, 47 n. 38

ša ekalli, 216
šadû, 166
šaḫṭu, 287
šakānu, 291–293, 299 n. 4
šalāmu, 241
šamru, 167
šamšu, 241
šamûm, 270
šanûm, 270–271
šaptā, 295
šarāṭu, 99–100
šaṭāru, 268

šâṭu, 166
šebû, 285
šemû, 287
šētu, 305 n. 110
šību, 101
šittu, 263
šizbu, 212–213
šubbû, 285
šuddû, 275 n. 51
šūḫuzu, 271, 328 n. 15
šūlû, 299 n. 4
šumī pašaṭu, 269
sumšu šaṭāru, 269
šumu, 291–293
šumu damqu, 309 n. 173
šupšuqiš, 191 n. 32
šurpu, 157
šuttatu, 173 n. 62, 305 n. 110
šuzuzzu, 299 n. 4
tarāṣu, 324
tukkulu, 280
tūltu, 315
tuppu, 275 n. 51

ṭayye, see *dayye*.

uḫḫuz, 310 n. 1963
ullû, 231, 235 n. 25, 289
ulṣu, 231
uṣurtu, 275 n. 51
uzuzzu, 280–281, 284, 291

wu"uru, 269, 328 n. 15

zakû, 243
zaqāpu, 299 n. 4
zikru, 291

Aramaic

אבד, 271, 314
אחד, 295, 310 n. 196
אחז, 94, 295–296, 310 n. 196
(see also אחד)
איתי, 29 n. 43
אכל, 315–317
אלב אש זר, 269–271
אלכסונא, 44
אלס, 75
אלף, 107
אמר, 271, 286
ארבה, 312ff
ארך, 285, 296–298
אש, 286–289
אשר, 287, 304 n. 94
אתר, 304 n. 94

בדקתא, 314
בי, 264
בזע, 19, 99
בסן, 107

גובא, 312
גוז, 26–7 n. 7
גזז, 27 n. 7
גוע, 275 n. 51
גלב, 70

דוי, 107
דחק, 81

הגע, 275 n. 51, 304 n. 94 (see also גוע)
הגע נצבא, 271
הרג, 267–272 *passim*

זחא, 312
זי, 287
זי לידע, 271
זין, 82
זיף, 34
זרז, 80, 82
זרח, 71

חבז, 321–323
חבל סותא, 271
חגר, 294–295
חוי־חוא, 39, 284–286
חזי, 296–297
חטר, 281–282, 284
חיב, 107
חכם, 54
חלבבה, 281–282, 284
חלק, 71
חצל, 81
חרטמים, 223

טבור, 41
טברר, 41
טוורד, 41
טוב, 309 n. 173
טוף, 221
טרף, 72, 99

יהב, 291
יסר, 107
יקר, 294
יש, 29 n. 43
ישיש, 101

כלל, 144 n. 19
כלמה, 314–317
כלמי, 315
כסן, 107
כרזבא, 312

לד, 271
לכד, 327 n. 9
לעס, 75
לקה, 42, 107, 112
לקח, 327 n. 9

מלל, 273, 274 n. 21
ממונא, 302 n. 55
מן, 314–317
מפס, 93
מצר, 189 n. 25

נגד, 39–40
נגע, 275 n. 51
נגרא, 71
נדן, 314 (see also נתן)
נוס, 271
נזק, 271

ניפולא, 312–313
נפול, 313
נקה, 327 n. 9
נתן, 283–285, 314

סס, 317
סעד, 281
ספר, 69–72, 107

עוזיאל, 168
עליה, 267
עלים, 300 n. 18
עלם, 278–280, 284
עמק, 294
ענה, 286–289, 306 n. 126
עקם, 35, 55
ערף, 272, 276 n. 56
עשא, 317

פום, 295–296
פטר, 72
פלח, 288
פצה, 81
פרחא, 312
פשט, 327 n. 9
פשך, 134

צדד, 43–44
צור, 295
צל, 20
צלא, 47 n. 38
צלב, 36, 47 n. 36
צלח, 19–20, 24, 26 n. 4,
צרח, 25

קדרה, 71
קום, 280–281, 284–286, 298–299
n. 4
קטל, 99
קלמתא, 315
קלקל, 35
קמל, 315–317
קעם, 281
קרא, 307 n. 140
קשי, 294

רגובלא, 71
רגלא, 71
רדה, 107
רזח, 71
רטש, 99
רמא, 275 n. 51
רשונא, 312
רשם, 274 n. 23

שאל, 283–284
שום, 291–293, 298 n. 4
שזב, 81
שחלין, 174 n. 77
שחת, 271
שחתה, 305 n. 110
שלח, 323
שם, 291
שמוטא, 312
שמחזאי, 168
שנם חוי, 284–286
שרי, 252

תוי, 312–317 *passim*
תולעה, 312–317 *passim*
תרע, 72

Hebrew

אבד, 314
אדר, 72
אדריכל, 72
אהבה, 229, 232-233
אימה, 135
אכל, 313
אלמנה, 122 n. 29
אמץ, 290
אסף, 82
אסר, 163
אפק, 211
אפריון, 229, 233
ארבה, 312–317 *passim*
ארגמן, 232
ארד, 72
ארז, 133
ארך, 285
ארשת, 30 n. 43 (see also ירשת)
אשכל, 132
אשר, 22 (see also ישר)

בדק, 314
בהט, 223
בור, 189 n. 25
בוש, 63
בחר, 72
בית, 264
בן, 297
בנה, 236 n. 31
בער, 24–25
בקע, 23, 25 n. 3, 26 n. 4, 100
ברד, 72
ברח, 72
ברית, 119
ברך, 71
בר־ברר, 241-243
בשם, 219
בשמת, 218–219

גאל, 257, 305 n. 110
גבירה, 216
גדל, 101, 126–128, 131–132, 147 n. 68 (see also דגל), 291 (גדל שם)
גוז, 26 n. 7
גוע, 275 n. 51
גזז, 27 n. 7
גזל, 276 n. 52
גזם, 312–317 *passim*
גזר, 72, 151–153, 165
גלב, 70
גלח, 70
גנן, 251
גער, 71
גרז, 72
גרש, 122 n. 29

דבר, 72, 111
דבש, 71
דגל, 126–135, 147 n. 68 (see also גדל)
דין, 21ff.
דלל, 191 n. 31
דלק, 24–25, 31 n. 68
דלת, 127, 133, 293
דמם, 66–7 n. 58
דקר, 118

דרש, 289

הדר, 126
הוכח, see יכח
הוללות, 56
הלך, 166
הלר, 173 n. 69
הפך, 35
הר, 187

זהב, 232
זך־זכך, 243–244
זכר, 290, 307 n. 143
זני, 122 n. 29
זקן, 110
זר, 175, 190 n. 30
זרח, 237–245 *passim*

חבס, 321
חגב, 312
חגר, 37, 72
חדר, 118
חומה, 127, 131–134
חזק, 94, 108
חטא, 57, 289
חכם, 55
חלב, 209–213 *passim*
חלל, 117–120, 326
חלץ, 79–89
חלק, 71
חמה, 244–245
חמץ, 29 n. 42
חסד, 289
חסיל, 312–3177 *passim*
חפז, 321
חצור, 224
חצרמות, 174 n. 78
חקק, 119, 268-269, 264 n. 23
חרב, 118, 171, 191 nn. 30–31
חרג, 72
חרגל, 312–313
חשך, 56, 172 n. 57

טבור, 41
טבליהו, 223
טוב, 223, 309 n. 173, (הטיב שם, 309 n. 170),
טחנות, 293
טירה, 127–128, 131–134
טף, 221
טפה, 220
טפח, 134 (טפחות, 223)
טפף, 221
טפת, 215–224
טרש, 71

יאור, 175–188
ידע, 308 n. 155
יכח, 108
ילד, 110
ילק, 312–317 *passim*
יסף, 285
יסר, 107–113
יפי, 126
יצא, 257
יצא שם, 292
יצב, 280–281
ירא, 288–289
ירד, 251
ירה, 108, 299 n. 4, 324
ירש, 283–284
ירשת, 30 n. 43 (see also ארשת)

יש, 29 n. 43
ישב, 263
ישוד, 173 n. 69
ישע, 280, 306 n. 110
ישר, 20, 35, 64 (see also אשר)

כבד, 111, 126, 294, 314
כלא, 121 n. 6, 172 n. 59
כליל, 123–136
כלל, 143–144 n. 17
כנים, 315
כסל, 65 n. 27
כסף, 131, 232
כף פעם, 191 n. 32
כרם, 72
כרת, 165
כתב, 268, 274 n. 23, 304 n. 94
כתר, 130

לוח, 127, 133, 146–7 n. 60
לחם, 330 n. 31
לחץ, 80
לטש, 99
לכן, 67 n. 58
למד, 108
לעס, 75–77
לץ, 108
לקח, 257

מבוע, 189 n. 25
מגדל, see גדל and דגל
מדבר, 151–169 *passim*
מות, 167–168
מים, 175, 191 n. 30
מלא, 209-211, 283–284
מליתה, 211

ממון, 302 n. 55
מס, 110
מעיל, 101–102
מערות, 122 n. 26
מצור, 175–188

נדגל, see דגל and גדל
נזל, 190 n. 30
נזר, 126, 144 n. 17
נטף, 221
נטש, 99
נמלה, 71
נער, 280, 300 n. 13, n. 16
נפל, 67 n. 58, 313
נפץ, 91–96
נפת דאר, 224
נצל, 257
נצר, 35
נקב, 118–119, 121 n. 10
נתן, 283–284, 291–293, 314
נתן חטר, 281–282
נתץ, 92

סבל, 110
סגר, 310 n. 196
סחט, 47 n. 38
סחק, 47 n. 38
סכל, 53–64
סלף, 33–45, 61
סלם, 71
סלעם, 312ff.
סמאל, 155
סס, 317
ספר, 69–72

עבד, 108, 111

עבה, 101
עבר, 26 n. 3
עולה (injustice), 306 n. 110
עור, 35
עות, 34
עזאזל, 151–169
עזה, 167
עזמות, 168
עזר, 290, 306 n. 110
עטר, 126, 130
על, 111
עלה, 191 n. 31, 305 n. 110
עלם, 263–265, 278–280, 300 n. 11
עמד, 280-281, 299 n. 4
עמס, 111
עמק, 294
ענה, 111
ענו, 288–289, 306 n. 121
עני, 306 n. 126
עקש, 35
ערבה, 173 n. 62
ערירי, 21, 29 n. 30
ערל, 71
עש, 317
עשה (שם), 292
עשק, 48 n. 53

פדה, 305 n. 110
פצר, 72
פרץ, 72
פרר, 57
פתל, 35, 55

צבא, 250–252
צבע, 71
צדד, 41–44
צדק, 60, 289
צוף, 221
צוק, 152
צור, 175ff.
צחצח, 88
צחק, 47 n. 38
ציח, 173 n. 62
צלב, 47 n. 36
צלח, 19–25, 63
צלמות, 172 n. 57, 173 n. 62
צלצל, 312ff
צלף, 33–45
צעיר, 101, 104 n. 25
צרח, 71
צרר, 175ff, 301 n. 32, 306 n. 110

קדם, 299 n. 11
קדרה, 71
קדש, 119–120
קום, 280–281, 299 n. 4, 301 n. 32
קור, 190 n. 29, 191 nn. 30–31
קטן, 101–103, 104 n. 25
קפץ, 19–20, 28 n. 26
קר, 190 n. 30
קרא, 290, 307 n. 143
קרץ, 329 n. 20
קשה, 111, 167

ראה, 296–297
רב, 101
רבה, 285
רבע, 296–297
רגע, 71
רדף, 31 n. 68, 71
רוח, 120 n. 6

רום, 299 n. 4
רחב, 209–213 *passim*
רחל, 71
רטש, 71, 99–100
רמח, 71
רעל, 71
רפא, 35
רצח, 71
רצף, 229–233, 235 n. 19
רשע, 289

שאל, 283–284
שאול, 167
שבט, 113, 282, (שבט משפט, 302 n. 49)
שבע, 285
שבר, 35
שגה, 57
שד (breast), 131
שד (demon), 156
שדד, 35
שואה, 173 n. 62
שוחה, 173 n. 62, 305 n. 110
שוט, 166, 173 n. 69
שות, 263
שחט, 47 n. 38, 79
שחלים, 174 n. 77
שחק, 47 n. 38
שחת, 305–306 n. 110
שטן, 155
שים, 291
שכל, 53–64, 108
שלח, 151, 316, 323–324
שלל, 35
שלם, 326
שלף, 83
שם, 291–293
שמר, 57
שמש, 241–245 *passim*
שנה, 263
שנהבים, 230
שניר, 72
שער, 72
שפה, 294
שפט, 21ff., 314
שפת, 263
שרות, 72
שרט, 100, 314
שריון, 72
שתי, 191 n. 31

ת (letter), 201–203
תאו, 312
תאי, 312
תהו, 312
תולעת, 313
תחפנס, 222
תמה, 35, 38
תמך, 290
תמם, 35
תער, 70
תפארת, 72, 126

Phoenician

אבד, 314
אדם שם, 308 n. 158
אר, 285
חטר משפט, 301–302 n. 49
חיי, 285–286
טנע, 299 n. 4
ישר, 288
כבד, 314
נעם, 309 n. 173
נער, 280
נתן, 314
סמל, 299 n. 4
צדק, 288
שים, 264
שלח, 325
שת שם, 291

Ugaritic

aḥd, 29 n. 43, 94 (see also *yḥd*)
aḥw, 286
arṣ dbr, 167, 173 nn. 75–76
'bd, 314
'rs, 283–284
'rš, 30 n. 43
'lm, 263–265
'z, 168
b'r, 24–5
dmm, 66 n. 58
gb', 166
ġr, 166
ḥpyr, 190 n. 29
ḥrt, 263
ḥwy, 286
ḫt mṯpṭ, 282, 301–302 n. 49
iṯ, 30 n. 43
kbd, 166, 173 n. 75, 314
kšth b'lm, 263–265
mrḥ, 71
nṣb, 299 n. 4
srd, 314
ṣḥq, 47 n. 38
ṣly, 47 n. 38
ṣwd, 166
š'ly, 299
šd šḫlmmt, 167
šḫl, 174 n. 77
šḫlm, 174 n. 77
šḫlmmt, 173 n. 77
šlḥ, 283
šth, 263–265
šyt, 263–264
thw, 312
ṯpd, 314
yḥd, 29 n. 43 (see also *aḥd*)
ylk, 166
ytn, 283–284, 314

Hebrew Bible

Gen. 22:3, 25 n. 3
Gen. 29:2, 27 n. 8
Gen. 31:28, 57
Gen. 48:14, 53–54, 61
Gen. 49:12, 212
Gen. 50:23, 296

Exod. 22:2, 237–245
Exod. 28:17, 209
Exod. 29:6, 126

Lev. 16, 151–169
Lev 21–22, 119
Lev. 24:11, 119

Num. 11:31, 26 n. 7
Num. 31:3, 82
Num. 32:17, 82
Num. 32: 20, 82
Num. 32:21, 80

Deut. 3:18, 88
Deut. 8:5, 113
Deut. 22:18–19, 109, 112
Deut. 25:3, 112
Deut. 25:9, 88
Deut. 32:22, 172 n. 58

Josh. 1:8, 63
Josh. 8:9, 131
Josh. 11:10, 219
Josh. 19:32–39, 219

Judg. 14:6, 19
Judg. 14:19, 19
Judg. 15:14, 19
Judg. 20:40, 125

1 Sam. 2:19, 101–103
1 Sam. 10:6, 19
1 Sam. 13:13, 57
1 Sam. 15:27, 97 n. 32
1 Sam. 16:13, 19
1 Sam. 18:10, 19
1 Sam. 21:14, 202
1 Sam. 26:21, 57

2 Sam. 1:21, 22
2 Sam. 13:18, 102
2 Sam. 15:27, 219
2 Sam. 15:36, 219
2 Sam. 16:31, 57
2 Sam. 16:34, 57
2 Sam. 17:17–21, 219
2 Sam. 19:18, 19, 26 n. 3
2 Sam. 24:10, 57

1 Kings 1:47, 309 n. 170
1 Kings 3:1, 217
1 Kings 4:1, 218–219
1 Kings 4:7–19, 218
1 Kings 5:29, 110
1 Kings 7:8, 217
1 Kings 7:9, 134
1 Kings 9:15, 220
1 Kings 9:16, 217

1 Kings 9:24, 217
1 Kings 11:1, 217
1 Kings 11:1–3, 215
1 Kings 11:28, 110
1 Kings 11:41, 218
1 Kings 12:1–19, 109ff
1 Kings 12:10, 101
1 Kings 18:12, 300 n. 13

2 Kings 12:10, 119
2 Kings 16:17, 235
2 Kings 17:6, 187–188
2 Kings 18–19, 175–188 *passim*
2 Kings 18:14–16, 256
2 Kings 18:21, 119
2 Kings 19:24, 175–188

Isa. 1:17, 22
Isa. 2:19, 122 n. 26
Isa. 5:29, 255
Isa. 7:18, 175
Isa. 10:8, 253
Isa. 10:29, 26 n. 7
Isa. 19:6, 191 n. 31
Isa. 31:4–5, 249–257
Isa. 35:7, 189 n. 25
Isa. 36–37, 182–184
Isa. 36:6, 119
Isa. 37:25, 175–188
Isa. 38:18, 22
Isa. 41:9–10. 290
Isa. 42:6, 290
Isa. 44:25, 57
Isa. 49:10, 189 n. 25
Isa. 51:8, 317
Isa. 51:9, 117
Isa. 51:10, 26 n. 7
Isa. 53:10, 296
Isa. 58:9, 324
Isa. 58:11, 83–86
Isa. 63:12, 300 n. 19
Isa. 64:1, 308 n. 155
Isa. 65:4, 263
Isa. 66:14, 87

Jer. 2:6, 172 n. 62
Jer. 2:31, 172 n. 62
Jer. 4:7, 255
Jer. 4:22, 56
Jer. 5:21, 56, 59
Jer. 5:28, 21–23
Jer. 8:14, 66 n. 58
Jer. 18:14, 190 n. 30
Jer. 22:30, 21
Jer. 25: 37, 66 n. 58
Jer. 49:26, 66 n. 48
Jer. 50:30, 66 n. 48
Jer. 51:4, 118
Jer. 51:6, 66 n. 58

Ezek. 9:4, 202
Ezek. 9:6, 202
Ezek. 16:13–14, 125–126
Ezek. 17:9–10, 20
Ezek. 21:19, 118
Ezek. 26:20, 171
Ezek. 27:3–4, 125
Ezek. 27:4, 143 n. 17
Ezek. 28:12, 126
Ezek. 31:14–18, 172 n. 58
Ezek. 32:22, 118
Ezek. 32:26, 118

Hos. 2:17, 300 n. 13
Hos. 10:2, 276 n. 57
Hos. 10:7, 213 n.18
Hos. 11:10, 255

Joel 1:4, 312

Amos 1:2–2:16, 195–204
Amos 5:1–17, 207 n. 27
Amos 5:4–6, 207 n. 26
Amos 5:6, 23–25
Amos 5:10–12, 207 n. 25
Amos 5:13, 61–63
Amos 7:14–15, 207 n. 25
Amos 8:8, 175
Amos 9:1–4, 207 n. 27
Amos 9:3–4, 207 n. 25
Amos 9:5, 175

Jon. 2:3, 166

Mic. 5:1, 300 n. 11
Mic. 7:11–12, 186–7

Nah. 1:12, 26 n. 7

Hab. 3:14, 119

Hag. 1:6, 119

Zech. 8:23, 95

Ps. 2:8, 283
Ps. 3:4, 290
Ps. 21:5, 283, 285
Ps. 22:16, 263
Ps. 31:11, 87
Ps. 32:3, 87
Ps. 45:5, 27 n. 8
Ps. 49:15, 263
Ps. 55:21, 326
Ps. 63:10, 172 n. 58, 173 n. 63
Ps. 74:74:23, 300 n. 32
Ps. 86:13, 172 n. 58
Ps. 88:7, 263
Ps. 88:10, 172 n. 59
Ps. 90:10, 26 n. 7
Ps. 91:6, 173 n. 69
Ps. 94:16, 280–281
Ps. 102:4, 87
Ps. 109:42, 280
Ps. 128:6, 296
Ps. 140:2, 88
Ps. 145:14, 305 n. 99
Ps. 146:8, 305 n. 99

Job 1:7, 166
Job 2:2, 166
Job 10:21–22, 172 n. 62
Job 11:4, 244
Job 17:13, 172 n. 57
Job 21:24, 87
Job 26:13, 117
Job 28:10
Job 30:33, 87
Job 31: 35, 202
Job 34:17, 60
Job 38:17, 172 n. 57
Job 40:24, 119
Job 40:26, 119
Job 42:16, 296

Prov. 6:12–13, 324
Prov. 11:20, 48 n. 53
Prov. 13:24, 113
Prov. 15:30, 87
Prov. 17:6, 296
Prov. 17:20, 48 n. 53
Prov. 21:12, 59–61
Prov. 21:17, 64
Prov. 21:19, 173 n. 75
Prov. 22:12, 38
Prov. 22:15, 113
Prov. 23:13, 113
Prov. 25:23, n. 6

Cant. 2:4, 135
Cant. 3:10, 229–234
Cant. 4:4, 132
Cant. 4:5, 132
Cant. 5:10, 88, 135
Cant. 5:10–15, 209
Cant. 5:12, 209–213
Cant. 6:4, 134–135
Cant. 6:8, 215
Cant. 7:4, 132
Cant. 7:5, 132
Cant. 7:8–9, 132
Cant. 8:6, 167
Cant. 8:8–10, 126–128, 133
Cant. 8:10, 132, 135

Ecc. 2:19, 56
Ecc. 7:17, 56
Ecc. 7:28, 215
Ecc. 10:3, 56
Ecc. 10:14, 56
Ecc. 12:3–4, 293
Ecc. 12:6, 189 n. 25

Lam. 2:15, 125
Lam. 4:7, 212
Lam. 4:8, 87

Esth. 1:6, 232
Esth. 8:7, 325

Dan. 11:42, 326
Dan. 12:1–7, 91–96
Dan. 12:5–6, 192 n. 33

Neh. 4:11, 110
Neh. 7:28, 168
Neh. 12:29, 168

1 Chron. 28:4–5, 307 n. 148
1 Chron. 28:10, 207 n. 140
2 Chron. 8:11
2 Chron. 16:9, 57

Apocrypha

1 Enoch 9:6, 162
1 Enoch 10:8, 162–3
Sir. 45:8, 126
Sir. 45:12, 126

Rabbinic Sources

Midrash Rabbah
Gen. Rab. 8:11, 43
Gen. Rab. 10:7, 26 n. 7
Gen. Rab. 86, 27 n. 8
Gen. Rab. 95, 211
Lev. Rab. 22:4, 26 n. 7
Lev. Rab. 34:15, 86–7
Deut. Rab. 2, 154

Cant. Rab., 236 n. 31
Esth. Rab., 232

Other Rabbinic Sources
ʾAggadat Šir Hašširim 2:14, 27 n. 8
ʾAvot de-Rabbi Nathan B:12, 146 n. 45
Hammidraš Haggadol, 41
Mekilta de-Rabbi Yišmaʿel Mišpaṭim 13: 238.
Pesiqtaʾ Rabbati 3:4, 54
Pirqe de-Rabbi Eliezer 46, 155
Sifra Šemînî 3:5, 313
Sifra Aḥare Mot 2:8, 153

Mishnah
Šabb. 19:2, 75
ʿErub. 3:9, 85
Yoma 5:2–3, 39ff
Yoma 6:4–6, 152
Pesaḥ. 2:7, 75
Menaḥ. 6:3, 51 n. 89
Kelim 3:3, 71
Kelim 20:7, 51 n. 89
Nid. 8:9, 75
Nid. 9:7, 75

Tosefta
Šabb. 12:8, 75
Pesaḥ. 6:11, 75
Yoma 3:19, 71

Yerushalmi
Yoma 5:4, 41

Bavli
Ber. 16b, 85
Ber. 44b, 76
Ber. 51b, 317
Ber. 60b, 118

Šabb. 32b, 312
Šabb. 55a, 207 n. 32
Šabb. 59a-b, 146 n. 44
Šabb. 119a, 26 n. 4
Šabb. 129a, 26 n. 4
Yoma 15a, 39
Yoma 19b, 329 n. 24
Yoma 37a, 43
Yoma 53a, 43
Yoma 54b, 39
Yoma 67b, 152–4
Yoma 72b, 26 n. 7
Beṣ. 34a, 71
Yeb. 102b, 87
Sot. 49b, 130–131, 312
Giṭ. 68b, 26 n. 4
B. Qam. 84a, 76
B. Qam. 113b, 26 n. 4
B. Meṣ. 79a, 26 n. 4
B. Bat. 99a, 43
Sanh. 56a, 119
Sanh. 72a-b, 238–239
Hor. 12a, 51 n. 89
Zeb. 38a, 39
Menaḥ. 75a, 51 n. 89
Menaḥ. 98b, 43
Menaḥ. 106a, 51 n. 89
Ḥul. 65b, 313
Ker. 5b, 51 n. 89
Nid. 20b, 317

Maimonides
Shabbat 19:6, 146 n. 46
Genevah 9:10, 239

CPSIA information can be obtained at www.ICGtesting.com
Printed in the USA
BVOW020014180712

295465BV00002B/1/P

9 781602 802162